Quakers and Politics

PENNSYLVANIA
1681-1726

Quakers and Politics

PENNSYLVANIA, 1681–1726

New Edition

BY

Gary B. Nash

Northeastern University Press

BOSTON

Northeastern University Press

Library of Congress Cataloging-in-Publication Data

Nash, Gary B.
Quakers and politics : Pennsylvania, 1681–1726 / by
Gary B. Nash.—New ed.
p. cm.
Includes bibliographical references (p.) and index.
ISBN 1-55553-166-0 (alk. paper)
1. Pennsylvania—Politics and government—To
1775. 2. Quakers—
Pennsylvania—Politics and government. I. Title.
F152.N25 1993
974.8'02—dc20   93-21914

Printed and bound by The Maple Press Company in York,
Pennsylvania. The paper is Sebago Antique, an acid-free
sheet.

MANUFACTURED IN THE UNITED STATES OF AMERICA

97   96   95   94   93   5   4   3   2   1

For Chrissie

Preface to the 1993 Edition
of *Quakers and Politics*

WHEN I began my study of the early Quaker experience in Pennsylvania more than three decades ago, the so-called consensus school of American history was in full sway. Stressing the tendency of Americans to compromise rather than hold to rigid positions, to adapt rather than cling tenaciously to inherited norms, to create a society without the class conflict and polarized politics that wracked European society, the consensus historians portrayed an American past well-suited to fortify mid-twentieth-century citizens of the United States in their contest against communism. I had learned first-hand of the silent war between the Soviet Union and the United States occurring in the 1950s for the allegiance of Third World countries, for as an officer on a U.S. Navy destroyer, I had engaged in many dockside arguments with young Eritreans, Sudanese, and Egyptians about the superiority of the American economic and political systems over those of communist powers, especially the Soviet Union and China. Not fully aware of it at the time (in spite of having majored in history as an undergraduate), the consensus school held up to the outside world an American past that was relatively free of the deep ideological divisions and the accompanying violence and human suffering that had occurred in countries now dominated by communism. It was the American way that would best lead developing nations, newly rid of their colonial masters, into the modern era.

Although in embarking on a study of early Quaker Pennsylvania I was not consciously trying to test the consensus interpretation of American history, I fully understood that one of the most widely read and discussed consensus historians of this era, Daniel Boorstin, had used the Quakers in Pennsylvania as the foil for his central argument. In *The Americans: The Colonial Experience,* Boorstin had laid down the foundations for a three-volume treatise on the "seamlessness" of American history—the quintessential pragmatism and adaptability of the Americans. In this scheme, slavery hardly received mention as part of the colonial experience, and Native Americans were merely a bedeviling "menace" that only cold steel and unsentimental minds could deal with. Once upon this scene in the forests of North America, the Quakers proved to have two fundamental flaws in Boorstin's view: their "urge toward martyrdom" and "a rigidity in all their beliefs." These quite un-American traits were their downfalling, Boorstin contended, because "neither the martyr nor the doctrinaire could flourish on American soil." Indeed, it was the rejection of ideology that enabled Americans to get along, to meet at the middle of the road, to split the difference rather than fight, and to solve the problems that had to be solved. Boorstin had special contempt for the Quakers' attempt to live together peacefully with Native Americans. Holding rigidly to their "peace testimony," he argued, the Quakers "misjudged the Indians" and left settlers on their western frontier unprotected against the onslaughts of the warlike native peoples.

The more I studied the early Quakers in Pennsylvania, the less I agreed with this attempt to use them as the fall guys for the consensus interpretation. If the Quakers were dogmatic, then was not this dogmatism—manifested, for example, in an unyielding commitment to pacifism—not a refreshing and progressive stance as they landed on the eastern seaboard of North America during a period of bloody wars with native people from Maine to the Carolinas? If the steadfast Quaker commitment to greater equality in human affairs and their universalist belief in the brotherhood of all mankind led to the first protests over slavery (six years after they arrived in Pennsylvania) was that not evidence that the Quakers, from the beginning, were a wellspring of reformist energy in American history rather than a set of utopian cranks who could not "get with" the American way? The post–World War II civil rights movement was already underway as the consensus historians were reformulating American history, and it was obvious to those participating in this "Second Reconstruction" that, as in virtually all the other periods of intense reform over the past two centuries, Quakers were prominent beyond their numbers in the reformers' ranks. It did not seem to me, involved in a small way in the early civil rights movement, that "men who set too much store by their dogmas and who will not allow themselves to be guided by the give-and-take between ideas and experience are likely to suffer defeat," as Boorstin said of the Quakers. Rather, the civil rights movement showed the nation that if the gap between the promise and reality of American life was ever to be closed, if white Americans were ever going to live up to the founding principles in the way they practiced capitalism and democracy, a lot more commitment to principles was going to be required. White America had been altogether too willing to compromise its principles and to set far too little store by its dogmas; this is why a multiracial democracy had never flourished in the United States. Perhaps if all America had been more Quakerly, American history would have been the better for it.

A generation ago, dissertation advisors did not allow their students to argue directly with established historians in their doctoral theses, so readers of my dissertation and of the book that emerged from it will find no mention of Daniel Boorstin, not even in a stray footnote reference. But Boorstin's ghost flits through the book from beginning to end. My announced purpose was to write an account of the struggle for political

ix

stability in early Quaker Pennsylvania. To do that, I wanted to examine the connections between the organization of society—the distribution of social and economic power—and the nature of politics. I was not very far into my research before I began to sense the awful complexities of founding a colony in the Americas. Even when the colonists were largely coreligionists, even when they were carving out a haven from a persecuting home society, even when they were fired by an annealing ethos that stressed family, peaceable relations with outsiders, and relative equality, they could squabble fiercely among themselves, niggle with a leader whom most professed to admire greatly, and sometimes respond to the opportunities that the new land seemed to offer in unbecoming ways. These did not seem at all like martyrs and doctrine-bound utopians; rather, they seemed to be people with strong reformist beliefs, healthy appetites for getting ahead, and the normal quotient of human frailties. Not a member of the Society of Friends myself, although I had grown up in the heartland of American Quakerism, I came to hold enormous respect for what the Quakers tried to do when given a government and a colony of their own along the violence-wracked coast of North America in the late seventeenth century. I also came to see that even the peaceable Quakers had the devil's time trying to build their "holy experiment."

In preparing this paperback edition of *Quakers and Politics,* I have decided to leave the original text intact. Partly this is because I have changed my mind very little on the main lines of argument and on the analysis of data and documents in the book as it was published in 1968. Partly it is because it may be useful for readers today to consider my unmediated and unexpurgated analysis, written in the 1960s, in the light of recent scholarship. A modest body of scholarship on society and politics in the first half-century of Pennsylvania's history has emerged in the last several decades. Most important are James T. Lemon's *"The Best Poor Man's Country": A Geographical Study of Early Southeastern Pennsylvania* (Baltimore, 1972), J. William Frost's *The Quaker Family in Colonial America* (New York, 1973), Stephanie Grauman Wolf's, *Urban Village: Population, Community, and Family Structure in Germantown, Pennsylvania, 1683–1800* (Princeton, N.J., 1976), Jean R. Soderlund's *Quakers and Slavery: A Divided Spirit* (Princeton, N.J., 1985), Sally Schwartz's *"A Mixed Multitude": The Struggle for Toleration in Colonial Pennsylvania* (New York, 1987), Barry Levy's *Quakers and the American Family: British Settlement in the Delaware Valley, 1650–1765* (New York, 1988), Sharon V. Salinger's, *"To Serve Well and Faithfully": Labor and Indentured Servants in Pennsylvania, 1682–1800* (New York, 1987), and the essays in Richard S. Dunn and Mary Maples Dunn's *The World of William Penn* (Philadelphia, 1986).

By far the most important new work, however, is the monumental five-volume edition of *The Papers of William Penn*, edited by Richard Dunn, Mary Maples Dunn, and various associate editors (Philadelphia, 1981–1987). As brilliant, heavy, and handsome as founder William Penn himself, these volumes gather together—with lavish footnotes and illuminating headnotes—hundreds of the most important letters and documents relating to early Pennsylvania. In doing research for *Quakers and Politics*, I had seen all but a few of these documents in manuscript or microfilm form. Readers can gain ready access to nearly all the primary sources cited in the footnotes in this book in *The Papers of William Penn*, where they will also find the editors' penetrating introductions and interpretations of the documents. In *The Papers of William Penn* readers will also find a wealth of material on the complex personality and tangled financial affairs of the proprietor William Penn, a topic to which I devote scant attention. From *The Papers of*

William Penn comes a picture of a leader who was anything but a martyr and anything but a rigid ideologue; he appears instead as a man of thought in action—arguing, negotiating, cajoling, remonstrating, and compromising in order to launch a colony, settle a colony, and see a colony through its infancy and adolescence.

I hope that this new edition of *Quakers and Politics* will contribute to the discussions of multiculturalism that have swept over the United States and the entire world in the last decade. The migration of British Quakers to Pennsylvania in the 1680s brought to the Americas a people whose outlook and customary modes of behavior differed markedly from those of other colonists. At the root of Quaker distinctiveness was a set of beliefs and ways of looking at the world that bears relevance to the arguments today about gender roles, racial and ethnic pluralism, religious freedom, and a world without war.

Quakers opened people to a new definition of community—a gathering of those whose success depended on ignoring or downplaying differences of birth, background, or belief. If the capital city of Philadelphia was not always the City of Brotherly Love that Penn had hoped for, it was at least a place where religious toleration and ethnic diversity came to be thought of as the natural state of human affairs—the norm rather than a debilitating defect. The eighteenth-century European philosophes took great encouragement in this, for in Pennsylvania they saw proof of their notion that men and women could live together peacefully, though they differed in belief, skin shade, and place of origin. Even though political harmony in early Pennsylvania was difficult to achieve—as I have tried to show there was a constant struggle against factionalism and misunderstanding—Penn's colonists had a profound effect on the reforming impulse in American life, and their early experiences still have a guiding force near the end of the twentieth century.

PACIFIC PALISADES, CALIFORNIA
MAY 1993

Preface

FEW CHAPTERS in the history of the American people have
been told more devotedly than the settlement of the Delaware Valley by the Society of Friends in the late seventeenth
century. By conventional accounts, the Quakers—indus-
trious, lower middle-class, equalitarian, and persecuted
for their mystical religious beliefs—fled the oppressive government of a corrupt English society for the freedom and
purity of a New-World wilderness. Social visionaries, they
projected a Quaker dominion between the already established colonies of New York and Maryland. Emerging as
their leader was William Penn, a towering figure who
dreamed of a new breed of Christians, transplanted across
the water and restored to Apostolic purity. Like John Winthrop's "citty upon a hill" of a half-century before, Penn's
"holy experiment" has been taken as illustrative of the
seventeenth-century search among enlightened Englishmen
for a better social order.

Sectarian histories of the Quaker migration have been
numerous and indispensably important to an understanding of colonial Pennsylvania. But they have largely avoided
any analytical inquiry into the agonizing struggle for political stability and maturity which absorbed the Quakers of
Pennsylvania for almost half a century after Penn's charter
was issued in 1681. Connections between the structure of
society and the nature of politics, between the behavioral
tendencies of the Quakers and their social outlook, between
environment and political aspirations—in short, the sociol-
ogy of politics—have been left unexplored. It is well known
that over the course of half a century a provincial Quaker
aristocracy emerged in Pennsylvania and assumed a leading

role in colonial affairs. However, many pertinent facts in the narrative seem at times to be dimly perceived: the struggle of an immigrant elite to establish itself at the center of colonial life in the early years, its subsequent defense of power in the face of internal and external threats, and the disarrangement of colonial politics which followed. The full story is of transcendent importance to an understanding of the first half-century in Pennsylvania, and the historian of the Revolutionary era who fails to comprehend the peculiar and often disorderly nature of politics in the initial stages of settlement may be attracted to dangerously simplistic explanations of the character and significance of the American Revolution in Pennsylvania.

Although this book is largely about Quakers in Pennsylvania, it purports to have a broader significance. The Friends, as will be shown, had distinctive characteristics and values which helped to shape the course of politics on the Delaware; and yet the Quaker response to the conditions of the New World may be likened to that of other Englishmen in North America. The Quakers' attempt to reconcile inherited ideas and institutions with a new environment was, in many respects, typical of the American colonial experience. Though one would generalize guardedly, admitting that sectional, regional, and even local differences make it necessary to trace out the political morphology of each of the colonies, it is hoped that this study of society and politics in early Pennsylvania will contribute to an understanding of the political dynamics of the American colonies in general in the early stages of their development.

In pursuing this study I have incurred a host of debts. I wish to thank the editors of the *William and Mary Quarterly* and the *Pennsylvania Magazine of History and Biogra-*

phy for permission to use material in chapters one and two which appeared originally in their journals. The quiet efficiency of the staff members at the Historical Society of Pennsylvania, Princeton University Library, Chester County Historical Society, American Philosophical Society, Delaware Archives, Library of Congress, New York Public Library, Haverford College Library, Henry E. Huntington Library, Friends House, London, and the Public Record Office, London, is gratefully acknowledged. Acknowledgment is also made to these institutions for permission to quote from materials in their possession. Nicholas B. Wainwright of the Historical Society of Pennsylvania was generous in granting me the use of important materials from a private collection. The Princeton University Research Fund, the New Jersey Society of Colonial Wars, and the Academic Senate, University of California, Los Angeles, provided financial assistance while this study was in progress. Richard S. Dunn of the University of Pennsylvania read the entire manuscript and provided many important criticisms. Frederick B. Tolles of Swarthmore College and Stanley Coben of the University of California, Los Angeles, were kind enough to read parts of the manuscript and offer suggestions. John Shy of Princeton University, Robert Birrell of Indiana University, and James T. Lemon of the University of Toronto were indispensable in discussing problems of historical interpretation and may find ideas of their own buried in the book. Marjorie Putney guided the manuscript through its final stages. My largest debt is to Wesley Frank Craven of Princeton University who supervised the doctoral dissertation from which this book grew, gave generously of his time, and provided criticism and encouragement in perfect proportions.

Contents

CONTENTS

Quakers and Politics

PENNSYLVANIA
1681-1726

CHAPTER 1

Planning a Wilderness Utopia

TEN SHIPS, the largest weighing only 300 tons, slipped past
the Delaware Capes between December 1681 and August
1682, pushing cautiously up the treacherously shallow waters of what was still known as the South River. Only infrequently, as the vessels passed the simple Dutch and Swedish
settlements at Whorekil, New Castle, Upland, and Shackamaxon, could passengers see signs of civilization amid the
dense forest growth. The New World had been reached.
Heavy with anticipation, the settlers quit their ships—the
*Bristol Factor, John & Sarah, Amity, Freeman, Hester &
Hannah, Lyon,* and others—eagerly seeking the feel of firm
ground, the smell and sight of the wilderness before them.
They were a varied lot—yeomen from Wiltshire in the
south of England, artisans from Bristol in the west, tradesmen from London, gentry from Ireland and Wales, former
officers of Cromwell's navy. A few were people of substance.
Many were indentured servants, bound for a period of service to adventurers in better circumstances, but willingly so
bound in order to have a chance to trade sides of the Atlantic. Most were simply people possessed of little more than a
trunkful or so of tools, clothes, and household possessions,
and of a deed of sale, paid for in England, for a freehold in
the uncharted expanses of what they called Pennsylvania.[1]
But in all of them, whether wealthy, middling, or poor,

[1] For an account of the ships reaching Pennsylvania in the first year
of settlement, with notes on their passengers and cargoes, see Marion
Balderston, "William Penn's Twenty-Three Ships," *Pennsylvania Genealogical Magazine,* 23 (1963), 27-67.

word of the new Quaker settlement in the valley of the Delaware had seemingly kindled a fire.

Eight more ships laden with immigrants would move up the river in September and October of 1682 before the *Welcome* hove into view at New Castle on October 27. This particular ship, though ordinary in size and appearance, bore special significance, for it carried one of the best-known Englishmen of the day—William Penn, "true and absolute proprietary" of Pennsylvania, an intimate of the King, and a venerated leader of the Quaker movement. For Penn, the sight of his province must have been in itself a measure of fulfillment. For seventeen frenzied months, since his charter had been granted in March 1681, he had wrestled with the problems of launching a far-distant colony—appointing officials who would precede him to the colony, signing land grants, drafting laws and constitutional documents, writing promotional literature, conferring with associates and friends, and preparing his own affairs for departure.[2] It was a complex and difficult business. For although Penn could seek guidance in the precedents set during nearly a century of English colonization in North America, the founding of his province presented unique and unexpected problems, and the methods adopted by earlier settlements provided only half-solutions at best.

A Restoration Financial Tangle

"I had an opening of joy as to these parts in the year 1661, at Oxford," Penn wrote to merchant friends in Dublin only days after receiving his charter for Pennsylvania.[3] The de-

[2] Catherine Owens Peare, *William Penn* (Philadelphia, 1957), 216-238.

[3] Penn to Robert Turner, Anthony Sharp, and Roger Roberts, April

scription is deceptive, for it suggests that Penn's plans twenty years later were part of a coordinated, long-standing design by the Quakers to establish a dominion of their own in America. Penn knew, of course, that the Society of Friends had sent Josiah Coale to the Susquehanna Valley as early as 1660 to investigate the possibilities of a Quaker settlement there. Twelve years later, George Fox, the revered leader of the Quaker movement in its early period, trekked twice through the wilderness on both sides of the Delaware, noting the dense forests, abundant streams, and lush fertility of the river basin.[4] But the colonization of the region between New York and Maryland by the Society of Friends grew out of no grand strategy for a Quaker domain in the New World. It sprang rather from a series of highly circumstantial and involved financial proceedings, relating in the first instance to the bankruptcy of one Edward Byllynge, former officer in Monck's cavalry, London brewer, and eventually Middlesex "gentleman" and prominent member of the Society of Friends.

Byllynge, in 1673, was not only failing in business but was under the charge of peculating nearly £40,000 of the Society's money that had apparently been entrusted to him as treasurer of the London Quakers. Under heavy attack from his associates in religion, he responded eagerly to the proposals of an old friend, John Lord Berkeley, who offered a timely solution to his acute embarrassment. If Byllynge could raise a suitable sum, Berkeley would sell him his interest in New Jersey, which he held jointly with Sir

---

12, 1681, in Samuel M. Janney, *The Life of William Penn* (Philadelphia, 1852), 172-173.

4 William C. Braithwaite, *The Second Period of Quakerism* (2nd edn., Oxford, 1961), 400; John L. Nickalls, ed., *The Journal of George Fox* (Cambridge, 1952), 618-619, 632-634.

George Carteret under a grant made in 1664 by James, Duke of York. Berkeley, with little interest in colonizing schemes, stood to harvest a tidy profit from a region which he had received as a gift less than ten years before. Byllynge, for his part, could now promote colonization in New Jersey, and thereby recoup his losses on the proceeds of land sales.[5]

The purchase of Berkeley's share in New Jersey was made in trust by a friend, John Fenwick, presumably because Byllynge was in bankruptcy. But to Byllynge's dismay Fenwick, who was also hot in pursuit of fortune, refused to convey the deed to him unless granted one-tenth of the total purchase. When Fenwick threatened to take the dispute to Chancery Court, important London Quakers, many of them Byllynge's creditors, intervened. It was Quaker policy to arbitrate disputes between Friends out of court. To this end, and to unravel Byllynge's tangled finances, Gawen Lawrie, Nicholas Lucas, and William Penn were appointed as trustees of Byllynge's estate in 1674. Lawrie was a wealthy London merchant; Lucas a maltster of Hertfordshire; and Penn, though only thirty years old at the time, was already widely known within the Society of Friends for his influence in high circles of government and his skillful advocacy of the Quaker cause.[6]

[5] John E. Pomfret, *The Province of West New Jersey, 1609-1702* (Princeton, 1956), 65-66.

[6] *Ibid.*, 66-68. A discerning biography of Penn is notably absent from studies of Quakerism and colonial Pennsylvania though several dozen stereotyped treatments exist. The best narrative of his life is Peare's *William Penn*. The first attempt to analyze the founder's political, social, and economic thinking was Edward C. O. Beatty's *William Penn as a Social Philosopher* (New York, 1939). Two recent additions to the literature on Penn have begun to close the gap. Joseph Illick's *William Penn the Politician; His Relations with the English Government* (Ithaca, 1965) considers Penn's relations with the government in England. Mary M. Dunn's *William Penn, Politics and Con-*

It was perhaps at this point that financial happenstance and visions of a Quaker colony began to converge. Entrusted with the oversight of Byllynge's debt-ridden estate, which had as its chief asset an unconfirmed title to some 4,600 square miles of trackless land in the New World, the Trustees decided to promote a Quaker colony in West Jersey. It was a nice case of turning misfortune into advantage, for in the process of expunging Byllynge's debts to his Quaker associates, the trustees would be enlisting the support of influential Quakers for the establishment of an American colony.[7]

From 1676 to 1681, when he relinquished his trusteeship of West Jersey, Penn was constantly involved in the business of launching the Quaker enterprise. The importance of his efforts in settling Byllynge's tangled affairs and in promoting the venture was large. This was Penn's training ground in matters of colonization. His work also put him in contact with the whole upper stratum of English and Irish Quakers, people whose resources would provide the financial underpinning for the Pennsylvania undertaking a half-dozen years later. Combing the ranks of substantial Friends, Penn must have been struck by the amount of fluid capital available within the community of Quaker merchants, craftsmen, shopkeepers, and landowners, for the hundred shares into which investment in West Jersey had been divided were quickly sold at £350 each. That Quakers would so readily

---

science (Princeton, 1967) succeeds admirably in unraveling Penn's political thought, which was never so consistent or idealistic as historians have maintained.

7 John E. Pomfret, "The Proprietors of the Province of West New Jersey, 1674-1702," *Pennsylvania Magazine of History and Biography*, 75 (1951), 117-146 (cited hereafter as *PMHB*), discusses the early plans for West New Jersey and analyzes the list of initial investors.

subscribe such amounts was indicative of the buoyant atmosphere of venture capitalism prevailing in Restoration England. Though religious non-Conformists, Quakers were eager participants in an age which witnessed the rise of global commerce and the development of English overseas markets as widely separated as Asia and America.

Penn's involvement on the east side of the Delaware River was not long in awakening far more grandiose schemes in his restless mind. In April 1680 he laid before the Privy Council a petition for a patent to the west bank of the river, a territory wrested from the Dutch in 1664 and governed as a part of James's ducal proprietary colony centered at New York.[8] Penn had compelling arguments to support his request, for he had a lien of £16,000 on the Crown, a debt to his father, who had served Cromwell and Charles II as an admiral of the fleet. He was also an intimate friend of the King's brother, the Duke of York, and in fact fitted perfectly the pattern of Restoration courtiers whose past services to the Crown were repaid by the King's chief disposable asset—land in the New World. From the royal point of view it was a seasonable bargain. The territory granted to Penn had earlier been offered for sale at £1,200 by the Duke without success;[9] now it could be used to discharge a far larger

[8] The petition, partially mutilated, is reprinted in Samuel Hazard, ed., *Annals of Pennsylvania, from the Discovery of Delaware, 1609-1682* (Philadelphia, 1850), 474.

[9] Penn to Lord Romney, Sept. 6, 1701, Penn Papers, Granville Penn Book, fol. 6, Historical Society of Pennsylvania. (All manuscripts cited hereafter are in the collections of the Historical Society of Pennsylvania unless otherwise noted.) Although Penn's statement concerning the Duke of York's inability to sell the west bank of the Delaware was written twenty years after the fact, he is not likely to have erred in his assertion, since Romney, close to the center of power in the English government, was in a position to know the accuracy of Penn's statements.

obligation. In addition, there was political advantage in encouraging an exodus of the Whiggishly inclined Quakers from England at a time when the King's Tory supporters were hard pressed to maintain an upper hand at home.[10]

Enjoying such advantages, Penn was able to guide his charter through the bureaucratic labyrinth in eleven months. "This day my country was confirmed to me under the Great Seal of England," he wrote in exuberance on March 4, 1681, to a wealthy merchant friend in Dublin. "My God that has given it to me . . . will, I believe, bless and make it the seed of a nation."[11]

Whereas plans for the Quaker settlement of West Jersey took shape almost accidentally, emerging unexpectedly out of a financial dispute adjudicated within the Quaker community, the colonization of Pennsylvania was carefully plotted from the first, as the result of both economic and altruistic goals entertained by Penn. Little has been said by

[10] See Fulmer Mood, "William Penn and English Politics, 1680-81," *Journal of the Friends Historical Society*, 32 (London, 1940), 3-21. Mood is criticized by Charles M. Andrews for overstating the importance of the King's political motives in granting Penn's charter; see *The Colonial Period of American History* (New Haven, 1934-38), III, 279n. That the uncertainty of the political situation was a contributing factor is nonetheless true. Mood, arguing deductively, overlooked the most direct statement supporting his thesis—Penn's own assertion that the English government, at the time, "was glad to be rid of us, at so cheap a rate as a little parchment, to be practis'd in a desart, 3000 Miles off." Penn to Lord Romney, Sept. 6, 1701, Penn Papers, Granville Penn Book, fol. 6.

[11] Penn to Robert Turner, March 5, 1680/81, *Memoirs of the Historical Society of Pennsylvania*, I, Pt. 1 (Philadelphia, 1826), 208-209 (cited hereafter as *HSP Memoirs*). Until September 1752, England and her colonies used the Julian calendar in computing dates. Though the historical year began on January 1, the church, civil, and legal year began on March 25. Double-dating between these two dates was common and this practice is followed throughout in footnote citations but not in the text.

9

historians concerning the economic aspect of the settlement of Pennsylvania. Fragmentary evidence, however, including the language of Penn's petition for the patent in America, suggests that Penn himself was in financial straits in 1680, perhaps as a result of his failing estates in Ireland and England.[12] He had not subscribed even a partial share in the West Jersey enterprise, of which he was a principal mover, and this may be further evidence of his strained resources. Careless in money matters and accustomed to an aristocratic style of living, Penn may have seen in Pennsylvania a means of recouping or at least bolstering his sagging finances. Certainly he expected the colony to return handsome profits through quitrents and the sale of land. He did not hesitate to express his thoughts at the time the enterprise was getting under way: "Though I desire to extend religious freedom, yet I want some recompense for my trouble."[13]

To mention the economic motive is not to deny the religious and political factors at play, for essentially there was no incompatibility between them. Penn was genuinely disturbed at which he saw around him in England: intolerance, oppression, Philistinism, and hypocrisy. A colony in America offered the prospect of escaping both political and religious corruption in England. Such motives, he wrote later, varied little from those of others who had established proprietary governments, the Carolinas excepted.[14] Pennsylvania, in short, offered the rare opportunity to serve at once God, personal fortune, and fellow Quakers. It needed a more timid man than Penn to decline the challenge.

[12] Andrews, *Colonial Period*, III, 278.

[13] Penn to ———, July 1681, quoted in William R. Shepherd, *History of Proprietary Government in Pennsylvania* (New York, 1896), 175.

[14] Penn to Lord Romney, Sept. 6, 1701, Penn Papers, Granville Penn Book, fol. 6.

The Business of Colonization

With his charter secured, Penn's basic need was not for colonists, whom he knew he would have little difficulty recruiting, but for capital to finance his visionary scheme. Even a man of his position could not singlehandedly underwrite a trans-Atlantic migration, even if his own resources were not low at the time. Penn later calculated that the cost of obtaining a patent and launching his colony had run to almost £12,000 in the first two years alone.[15] As an experienced colonial promoter, Penn must have recognized that the success of his colony hinged in no small part on his ability to recruit wide financial support. The lessons of nearly one hundred years of English colonization were clear: success was unthinkable without the steady infusion of capital during the initial stage of settlement. Again and again colonial ventures had foundered on the rocks of inadequate financial backing, especially proprietary experiments such as that of Sir Ferdinando Gorges in New England and those in the Carolinas.

Fortunately for Penn, the problem was not without its solution. By the 1680's, English Quakerism, though identified chiefly with yeomen and shopkeeper-artisans, had attracted a considerable number of merchants and well-to-do gentry. Within a decade or so the "Richest Trading Men in London" were Quakers, according to one contemporary

[15] Penn to James Logan, Sept. 14, 1705, Edward Armstrong, ed., *The Correspondence of William Penn and James Logan* . . . (Philadelphia, 1879-80), II, 71 (cited hereafter as *Penn-Logan Correspondence*); Penn to Robert Harley, Feb. 9, 1704, Duke of Portland Manuscripts, *Historical Manuscripts Commission, Report*, IV (London, 1897), 80 (cited hereafter as *HMC Reports*).

observer.[16] Upon these men Penn would count initially for support.

Penn was singularly well-connected in Quaker society to make his appeal. Not only in his endeavors for West New Jersey but as one of the intellectual leaders of the Quaker movement, he had circulated for years among the most affluent Friends, establishing cordial relations with merchants of note in all the urban centers of Quakerism—Dublin, Cork, Bristol, and London—and with the Quaker gentry in the countryside. His courageous efforts in the law courts and at Whitehall on behalf of the faith had made his name almost a household word among Quakers. No less intimate was his association with the religious leaders of the movement— George Fox, William Meade, Alexander Parker, George Keith, Robert Barclay, Benjamin Furly, and others. Penn was often a companion on their evangelical trips through England, Scotland, and Ireland, and even to the Rhineland and Holland.[17] When the Pennsylvania charter was granted in 1681, these friendships paid dividends. Every "Publick Friend," as the traveling religious leaders were known, was a potential spokesman for Penn's undertaking. There were few who did not respond. Over the Society's well-developed lines of communication word went out: Penn's charter had passed; a plan of government was being drawn; land grants could be obtained through Penn's agents in most of the major towns.

But even the exciting word of Penn's grant was probably

16 Charles Leslie, *The Snake in the Grass* (London, 1698), quoted in Frederick B. Tolles, *Meeting House and Counting House: The Quaker Merchants of Colonial Philadelphia, 1682-1763* (Chapel Hill, 1948), 48.
17 The intimacy of Penn with the leading figures of the Society of Friends can be traced in Peare, *William Penn*, and Nickalls, ed., *Journal of George Fox*, passim.

not enough to attract the broad support of affluent Friends. By 1682 a Quaker intent on emigration or with capital to invest could choose among three New-World colonies dominated by Friends: Pennsylvania, West Jersey, or East Jersey. Twelve Quaker proprietors, including Penn, had purchased East Jersey while plans for Pennsylvania went forward. Like colonial promoters before him, Penn had to appeal for backing with the argument that his colony would be not only a haven for the oppressed, but a highly promising investment. He recognized that the support of well-to-do Friends could best be mobilized by presenting Pennsylvania not only as a religious refuge—a place for the English Quakers to build their own "city on a hill"—but also as an area ripe for economic exploitation. The same motives which induced Quaker men of means to purchase shares in East and West Jersey, and to trade them speculatively throughout the 1680's, were at play in the purchase of large blocks of land in Pennsylvania.[18] Penn, in effect, was competing for investors with the other Quaker colonies. Robert Barclay, his promotional agent in Scotland, reminded him of this in 1681, warning that the cheap price of East Jersey land "makes thine seem dear." "Thou has land enough," cautioned Barclay, "so need not be a churle if thou intend to advance thy plantation."[19]

Penn's promotional tracts of 1681 and 1682, addressed to both investors and potential settlers, reflected his awareness

[18] For trading of East New Jersey shares, see, for example, James Claypoole to Thomas Cooke, Nov. 14, 1682, Marion Balderston, ed., *James Claypoole's Letter Book, London and Philadelphia, 1681-1684* (San Marino, Calif., 1967), 170.

[19] Robert Barclay to Penn, Nov. 29, 1681, Francis F. Hart Collection. Competition for settlers led to serious friction between Pennsylvania and West New Jersey in the early years of settlement. See *New Jersey Archives*, 1st Ser., I (Newark, 1880), 415-421.

that support depended upon advertising the colony as a field for economic development and as a future center of overseas commerce in North America.[20] It is not surprising that the proprietors of West Jersey were currently presenting their colony in precisely this manner, combining glowing statements about the opportunities for small landowners with predictions of the region's great commercial future.[21] Penn's first advertisement, *Some Account of the Province of Pennsilvania*, made much of the commercial prospects, discussing the natural channels of trade to other mainland colonies and the West Indies, the fur trade, the rich timber resources, and the ripe prospects "for those that will follow merchandize and Navigation."[22] A flurry of such promotional essays followed, culminating in 1683 with the ebullient claim that not only the Delaware River but its tributaries, the Christina, Brandywine, Shelpot, and Schuylkill, had "room to lay up the Royal Navy of England."[23]

Penn's sober concern for the mercantile development of his colony was always curiously mixed with more nostalgic visions of an agrarian utopia in the New World. In more philosophical moments he dreamed of a "greene country towne" serving the commercial needs of a basically agricultural society. He advised his children to eschew trade for agriculture, for the latter was a calling which led men to ponder the works of God and diverted the mind "from being

20 The tracts are listed and described by Hope Frances Kane, "Notes on Early Pennsylvania Promotion Literature," *PMHB*, 63 (1939), 144-168.

21 *The Present State of the Colony of West-Jersey* (London, 1681), in Albert C. Myers, ed., *Narratives of Early Pennsylvania, West New Jersey, and Delaware* (New York, 1912), 191-195.

22 *Ibid.*, 202-215.

23 *Letter from William Penn to the Committee of the Free Society of Traders, 1683* (London, 1683), in Myers, ed., *Narratives*, 224-244.

taken up with the vain arts and inventions of a luxurious world."[24] This was Penn in his pastoral mood, the social critic of Restoration England. But he was involved in trade himself, and in less ruminative moments recognized that commerce in Pennsylvania would be the springboard to growth and prosperity.

The campaign to present Pennsylvania not only as a religious haven but also as a prudent and promising investment was waged vigorously throughout 1681 and 1682. Assisting Penn in his appeal to the affluent members of Quaker society were a few close merchant friends. Robert Turner, a rising cloth merchant of Dublin, acted as a go-between in that city. In London, merchant James Claypoole, with commercial ties to the West Indies, the Baltic, and other centers of English commerce, played a central role, encouraging fellow traders to subscribe to the cause. In Rotterdam, Benjamin Furly, a great Quaker trader, functioned similarly, as did James Harrison in Bolton and Robert Barclay in Scotland. By the summer of 1682, nearly 500,000 acres had been sold, yielding Penn—at least on paper—receipts of about £10,000.[25]

The success of Penn's appeal to substantial Quakers is evident in an analysis of the men who bought land directly

24 Quoted in Thomas Clarkson, *A Portraiture of Quakerism* . . . (New York, 1806), II, 44.

25 For the assistance of Penn's merchant friends see John E. Pomfret, "The First Purchasers of Pennsylvania, 1681-1700," *PMHB*, 80 (1956), 145, and Balderston, ed., *Claypoole's Letter Book*, passim. Land sales as of about August 1682 are listed in Hazard, ed., *Annals*, 637-642. Hazard dates the list May 22, 1682, but is probably incorrect since deeds of purchase for some of those listed (as recorded in Lease and Release A-1 and B-2, Bureau of Land Records, Department of Internal Affairs, Harrisburg, Pa.) are dated as late as Aug. 6, 1682. By late 1684, Penn's secretary in London had received nearly £8,000 from the sale of Pennsylvania land. Shepherd, *Proprietary Government in Pennsylvania*, 186n.

from the proprietor in the first years of settlement. One surviving list of "First Purchasers," tabulating land sales as of mid-1682, reveals that of some 469 buyers, 41 subscribed to 241,000 acres, or nearly half the land purchased. Another list, which probably records purchases through 1684, itemizes 751 purchasers, 69 of whom absorbed 380,000 of the 860,000 acres sold. In both lists each large purchaser—Penn called them "lords" or "barons"—took 5,000 acres or more. It is also notable that while about two-thirds of the early purchasers immigrated to Pennsylvania, only about one-third of the baronial buyers—men with 5,000 acres or more —did so. Of 56 large purchasers in the first list, only 13 moved to Pennsylvania. On the 1684 list, only 20 of 69 purchasers left the Old World.[26]

This upper stratum upon which Penn depended so heavily was studded with Quaker merchants, particularly from London and to a lesser degree from Bristol and Dublin. Regardless of which list of purchasers is used, mercantile wealth is identifiable in more than half of the names. Richard Marsh, Robert Turner, Thomas Callowhill, Samuel Carpenter, Samuel Claridge, James Claypoole, Joseph Fisher, John Fuller, James Lyell, and many more—practically a roll call of the better-known Quaker merchants in England and Ireland, with a scattering from other places— make up the list. The other major investors formed a potpourri of professional men, prosperous landowners, and Penn's relatives and personal associates.[27] The purchases of

[26] Pomfret, "The First Purchasers of Pennsylvania," *PMHB*, 80 (1956), 148-150, and statistics based on my own analysis of the lists. The 1684 list of purchasers is in the Penn Papers, Pennsylvania Cash Accounts. Technically, "First Purchasers" were the buyers of the first 500,000 acres of land in Pennsylvania.

[27] Biographical data on the first generation of colonists must be sought in widely scattered sources. The most important are the 91 vol-

some of these investors represented venture capital advanced primarily for speculative purposes by men who had no intention of going to Pennsylvania. Of those who planned to live in the province, most, including the merchants, purchased land on the assumption that it would appreciate rapidly as new settlers sought property in Philadelphia and the surrounding countryside. A few of the gentry and a handful of prosperous yeomen, men like Phineas Pemberton, Nicholas More, Joseph Growden, and the landed leaders of the Welsh migration, sought a new life in the colony as country gentlemen. But of greatest numerical importance in early Pennsylvania were the yeomen and artisans who left England for both religious and economic reasons. While seeking such sturdy settlers, Penn relied on a far smaller number of prosperous men for the purchase of nearly half of the land and, what is more, counted on them for political leadership.[28]

---

umes of the *PMHB* for which the *Index* to volumes 1-75 is an invaluable aid; editorial notes in Norman Penney, ed., *The Journal of George Fox* (2 vols., Cambridge, 1911), and Norman Penney, ed., *The Short Journal and Itinerary Journals of George Fox* (Cambridge, 1925); John W. Jordan, ed., *Colonial Families of Philadelphia* (2 vols., New York, 1911); Wilfred Jordan, ed., *Colonial and Revolutionary Families of Philadelphia* (16 vols., New York, 1933-60); Joseph Besse, *A Collection of the Sufferings of the People Called Quakers . . .* (2 vols., London, 1753); William H. Hinshaw, ed., *Encyclopedia of American Quaker Genealogy* (6 vols., Ann Arbor, 1936-50); and the extensive collections, both manuscript and published, at the Genealogical Society of Pennsylvania, the Historical Society of Pennsylvania, and Friends House, London.

[28] For the motivation and social origins of the early settlers see Tolles, *Meeting House*, 33-44, and Alan Cole, "The Social Origins of the Early Friends," *Journal of the Friends Historical Society*, 48 (London, 1956-58), 99-118.

Mobilizing Support

In recruiting the support of the upper stratum of English Quakers, Penn offered handsome rewards to those who would join him in the work of nation-building in the wilderness. It is not too much to say, in fact, that in forging plans for his colony Penn placed himself and his principal associates at the vital center of economic and political affairs. The distribution of land, the establishment of a joint-stock company to trade between Pennsylvania and London, the conferral of profitable offices, and the organization of government were all a part of this pattern.

Among the inducements which Penn offered to men of wealth was an alluring plan of land allocation in the capital city—later named Philadelphia. From the earliest stages of planning, Penn envisioned a colony built around a river capital which would serve as the seat of government and the hub of commercial activity. His plan reflected not only his familiarity with London and the surrounding countryside and a natural tendency to borrow from English precedents, but more practical considerations as well. Penn intended to sell no property in the city outright, but to reserve Philadelphia as a bonus for the purchasers of the first 500,000 acres of country land. The land in the capital city would be distributed by lot at the rate of 10 acres for every 500 purchased in the country.[29] The larger the purchase of country land, the larger the dividend in the city. Naturally, the city lots would appreciate more rapidly than other real estate in the province. Small purchasers, if they acted promptly,

[29] A statement of terms on which land could be purchased and held, "Certain conditions and concessions agreed upon by William Penn . . . ," was issued in July 1681. It is given in Hazard, ed., *Annals*, 516-520.

would also profit, but it is clear that Penn was primarily attempting to attract wealthy buyers. In fact, one of the first promotional pamphlets emphasized that land would be sold only in shares of 5,000 acres.[30]

The land bonus scheme worked to the mutual benefit of Penn and the major investors. The tantalizing offer of a dominant position in city realty stimulated large purchases of land; the buyers, in turn, only a third of whom would emigrate, could savor the prospect of a handsome return on their investment as incoming settlers bid for property in the commercial center of the province. Whether Penn privately offered the largest investors priority to waterfront property at this time is not known. It is not unlikely, though, for when Penn actually allocated the city lots after his arrival in October 1682, he did just this, placing his relatives and those "that he had the Greatest regard for" on the most advantageous sites.[31]

It was not only through concessions relating to land that Penn attracted the support of able and affluent Quakers. An integral part of his overall plan was a joint-stock company which, capitalizing on special privileges granted by Penn, was to occupy a central position in the economic life of the young colony. Named the Free Society of Traders in Pennsylvania, the company was primarily the work of a small group of London Quakers, mostly merchants, who from the outset enjoyed Penn's warm support.[32] Leading the enter-

[30] *Some Account of the Province of Pennsilvania* (London, 1681). Myers, ed., *Narratives*, 208. Those unable to purchase 5,000 acres could either rent land from the purchasers or come as indentured servants. *Ibid.*

[31] Minutes of the Board of Property of the Province of Pennsylvania, *Pennsylvania Archives*, 2nd Ser., XIX (Harrisburg, 1890), 532.

[32] The Free Society of Traders is discussed by Simeon E. Baldwin, "American Business Corporations before 1786," *American Historical*

prise were three Londoners, Nicholas More, James Claypoole and Philip Ford. More, a wealthy physician, had long
been interested in seeking a fortune in the Quaker colony
to be established on the Delaware. In 1670 he had married
Mary Hedge, daughter of a prosperous Quaker merchant
of London. Five years later More's brother-in-law, Samuel
Hedge, immigrated to Salem in West Jersey with John Fenwick, founder of that settlement, and married Fenwick's
daughter.[33] Already a large landholder, Hedge may have
interested More in the possibilities of the area. In 1681 More
made his move, purchasing from Penn a 10,000 acre tract,
later called the Manor of Moreland. More invested £300
in the company and was appointed president, perhaps in
recognition of his substantial investment.

Merchant James Claypoole, another dominant figure, also
purchased 10,000 acres in the colony. Penn "is so much my
friend," he wrote his brother in 1682, "that I can have anything in reason I desire of him." Claypoole functioned as
the chief promotional agent of the Society, a position for
which he was admirably suited by his extensive mercantile
contacts. Philip Ford was also a London merchant, and
since 1670 had been in charge of Penn's business and financial affairs. Like Claypoole and More, he invested liberally
in Pennsylvania, purchasing 5,000 acres from Penn and sink-
ing an additional £400 into the Free Society.[34]

Widening the Society's circle of leadership were six other

Review, 8 (1902-03), 453-456; and in greater detail in Meredith B.
Colket, Jr., "The Free Society of Traders in Pennsylvania" (unpublished
M.A. thesis, Haverford College, 1940).

33 Myers, ed., *Narratives*, 281-282.

34 A list of subscribers is in *PMHB*, 11 (1887), 175-180. Claypoole's
central role in the early history of the Free Society is revealed in his letter book, edited by Marion Balderston; for the comment on Penn see
Claypoole's Letter Book, 111.

men, all investors in Pennsylvania land. Four of them—
William Sharlow, Thomas Barker, Edward Pierce, and Edward Brooks—were London Quakers, each active in the
world of commerce. The other two, John Simcock and
Thomas Brassey, were substantial yeomen of Cheshire and
staunch friends of Penn.

Under the leadership of these men the Free Society projected bold plans for the economic development of Pennsylvania. As a beginning, 200 indentured servants were to be
sent to the colony. Hopefully this agricultural labor force
would quickly produce commodity surpluses on the Society's
20,000 acres. Further profit was anticipated from the lease of
land to incoming settlers, who would pay quitrents to the
company while living under its administrative shelter.[35]

More advanced projects would follow this initial utiliza-
tion of land. Extraction of whale bone and oil, the manufacture of hemp and linen, mining enterprises, and fisheries
were projected. Two thousand pounds was allocated to
launch a fur trade with the Indians. But the greatest profits
were expected to come from "factories" to be situated in
Philadelphia and on Delaware and Chesapeake bays. These
were to be the supply centers of the colony, manned by
agents of the Society who would barter or sell a wide array
of imported manufactures needed in the colony in exchange
for tobacco, fish, grain, and other produce brought in by
the settlers.[36]

Recognizing the need for ample capital to initiate such

[35] Penn's charter to the Society is in Hazard, ed., *Annals*, 541-550. For
the company's early plans see *The Articles Settlement & Offices of the
Free Society of Traders in Pennsilvania* . . . (London, 1682) , reprinted
in *PMHB*, 5 (1881) , 37-50.

[36] *Ibid.*; see also James Claypoole to Edward Claypoole, April 20,
1682; same to Norton Claypoole, July 14, 1682, Balderston, ed., *Claypoole's Letter Book*, 109-111, 132-134.

ambitious plans, the Society's leaders set out to raise £20,-
000 in subscriptions. Both large and small investors were
courted in an enthusiastic prospectus which proclaimed
the advantages of this "very Unusual Society." Pennsylvania,
England, and the investors would all bask in the benefits of
the Free Society of Traders. And like all such companies
before and since, it would be "a great and prudent body, a
kind of perpetual Trustees; the Friend of the Widdow and
the Orphan."[37]

There can be little doubt that from the outset Penn regarded the Free Society as an integral part of his plans for
the colony. In selling the company 20,000 acres, Penn
charged the usual price of £100 per 5,000 acres, but agreed
to forego quitrents on the tract. The Society was promised
three seats on the provincial council and its charter was ratified by the so-called Laws Agreed Upon in England.[38] Ultimate confirmation of the laws—and thus of the Society's
charter—was deferred until the first assembly convened in
Pennsylvania, but there seemed no reason to doubt that this
approval would be given. Penn personally promoted the
company by publishing a lengthy *Letter to the Free Society
of Traders* . . . (1683), a promotional pamphlet which expressed in glowing terms the central role he had reserved for
the company in the economic development of his colony.[39]

An analysis of stock subscribers to the Free Society reveals

[37] *The Articles Settlement & Offices of the Free Society* . . . , *PMHB*,
5 (1882), 49.

[38] "List of Subscribers to the Free Society of Traders . . . ," in *PMHB*,
11 (1887), 175-180; *The Articles Settlement & Offices of the Free
Society* . . . , *PMHB*, 5 (1881), 37-50; Francis N. Thorpe, ed., *The
Federal and State Constitutions, Colonial Charters, and Other Organic
Laws* . . . (Washington, 1909), v, 3,062.

[39] *The Articles Settlement & Offices of the Free Society* . . . , *PMHB*,
5 (1882), 44-45; Penn's *Letter to the Free Society of Traders* . . . in
Myers, ed., *Narratives*, 224-244.

that the principal investors, like the major land purchasers, represented chiefly a small circle of Quaker merchants, joined by Penn's relatives and close associates, and a handful of prosperous landowners. Of 32 purchasers investing £100 or more, 7 were related to Penn or in his employ, 5 were substantial landowners (2 of them gentry), 14 were merchants, 3 were shopkeepers, 1 was a doctor, and 2 are unidentifiable. Two-thirds of them purchased land in the early years, most of them investing in large tracts. The list of subscribers to the Free Society's stock diverges from that of the early land purchasers at the lower levels. Among the First Purchasers, the small buyers tended to be modest landowners, craftsmen, and artisans who planned to immigrate to Pennsylvania. In the Free Society the lesser subscribers were typically merchants, shopkeepers, artisans, and yeomen, who intended to remain in England.[40]

The election of company officers and a twelve-man governing committee to manage affairs in Pennsylvania also revealed the interlocking nature of principal land purchasers and prominent members of the Society. More, Claypoole, and Simcock, the first three officers of the company, had purchased respectively 10,000, 10,000, and 7,875 acres. On the committee of twelve were many of Penn's closest associates: merchants Robert Turner, William Haige, Francis Plumstead, and Griffith Jones; Thomas Holme, Penn's gentleman neighbor at his Irish estates; and James Harrison, shopkeeper of Lancashire and Penn's promotional agent in that area. Four were proprietors of West Jersey, well known to Penn in that capacity—Turner, Haige, Anthony Elton, and Isaac Martin—and three served as proprietors for East Jer-

[40] Based on an analysis of the lists of First Purchasers and subscribers to the Free Society previously cited, and on biographical data compiled from sources listed in note 27.

sey—Turner, Haige, and Francis Plumstead. Collectively the officers and committeemen of the Free Society had invested more than £1,200 in about 61,000 acres of Pennsylvania land.[41]

Penn used his extensive patronage power as an additional means of recruiting prosperous adherents to follow him to Pennsylvania. Initially the proprietor reserved the right to appoint all proprietary, provincial, and county officers; each would serve, barring misbehavior, for life. Penn put this broad appointive power to good use. As the table below indicates, positions of profit and power went almost uniformly to men whose tangible commitment to the "holy experiment" was substantial. In striking contrast to both East and West New Jersey, the other Quaker colonies in the New World, dual office-holding was not forbidden in Pennsylvania; in fact, it was common practice.

Nicholas More, the President of the Free Society of Traders, was appointed Provincial Secretary and Clerk of the Council, both positions of high importance. Once in Pennsylvania, Penn augmented More's importance by commissioning him Chief Justice of the Provincial Court. Robert Turner, Penn's former agent in Dublin and a purchaser of 6,000 acres, gained a seat on the powerful Board of Propriety, created to administer the allocation of land in Penn's absence. Turner also sat as a provincial judge and a justice of the peace for Philadelphia County. William Markham, Penn's kinsman and purchaser of 5,000 acres, functioned before Penn's arrival as his deputy governor and thereafter as Proprietary Secretary and a member of the Board of Propriety. Thomas Holme, another large landholder, was ap-

[41] The officers of the Society are given in the minutes of the first meeting of the company in London, May 29, 1682. See Hazard, ed., *Annals*, 576-577.

pointed first as Markham's assistant and then as Receiver General for the Lower Counties (later the province of Delaware), Surveyor General, and justice of the Philadelphia County Court. Thomas Rudyard, Penn's trusted solicitor and legal draughtsman in London, was rewarded for his 5,000-acre purchase with the important offices of Master of the Rolls and Keeper of the Seal. Hardly a position of influence or profit in the early years was conferred on a man who invested in less than 5,000 acres in the province. Most appointees were also stockholders in the Free Society of Traders.

Of the First Purchasers of 5,000 acres or more who came to Pennsylvania before 1684, only four—Simcock, Growden, Brassey, and Jones—were not rewarded with important offices, all but the last simply because they chose to establish estates in the country where they were appointed to the county courts and assumed leading roles in local affairs. Looking at the question in another way, it can be said that of all the important officeholders, only three—Clarke, Welch, and Haige—were not large land buyers. Each of these men, however, was a proprietor and vast landowner in West Jersey, and earlier an intimate of Penn in England. All were merchants, all were Quakers; Haige and Clarke, who preceded Penn to the Delaware, were already experienced in matters of settlement. Haige and Welch died within a few years, but Clarke lived on to become Penn's most trusted officeholder in the Lower Counties and the most influential figure on the lower Delaware Bay.

That Penn should establish a system of economic and political control which delivered power and advantage to those who invested most heavily in his plan is hardly surprising. Like any enterpriser, colonial or otherwise, he sought support among the wealthiest and most experienced members

INITIAL APPOINTMENTS TO PROVINCIAL AND PROPRIETARY OFFICES
IN PENNSYLVANIA[42]

Office	Appointee	Land Purchased, Acres	Religion	Occupation in England
Deputy Governor	William Markham	5,000	Anglican	Gentleman
Assistant Deputy Governor	Silas Crispin*	5,000	Quaker	Gentleman
	Thomas Holme	5,000	Quaker	Gentleman
Commissioners for Settling the Colony	Silas Crispin*	5,000	Quaker	Gentleman
	William Haige	500	Quaker	Merchant
	Nathaniel Allen	2,000	Quaker	Cooper
	John Bezar	1,000	Quaker	Maltster
Keeper of the Seal	Thomas Rudyard**	5,000	Quaker	Lawyer
	Thomas Lloyd	5,000	Quaker	Gentleman
Master of the Rolls	Thomas Rudyard**	5,000	Quaker	Lawyer
	Thomas Lloyd	5,000	Quaker	Gentleman
Surveyor General	Thomas Holme	5,000	Quaker	Gentleman
Receiver General	Christopher Taylor	5,000	Quaker	School teacher
Receiver General for the Lower Counties	Thomas Holme	5,000	Quaker	Gentleman
Register General	Christopher Taylor	5,000	Quaker	School teacher
Provincial Secretary and Clerk of Provincial Council	Richard Ingelo***	500	Quaker	?
	Nicholas More	10,000	Anglican	Gentleman

Position	Name	Acres	Religion	Occupation
Provincial Treasurer	Robert Turner	6,000	Quaker	Merchant
Chief Justice of Provincial Court	Silas Crispin*	5,000	Quaker	Gentleman
	Nicholas More	10,000	Anglican	Physician
Provincial Judges	William Welch	?	Quaker	Merchant
	William Wood	2,500	Quaker	Merchant
	Robert Turner	6,000	Quaker	Merchant
	John Eckley	1,250	Quaker	Yeoman
Attorney-General	John White	1,000	Quaker	Attorney
Commissioners of Propriety	James Claypoole	10,000	Quaker	Merchant
	Robert Turner	6,000	Quaker	Merchant
	Thomas Lloyd	5,000	Quaker	Gentleman
	Samuel Carpenter	5,000	Quaker	Merchant
Proprietary Secretary	Philip Lehmann	1,000	Quaker	Gentleman
Proprietary Steward	James Harrison	5,000	Quaker	Shopkeeper

* Died en route to Pennsylvania
** Relinquished appointment to assume lieutenant governorship of East New Jersey
*** Served only five months

42 Many of Penn's early appointments are listed in John Hill Martin, *Martin's Bench and Bar of Philadelphia* . . . (Philadelphia, 1883) and in *Pennsylvania Archives*, 2nd Ser., IX, 607-766. Neither compilation, however, is wholly accurate or complete; they have been corrected and supplemented by consulting the multitude of commissions found in the Penn Papers, Pemberton Papers, Etting Collection, and Society Miscellaneous Collection; Penn Manuscripts and Ancient Documents, American Philosophical Society; and Deed Books C-1, E-1/5, and E-2/5, Recorder of Deeds, City Hall, Philadelphia.

of the community. Conversely, these men expected compensation for their financial backing and their willingness to start life anew in a distant wilderness. Notwithstanding what has been written about Quaker equalitarianism, one searches in vain for evidence that Pennsylvania was ever conceived as an economic or political democracy in nineteenth- or twentieth-century terms. Nothing could have been more natural than the transplanting of an ordered society in which position and power belonged to those whose stake in the venture was the largest.

Fashioning a Constitution

In addition to the terms of land allocation, the chartering of the Free Society of Traders, and the distribution of patronage, one must consider the most central aspect of the governmental apparatus which was constructed in London prior to colonial settlement—the Frame of 1682, a constitutional scheme under which Pennsylvania was to be governed. Little is known of the pressures and influences to which Penn was subjected as he pieced together the instruments of government in the crowded months after his charter was granted. Most writers are content to believe that he was given the rare opportunity of forging a government of his own, and that the result was a pure distillation of his philosophy, drawn from studies of classical Republican writers, his practical experience in the affairs of West New Jersey, and the counsel of a few intimate advisors such as Algernon Sidney, the radical parliamentarian, and Benjamin Furly.

This uncomplicated view assumes a confidence in Penn on the part of his principal supporters that probably never existed. Penn was probably far from a free agent in the work of constituting a government. William Markham, his cousin and a trusted adjutant in the colony for many years, indicated as much when he wrote later: "I knew very well it [the Frame of Government] was forced upon him by friends who unless they received all that they demanded would not settle the country."[43] But beyond this intriguing comment little direct evidence of such pressures survives to illuminate the government-making process in 1681; nor is it likely that any interplay between Penn and his supporters was recorded at the time. Nonetheless, it was to be expected that men prepared to invest heavily in Pennsylvania, and especially those who were transferring their fortunes to the province, should demand a voice in constructing the framework of government, just as they had expected special concessions in the allocation of land and first consideration in the distribution of profitable offices. The absence of conclusive evidence leaves any hypothesis open to question, but there are strong indications that Penn's circle of backers caused him to deviate markedly from his own ideas on government in favor of a system more to their liking and advantage. At the same time, in accommodating their demands, Penn seems to have taken a second hard look at the experiment he was promoting and to have sought powers as proprietor and governor that earlier he might have considered extreme.

It needs to be understood, in discussing Penn's political ideas, that consistency was never a characteristic of the proprietor's thinking, and that even at the time when plans for Pennsylvania were going forward Penn's political philosophy was far from frozen.[44] On the one hand, he had long

[43] William Markham to Governor Benjamin Fletcher, May 20, 1696, *Calendar of State Papers, Colonial Series, America and West Indies, 1696-97* (London, 1904) , #27xi.

[44] On the discordant tendencies in Penn's political philosophy see

been in the vanguard of those Restoration critics who contended that English rights and liberties were being endangered by creeping licentiousness and authoritarianism. His
efforts on behalf of religious toleration and civil liberties in
the 1670's were unmatched by any Englishman of his time.
Penn had enunciated a call for moderation and sympathy in
affairs of church and state and for recognition of the populace as the ultimate source of political authority in memo-
rials to Parliament, to the sheriffs of London, and to the
justices and lords; in speeches before parliamentary committees and Charles II; and in pamphlets.[45] Here was a
man entirely at home with the "commonwealth-men" of his
era, who sought to follow Milton's injunction that Englishmen must teach the nations how to live. But in other ways
Penn was essentially a conservative thinker, committed to a
political order based on property, in favor of a social system
which upheld "all reasonable distinction and those civil degrees that are amongst people," and he was filled with a
downright aversion to the "mob" and the "rabble."[46] He
wrote in the 1670's that freedom was endangered "by the

Beatty, *William Penn as a Social Philosopher*, 20-41. By far the most
perceptive investigation of Penn's political theory is Dunn, *William
Penn, Politics and Conscience*. For a different view see Richard J.
Oman, "William Penn: A Study in the Quaker Doctrine of Political
Authority" (unpublished Ph.D. dissertation, University of Edinburgh,
1958) .

[45] *The Great Case of Liberty of Conscience* . . . (London, 1670) ;
England's Present Interest Discovered . . . (London, 1675) ; *An Address
to Protestants of All Persuasions* . . . (London, 1679) ; *England's Great
Interest in the Choice of This New Parliament* (London, [1679]) ;
and *One Project for the Good of England* . . . (London, [1679]) .

[46] Joseph Dorfman, *The Economic Mind in American Civilization,
1606-1865* (New York, 1946) , I, 80, quoting Penn, *An Address to Protestants*.

ambitions of the populace which shakes the constitution,"[47] and at moments seemed filled with a nostalgic longing for the feudal past with its well-ordered society and its "old time Nobility and Gentry."[48] Even in America Penn sometimes likened his provincial councilors to the English "Knights of Shires."[49]

Despite these sometimes ambivalent tendencies in his thought, Penn did commit himself wholeheartedly to one constitutional document of the 1670's—the West New Jersey Concessions and Agreements of 1677, published as fundamental law for the western half of the Jerseys. Although Penn's authorship of the Concessions and Agreements has been questioned, there is little doubt that many of his ideas found expression there and that as a trustee of the colony he gave his full consent to it.[50] In this sense it is indicative of his thinking on matters of civil polity during this period. By its provisions the Concessions delivered all legislative power to an assembly, chosen by the "inhabitants, freehold-

[47] Quoted in Beatty, *William Penn*, 38.

[48] William Penn, *Some Account of the Province of Pennsilvania* (London, 1681), in Myers, ed., *Narratives*, 205. For this vein in Penn's thinking see also Anthony N. B. Garvan, "Proprietary Philadelphia as Artifact," in Oscar Handlin and John Burchard, eds., *The Historian and the City* (Cambridge, Mass., 1963), 177-201.

[49] Penn to William Clarke, ca. Feb. 1683, *Pennsylvania Archives*, 2nd Ser., VII, 6.

[50] See John L. Nickalls, "The Problem of Edward Byllynge: His Writings and Their Evidence of his Influence on the First Constitution of New Jersey," in Howard H. Brinton, ed., *Children of Light* (New York, 1938), 111-131; and John E. Pomfret, "The Problem of the West Jersey Concessions of 1676/77," *William and Mary Quarterly*, 3rd Ser., 5 (1948), 95-105. Despite such arguments, the authorship of Byllynge is not wholly proven. In all likelihood Byllynge participated in the preparation of the Concessions but played a secondary role to the more active Quaker trustees of West New Jersey—Nicholas Lucas, Gawen Lawrie, and Penn.

ers and proprietors" of the colony. The legislature was to constitute courts and define the jurisdiction of each, appoint the principal public officers, choose its own speaker, meet and adjourn as it saw fit, and appoint a ten-man commission to act in an executive capacity. Justices of the peace and local officeholders were also to be elected. Complete freedom of religion and explicit guarantees of trial by jury were included.[51] As Penn and five other trustees wrote even before the document was published, "we lay a foundation for after ages to understand their liberty as men and christians, that they may not be brought in bondage, but by their own consent; for we put the power in the people."[52]

The West Jersey Concessions perhaps went farther than even Penn might have been expected to go. By personal preference, he might have hewed closer to the enlightened constitutional theory of the time, which prescribed a balance of strong and independent governmental powers as the best safeguard against tyranny.[53] Just such a system was believed to be embodied, at least theoretically, in the English government—an equilibrium of monarchy, aristocracy, and democracy as represented by King, Lords, and Commons. Most of the colonies, in distributing power among governor, council, and assembly, followed the English example with its emphasis on equipoise. Also, Penn might logically have made other modifications of the concept of limited government simply because his charter to Pennsylvania was proprietary in form.

[51] Aaron Leaming and Jacob Spicer, *The Grants, Concessions, and Original Constitutions of the Province of New Jersey* . . . (2nd edn., Philadelphia, 1881), 382-411.

[52] Gawen Lawrie, William Penn, Nicholas Lucas, Edward Byllynge, John Eldridge, and Edmond Warner to Richard Hartshorne, Aug. 26, 1676, *New Jersey Archives*, 1st Ser., I, 228.

[53] Dunn, *Politics and Conscience*, 81-83.

Beyond such conjectures one can move to firmer ground, guided by a series of seventeen constitutional drafts in which the evolution of the Frame of 1682 can be traced.[54] That the end product varied so significantly from Penn's expressed views of earlier years and even from his initial attempts to formulate a constitution suggests that either his political philosophy underwent a complete reorientation in 1681 and 1682, or, as is more likely, that in gathering support for his colonial undertaking he yielded to the demands of persons he was in no position to ignore.

The first draft of the Frame of 1682 projected a system far less liberal than that which Penn had approved for West New Jersey. The governor was to be assisted by a parliament consisting of two houses. The upper chamber, analogous to the House of Lords, would include the first fifty purchasers of 5,000 acres or more; they would comprise a self-perpetuating aristocracy, their seats devolving to their heirs. The members—called "lords"—were to sit and adjourn at their own pleasure, nominate all officers in church and state, and delegate committees drawn from both houses to supervise financial and military affairs. Laws could be passed only with their consent. The lower house contained "renters"—the smaller landowners—or their delegates. Theirs was the function of initiating laws.[55]

Although it has been suggested that Penn was not the author of such a "government by a landed aristocracy," the two-house parliament, stripped of the hereditary feature in the upper chamber, was the organizing principle of the next five drafts, some of which were interlineated in Penn's

[54] The drafts are in the Penn Papers, Charters and Frames of Government, foll. 49-149.
[55] *Ibid.*, 49-51.

hand.[56] The only major innovation was the addition of a council, chosen by the proprietor from a double list of names nominated by the parliament, to assist in the executive functions of government. Untouched was the power of the lower house to initiate legislation and the right of the large landowners to sit as an upper house, nominating most provincial and county officers and passing bills presented by the lower chamber. Though somewhat unwieldy, it was a scheme of government which aimed at a rough division of power among the governor, the two houses of parliament, and the executive council.

But abruptly, after the first six drafts, an entirely new direction was taken. Departing from the previous formula, the seventh draft greatly magnified the power of both proprietor and large landowners while reducing that of the lower house. Behind the shift, apparently, was a lengthy critique of the earlier drafts by Thomas Rudyard, Penn's lawyer and one of his closest advisors.[57] Although there is no direct evidence that Rudyard's criticisms reflected the ideas of the men around Penn, a number of factors point to this conclusion. As a prominent London Quaker and a man of affairs, Rudyard was in close touch with almost all of Penn's substantial supporters. He had first been connected with Penn in 1670 at the renowned Penn-Meade trial, and by 1681 was deeply involved in Quaker affairs in East and West New Jersey. It was to Rudyard's home in George Yard, Lombard Street, that prospective emigrants came in that year to obtain details about West Jersey or to purchase land. Similarly,

[56] Sydney G. Fisher, *The True William Penn* (Philadelphia, 1906), 222. Drafts 2-6 are in Penn Papers, Charters and Frames of Government, foll. 53-61, 71-77. The following discussion of the efforts to fabricate a constitution is based on an analysis of the various drafts in this collection.

[57] *Ibid.*, fol. 63.

34

throughout the period when Penn was piecing together a model of government, Rudyard, himself a purchaser of 5,000 acres, was drawing up land deeds and other documents for Pennsylvania.[58] His appointment as deputy governor of East New Jersey only six months later was a measure of the confidence which moneyed Quakers placed in him. It is difficult to believe that his appraisal of the drafts of government, as they had evolved by late 1681, was not related to the objections of other important Pennsylvania investors.

The interest of such men in the pattern of government was doubtless great—and hardly unexpected. This was an era alive with the controversial questions of a possible Catholic succession, foreign domination, parliamentary privileges, and the legitimate boundaries of the King's power. Living in the urban centers of England, leading Quakers were keenly aware of these significant political issues even if they were not actually involved in them. What is more, ten of Penn's major land purchasers, as proprietors of West New Jersey, were a part of the dispute raging between Edward Byllynge and the inhabitants of the colony even as the plans for Pennsylvania went forward. The issue involved the right to elect a deputy governor. Byllynge, as chief proprietor of the colony, claimed the privilege of appointing the deputy governor and cited the Duke of York's confirmation of his title to West Jersey in 1680, which vested the right of government in him. The popularly elected Assembly, on the other hand, viewed this as an invasion of a right

[58] John E. Pomfret, "The Proprietors of West Jersey," *PMHB*, 75 (1951), 136-137; *The Present State of the Colony of West-Jersey, in America* . . . (London, 1681), in Myers, ed., *Narratives*, 195; William Penn, *Some Account of the Province of Pennsilvania* (London, 1681), *ibid.*, 215. On Rudyard see also Alfred W. Braithwaite, *Thomas Rudyard*, Supplement No. 27 to the *Journal of the Friends Historical Society* (London, 1956).

belonging solely to it under the Concessions of 1677.[59] The controversy was an object lesson in the potential dangers of a proprietary government, especially should the proprietor attempt to exercise his authority from England. It was natural that as prudent businessmen Penn's supporters should act to protect their investment in Pennsylvania by safeguarding against such possibilities. Who knew when Penn, the "true and absolute Proprietor," might die, to be succeeded by a son or heir whose interests might diverge from their own? Or who could guarantee that Penn, like Byllynge, might not become a distant source of authority, an absentee proprietor exercising prerogative power from England?

In his appraisal of Penn's drafts of government, Rudyard argued that the proprietor must alter his initial conception of a landed aristocracy, sitting as an upper house with powers analogous to the Lords in England. Such a system was based on an early plan, copied from West Jersey, to sell one hundred "proprieties" of 5,000 acres or more, allowing men of more slender means to buy or rent land from these proprietors.[60] This scheme had already been discarded in favor of a more flexible program whereby Penn offered small tracts to husbandmen and yeomen while advertising baronial estates to a limited number of wealthy men who would be allowed to rent land to tenants, hold seignorial courts, and exercise administrative authority within their domains.[61] In view of the sluggish market for manorial tracts, Rudyard questioned whether there would be enough proprietors for the upper house of the bicameral parlia-

59 Pomfret, *West New Jersey*, 111-112.

60 Penn, *Some Account of Pennsilvania*, in Myers, ed., *Narratives*, 208-209.

61 Penn Papers, Charters and Frames of Government, fol. 63; Pomfret, "First Purchasers of Pennsylvania," *PMHB*, 80 (1956), 146.

ment. Even if there were, he argued, such an aristocratic system would "reflect on us as a people who affect Grandure beyond our pretensons, and sett up that in state pollity which in our religious Capacity we have struck against beyond any people whatsoever." Rudyard pressed the need for a less formal system based on a working aristocracy vested with a central and functional role in the government, not on a provincial nobility. Legislative power, he suggested, should be concentrated in a single house controlled by the wealthiest men of the colony—not by prescription but simply out of the deference which lesser members of the community had traditionally shown to such men. Rudyard pointed out that in England persons of modest income who were entitled to vote outnumbered twenty to forty times those of great estate. But rarely, if ever, was a man of less than £500 to £1000 yearly income elected. So it would be in Pennsylvania. To concentrate the 5,000-acre proprietors in an upper house as planned would be doubly disadvantageous. Not only would they lack the power to initiate legislation, but the lesser freemen, seeing their betters congregated in an upper house, would be encouraged to elect men of their own station to the lower house—a situation which "may in all probability breed differences and Emulations between the upper and lower houses, and hinder dispatch of busyness."[62]

It may have been at this point, though the absence of dates on many of the drafts makes sequential ordering difficult, that Penn wrote his most liberal draft of government, "The Fundamentall Constitutions of Pennsilvania."[63] The document, which is among the most carefully written of Penn's constitutional drafts, is prefaced by the proprietor's

[62] Penn Papers, Charters and Frames of Government, fol. 63.
[63] *Ibid.*, foll. 73, 119-125, and reprinted in *PMHB*, 20 (1896), 283-301.

reflections on theories of government—an essay which in content and phraseology closely parallels the preamble to the Frame of 1682. Central to the Fundamental Constitutions was the idea that the bulk of governmental power should rest with the freeholders. The legislative assembly would consist of two houses. The lower house, comprising 384 members, elected annually, and enjoying all the privileges known to the English House of Commons, would alone propose and pass laws. By an extraordinary clause, each member was required to bring instructions from his electors to the first session of the assembly where a copy would be made and registered. No money bill could be voted upon until referred back to the freemen in each of the electoral districts. The second branch of government, the council, would include 48 members chosen for three-year terms by the lower house from among its own members. In legislative matters the council was purely a consultative body, sitting with the governor to make recommendations upon bills initiated in the assembly, but possessing no veto power. The council's most important function was to exercise executive oversight in the colony through its committees of justice, trade, treasury, and "manners and education." Further articles in the Fundamental Constitutions provided for the annual election in cities and towns of justices of the peace, bailiffs, sheriffs, and constables. In the counties the governor or his deputy would choose sheriffs and justices from a double list presented by the electorate. Individual liberties were protected by guarantees of freedom of religion, due process, jury trial in the vicinage, habeas corpus, monthly sessions of county courts, and the prohibition of imprisonment for debt. The fact that the Fundamental Constitutions contrasted so sharply with earlier drafts of government and was given close consideration is indicative of Penn's fluid state of mind at the time the blueprints for his government were on the drawing board in London.

Benjamin Furly, Penn's close associate in Rotterdam, was among those consulted in the drafting of the Fundamental Constitutions. Furly, in fact, believed that Penn had adopted this plan, which he deemed excellent.[64] But at some point in the early months of 1682 Penn reverted to a far less liberal scheme of government. A new plan was drafted, providing for an elective upper house of the 72 men in the colony "most eminent for vertue Wisdom and Substance." The right of initiating legislation, except in bills related to "Publick moneys," was transferred from the lower to the upper house. Several drafts later the lower chamber was stripped of any role whatsoever in initiating legislation, and left with only the right of consent. The ultimate step came in the fourteenth draft. The functions of the governor's council and the upper house of the legislature were combined, fusing in one body control of legislative, executive, and judicial matters—a pattern often found in other colonies.[65]

What remained was an emasculated lower house which was restricted to a nine-day annual session and allowed only to approve or negate laws proposed by council, to impeach criminals, and, after Penn died, to nominate county sheriffs, coroners, and justices of the peace. It could not initiate legislation as could Parliament at home or the lower houses in some neighboring colonies. Nor could it elect its own speaker, as had been allowed in earlier drafts, or sit on its own adjournment, another right commonly enjoyed in adjacent provinces. In fact, as Penn subsequently pointed out,

[64] "B[enjamin] F[urly] Abridgm^t out of Holland and Germany . . . ," in Julius K. Sachse, "Benjamin Furly," *PMHB*, 19 (1895), 303-304.
[65] Penn Papers, Charters and Frames of Government, foll. 79-117, 127-141.

the lower house had no real existence of its own, but represented simply those delegates chosen annually to sit in a "General Assembly" with the councilors for the purpose of passing laws initiated by the governor and council. It did not possess the power even to debate a proposed law or to ask for the amendment of a clause within it. "The Assembly, as they call themselves," wrote Penn later in attacking the ambitions of the self-named lower house,

> is not so, without the Governor and P[rovincial] councel, and . . . no Speaker, clarke [clerk] or book [minutes] belong to them . . . the people have their representatives in the Pro. Councell to prepare, and the Assembly as it is called, has only the power of I or no, yea or nay. If they turn debators, or Judges, or complainers, you overthrow the Charter quite in the very root of the constitution of it, for that is to usurp the P[rovincial] councels part in the Charter and to forfit the Charter itself: here would be two assemblys and two representatives, wheras they are but one . . . one prepares and proposes, the other assents or denys—the negative voyce is by that in them, and that is not a debateing, mending, altering, but an accepting pow'r.[66]

The council, on the other hand, was endowed with sweeping legislative, executive, and judicial powers. Included was the all-important right of initiative and also authority (with the governor) to establish courts; preserve the peace and safety of the province; determine the location of cities, ports, and market towns; regulate all matters relating to public buildings, roads, and marketplaces; judge impeached

[66] Penn to Commissioners of State, Sept. 18, 1688, in Samuel Hazard, ed., *Register of Pennsylvania*, IV (Philadelphia, 1829), 105.

criminals; execute the laws; and supervise the treasury. The proprietor, as governor, also possessed extensive powers. He sat as the presiding officer in the council where he held a triple vote. More important he held sole power of appointment of all proprietary, provincial, and county officers— judges, treasurers, masters of the rolls, sheriffs, justices of the peace, and coroners. Only after the initial round of appointments—the appointees would serve for life barring misbehavior—would the power devolve on the council to nominate a double list of officers for the governor's choice of provincial officers, and devolve on the electorate to nominate men in each county for his choice of county officers.[67]

In comparison with either the West New Jersey Concessions and Agreements of 1677 or the New York Charter of Liberties of 1683, Penn's Frame of 1682 represents a rather restrictive system of government. In both neighboring colonies the lower house existed as a discrete legislative body, possessing power of initiative and the right to meet on its own adjournment, without time limitations. West New Jersey adopted a far more liberal voting requirement—in effect, all free male inhabitants were qualified—and provided, in contrast to Pennsylvania, that administrative and judicial officers should be chosen either by public election or by the assembly.[68] Even in East New Jersey the impossibly complex Fundamental Constitution of 1683 conferred greater power on the elected assembly than was allowed in Pennsylvania, and provided for the election of jus-

[67] The final version of the Frame of 1682 is printed in Thorpe, ed., *Federal and State Constitutions*, v, 3,052-3,059.

[68] Pomfret, *West New Jersey*, 95-99; for a recent appraisal of the New York Charter of Liberties, see David S. Lovejoy, "Equality and Empire; The New York Charter of Libertyes, 1683," *William and Mary Quarterly*, 3rd Ser., 21 (1964), 493-515.

tices of the peace, sheriffs, and petty officers by the freemen of the towns.[69]

Penn, in short, had finally settled on a constitutional system where political power was concentrated in the governor and his council. Belatedly he had realized, or had been made to understand, that neither his initial plans for a parliamentary system nor his later more liberal schemes were feasible or acceptable. Men of substance, upon whom he relied for leadership and financial backing, would not exchange carefully cultivated estates in England for the uncertainties of a proprietary wilderness unless they were promised far-reaching power.

The provision that the 72 councilors were to be elected by the freemen has obscured the vision of many historians when viewing the division of power in the final Frame of 1682. Historians have sometimes read twentieth-century democracy into seventeenth-century documents. But men of influence at the time, as Thomas Rudyard stated, knew what sort of man should—and would—reach office. The "Laws Agreed Upon in England," a series of 40 statutes to be ratified in Pennsylvania, indicated plainly that any Christian of twenty-one years who possessed 100 acres of land (50 acres if he had been released from indenture within the preceding year) or who paid scot and lot, a property owners' municipal tax, was eligible to vote.[70] This probably enfranchised about half the adult males or one-eighth of the total population.[71] But the actual recruitment of councilors

[69] John E. Pomfret, *The Province of East New Jersey, 1609-1702* (Princeton, 1962) , 140-143.

[70] Thorpe, ed., *Federal and State Constitutions*, v, 3,060.

[71] Two samples of early immigrants yield information on the ratio of indentured servants to freemen. "A Partial List of the Families Who Arrived at Philadelphia between 1682 and 1687," *PMHB*, 8 (1884) 328-340 records 89 heads of families and 192 indentured serv-

was another question. Men of this era understood—and early elections in Pennsylvania would confirm their belief —that only men of considerable estate, demonstrably successful in their private affairs and proven leaders at the local level, could expect to reach the council. Early Pennsylvania was expected to be a well-ordered, structured society. Quakers had no more difficulty than other Englishmen in reconciling spiritual equalitarianism with a traditional view of the natural layering of social classes. A large elective council posed no threat to the pivotal position which Penn's principal supporters expected to occupy.

Two of Penn's advisors, neither of whom intended to immigrate to Pennsylvania, did not hide their dismay that Penn had forsaken earlier ideals of balanced government by concentrating political power in the hands of a small circle of followers. Algernon Sidney, Penn heard, attacked the Frame of Government as "the basest laws in the world, and not to be endured or lived under." Even "the Turk was not more absolute" than the Proprietor, claimed Sidney, according to reports reaching Penn's ears.[72]

Benjamin Furly, Penn's learned friend in Rotterdam, was equally disillusioned. He had seen earlier drafts of government, especially the Fundamental Constitutions, which had given the lower house far more power. "I wonder who should put thee upon altering them [the earlier drafts] for these, And as much how thou couldst ever yield to such a thing. . . . Who has turned you aside from these good beginnings to establish things unsavory and unjust," demanded Furly. Specifically the Rotterdam merchant de-

---

ants. A Bucks County census taken in 1684 tabulated 61 heads of family and 80 servants. For the latter see *PMHB*, 9 (1885), 223-233.

[72] Quoted in William T. Hull, *William Penn; A Topical Biography* (London, 1937), 229.

plored the elimination of the assembly's initiative power
and its right to sit on its own adjournment; he predicted
that this "divesting of the peoples representatives (in time
to come) of the greatest right they have . . . will lay morally
a certain foundation for dissention amongst our successors."
The "patronizers" of this final frame, he warned propheti-
cally, would later be brought under attack for dispossessing
Englishmen of "that naturall right of propounding laws to
be made by their representatives." To have a "great nation"
ruled by only such laws as 48 men (a quorum of council)
should think fit, and they likely to be "corrupted" by a governor with a triple vote in council, was a step backward,
not forward. Finally, Furly expressed his dismay that the
assembly had lost its voice in the appointment of public officials and that nowhere in the frame was the legislative veto
power of the governor explicitly denied.[73]

Among other critics of Penn's frame of government
were George Hutcheson and Jasper Batt, two of the best-
known Quakers in the west of England in the late 1670's.
Hutcheson, a proprietor of West New Jersey and one of
that colony's most important officeholders and political leaders after immigrating to the Delaware in 1681, reported that
Penn was "reflected upon" in West Jersey for his government and laws.[74] Batt, who was singled out by the Bishop
of Bath and Wells as the greatest Quaker proselytizer "in all

[73] Furly's lengthy criticism of the Frame of 1682 is reprinted in
PMHB, 19 (1895), 297-306. John Locke, who lived in exile at Furly's
house in Rotterdam in 1687 and 1688, studied a copy of Penn's Frame
in 1686. Locke found the constitution imprecise, disjointed, and occasionally arbitrary in the large powers conferred upon the council, although he made no comments on the limited role of the lower house.
See Maurice Cranston, *John Locke* (London, 1957), 261-262.

[74] Hutcheson to Penn, March 18, 1683, Penn Papers, Friends House,
London.

the West," was more specific.[75] When he first scanned the Frame of 1682 in the company of Penn's London associates, Batt confided, he had been ready to accept it. But he had met with heated criticisms of the constitution in the west country, and upon scrutinizing the document was convinced of the nearly unshakable control which the governor and those close to him could potentially exert. The constitution, Batt pointed out, did not specifically allow the governor a negative voice in the passage of laws. But four distinct clauses of the Frame stated that all laws must be prepared by the governor and the provincial council. "What need the Governor a negative voyce in passing of lawes," chided Batt, "when he have it before, and none must be prepared or offered but what he first assents unto . . . . Indeed if no bills were to be past into law in England by the Commons but what the king first with his Council prepared for them, there were no need of the kings passing them at last. To me here is all the difference, the Governor there must first passe it, and here the king after passe it." Penn, concluded Batt, exercised more power in government than the King in England, not to mention his expansive tenurial rights as proprietor.[76]

No conspiratorial overtones need be attached to this apparently conscious attempt of Penn and the principal colonizers to vest themselves with prescriptive political authority. These were men whose sufferings as members of a persecuted sect had bred in them a keen sense of history and a watchful attitude toward their fellowmen. Also, they were transferring their estates to a colony granted under semifeudal conditions. It is not surprising that those who risked their for-

[75] John Whiting, *Persecution Exposed* . . . (London, 1715) , 108.
[76] Jasper [Batt], "Ans[wer] to W[illiam] P[enn']s Letter," ca. 1684, Swarthmore Manuscripts, VI, Friends House, London.

tunes and uprooted their lives would seek a system of government which they could control in the Delaware wilderness. Likewise they felt entitled to special consideration in the allocation of land and the distribution of profit-bearing offices.

Penn did not find the arguments for a weak assembly and a strong council unconvincing. He was highly aristocratic himself and in political theory no dogmatist. "I do not find a model in the world," he wrote in the preface to the Frame of 1682, "that time, place, and some singular emergences have not necessarily altered; nor is it easy to frame a civil government, that shall serve all places alike." To this statement he added another defense of his pragmatic approach —and one which suggests that he felt obliged to rationalize his scrapping of earlier, more liberal plans:

> There is hardly one frame of government in the world so ill designed by its first founders, that in good hands would not do well enough; . . . Governments, like clocks, go from the motion men give them, and as governments are made and moved by men, so by them they are ruined too. Wherefore governments rather depend upon men, than men upon governments.[77]

It was this emphasis on the personnel rather than on the structure of government, quite the reverse of conventional Whiggish dogma, that permitted Penn to be swayed from initial plans for a government modeled on more advanced thinking. Moreover, his outlook on man at this time, while he was in the full euphoria of establishing a Quaker utopia, was Lockean rather than Hobbesian.[78] Almost all of the great early purchasers were fellow Quakers, many of them

[77] Thorpe, ed., *Federal and State Constitutions*, v, 3052-3054.
[78] Beatty, *William Penn*, 17.

close associates and intimate friends. Penn had every reason to believe that his "holy experiment" would be safe in their hands, especially since he planned personally to assume the role of governor in Pennsylvania. "Let men be good," he pronounced, "and the government cannot be bad."[79]

Furthermore, Penn had compromised only one element in his plans for government. Inviolably secure was the corner-stone of religious toleration, the object of a whole decade of labors in England. Also firmly rooted were an enlight-ened judicial system and penal code, positive safeguards for property and individual liberty, and such Harringtonian devices as the secret ballot, controls against political chi-canery, and the rotation of offices.[80] Here was a constitu-tion which, despite its departures from some of his earlier concepts of government, could translate Penn's noble vision into reality.

[79] Frame of 1682 in Thorpe, ed., *Federal and State Constitutions*, V, 3054.

[80] Penn's emphasis upon these requisites of good government is con-sidered in Beatty, *William Penn*, 24-32; and Mary Maples [Dunn], "William Penn the Classical Republican," *PMHB*, 81 (1957), 152-1

CHAPTER 2

Problems of a New Society

IN three-quarters of a century of English colonization no settler had come to a colony where more had been done to pre-establish the machinery of government than in Pennsylvania. Colonists in Virginia, Plymouth, and Massachusetts Bay had little more than a patent from the Crown or a preliminary social "compact" to guide them as they stepped ashore in the New World. New Yorkers and Marylanders had only their proprietors' instructions regarding the distribution of land and the general conditions of settlement. Some attempt at devising organic law had preceded settlement in the Jerseys and Carolinas, but the "Concessions and Agreements" of these colonies were not to be compared for comprehensiveness with Penn's "Concessions and Conditions," the Frame of 1682, and the accompanying civil and criminal code—all fashioned in England.

Yet for all the preliminary work done in England, the first years in Pennsylvania were distinguished not by the orderly establishment of political institutions and purposeful development of the economy, but rather by wholesale confusion and chronic friction between sections, groups, and individuals. In the first rush of enthusiasm settlers wrote fervently of "the Joy of the wildernes, & . . . that gladnes that did break forth of the solitary & desolate Land"; or they saw in Pennsylvania "an honorable place within Zions walls" where the divine hand was "setting up a remnant in these parts as an ensign to the Nations."[1] Similarly, Penn wrote letters, meant for consumption in England, that de-

[1] George Hutcheson to Penn, Feb. 17, 1682/83, Penn Papers, Friends House, London.

scribed a "precious Harmony" in the meeting of the legislature and a "heavenly Authority" which bound together in
common purpose all members of the "holy experiment."[2]
But in reality, few things were more elusive in early Pennsylvania than "authority" and "harmony." The plans of the
Free Society of Traders for a pivotal position in economic
affairs were resented and resisted from the outset. In the political sphere elements of the legislature matched strength,
the Lower Counties jockeyed for power with the three
Quaker counties established around Philadelphia, pro- and
antiproprietary factions emerged, and within factions individuals vied for position. "For the love of God, me and the
poor country, be not so governmentish, so noisy and open
in your dissatisfactions," Penn wrote only three years after
the colony had been launched. A year later he was writing
in disgust that he was tempted to give Pennsylvania back to
the King and let "a mercenary government" tame the
Quakers if it could.[3]

The Structure of Immigrating Society

The human ground swell that broke upon Pennsylvania's
shores in the first four years of settlement was evidence of
the hopes and aspirations which Penn had aroused with his
strenuous promotional efforts. Twenty-three ships from
England sailed up the Delaware between December 1681
and December 1682, disgorging some two thousand settlers.[4]

[2] Penn to John Alloway, Nov. 29, 1683, Swarthmore Manuscripts,
VI, No. 68, Friends House, London. See also Penn's *Letter . . . to the
Free Society of Traders . . .* (London, 1683) in Myers, ed., *Narratives*,
239.
[3] Penn to Council, Aug. 19, 1685, Gratz Collection; Penn to Thomas
Lloyd, Nov. 7, 1686, Parrish Collection, Proud Papers, II, 5 (copy).
[4] Balderston, "William Penn's Twenty-Three Ships," *Pennsylvania*

In 1683 twenty ships followed with an additional two thousand immigrants.[5] James Claypoole estimated that toward the end of that year almost one thousand settlers arrived in one six-week period alone. By the close of 1685, when the first great wave of immigration ended, almost ninety ships had delivered about eight thousand immigrants to Pennsylvania, a population buildup unmatched in the annals of English colonization.[6] Even the great Puritan migration to Massachusetts Bay Colony in the early 1630's did not quite equal the initial movement to Pennsylvania. It had taken Virginia three decades to reach the population Penn's colony attained by 1685.[7]

At the bottom of immigrating society, if one excludes the small number of Africans who were brought into the colony in the first two years, were the indentured servants. It is likely that at least one-third of all the early settlers were indentured, and probably one-half of the adult males arriving in the early years came as servants.[8] This was no perma-

---

Genealogical Magazine, 23 (1963), 27-67; for the number of arrivals see James Claypoole to Robert Turner, Jan. 9, 1682/83, *PMHB*, 10 (1886), 201; same to Abel Ram, Feb. 13, 1682/83, *Claypoole's Letter Book*, 193; "Epistle from Pennsilvania's friends," March 17, 1682/83, Penn Letters and Ancient Documents, I, 35, American Philosophical Society, Philadelphia.

[5] Marion Balderston, "Pennsylvania's 1683 Ships and Some of Their Passengers," *Pennsylvania Genealogical Magazine*, 24 (1965), 69-114.

[6] James Claypoole to Edward Claypoole, Dec. 2, 1683, *Claypoole's Letter Book*, 222-224. William Penn to Henry Sidney, July 24, 1683, quoted in William J. Buck, *William Penn in America* (Philadelphia, 1888), 44; Penn to Lord Keeper North, July 24, 1683, *ibid.*, 116.

[7] Evarts B. Greene and Virginia D. Harrington, *American Population before the Federal Census of 1790* (New York, 1932), 12-13, 113-114, 135-136.

[8] Of 788 persons recorded on two lists of early settlers 34 percent of all persons and 49 percent of adult males were indentured. "A Partial List of the Families Who Arrived at Philadelphia between 1682 and

nently depressed class of individuals, however. Frequently the indentured servant was an ambitious person whose only chance of reaching America lay in contracting his labor for a limited period. Though no statistical analysis of his progress is possible, one sees frequent evidence of a rapid ascent in society. John Clows of Cheshire, England, a purchaser of 1,000 acres of land, brought three indentured servants with him to Pennsylvania. One became a substantial landowner and constable of Newtown and Wrightstown in Bucks County; another was a constable in Bucks County by 1689 and later an innkeeper and operator of a Delaware River ferry; and the third became a yeoman farmer. Of Joseph Fisher's eleven servants, four became landowners, one a deputy sheriff of Bucks County, two were women who married landowners, and four died or dropped from sight.[9]

Above the indentured servants stood the colonists of yeoman and artisan origin. These were typically men of skill and drive. For in seventeenth-century England the riffraff and ambitionless generally refused to trade their parish alms for the rigors of fashioning life anew in the American wilderness. When Penn proposed to transport poor Scots to Pennsylvania and "set them downe at easy raits," his chief agent and promoter in Scotland advised that "such is the humeur of that gang of people here" that none would "stir from home [for] such a journey."[10] Those who sought land and wider opportunity in the New World were the crafts-

1687," *PMHB*, 8 (1884), 328-340; "A Partial List of the Families Who Resided in Bucks County, Pennsylvania Prior to 1687," *ibid.*, 9 (1885), 223-233.

9 Balderston, "Pennsylvania's 1683 Ships," 82n, 92n-93n.

10 Robert Barclay to Penn, Oct. 10, 1681, Society Miscellaneous Collection (photostat). See also Mildred Campbell, "Social Origins of Some Early Americans," in James M. Smith, ed., *Seventeenth-Century America: Essays in Colonial History* (Chapel Hill, 1959).

men and farmers in whom the fires of ambition had not yet been snuffed out by years of destitution. This was especially true among Quakers. Friends in England were rarely recruited from the truly impoverished class. The Society's strongest appeal was to the urban worker or shopkeeper and in the country to the yeoman or husbandman.[11]

One estimates that 80 to 90 percent of the nonindentured immigrants were of the artisan-yeoman class. A study of landholding in the first decade of settlement tends to support this view of a society in which the "middling sorts" predominated. It is tempting, upon analyzing land purchases made in England, to conclude that Pennsylvania began as a rather sharply stratified society. As Table A indi-

TABLE A

DISTRIBUTION OF LAND PURCHASERS, 1682

Size of Purchase	Number of Purchasers		Total Acreage Purchased	
100-500 acres	252	(56.0%)	96,325	(17.6%)
501-1000	90	(20.0%)	85,750	(15.6%)
1001-2500	63	(14.0%)	109,400	(20.0%)
2501-5000	39	(8.7%)	193,000	(35.2%)
5001-	6	(1.3%)	63,375	(11.6%)
TOTAL	450	(100.0%)	547,850	(100.0%)

cates, three-quarters of the purchasers, having invested no more than £20 in Pennsylvania land, were concentrated in the lower brackets where they accounted for about one-third of the total land purchased.[12] At the other end of the scale were a relatively small number of men (10 percent of the total purchasers) who could lay claim to nearly half of the pur-

[11] Cole, "Social Origins of Early Friends," *Journal of the Friends Historical Society*, 48 (London, 1956-58), 99-118.
[12] An Account of the Lands in Pennsylvania Granted by William Penn . . . , *Pennsylvania Archives*, 1st Ser., I (Philadelphia, 1852), 42-46.

chased land in Pennsylvania. What changed this picture markedly was the fact that whereas more than two-thirds of the smaller purchasers immigrated, less than one-third of the wealthy buyers did so. The first rent roll for Pennsylvania, completed in 1689, gives evidence of a far less stratified society than the list of First Purchasers would tend to suggest. A glance at Table B reveals both the degree to which smaller landowners predominated in the countryside and the general absence of men with large estates.[13] Kent and Sussex counties showed a somewhat more differentiated society, perhaps because the area had been settled a decade or more before Pennsylvania was founded.

TABLE B

DISTRIBUTION OF LAND OWNERS, 1689

Number of Landholders

Acres Owned	Chester County		Philadelphia County		Kent-Sussex Counties		First Purchasers (1682)	
1-250	95	(49.5%)	80	(43.5%)	20	(9.1%)	111	(24.6%)
251-500	65	(33.8%)	71	(38.6%)	79	(35.7%)	141	(31.4%)
501-750	13	(6.8%)	9	(4.9%)	41	(18.6%)	13	(2.9%)
751-1000	13	(6.8%)	9	(4.9%)	40	(18.1%)	77	(17.1%)
1001-1500	4	(2.1%)	6	(3.3%)	27	(12.2%)	35	(7.8%)
1501-2000	—		3	(1.6%)	5	(2.3%)	11	(2.4%)
2001-3000	—		—		6	(2.7%)	18	(4.0%)
3001-5000	2	(1.0%)	5	(2.7%)	2	(0.9%)	38	(8.5%)
5001-	—		1	(0.5%)	1	(0.4%)	6	(1.3%)
	192		184		221		450	

In the city of Philadelphia the preponderance of humble settlers was much the same. Penn had made a strong appeal

[13] Compiled from Gov. John Blackwell's Rent Roll in Penn Papers, Blackwell's Rent Roll. Kent and Sussex Counties have been combined because property owners in the Lower Counties frequently held land in both counties.

in the urban centers of English society, for he knew that the Society of Friends had thrived in London, Bristol, Dublin, and smaller towns, and he recognized that men of the "laborious Handicrafts" would form the backbone of his "great city." In 1685 he boasted of the wide range of crafts represented in Philadelphia. Later statements confirm the impression that Philadelphia was typically a town of ambitious artisans and shopkeepers.[14]

If society in Pennsylvania seemed to huddle on the lower and middle rungs of the ladder, though the bottom-most rung was scarcely occupied, it did not lack at least the nucleus of an upper class. Though unpretentious landowners and struggling urban artisans predominated, there was a small number of more substantial men among the initial immigrants. In the country, men like John Simcock, John Blunston, and Caleb Pusey of Chester County, Phineas Pemberton, James Harrison, and Joseph Growdon of Bucks County, and Jasper Farmer, Nicholas More, and Thomas Holme of Philadelphia County were representative. Usually they had purchased at least 5,000 acres of land, had invested £50 or more in the Free Society of Traders, and had arrived with at least a half-dozen indentured servants. From an early date they were able to establish small commercial farms which produced grain and foodstuffs for the West Indian market. But in spite of their relative affluence, these men lived remarkably like their poorer neighbors. Because everyone started from scratch in the Delaware wilderness, the colonial gentry, if it can be called that at all, was distinguished chiefly for its rough-hewn appearance. It would take at least a generation in Pennsylvania for the wealthier immigrants to carve out estates which in size and appearance would clearly differentiate them from their neighbors.

[14] Tolles, *Meeting House*, 38-43.

More important in the formation of a colonial upper class was the rapid gathering of a community of merchants. About thirty-five traders, Quaker with few exceptions, converged on Pennsylvania during the first four years. The largest group was from London. It included William Haige, Christopher Taylor, William Welch, James Claypoole, John Eckley, and Griffith Jones—men who were to figure prominently in Penn's proprietary circle. From Bristol came Samuel Cart and George and Joseph Wilcox. Dublin contributed Joseph Fisher and Robert Turner. Maurice and William Trent, the only non-Quakers among the early arrivals, emigrated from Leith, Scotland. From scattered towns, mostly in south and southwestern England, came William Hudson, William Salway, Hugh Durborrow, John Richardson, Robert Ewer, and Thomas Wharton.[15]

Others outside of England also saw fortune awaiting them in Pennsylvania. Isaac van Bebber and Jacob Telner, merchants of Amsterdam and leaders of the Dutch migration, transferred their estates to the colony. From the West Indies came Samuel Carpenter, Henry Jones, Jasper Yeates, and John Jones. Arthur Cooke, earlier a noted Friend in London and since 1678 a merchant in Portsmouth, Rhode Island, moved south to the Delaware. New York added George Foreman, William Darvall—the former Anglican mayor of the city—and three Quaker merchants, William Frampton, Humphrey Morrey, and Abraham Whearley. From across the Delaware, in West New Jersey, came William Clarke, Joshua Barkstead, and Anthony Morris, men

[15] The sources for tracing the gathering of the merchant community are too numerous and varied to list here. Biographical sketches of the seventeenth-century Pennsylvania merchants and bibliographical references can be found in Appendix C of my unpublished doctoral dissertation, "Economics and Politics in Colonial Pennsylvania, 1681-1701" (Princeton University, 1964) .

quick to perceive the economic control which Philadelphia would soon exert over the entire length of the river. Most of these adventurers gravitated toward Philadelphia. Only a few, such as Clarke, Darvall, Maurice Trent, Yeates, Barkstead, and Richardson, sought success down-river at Chester, the oldest settlement in the province, or in the lower Delaware ports of New Castle and Lewes.

The significance of the structure of immigrating society lay in the heavy concentration of yeomen and artisans and in the relatively narrow distance that separated the upper and lower classes. The effect of this telescoping of the social structure was ambivalent. In terms of economic development, the presence of so many sturdy yeomen and artisans, together with the general absence of a fixed upper class, which might block the ascent of ambitious persons of humble origin, was probably a major factor in Pennsylvania's phenomenally rapid growth. In political and social affairs, however, severe strains were placed on traditional concepts of political organization.

The Pattern of Economic Development

There are few parallels in colonial history to the economic success of Pennsylvania in the first two decades. Only three years after settlement, its capital city was firmly established in the Barbados provisioning trade and had cut deep inroads into New York's control of the middle-Atlantic fur and tobacco markets. By 1700 Philadelphia was second in size only to Boston in the English colonies.[16] Prosperity

[16] The rise of Philadelphia as a competitor of New York in the Barbados provisioning trade can be traced in Barbados Shipping Returns, 1678-1714, CO 33/13-15, Public Record Office, London, from which the following figures are collated:

stemmed not only from the fertile soil of the Delaware River Valley and Penn's effectiveness in promoting immigration to his colony. At least as important was the fact that from the outset Pennsylvania possessed a large number of highly skilled craftsmen, men who formed the nucleus of a thriving urban community and gave impetus to the infant economy. Equally important in the rapid economic development of the colony was the immediate arrival of an experienced body of merchants, men long established in other seaports of the English world, men with sound credit and reputation, men whose close mercantile contacts throughout the world of English commerce gave the economy a kind of headstart. Many were closely connected with a far-flung circle of Quaker merchants, some of whom had invested liberally both in Pennsylvania land and the Free Society of Traders. Almost automatically, Pennsylvania merchants took their place in this intercolonial and intercontinental league of Quaker commerce.

Pennsylvania's rapid growth and the general success of

TONNAGE OF SHIPPING FROM NEW YORK
AND PHILADELPHIA TO BARBADOS

Year	New York	Philadelphia
1682	713	70
1683	980	410
1684	612	175
1685	383	260
1686	727	407

For incursions into New York's fur and tobacco trade see petition of the mayor and aldermen of New York to Sir John Werden, May 1685, Edmund B. O'Callaghan and Berthold Fernow, eds., *Documents Relative to the Colonial History of the State of New York* (Albany, 1856-87), III, 361 (cited hereafter as *N.Y. Colonial Documents*); and Beverly McAnear, "Politics in Provincial New York, 1689-1761" (unpublished Ph.D. dissertation, Stanford University, 1935), 72-87.

the economy in the first two decades should not conceal the fact that almost from the start there were tensions and at times even open conflict within the mercantile community. On the surface the emergent merchant class appeared homogeneous enough. Almost all of the merchants were Quakers. Most of them were English, proceeding to Pennsylvania from various way stations in the English mercantile world, but acquainted even before arrival through previous commercial and religious contacts. Those who took up trade on the lower Delaware mixed easily with the early settlers who had drifted into the region in the 1660's and 1670's. However, despite the outward appearance of unity, the merchants were deeply divided. The sources of tension related not so much to their ethnic or religious background as to other considerations. Only nine of the merchants had participated in the launching of Pennsylvania. As members of Penn's circle, they had received important provincial and proprietary offices and appeared to hold special claims to the proprietor's favors.[17] Probably few of them doubted that once in Pennsylvania they would be uniquely situated to control the colony's trade. At least as important, only five of the early merchants belonged to the Free Society of Traders, which Penn had projected as a vital part of his plans.[18] Finally, about one-quarter of the total had cast their lot in the down-river ports south of Philadelphia from which they gazed apprehensively at the burgeoning Quaker capital.

The immediate difficulties of the Free Society of Traders can be taken as an indication of the divisions within the

[17] William Clarke, Christopher Taylor, William Welch, Samuel Carpenter, James Claypoole, John Eckley, Robert Turner, Arthur Cooke, and William Haige.

[18] Claypoole, Turner, Haige, Griffith Jones, and Nicholas More.

mercantile ranks. The hope entertained by the Society that it might assume a controlling role in the economic development of Pennsylvania was quickly lost. Only a handful in number, Penn's merchant associates found themselves swamped by a larger group of entrepreneurs who had no intention of allowing such a closed body to monopolize the colony's trade. Instead the early commerce fell largely into the hands of individual merchants, acting for themselves or as agents for merchants in England. This overshadowing of the Free Society had repercussions far beyond the economic realm.

In a sense the Free Society of Traders was defeated before it entered the race. The first phase of commercial activity involved provisioning the successive waves of immigrants that disembarked on Pennsylvania shores; by the time the Society was on the scene in late 1682 this function was already in the hands of other men. During the earliest stages of immigration merchants who had established themselves on the Delaware in the 1670's, when the region was still a part of the Duke of York's grant, assumed the leading role, selling supplies to the newcomers and capitalizing on the needs of those who arrived too late in the year to get crops in the ground. The "ancient lowly inhabitants come to sell their produce to their profit and our accomodation," reported Penn after his first winter.[19]

Merchants in other colonies were also quick to exploit the new market on the Delaware. At first coin was plentiful, for most immigrants converted their assets into specie before leaving England. According to Penn, about forty ships came to trade in Pennsylvania during the first year, eager

[19] Penn to Lord Keeper North, July 24, 1683, in Buck, *William Penn*, 116.

to exchange provisions for the always coveted money. "New York, New England and Road Island did with their provisions fetch our Goods and Money," he disclosed.[20]

Among those who came to trade, some found the promise of Pennsylvania irresistible. William Frampton was one. An established New York merchant with an eye to the main chance, he made his move early. During the first winter of settlement he was in Philadelphia selling cargoes on consignment from his friend, Walter Newberry, a Quaker merchant of Newport, Rhode Island. With two sloops, owned jointly with Francis Richardson of New York, another Quaker merchant and ship captain, Frampton also traded extensively in the Lower Counties where nearly every tobacco planter in Kent, Sussex, and New Castle counties was soon in his debt.[21] Early in 1683 Frampton purchased the land rights for 5,000 acres and two city lots from one of Penn's earliest supporters and moved his family to Philadelphia. Two years later he was operating one of the largest wharves on the Philadelphia waterfront and had acquired a brewery, a bakery, and an inn. In addition, he became the Pennsylvania agent for Charles Jones & Company, Quaker merchants of Bristol, England, and for London merchants Walter Benthall and Thomas Hart.[22] Although neither a

20 Penn to Earl of Sunderland, July 28, 1683, Society Miscellaneous Collection; William Penn, *A Further Account of the Province of Pennsylvania* . . . in Myers, ed., *Narratives*, 266-267.

21 Bruce M. Bigelow, "The Walter Newbury Shipping Book," *Rhode Island Historical Society Collections*, 24 (1931), 87; *Minutes of the Common Council of the City of New York, 1675-1776* (New York, 1905), I, 128; *Minutes of the Provincial Council of Pennsylvania* (16 vols., Philadelphia and Harrisburg, 1852-53), I, 82-84 (hereafter cited as *Minutes of Council*). See also Bibliographical Note on this source.

22 Warrants and Surveys of the Province of Pennsylvania, 1683-1750, 1/335-336; 3/227; 3/602, Municipal Archives, City Hall, Philadelphia; Exemplification Book 1/23-25, Deed Book E1-5/37-39, Recorder of Deeds

First Purchaser nor a member of the Free Society few in Pennsylvania could match his success in the early years.

Another merchant who exemplified the pattern of early economic development was Samuel Carpenter. For ten years a Quaker merchant in Barbados, Carpenter arrived in Philadelphia in early 1683 and immediately set about spinning a network of enterprises that made him the wealthiest merchant in the province within a decade. His fine wharf, capable of accommodating ships of 500 tons, was the first in Philadelphia; by 1685 he had an interest in several grain mills, timber lands on both sides of the Delaware, and a lime burning business. His trade with the West Indies was extensive. Like other merchants he was deeply involved in land speculation, both in Pennsylvania and West New Jersey.[23]

Even those who had launched the Free Society and invested substantial sums in it, merchants such as James Claypoole and Robert Turner, were quick to pursue their own mercantile interests apart from company affairs. Claypoole, who was treasurer of the Society, was one of Philadelphia's most eager entrepreneurs. More than a year before his departure from England, he had plied his brother, already in Pennsylvania, with questions about trade possi-

---

Office, City Hall, Philadelphia. The relations between Frampton and Charles Jones & Company can be traced in a collection of early Philadelphia mercantile correspondence designated Early Letters from Bristol and Philadelphia (Am. 2532) , 10-45. Frampton's activity as agent for Benthall and Hall is described contractually in Deed Book E2-5/ 13-20.

[23] Edward and Louis H. Carpenter, *Samuel Carpenter and His Descendants* (Philadelphia, 1912) , 5-7; John Clement, *Sketches of the First Emigrant Settlers in Newton Township* (Camden, N.J., 1877) , 346-347; Penn, *A Further Account of Pennsylvania*, Myers, ed., *Narratives*, 261; Jordan, ed., *Colonial Families of Philadelphia*, I, 469.

bilities in the new colony and had sent a trusted servant ahead to launch his mercantile affairs. Once in Philadelphia he quickly established a vigorous trade, importing pork, beef, butter, cheese, and a variety of dry goods and tools from England and sending pipe staves, timber, silver, pelts, furs, and whale oil and bone in return. Trade lines were quickly opened to Barbados where another brother, a prospering planter-merchant, acted as correspondent.[24]

By 1684, individual merchants had firmly established the Delaware River as a center of no small promise in the English mercantile world. Boston, Newport, New York, Bristol, London, and Barbados were all within the orbit of trade for Philadelphia and New Castle. Penn reported in July 1683 that since the previous summer almost sixty ships had put into Philadelphia to trade. "This we esteem a good beginning," he remarked. James Claypoole, no less optimistic, expressed the general belief that within a few years Pennsylvania would rival any of her neighboring colonies in matters of commerce.[25]

Amidst the buoyant beginnings of such individual enterprisers, the Free Society of Traders encountered little but adversity. From the beginning the company was crippled by the disinterest of some of its officers and the erratic behavior of others. Nicholas More, the president, was no man to lead the venture. Aristocratic, unstable, and condescending by nature, he was poorly equipped to guide the Society's affairs. Most of his time was spent establishing his manor

[24] *Claypoole's Letter Book*, passim, especially the letters of Oct. 28, 1681, Jan. 11, 1682/83, Jan. 16, 1682/83, Dec. 2, 1683, Feb. 1, 1683/84, Feb. 13, 1683/84.

[25] James Claypoole to Thomas Cooke, Feb. 1, 1683/84, *Claypoole's Letter Book*, 232; Penn to Lord Keeper North, July 24, 1683, in Buck, *William Penn*, 116.

outside of Philadelphia. Simcock, the vice-president, settled in Chester County, far away from the Society's offices, and became a farmer. Claypoole, the treasurer, did not arrive in Philadelphia until late 1683 and then, seeing the already fallen state of company affairs, followed his own trading interests while grumbling of the incursions which Society business made on his time. One of the committee men complained about the Society's governing board: "particular men do[e]th for themselves."[26] Of the twelve members elected as resident commissioners, three decided to remain in England and three others took up land outside of Philadelphia, the Society's center of business.

Despite personnel problems, efforts were made to establish the Society at the heart of the province's economic life. The first cargo of English goods and about sixty indentured servants of the company arrived in September 1682 with President More. Eager buyers snapped up the wares. But already the necessity of buying provisions from other colonies was draining Pennsylvania of money and the Free Society was forced to take credit when the supply of coin was exhausted.[27] A second cargo reached Pennsylvania the following summer. Again the shipment was quickly disposed of, but as before the goods had to be retailed on credit. "We are forced to trust most what we sell, and People will not pay in 6 or 9 months," the treasurer reported. Within a year he was obliged to admit that "we have neither credit

[26] John Blunston to William Sharlow, Jan. 23, 1683/84, Logan Papers, XVI, 14.
[27] James Claypoole to Thomas Loveday, Sept. 21, 1682. *Claypoole's Letter Book*, 154; the Free Society's cargo is listed in London Port Book E 190/109/1, Public Record Office, London, as cited in Balderston, "William Penn's Twenty-Three Ships," *Pennsylvania Genealogical Magazine*, 23 (1963), 60-61.

nor money, and now must sue people at law, or be forced to loose all."[28]

Compounding the financial difficulties of the Society was the unwillingness of English stockholders, apprehensive at reports of mismanagement in Pennsylvania, to pay in their full subscriptions. "Wee understand but halfe of the subscription money is paid in," wrote an alarmed member of the governing board in January 1684.[29] Added to the growing shortage of specie in the province, the default of English stockholders was nearly a crushing blow. It was apparent that the Society lacked sufficient capital to sell goods on credit for the one or two years required until Pennsylvania could develop exportable commodities to balance her trade.

Although crippled by inadequate capitalization, the Society attempted to carry out some of the expansive schemes projected in London in 1682. Fishing and whaling expeditions were initiated at the mouth of Delaware Bay; a grist mill was purchased from early Swedish settlers and operated for a few years; a glass factory, a brick kiln, and a tannery were begun; and Lasse Cock, an early Swedish settler

[28] John Blunston to William Sharlow, July 23, 1683, Logan Papers, XVI, 7; James Claypoole to Edward Haistwell, July 29, 1684, *Claypoole's Letter Book*, 242. The chronic lack of specie which plagued the colony almost immediately was mentioned by many of the early settlers. See, for example, John Blunston to William Sharlow, Feb. 2, 1682/83, Logan Papers, XVI, 11; Samuel Carpenter to Penn, Dec. 25, 1684, Albert C. Myers Collection, Box 2, #9, Chester County Historical Society, West Chester, Pa. (cited hereafter as CCHS); F. Pastorius, *Circumstantial Geographical Description of Pennsylvania . . .* (Frankfurt, 1700), translated in Myers, ed., *Narratives*, 376. Illustrative of the specie drain was the arrival in Philadelphia of a ship from Bristol with a cargo of 150 African slaves. "All the Negros where sould for redy money, which has Caused Money to be very scarce," wrote the president of the Free Society to Penn. See Nicholas More to Penn, Dec. 1, 1684, Myers Collection, Box 2, #6, CCHS.

[29] John Blunston to William Sharlow, Jan. 23, 1683/84, Logan Papers, XVI, 14.

and experienced Indian trader, was engaged to launch the fur trade of which so much was expected. Two small vessels were purchased to establish a trade with the West Indies.[30] But in spite of these attempts commerce in Pennsylvania after 1684 progressively fell into the hands of men who had played no part in the original promotion of the colony or who were steadily shying away from the proprietary group. Supplies from England were controlled not by the Free Society but by Charles Jones & Company of Bristol whose factors in Philadelphia, William Frampton and Andrew Robeson, remained aloof from the proprietary circle. The growing grain trade with the West Indies, which would become the foundation of Pennsylvania's economy for the next two decades, was likewise dominated by independent merchants who shunned any involvement with the Free Society. Their efforts only signified a continuation and reemphasis of the earlier attempts to outflank the proprietary-supported joint-stock company and its handful of London Quaker merchants.

A succession of suits brought against the Society between 1684 and 1686 caused its final collapse as a significant factor in Pennsylvania's trade. Thereafter, the Society functioned solely as a land company, gradually selling its extensive property to settle debts.[31] The first suit, an action for outstanding debts, was brought by Samuel Carpenter, who was emerging as the leading merchant of the province. "The Society would not pay me," he informed Penn, "but told me I must take my Course at Law." Carpenter won his case be-

[30] The early activities of the Free Society can be traced in *Claypoole's Letter Book*, passim. Details are also given in Myers, ed., *Narratives*, 241n; and John Blunston to William Sharlow, July 23, 1683, Logan Papers, XVI, 7.

[31] Early land sales to discharge debts are recorded in Philadelphia Deed Book E1-5/639-647; H8/357-361; I12/180-181.

fore the County Court at Philadelphia, a decision upheld by the Provincial Court when the company appealed the verdict.[32] On the heels of Carpenter's suit came an action by Henry Bowman, who had supervised the company's whaling enterprise. The court's award of £500 to Bowman in a breach of contract suit came as the final crushing blow to the embarrassed company.[33]

Debt-ridden as it was, the Society still hoped to salvage its fading fortunes—by political influence if necessary. Many of its officers still occupied positions of executive and judicial importance as members of Penn's circle. On the Philadelphia County Court, for example, sat some of Penn's closest supporters: Thomas Holme, Robert Turner, Francis Daniel Pastorius, John Goodson, Hugh Roberts, and William Clarke. The Provincial Court was an even stronger proprietary stronghold. Nicholas More sat as presiding judge while Clarke, Eckley, Turner, and Wood, all partisans of Penn and all save Clarke members of the Free Society, completed the bench. It was Eckley and Clarke who heard the appeal of James Claypoole, acting for the Society in the Carpenter case. Although the decision was upheld, Clarke "refused to sett his hand to it, notwithstanding he had given his Judgment for it in Court."[34] Claypoole attempted another tactic, denying the validity of the judgment on the ground that he was appealing the case to England. When it was disclosed that he had given no security —in cases of equity the appellant was required to post bond for the amount of the judgment as a condition of appeal—

[32] Carpenter to Penn, Dec. 25, 1684, Myers Collection, Box 2, #9, CCHS.

[33] Charles H. B. Turner, ed., *Some Records of Sussex County, Delaware* (Philadelphia, 1909), 115; Benjamin Chambers v. Nicholas More, Sept. 24, 1686, Gratz Collection, Supreme Court of Pennsylvania.

[34] *Minutes of Council*, I, 146-147.

Carpenter's petition to execute the decision was upheld by Council.[35]

As Carpenter informed Penn, far more had been at stake than an overdue debt. For if Penn's appointees, many of them personally involved in the Society's affairs, continued to exploit their connections and to misuse their offices in defense of a bankrupt and restrictive trade company, they would bring discredit to both Penn and his colony. "Nothing but Shame and Confusion will attend them," wrote the embittered Carpenter; "the way they Endavor to uphold themselves pulls them downe with both hands . . . . Their debts lyes out notwithstanding all their Counsells Courts and Comitties and grandure therein, and people unpaid to their Perpetuall Shame and the dishonor of the Province."[36]

Early Political Tension

In political as in economic affairs the "holy experiment" was hobbled from the beginning by controversy. The trouble began shortly after Penn's arrival. Eager to obtain final approval of his constitutional apparatus, Penn convened an assembly, or ratifying convention, to endorse the Frame of 1682, the 40 "Laws Agreed Upon in England," and about fifty additional laws newly submitted after his arrival in Pennsylvania. On December 4, 1682 the convention of 42 men, 7 from each of 6 established counties, gathered at Chester. It was no surprise that almost all of Penn's supporters and officeholders, including 6 officers of the Free Society of Traders, had secured places.[37] But from the 3 Lower Coun-

[35] *Ibid.*; Carpenter to Penn, Dec. 25, 1684, Myers Collection, Box 2, #9, CCHS.
[36] *Ibid.*
[37] Though not all the members of the convention are known, the

ties came representatives of the older Swedish, Dutch, and
English settlers, most of them disgruntled at the sudden
takeover of territory and government by the proprietor and
his small circle. For nearly a decade English tobacco planters had been drifting into the lower Delaware area from
adjacent counties in Maryland, taking up land patents under the Duke of York's deputies and gradually replacing
the Swedes. When Penn received his charter, more than a
thousand people populated the Lower Counties—Sussex,
Kent, and New Castle—arranged in a tier from the mouth
of Delaware Bay northward to the town of New Castle.[38]
Now their representatives seemed reluctant to yield to the
proprietor's requests. The speakership of the Assembly
nearly went to a non-Quaker, and Penn wrote in dismay,
"Friends carrying it but by one voyce, and that through the
absence of 2 of the other side that were not Friends."[39]

The confrontation between old and new, Quaker and
non-Quaker, Penn's friends and independent adventurers
had grave consequences for the Free Society of Traders and
for the entire machinery of proprietary management. In a
series of moves the ratifying Assembly struck at Penn's system. Proposals were made to overthrow the Council's monopoly in initiating legislation by allowing any member of
the Assembly to propose a bill "except in Case of levying
Taxes." Nineteen of the 90 laws proposed by Penn were rejected outright. Most significantly, both the Frame of 1682

---

names of 17 delegates are given in Gertrude MacKinney, ed., *Votes and
Proceedings of the House of Representatives of the Province of Pennsylvania, Pennsylvania Archives*, 8th Ser. (Harrisburg, 1931-35), I, 1-
13 (cited hereafter as *Votes of Assembly*).

[38] For the early settlement of the Lower Counties see J. Thomas
Scharf, *History of Delaware, 1609-1888* (2 vols., Philadelphia, 1888),
II, 1029.

[39] Penn to Jasper [Batt], Feb. 5, 1682/83, *PMHB*, 6 (1882), 467-472.

and the law confirming the charter of the Free Society were voted down. Though evidence of their motives is lacking, one surmises that many of the delegates, especially those from the Lower Counties, were unready to accept the tightly knit economic and political partnership which had been put before them, even though the Quakers had consented to an "Act of Union" between the Lower Counties and the province of Pennsylvania and had joined in passing a Naturalization Act under which the Dutch, Finns, and Swedes inhabiting Penn's grant were to be "as free as other Members of this Province."[40]

If the dispute over the ratification of the Frame of 1682 gave warning of tensions within the infant community, the General Assembly (the Assembly, Council and Governor) which met the following year confirmed their existence. As expected, Penn's associates dominated the Council. Half of the councilors chosen were important provincial officers and large landholders, while several others, Quakers who had settled on the Delaware before Penn's grant, were equally bound to the proprietor. In the Assembly, sat an uneasy company of Quaker and non-Quaker, old settler and new, English and non-English. One characteristic alone bound them together: almost none was tied to the proprietor by appointive office or involvement in the Free Society of Traders. Those from the upper counties were Quakers with few exceptions and those from the Lower Counties were mostly non-Quaker settlers of the pre-Penn era.[41]

The principal task of the General Assembly was to model a new frame of government in place of the rejected Frame of 1682. Debate focused on the proper distribution of power

[40] *Votes of Assembly*, I, 1-13.

[41] For membership of the General Assembly see *Minutes of Council*, I, 57-69; and *Votes of Assembly*, I, 13.

among proprietor, Council and Assembly—the same thorny problem controverted so laboriously in England.[42] But now assent was needed from the very body which had been relegated to virtual impotency—the Assembly. Penn had not anticipated this; he had expected the Frame of 1682 to be endorsed by a ratifying convention dominated by his associates. Even should the Frame fail, as it had, Penn probably had few doubts before he arrived that such Quakers as were elected to the lower house would defer to the "wisdom, virtue, and ability" of the provincial leaders gathered in Council. Now the Assembly was showing signs of becoming instead the crucible of antiproprietary sentiment. Half the seats were occupied by non-Quakers from the Lower Counties and others by men eager to enlarge the Assembly's role. Only a minority, composed of Quakers from the upper counties, remained firm in their support of Penn.[43] And even the Council, though supporting Penn on the whole, sought subtle reductions of his power.

Upon one issue, the unmanageable size of both legislative bodies as specified in the Frame of 1682, there was general agreement. Accordingly, the Council and Assembly were reduced from 72 and 200 respectively to 18 and 36. This, of course, only concentrated the extensive power of the Council in the hands of a much smaller number of men. Consensus was found on little else. Of foremost concern was the question of the governor's vote in legislative matters, the point that had alarmed Sidney, Furly, Batt, and others in England. In 1681, eager to promote his colony, Penn had at

[42] Proceedings of the General Assembly are in *Votes of Assembly*, I, 13-43.

[43] Penn's adherents comprised about one-sixth of the lower house. Included were John Songhurst, Thomas Wynne, William Yardley, Nicholas Waln, Thomas Fitzwater, John Blunston, Thomas Brassey, and John Bezar.

first reserved for himself only a single voice in the Council and no power to reject laws passed by the General Assembly. In its final form, however, the Frame of 1682 allowed him a treble vote in the Council and power to withhold approval of any constitutional alterations. But sometime before his arrival in the colony Penn apparently took a harder look at his charter from the King. Two provisions were clear: first, laws were to be made *by* the proprietor "with the advice, assent, and approbation of the freemen." To strip himself of a veto power, as was later pointed out, would technically have violated the terms of the charter, which he could in no way alter.[44] Secondly, Penn was obliged to "stand security" to the Crown for any damages resulting from colonial violations of the Acts of Trade, as ascertained in any English court. In effect, this required Penn to assume financial liability for the good behavior of his entire colony in commercial affairs. It was a provision unknown to earlier colonial charters and indicative of England's new determination to obtain colonial obedience to the Navigation Acts, which had been frequently evaded and ignored during the previous decade.

Meeting with Council, Penn argued that he must have either the right to override legislation or the colonists' counter-security for their observance of the Navigation Acts. After lengthy debate, Council agreed to allow the governor a negative voice rather than put their own estates on the line.[45] In return for this concession, Penn agreed that the

[44] James Logan to Penn, Dec. 20, 1706, *Penn-Logan Correspondence,* II, 184.

[45] Edwin B. Bronner, who has written most recently and extensively on the Frame of 1683, concludes that Penn lost his treble vote in the Council while gaining no compensatory legislative veto. It is suggested that in this "rosy period" Penn may have considered "abdicating his supremacy" and entrusting the management of public affairs to

governor should act in matters of justice, trade, finance, or defense—the major areas of legislation—only with Council's "advice and consent."[46]

The Assembly reluctantly accepted the innovation of the governor's veto power, for a majority in that body continued to rankle at the insignificant role allowed them. Chagrined, they reintroduced the proposal of the previous December that the Assembly be given the power of initiating legislation. But neither Penn nor the Council would accept this change, though they conceded that the Assembly should at least be allowed to confer with the Council. It was, however, a concession large enough to whet the appetite of the Assembly where some, according to Penn's supporters, were now leveling "undeserving Reflections and Aspersions upon the Governor."[47] Nonetheless, the new Frame of Government was approved.

At a second session of the General Assembly, convened in Philadelphia in October 1683, the Assembly again pressed for the right to initiate legislation. Penn gave ground slightly by agreeing that after the General Assembly was adjourned the members of the Assembly might consult informally with the governor and Council and suggest "such

the Council. See *William Penn's "Holy Experiment"* (New York, 1962), 41-42. There is little evidence to sustain this view. Penn never considered this a "rosy period" and it is clear that the colonists agreed, however reluctantly, that Penn must be given the right to confirm or withhold his assent from laws passed by the General Assembly. See *Minutes of Council*, I, 60-61 and Penn's later discussion of the debate over this point in his letter to James Logan, May 10, 1705, *Penn-Logan Correspondence*, II, 17. Also, Logan to Penn, Dec. 20, 1706, *ibid.*, 184. In 1686 Penn even rashly threatened to plunge the colony into a state of confusion by refusing to confirm the annual continuation law by which all previous laws were continued in force for another year. Penn to Thomas Lloyd, Sept. 21, 1686, *PMHB*, 80 (1956), 246.

[46] *Votes of Assembly*, I, 18-19.   [47] *Ibid.*, 14-15, 18.

Proposals ... as might tend to the Benefit of the Province."[48] But beyond this modest concession nothing was done to alter the existing distribution of power. Although he had been unable to secure the Free Society's charter, Penn had held the line in the face of growing opposition on the part of those not involved in the early planning of the colony. In obtaining passage of the Frame of 1683, and in resisting the Assembly's aspirations, he had completed the work begun in England of reaching a compromise in government with his principal associates.

As vexing as the work of passing a Frame of Government had been, Penn had experienced only the beginning of political turmoil in his colony. In 1684 tensions rose sharply, and at one time presented the prospect of open conflict. Trouble struck first in the Lower Counties with a militant display of antiproprietary sentiment. It was not surprising that old settlers and merchants there should resist Penn's authority. Many of them had lived for nearly two decades under the light rein of the Duke of York's deputy governors, who had allowed a wide measure of local government. Historians have pictured the joyous reception of Penn by the old settlers, who are said to have followed medieval custom in offering turf and twig to the new proprietor as he stepped ashore in October 1682. Though less romantic, it would be more accurate to say that neither Penn nor the old settlers harbored any illusions about the union being effected. Control of the Lower Counties gave Penn uninterrupted access to the sea, but in absorbing a territory which would send representatives to the General Assembly equal in number to those of the Quaker counties of Philadelphia, Chester, and Bucks, he endangered Quaker political control. "Should they outnumber us we are gone,"

[48] *Ibid.*, 46.

Penn wrote after the ratifying convention in December 1682, referring to the non-Quakers concentrated in the Lower Counties. He had just witnessed the defeat of the Frame of 1682 by an Assembly in which the Quakers had prevailed by the narrowest of margins.[49]

As for the earlier settlers, their choice was clearly limited. Once Penn presented his deeds to the region, which he had obtained from the Duke of York only days before sailing for America, they accepted the inevitable and simply worked to obtain equivalent power with their Quaker neighbors to the north. Their submission to Penn, however, was given grudgingly. Many held land under patents from Lord Baltimore, who claimed parts of Sussex and Kent counties, and some still regarded him as their rightful proprietor. Baltimore, for his part, had no intention of submitting to Penn's claims. Since the initial grant to Penn, he had disputed the boundaries of the Quaker colony, basing his title to the Lower Counties on his charter from Charles I in 1632. For almost two years after Penn's arrival the two proprietors argued their conflicting claims without finding a basis for settlement.[50]

During the first three years of settlement, from 1682 to 1684, Baltimore's agents periodically probed Kent and Sus-

49 Penn to Jasper [Batt], Feb. 5, 1682/83, *PMHB*, 6 (1882), 467-472. The disputed election is detailed in *Votes of Assembly*, I, 1-2. For evidence of the Quakers' reluctance to join with the Lower Counties see Assembly and Council to Penn, May 18, 1691, Penn Papers, Autograph Petitions, 11; and Joseph Growdon to Penn, April 28, 1691, photostat in Myers Collection, CXLVIII, folder 23, CCHS. For a general discussion of this regional tension see Robert W. Johannsen, "The Conflict between the Three Lower Counties and Pennsylvania, 1682-1704," *Delaware History*, 5 (1952), 96-123.

50 Bronner, *Penn's "Holy Experiment,"* 65-67. Accounts of the transactions between Baltimore and Penn are given in Clayton Colman Hall, ed., *Narratives of Early Maryland, 1633-1684* (New York, 1910), 407-448.

sex counties, stirring up the planters with promises of more favorable land terms than Penn extended. The Quaker, they promised, would lose title to the territory as soon as proceedings in England came to judgment. Prudent men would declare their allegiance to Baltimore while time remained. When words failed, the Catholic proprietor resorted to more direct methods. Armed "musqueters" invaded homesteads and threatened freeholders: if they would not swear allegiance to Baltimore and pay quitrents to him, "he would Turne them out of their homes and take their land from them."[51] In late March 1684, Baltimore's agents began constructing a fort at Christina Bridge in New Castle County. This amounted to an armed invasion of the Territories, as the Lower Counties were called, but Penn's deputies, as pacifists, were powerless to halt it.[52]

By April 1684, dissension in the Lower Counties had reached the boiling point. Baltimore's agent scoured Kent County attempting "to seduce the people from their obedience and fidelity to the Governor [Penn]." New Castle, it was reported, was filled with defectors.[53] In Philadelphia, the Council listened in fear to a Kent County landholder who reported that most of the local merchants were "resolved to revolt" because Penn had broken his promise to require all Delaware shipping to enter and clear their cargoes at New Castle—the only means by which that port could maintain its economic position in the face of Philadelphia's vigorous growth. Should they rebel, he continued, Baltimore would give them full support.[54] Worse still, the

[51] *Minutes of Council*, I, 113.

[52] William Welch to Penn, April 5, 1684, Dreer Collection.

[53] William Clarke to Penn, April 19, 1684, *Pennsylvania Archives*, 2nd Ser., VII, 8; William Welch to Penn, Feb. 18, 1683/84, Personal Miscellaneous Papers, Library of Congress.

[54] *Minutes of Council*, I, 101.

representatives of Sussex and Kent counties boycotted the Council sessions and stood ready to throw in their lot with Baltimore, who for the moment appeared the stronger of the two proprietors. Merchant William Darvall, former mayor of New York and justice of the peace in Kent County, warned the people not to pay quitrents to Penn.[55]

To stifle the uprising Penn sent four trusted agents to the Territories armed with a letter demanding recognition of him as their proprietor; at the same time Penn extended a promise of more favorable land terms than Baltimore was offering.[56] Though Penn's timely action checked the dangerous tide of rebellion, the seeds of disaffection could not be destroyed. Divided from the Quaker counties by religion and economic interest, the Territories could never again equate their goals with those of their northern neighbors. Their leaders remained chronically restless, always prepared to side with Quaker malcontents on particular issues. Occupying half the seats in the General Assembly, they sometimes seemed almost to control the political fate of Pennsylvania.

On the heels of dissension in the Lower Counties came disunity and discord among Quakers. To some extent the problem was a continuation of the tacit challenge to Penn and his inner circle thrown down earlier by the large number of merchants and substantial landholders who sought opportunity outside the Free Society of Traders or who

[55] *Minutes of Council*, I, 102-104; William Clarke to Penn, April 19, 1684, *Pennsylvania Archives*, 2nd Ser., VII, 8.

[56] Penn to James Harrison, John Cann, William Welch, John Simcock, April 2, 1684, Society Miscellaneous Collection (photostat of original in Delaware Archives, Hall of Records, Dover, Del.); William Clarke to Penn, April 19, 1684, *Pennsylvania Archives*, 2nd Ser., VII, 8-9; Penn to James Harrison, Dec. 4, 1685, Penn Papers, Domestic and Miscellaneous Letters, 22.

76

chafed at the proprietor's extensive powers. But fresh causes of dissatisfaction fanned the antiproprietary fires, causing some of Penn's most faithful followers to question his policies.

Property was the foremost issue. As Penn's land policy unfolded after his arrival, a chorus of voices arose to protest that the proprietor, motivated by a desire to increase his own income, was altering the terms upon which Quakers in England had been attracted to Pennsylvania. In July 1684, Quaker leaders in Philadelphia, most of them early purchasers of land, presented Penn with a list of grievances. Penn, they objected, had promised the city as a bonus to "First Purchasers"—subscribers to the first hundred blocs of 5,000 acres. The promise that 2 percent of their purchases would be contained within the capital city had been of no little importance in the decision of many to immigrate.[57] But once in Pennsylvania, they found a radically different situation. Ascertaining that the city was not large enough to contain the collective bonuses of all First Purchasers, Penn had decided to grant the dividends in the "liberties," a broad belt of land girdling the city, and in addition to award each purchaser city lots in proportion to his purchase. Large purchasers were to be given the choicest property fronting on the river and the market street; smaller buyers would receive "back lots" in the interior of the city. This much was agreed to by a number of the First Purchasers, and the allocation had been carried out accordingly in late 1682 and early 1683.[58] Now it was realized that the city lots

[57] Petition of "Persons considerate in this City" to William Penn, Proud Papers, Box 2. A copy is in Parrish Collection, Proud Papers, I, 33-37. The original terms of land settlement, published in 1681 as *Certain Conditions or Concessions agreed upon by William Penn* . . . , are in *Votes of Assembly*, I, xli-xlvi.

[58] Penn's plan is detailed in Lawrence Lewis, Jr., *Land Titles in*

assigned to the First Purchasers comprised only a fraction of the city. Penn was renting lots to incoming artisans and using the remainder to promote new land sales.[59]

Furthermore, it was complained, Penn had imposed heavy quitrents on Philadelphia property, arguing that the city lots were not a part of original land purchases but merely "the Proprietary's Gift." To the petitioners this seemed a flagrant breach of trust. In their view the city lots were no tokens of Penn's generosity but part of a contractual bonus to First Purchasers. To many, Penn appeared intent on reaping the greatest possible profits from his proprietary grant even at the cost of violating earlier promises. Penn's indignant answer to the remonstrance only increased this feeling and showed the atmosphere of disillusionment that now prevailed between the proprietor and the people.[60]

Compounding the dissatisfaction was the allocation of city property, which inevitably left some parties more advantageously situated than others. It was no secret that the commercial center of town, containing the most valuable real estate, would stretch along the Delaware River waterfront and perhaps westward from the river for two or three blocks. While Penn was still in England his deputies in the colony agreed that city lots should be assigned by lottery. A drawing for lots was actually held, but upon his arrival Penn discarded the plan and personally situated buyers in his capital city according to the size of their purchase and the

---

Philadelphia (Philadelphia, 1880), 101-102, 118-120. The original allocation is in Warrants and Surveys of the Province of Pennsylvania, 1683-1750, II, 136-154, Municipal Archives, Philadelphia. It was published for promotional purposes as T. Holme, *Portraiture of the City of Philadelphia* . . . (London, 1683).

59 Petition to Penn, Proud Papers, Box 2.

60 *Ibid.*, and Penn's reply, Proud Papers, Box 2.

strength of their commitment to him. Lots along the Delaware waterfront went to the largest First Purchasers present in the colony or to buyers in England whose agents in Philadelphia were promoting their interests. Most of the other First Purchasers, not present to press their claims, were relegated to the western half of town which would not be developed for years. It was no coincidence that the property adjacent to Dock Creek, projected as the wharving center of the port, was parceled out to the Free Society of Traders and to Penn's closest associates.[61]

It was not surprising that Penn should favor immigrating purchasers over those who remained in England and therefore had a purely speculative interest in the colony. Nor was it unnatural that older acquaintances should receive preferential treatment. Nevertheless, discontent inevitably arose over the distribution of land. Nothing contributed more to disillusionment with Penn, and with proprietary government in general, than this seemingly ambiguous and opportunistic land policy. Property rights, even more than political rights, were of utmost importance to Englishmen, both native and colonial, since land was the principal basis of the political, economic, and social structure. Land policy seemed no longer equitable or consistent and was felt to rest on proprietary whim, and the landowners believed that previous agreements had been broken. Consequently, political harmony between Penn and the Pennsylvanians was now all but impossible. The fact that dissatisfaction with Penn's land policy in Philadelphia often reflected personal

[61] The distribution of city lots by lottery is published in Hazard, ed., *Annals*, 642-643. For a detailed discussion of the allocation of city property and the political repercussions of Penn's policy see Gary B. Nash, "City Planning and Political Tension in the Seventeenth Century: The Case of Philadelphia," *Proceedings of the American Philosophical Society*, 112 (1968), 54-73.

disappointment and even rapaciousness on the part of the settlers mattered little. Penn later argued that there had been substantial agreement among the First Purchasers present in 1683 that in laying out and allocating his capital city he should not be held inflexibly to a plan which had been drawn up 3,000 miles away and long before the topographical features of the city or even its location were known.[62] This was probably true, but it did little to assuage the anger of those who had not been present at the time or had not consented to discarding the initial plans.

Resentment over Penn's land policy and a creeping skepticism of proprietary intentions were unmistakably reflected in the General Assembly of 1684. Council, as before, was dominated by Penn's firmest adherents, but the Assembly was hostile from the outset. When Penn announced his intention to appoint a provincial court, the Assembly questioned whether the proprietor should be allowed the power to choose the judiciary. Should laws have a continuing life, once passed, or should they be put before the General Assembly annually for review? Should the bill before the house for the protection of the proprietor's person and reputation be so broadly framed? And should not two or more witnesses against a libeler be required for conviction? Pushing its quest for power a step further, the Assembly asked whether it could not disallow current laws. As if the meaning of these queries was not clear enough, the Assembly pushed to revoke the statute which forfeited the lands of any freeholder who refused to take a pledge of fidelity to William Penn.[63]

62 Penn's reply to the petition of "Persons considerate in this City," Proud Papers, Box 2; for a further defense of his policy, see Penn to Stephen Crisp, Feb. 28, 1684/85, Myers Collection, Box 1, #7, CCHS.

63 Minutes of Council, I, 104-110; Votes of Assembly, I, 46-58.

Angered at the Assembly's unwillingness to play the passive role expected of it, Penn sent councilors William Welch and Thomas Lloyd to admonish the house for debating their privileges rather than voting on the bills proposed by Council. By exerting all of his influence, Penn was finally able to repulse the contentious lower house. Council refused to consent to the Assembly's right to revoke laws and authorized Penn to appoint a provincial court. At the same time, a comprehensive libel and sedition act, designed to neutralize the near-anarchy in the Lower Counties, was pushed through with the support of Quakers in the lower house.[64]

By the end of 1684, after two years of political fencing among proprietor, Assembly, and Council, and by elements within the two legislative bodies, political groups began to form. Three factions, still shifting and amorphous, but progressively recognizable, had emerged. Each was led by an alliance of merchants and large landholders. In legislative matters cooperation between any two of the groups could overpower the third.

The first faction was made up of the inner circle of Penn's staunch supporters and officeholders—men such as Holme, Markham, Lloyd, Harrison, Claypoole, More, Taylor, Haige, Clarke, and Welch. A few of them operated from the Lower Counties, notably Clarke at Lewes and Welch at New Castle, but most resided in Philadelphia or took up country estates in Bucks or Chester counties. Never numerous, this group had been shaken by the failure of the Free Society of Traders. Nonetheless, their power was great since they occupied almost every position of importance in proprietary

[64] *Minutes of Council,* I, 109-110. For the laws passed by the General Assembly of 1684 see *Laws of Pennsylvania,* 166-175. See Bibliographical Note on this source.

and provincial affairs. With few exceptions the members of this group were Quakers. The Council was their citadel, although a few sat in the Assembly from time to time.

The second group was also composed of Quakers, but its members were strikingly different in their attitude toward Penn. Increasingly resentful of the proprietor's prerogatives, they sought an autonomy in local and provincial affairs that clashed directly with Penn's political concepts. Many of this group, men like Joseph Growdon, John Simcock, Nicholas Waln, John Songhurst, John Blunston, and George Maris, had been strong supporters of Penn in the evolutionary stages of the "holy experiment." But transplanted to the Delaware, they began to chafe under what they were coming to regard as a restrictive proprietary policy. Joining them were a sizable number of newly arrived merchants—men from New York, the West Indies, and England—who, though Quakers, were rarely First Purchasers, officeholders, or members of the Free Society of Traders. Using the lower house as their forum, they questioned the exclusive power structure set up by Penn and his supporters. So long as Penn was in Pennsylvania their demands were moderate; but once the proprietor returned to England their drive for power became far more determined.

A third faction was centered in the Lower Counties. Since Penn's arrival it had been evident that congenital differences would make a true union of interests between upper and lower counties difficult if not impossible. In the upper counties Quakers predominated. In the Territories the minority who maintained any church affiliation were Anglican or Lutheran. The upper counties were populated by newly arrived English and Welsh; to the south Swedes and former Marylanders, many of them landholders in the area for a decade or more, formed the bulk of the population. The

82

upper counties saw no need for defensive fortifications or a militia, relying on a benevolent Indian policy to obviate such needs; the Lower Counties, vulnerable to marauding pirates and later to French raiders, demanded river forts and an armed citizenry. Perhaps most important was economic rivalry. With the growth of Philadelphia the down-river ports of New Castle and Lewes saw their control of the Delaware River vanish. Finally, the Lower Counties were confined territorially, hemmed in on their western border by Maryland and to the east by Delaware Bay. It was obvious that as fresh waves of immigrants took up land, new counties would be required—a process which could only diminish the power of the Lower Counties in the legislature. In both Council and Assembly, representatives of the Lower Counties, save for a few loyal adherents of Penn, were intent on preserving their own autonomy from both Quaker factions to the north.

Penn's Departure

While independent-minded men in the Lower Counties rose in opposition to Penn and an antiproprietary Quaker faction took form, the proprietor did what he could to rally support behind his interests. To accommodate the merchants and encourage trade he set aside a bill passed in 1683 which had levied a proprietary duty on all imports and certain exports. In 1684, at the request of prominent merchants and landowners, Penn agreed to give up proprietary duties altogether and to accept instead a lump sum of £500, which was to be raised by subscription.[65]

Penn undertook further measures to consolidate his in-

[65] *Laws of Pennsylvania,* 138-139; Petition to William Penn, May 30, 1684, Norris Papers, Family Letters, I, 101.

terests in the summer of 1684 when he realized that he must return to England to defend his claim to the Lower Counties which Lord Baltimore, already in England, was contesting before high officials at Whitehall. As plans for his voyage were made, Penn pressed for the incorporation of Philadelphia, a move which would allow the city its own representatives in the General Assembly. Since the capital city was already displaying a potential for growth far beyond that of the outlying areas, it seemed logical that Philadelphia should have its own representatives. For Penn and the Friends the innovation would mean additional support against the Lower Counties since Philadelphia was a Quaker stronghold and, what is more, most of Penn's supporters lived there. The bill passed in Council, but it was defeated by the Assembly where the Lower Counties commanded half of the votes.[66]

Ultimately, Penn's best hope for protecting his interests in Pennsylvania rested in the appointment of public and proprietary officials sympathetic to his cause. By his charter and by the Frame of 1683 he possessed sole right to commission a vast array of officers, both public and proprietary, who, barring malfeasance, would serve for life. These officers could give continuity to proprietary policy and insulate it from jealous encroachers.

Penn, before his departure, employed this power to the fullest extent. To the Provincial Court, which was to assume the appellate jurisdiction exercised until now by the Council, went five firm supporters: Nicholas More, William Welch, William Wood, Robert Turner, and John Eckley. All of these men were old friends and early participants in the colonization of Pennsylvania: four were members of the Free Society of Traders, and all but More represented the

[66] *Minutes of Council,* I, 98-99.

older, conservative Quaker faction. To the Philadelphia County Court went Welch, Turner, William Clayton, and Francis Daniel Pastorius. Clayton was an old settler, who had purchased land before 1680. Pastorius was the German agent for the Frankfurt Company and a friend of Penn since the proprietor's journeys through the Rhineland in 1677. Other county courts, appointed before Penn's departure, were also filled with large landholders and men who inspired Penn's confidence.[67]

Two powerful bodies were commissioned to administer proprietary land affairs. To one, the "Commissioners of my Estate & Revenues In America," Penn appointed five trusted friends: Thomas Holme, Robert Turner, Samuel Carpenter, James Harrison, and Philip Lehnman. All were Quakers, each was a large purchaser of land, and each held a proprietary position in another capacity as well. The commissioners were instructed to draw up a master quitrent roll, to superintend the work of the rent collectors and the Proprietary Steward of Penn's countryseat at Pennsbury, and to make annual financial reports to Penn.[68]

The second body, the Commissioners of Propriety, possessed even greater influence, for it acted directly for Penn in the allocation and sale of land. Not an acre of soil could be taken up without a warrant signed by the Commissioners; all property patents originated with them; and all matters relating to land policy required their approval. To this vitally important committee Penn named Thomas Lloyd, Robert Turner, and Samuel Carpenter, all merchants and three of the most important men in Pennsylvania.[69]

[67] Martin, *Martin's Bench and Bar*, passim; *Pennsylvania Archives*, 2nd Ser., IX, 629-630, 700.
[68] Penn to Commissioners of My Estate, ca. July 1684, J. Henley Smith Papers, I, 3, Library of Congress.
[69] Robert Proud, *History of Pennsylvania in North America . . .* (2

Rather than appoint a lieutenant governor, Penn attempted to satisfy all factions by vesting the executive functions of government in the Council as a whole. As president of that body he named Thomas Lloyd, graduate of Jesus College, Oxford, and son of the eminent and affluent Welsh Quaker, Charles Lloyd. The younger Lloyd had arrived in Pennsylvania in August 1683, and immediately caught Penn's eye as the kind of dedicated and competent Quaker who could assist at the controls of the "holy experiment." In the year that followed, Penn's esteem for Lloyd was evident in the Welshman's meteoric rise to power. In rapid succession he was appointed Master of the Rolls, President of Council, and member of the Board of Propriety. Just prior to his embarkation for England in August 1684, Penn further augmented Lloyd's powers by commissioning him Keeper of the Great Seal.[70]

With the network of offices delegated to his most unswerving supporters, Penn set sail for England on August 18, 1684. Not quite two years had passed since he had stepped ashore in the Delaware Valley filled with hopes for the creation of a regenerated society. Much had been accomplished during the 22 months Penn had been in his colony. He could look with satisfaction upon the rapid population buildup and the colonists' success in establishing farms

vols., Philadelphia, 1797-98), I, 287; all patents issued after Penn's departure were signed and executed by Lloyd, Turner, and Carpenter. See Exemplification Book 1, pp. 53-54 and all succeeding entries, Recorder of Deeds, City Hall, Philadelphia. In the Lower Counties land affairs were in the hands of the same Commissioners of Propriety, assisted by William Clarke, Commissioner of Quitrents, and Thomas Holme, Surveyor General. See *Governor's Register, State of Delaware* (Wilmington, 1926), 3.

70 Penn to Council, Aug. 16, 1684, Penn Papers, Domestic and Miscellaneous Letters, 78.

which kept the colony, almost from the beginning, free of the serious privation that had always characterized the early stages of colonization in North America. A dozen Quaker meetinghouses, completed or under construction throughout the colony, testified to the Friends' success in transplanting their church. Relations with the Indians, always a problem in new colonies, had been conducted with unusual success.[71]

And yet Penn left the colony not in a state of exhilaration but in a state of despair. To the south Baltimore disputed his claim to the indispensable Lower Counties and encouraged rebellion among the inhabitants, who responded all too readily. To the east, Byllynge's agents in West Jersey poisoned relations with reports to England of chaos in Pennsylvania. Worst of all, unity and accord among the Quakers had been difficult to achieve. The Assembly strained restlessly for more power. Council showed divisive tendencies. Individuals everywhere, Quaker and non-Quaker alike, put their individual interests above those of the community, with only a handful demonstrating unmixed loyalty to the proprietor.

[71] Early economic conditions outside of Philadelphia are described in Bronner, Penn's "Holy Experiment," 77-86. The institutional growth of the Quaker church in Pennsylvania in the first decades is portrayed in Ezra Michener, Retrospect of Early Quakerism (Philadelphia, 1860). Indian relations are most extensively treated by Francis P. Jennings, "Miquon's Passing: Indian-European Relations in Colonial Pennsylvania, 1674-1755" (unpublished Ph.D. dissertation, University of Pennsylvania, 1965). Quaker-Indian contacts in seventeenth-century Pennsylvania were far less abrasive than in other colonies, but historians have exaggerated the state of harmony between the two cultural groups. For evidence of the tension between the Quakers and Indians in the 1680's, see Gary B. Nash, "The First Decade in Pennsylvania: The Letters of William Markham and Thomas Holme to William Penn," PMHB, 90 (1966), 314-352, 491-516.

Penn's parting prayer for Philadelphia expressed the fears and anxieties aroused by two years of wearying dissension. "What love, what care, what service, and what travail, has there been to bring thee forth and preserve thee from such as would abuse, and defile thee," the troubled founder wrote from his ship, anchored in lower Delaware Bay. "O that thou mayest be kept from the evil of that [which] would, overwhelm thee. . . . My soul prays to God for thee that thou mayest stand in the day of trial . . . and thy people saved by his power."[72]

[72] Penn to Thomas Lloyd, James Claypoole, John Simcock, Christopher Taylor, and James Harrison, Aug. 12, 1684, in Proud, *History of Pennsylvania*, I, 288-290.

CHAPTER 3

Dismantling the Proprietary System

THE LINES of conflict which Penn found so disheartening during his brief stay in Pennsylvania were only etched deeper by events following his departure. With the proprietor in England, men of ambition had greater scope for action and the feeling mounted that, far from sustaining the new colony, Penn's proprietary government only hindered its development. Gradually in the 1680's, the antiproprietary faction grew in strength until it included most of the important merchants and landowners in Pennsylvania. However, the proprietary system did not go uncontested by lesser men also struggling for a share of power and status. It was this dual struggle of the emerging elite—to resist proprietary policy imposed from above, while warding off the threats of ambitious men lower on the social ladder—that characterized the politics of the first decade in Pennsylvania. By the end of the 1680's it was clear that the "holy experiment," as originally conceived, was floundering in an atmosphere of recrimination, chronic friction, and struggle for position.

A Waning of Confidence

No issue after 1684 was more important in diminishing confidence in Penn than his land policy. Even while Penn was in his province, this had been a source of dissatisfaction. Following his departure discontent mounted. At the root of the problem was the belief that Penn, in disposing of his vast wilderness domain, held the settlers to impossibly idealistic principles concerning the use of the land, while in his own dealings with the settlers he emphasized profit rather than their needs or rights.

Nothing illustrates better this tension between idealistic plans and practical realities than Penn's attitudes toward land speculation and the pattern of settlement. When this colony was still in the planning stage, Penn projected a township system of settlement which provided for the systematic settlement of blocs of settlers in agricultural villages with each purchaser's land radiating outward from the center. It was a system that would not only preserve the Quaker spirit of community in Pennsylvania, but would allow Penn a maximum return on his land.[1] To discourage land speculation, Penn required all purchasers to settle their land within three years after purchase. This regulation had a dual purpose. On the one hand, it would prevent the largest purchasers from staking out tracts of 2,500 or 5,000 acres near Philadelphia and then waiting for the market to rise while newcomers were forced into the interior. New settlers, wrote Penn, "must not suffer to be drove back by them [land speculators] from comeing or [be driven] into other Provinces. . . . Let this not become like desolate Virginia and Maryland."[2] At the same time, Penn recognized that he must dampen the speculative urge because of the effect it would have in undermining the guiding principles of the "holy experiment" which stressed the needs of the com-

[1] Myers, ed., *Narratives*, 263, 274-275. For a fuller discussion of Penn's attempts to establish organic agricultural communities see James T. Lemon, "A Rural Geography of Southeastern Pennsylvania During the Eighteenth Century: The Contributions of Cultural Inheritance, Social Structure, Economic Conditions and Physical Resources" (unpublished Ph.D. dissertation, University of Wisconsin, 1964) , Chap. 6.

[2] Penn, *A Further Account of Pennsylvania*, in Myers, ed., *Narratives*, 263; Penn to Thomas Holme, Aug. 8, 1685, Ford MSS Collection, New York Public Library.

munity rather than the individual. If land speculation were allowed to run rampant in Pennsylvania it would lead to profiteering and acquisitiveness as it had in other colonies, and the ligaments of the Quaker community would soon be severed.

However sound in theory, Penn's land policy was an attempt to stop the unstoppable. In their hunger for land and their eagerness to speculate in it, Quakers on the Delaware differed little from Puritans in New England or Anglicans on the Chesapeake. Rather than settle in agricultural villages, where the emphasis was on cohesion and order, the Quakers sought the best land available, especially along the numerous streams that fed the Delaware and Schuylkill rivers. Dispersed farms and irregular holdings were the rule; and with new settlers pouring in almost everyone in Pennsylvania with capital to invest, merchants foremost among them, realized that no greater opportunity for profit-making existed than land speculation. Penn employed reasoning, appeals to conscience and religious convictions, and even threats, but nothing could stem the tide of speculation that overtook the land-starved and ambitious Quakers who found themselves surrounded by endless expanses of virgin land.[3]

As abstract as it was, Penn's land policy was even more deeply resented because it was so inconsistently applied. Just one day before he embarked for England, for example, Penn negotiated the sale of 40,000 acres to Ralph Fretwell, a wealthy Quaker merchant of Barbados. When the word

[3] Lemon, "A Rural Geography of Southeastern Pennsylvania," Chap. 6. Penn's attempts to curb land speculation can best be seen in his letters to Thomas Lloyd, Oct. 2, 1685, and April 21, 1686, Penn Papers, Domestic and Miscellaneous Letters, 15, 83; and to Phineas Pemberton, Feb. 8, 1686/87, Etting Collection, Early Quakers and the Penn Family, 4.

leaked out that Penn not only had sold the land at a price below the established rate and relieved the purchaser of the usual obligation to settle families on the tract within three years, but had ordered his Board of Propriety to locate the immense purchase on choice land within the immediate area of settlement, a storm of opposition arose.[4] The rancor aroused by the Fretwell case was increased by Penn's strict application of the "Conditions or Concessions" which specified that one-tenth of every 100,000-acre section of land must be reserved for proprietary use. The sight of so much reserved land lying unused, while the proprietor in England harped on the subject of unsettled land, rankled many in Pennsylvania. Penn's Surveyor General reported that complaints rang out from old and new purchasers alike that they must take up land far distant from Philadelphia while large proprietary tracts lay vacant near the city.[5]

As unrealistic and inconsistent as Penn's land settlement policy was felt to be, it never met with the opposition aroused by another proprietary device—the quitrent. Recognizing that many had exhausted their resources in immigrating to the colony, Penn had promised that quitrents would not begin "till after 1684." But in 1684, before embarking for England, he instructed his commissioners to collect the rents for that year, requiring payment in coin no later than March 1685.[6] What had been accepted by pur-

[4] For the grant of land to Fretwell see *Pennsylvania Archives*, 3rd Ser., II, 700; and Penn Papers, Philadelphia Land Grants, 89-95. The colonial reaction is recorded in the letters of Philip Lehnman, Nicholas More, Samuel Carpenter, and Robert Turner to Penn, Myers Collection, Box 2, #5, 6, 9, and 16, CCHS; and a series of letters from Fretwell to Penn, *ibid.*, #8, 11, and 14.

[5] Thomas Holme to Penn, March 24, 1688, *PMHB*, 90 (1966), 502.

[6] Hazard, ed., *Annals*, 510; Penn to Commissioners of My Estate, ca. July 1684, Smith Papers, Library of Congress.

chasers in England, however, no longer seemed an obligation in Pennsylvania. Lacking specie, struggling to subdue
the wilderness around them, and still in the early stages of
developing the land, the vast majority of landowners looked
upon the rents as an onerous tax which would serve only to
increase Penn's already sizable fortune.

In the face of strong opposition Penn withdrew his instructions to collect rents in 1684. But in the next year, when
the settlers argued for a further postponement, he rightly
concluded that quitrents would never be collected except
under duress. Though Penn exhorted and admonished the
colonists, even threatening legal proceedings, quitrents went
uncollected month after month, year after year. Even Penn's
officeholders would do nothing. To his dismay Penn learned
that William Clarke, the chief pillar of proprietary policy
in the Lower Counties, refused to support the collector of
quitrents and publicly stated "that the governor did not expect the full rents." No wonder the collectors in the Territories received "cold entertainment," remarked Penn's informant.[7]

Compounding the mounting irritation with Penn's land
policy was the common feeling that some of the proprietor's
officeholders, like their patron, seldom overlooked an opportunity to turn a profit at the expense of the hard-pressed
settlers. Thomas Holme, who as Penn's Surveyor General
was the key official in the proprietary land system, was
charged with chronic drunkenness, taking bribes, and charging extortionate fees. Other officers of government were
characterized as oppressive or "designingly partiall" to
Penn's interests.[8] The feeling grew in Pennsylvania that

[7] Bronner, Penn's "Holy Experiment," 72; Holme to Penn, Nov. 25,
1686, PMHB, 90 (1966), 351.

[8] Penn to Thomas Lloyd, Aug. 15, 1685, Penn Papers, Domestic and

men did not earn the right to govern by dint of the estates they had carved out in the Delaware wilderness but because of their earlier connections with Penn. "There are gridges in some," admitted one of Penn's closest advisors, "that none are put in places of power but friends and tis not profession qualifies men for places and powers; offices show it too much."[9]

In 1687, still determined to hold the colonists to the land policy formulated in London before colonization began, Penn appointed a new Board of Propriety and attempted to inspire its members with lengthy letters of instruction and proprietary proclamations demanding strict adherence to his land policies. Speculators who were waiting for large tracts of unsettled land to rise in value were to be prosecuted in the courts and, if necessary, half of their lands reclaimed. "Though I doubt not but you may meet with contradictions with some of the greater purchasers," Penn wrote, "Govern not yourselves by that, for 'tis just, 'tis wise, 'tis equal." Newly purchased land must be laid out contiguous to settled areas, ore lands were not to be warranted to private individuals without his express permission, and quit-rents were to be collected in silver at once.[10]

To order such things was one thing; to enforce them was another. Thomas Holme made it plain to Penn that he could never win a case relating to land, rents, or any other

Miscellaneous Letters, 81; Penn to Council, July 13, 1685, *ibid.*, 80; Ralph Fretwell to Penn, Oct. 1684 and May 23, 1685, Myers Collection, Box 2, #7, 11, CCHS.

9 Thomas Holme to Penn, Nov. 25, 1686, *PMHB*, 90 (1966), 350.

10 The commission, letters of instruction, and proprietary proclamations concerning land policy are in Minutes of the Board of Property of the Province of Pennsylvania, *Pennsylvania Archives*, 2nd Ser., XIX, 3-13.

proprietary matters in the common law courts.[11] But Penn
was determined now to put teeth into his policy. If the proclamation regarding the settling of land was not obeyed, the
Board of Propriety was to constitute itself as a prerogative
court. "You are my Court for land and I need not submit to
ordinary Courts," ordered Penn. It was a bold innovation
and one which he sensed would not be passively accepted. If
juries could be trusted, he added, cases might be put before
them, though he was not obliged to use the civil courts. As
for quitrents, Penn warned that if they remained unpaid he
would repossess the land, an action which "the best Lawyers
here assure me I may do."[12]

In spite of administrative changes and proprietary dicta,
land speculation could not be stopped by the absentee proprietor. The new Commissioners of Propriety faithfully
published proclamations warning that unsettled land would
be offered for sale. William Markham appended a plea to
prominent Friends in each county, asking their cooperation
in executing Penn's demands.[13] But beyond such appeals the
Board could do little. William Markham pointed out the
limits of the Board's power a year after the proclamation
was issued. He had broached the subject of Penn's order "of
Disposeing of mens lands not seated according to Regulation" with John Simcock and Arthur Cooke, Quaker leaders in Chester and Philadelphia counties upon whom Penn
depended for support. But Simcock warned him, Markham
related, that to attempt an enforcement of proprietary land

---

[11] Holme to Penn, March 24, 1686/87, *PMHB*, 90 (1966), 504-505.

[12] Penn to Commissioners of Propriety, Feb. 8, 1686/87, *Pennsylvania Archives*, 2nd Ser., XIX, 12; Penn to Commissioners of State, Sept.
17, 1687, Penn Papers, Domestic and Miscellaneous Letters, 86.

[13] The proclamation and Markham's letter to the Quaker leaders is
in *PMHB*, 24 (1900), 245.

policy was to court disaster. It was pointed advice from one of Penn's early supporters, who, like so many others, had drifted into the antiproprietary camp. Nor could the Board of Propriety employ a proprietary court of exchequer authorized by Penn as a last resort. The landowners would never admit its legitimacy, Markham warned, even if the members of the Board risked their own position in the community by establishing such a prerogative court. Of the new Commissioners of Propriety, only Samuel Carpenter was sympathetic to the proprietary cause and even he had now weakened in his support of Penn's demands, complaining that the proprietor asked "hard things."[14]

It was no different with the collection of quitrents and the demand for their payment in silver. The issue came to a boil in early 1688 when John Simcock discovered a proclamation that had been posted on Penn's order and which he threatened to pull downe "ffrom off the Cour[t] house Door at Upland [Chester] and burne it." The proclamation ordered the collection of rent in specie in conformity with Penn's instructions. Simcock charged that Penn had agreed to collect rents in corn in lieu of specie and argued that a law passed in 1683, which made "country produce" lawful pay, obliged Penn to accept corn. Markham replied that Penn had given a "positive order to the Contrary" which must be obeyed. Then the Board of Propriety must sue for the rents, retorted Simcock, and predicted that a jury could not be found in all of Pennsylvania that would uphold the Board. "I hope," returned Markham, "you doe not think the Governor would Submitt his Cause between him and the people to the Judgment of the people." But he dared not give any further hint of the proprietary court of exchequer which Penn had authorized. Sim-

14 Markham to Penn, May 2, 1688, *PMHB*, 90 (1966), 506-508.

cock ended the confrontation by charging that the people intended "nothing but Honesty" with Penn, but Penn not so with them, and complained bitterly that the proprietor had "kidnapped them into the Country" with false promises.[15]

The Struggle for Power

A capriciously administered and hopelessly idealistic land system, resentment over quitrents, dishonest or distrusted placemen, and what seemed a distant and unresponsive proprietor—all combined to produce a crisis of confidence in Penn which refashioned the political dynamics of Pennsylvania. Earlier one group in Pennsylvania, composed of inhabitants of the Lower Counties and men who had not participated in the original planning, had opposed the monopoly of power enjoyed by Penn's early supporters— merchants and gentry. But now many in Penn's select circle, disillusioned by his inflexible policies and reacting to unforeseen contingencies in primitive Pennsylvania, forsook their loyalty to the proprietor. Joining the new merchants, they formed a new Quaker elite—proud, aggressive, preeminent in trade, and intent on substituting local autonomy for proprietary control. Facilitating their rise to power was the sudden depletion of the proprietary ranks after 1684. A few months after Penn left the colony, William Welch died and William Haige moved to East New Jersey. Christopher Taylor died in 1686 and by the end of the following year James Claypoole, Nicholas More, and James

---

[15] *Ibid.* In his parting instructions to the Board of Propriety, as Simcock argued, Penn had authorized the collection of quitrents in wheat. See Penn's commission to the Commissioners of Propriety, Smith Papers, I, 3, Library of Congress.

Harrison were dead.[16] The new Quaker alliance, moving into the vacuum left by the disintegrating proprietary circle, became, half by default and half by aggressive action, the new locus of economic and political power in Pennsylvania.

The clash between the new Quaker faction and the proprietor was intensified by the drift of both Penn and the provincial leaders in Pennsylvania toward new concepts of government. Both sides became more conservative but in a way that only increased the area of disagreement between them. In Pennsylvania leaders of the Quaker society found themselves cast in a new role; no longer the fanatical sectarians of Restoration England—persecuted, martyred, and excluded from places of power—they now found their efforts rewarded with political prominence and a measure of economic success. Controlling their society and representing the majority religious view, these social firebrands of the Old World turned conservative in the New. The right of minority protest—whether political or religious—lost its appeal, for now it took on the appearance of a challenge to their hard-won reprieve from the persecution they had suffered on the other side of the Atlantic. The emerging Quaker elite, composed of the leading merchants and landowners, steadfastly utilized their power to resist pressure from both above and below. In their view, the pattern of political and economic development in Pennsylvania must not be decided by an absentee proprietor. Nor should it be left to the "lesser sorts," including non-Quakers in the Lower Counties, who were maneuvering for a larger role in

16 For the deaths of Welch, Taylor, Claypoole, More, and Harrison see Philadelphia Wills and Inventories, Book A, 1682-1699, photostats at the Genealogical Society of Pennsylvania, Philadelphia. For Haige see Pomfret, *East New Jersey*, 209.

the economic and political process. Their concept of government was essentially elitist but antiproprietary.

For Penn, the years following his return to England were filled with grave misgivings at the system of government he had fashioned for Pennsylvania. As antiproprietary sentiment rose and only a small cluster of the faithful remained to defend his interests, his conviction grew that the colonists were incapable of self-government. Only a less permissive system would restore stability and quietude. "I hope," he wrote in 1686, "some of those that once feared I had too much Power, will now see I have not enough, and that excess of Power does not the Mischief that Licentiousness does to a State."[17] Abstract political theory and practical statecraft, Penn discovered, were not the same thing. As the 1680's wore on, his defense of proprietary powers stiffened.

Illustrative of the rising antiproprietary spirit were the evasive tactics of the leading merchants and councilors in collecting the £500 subscription promised Penn in 1684 in lieu of proprietary customs. After his arrival in England, Penn repeatedly reminded the merchants of their obligation. Finally, more than a year after his departure, the Council ordered the merchants to explain the "urgent business ... about the Subscriptions." The merchants produced a list of subscribers who had pledged some £200, but explained that outside of Philadelphia County nothing at all had been promised. If the Council would invest them with legal authority to levy assessments, the merchants did not doubt that they could raise the money. But the Council, persuaded by the arguments of President Lloyd, whose allegiance to Penn was rapidly withering, refused to support this request or

---

[17] Penn to Thomas Lloyd, Nov. 7, 1686, Parrish Collection, Proud Papers, II, 5 (copy). For a discussion of Penn's changing political philosophy see Dunn, *Politics and Conscience*, 132-161.

even to contribute to the fund.[18] A year later it was evident that no one in the colony really cared about honoring a promise made two years before. Though Penn wrote in anger of "that gross delusion of the marchants about the supply" and attacked the faithlessness of the provincial leaders, nothing could move the colony to action. "The Subscriptions are laid aside like an old Tayle told," wrote William Markham. Later in the year Penn learned that not a penny had been raised.[19]

Penn made attempts to stem the tide of feeling running against him. "Assure my servants," he wrote to James Harrison in 1685, "that if they be of aid to me and Dilligent, I will be kind to them in land and other things at my returne."[20] But promises from afar had little effect. When inducements failed, Penn tried threats. "Lett them know how much they are in my power not I in theirs," he wrote in reference to the merchants a year later. Two swords would be suspended over their heads to end their obduracy, he cautioned: he would refuse confirmation of all laws passed since his departure, and thus void them; or, failing that, he would reclaim all land sold to First Purchasers but not yet patented. "And that will be Supply enough to me and myn," Penn concluded grimly.[21]

18 *Minutes of Council,* I, 162-163; "A true & full Narrative of the Beginnings progress and Conclusion of the Voluntarie Contribution for the Maintenance of the Government in Lieu of the Act of Excise . . . ," Penn Papers, Penn vs. Ford.

19 Penn to Council, Sept. 25, 1686, Dreer Collection, Penn Letters, 17; Markham to Penn, Oct. 5, 1686 and Holme to Penn, Nov. 25, 1686, *PMHB,* 90 (1966), 347, 349.

20 Penn to Harrison, Oct. 4, 1685, Penn Papers, Domestic and Miscellaneous Letters, 16.

21 Penn to Thomas Lloyd, Sept. 21, 1686, in *PMHB,* 80 (1956), 236-247 with notes by Frederick B. Tolles.

Neither carrot nor stick cured the spirit of disaffection. Penn's letters to Council were frequently ignored. "After they are Read there is no more notice taken of them," reported Markham in August 1686. Men grumbled that they came "so far for so little," when called from their farms to hear Penn's instructions read before Council. His name was even omitted from public acts, Penn heard. "Hold fast what you have," his Secretary warned in 1686, "[for] Every inch you part with will be an Ell to yor successors loss."[22] Holme divulged the undisguised hostility among men of position to raising a tax for the support of proprietary government, and revealed that a prominent Quaker landowner had publicly asserted that Penn "had not so much power as he hath." Warned another of Penn's supporters: "Whatever privilidg you once grant you must never think to Recall without being Reflected on and Counted a Great oppressor."[23]

Once convinced that Penn would not—or could not—adapt proprietary policies to the needs of the colony, the rising Quaker elite undertook to absorb, or, if that was not possible, to ignore, his prerogative power. Heading the anti-proprietary movement was Thomas Lloyd, the educated and influential Welsh leader in whom Penn had invested the most important offices in the colony: President of Council, Keeper of the Seal, Master of the Rolls, and member of the Board of Propriety. In 1684 Lloyd had become suitor to the widow of a wealthy Quaker merchant in New York and for the next year spent most of his time there, coming

[22] Markham to Penn, Aug. 22, 1686, *PMHB*, 90 (1966), 326; Penn to James Harrison, Jan. 28, 1686/87, Penn Papers, Domestic and Miscellaneous Letters, 32; Markham to Penn, Oct. 5, 1686, *PMHB*, 90 (1966), 347.

[23] Thomas Holme to Penn, Nov. 25, 1686 and Markham to Penn, Aug. 22, 1686, *PMHB*, 90 (1966), 349, 321.

to Philadelphia only as Council business required.[24] Possibly his experiences in New York, where merchants dominated municipal and provincial government, added to Lloyd's disillusionment with Penn and to his conviction that the leaders of Pennsylvania must acquire a greater degree of autonomy and a layer of insulation from proprietary influence. Lloyd, however, was not motivated by a deep-seated hostility toward Penn as were several members of the Council. Rather he was inspired to assume the leadership of the antiproprietary faction by his awareness that proprietary policy was not only badly suited to the needs of the colony but was impossible to enforce in a community where force, in and out of government, was disavowed.[25]

In reducing Penn's powers Lloyd and the Council relied

[24] Samuel Carpenter to Penn, Dec. 25, 1684 and Robert Turner to Penn, Oct. 31, 1685, Myers Collection, Box 2, #9, 16, CCHS.

[25] The tendency to view the early politics of Pennsylvania as a struggle for power between the Council and Assembly, with the Council defending the proprietary interests, has almost wholly obscured the role of Thomas Lloyd as a leader in the movement to develop the autonomous power of the leading Quaker merchants and landowners at Penn's expense. Isaac Sharpless entirely ignored Lloyd's activities in the five years after Penn's departure, focusing on his later struggles against Governor John Blackwell and the Quaker apostate, George Keith *History of Quaker Government in Pennsylvania* (Philadelphia, 1898-99) and *Political Leaders of Provincial Pennsylvania* (New York, 1919). Frederick Tolles calls Lloyd the "acknowledged leader of the conservative or Proprietary party" and states that the Council from the outset was "friendly to the Proprietor's interests." (*Meeting House*, 117, 120). Bronner, who has treated the politics of the seventeenth century most recently and extensively, also ignores the antiproprietary thrust of Lloyd and his followers, asserting simply that Penn was "fortunate in his choice" of Lloyd as president of the Council but mistaken in giving him too little power (*Penn's "Holy Experiment,"* 88-89). Only Roy N. Lokken in his biography of David Lloyd, recognizes that Thomas Lloyd was "indifferent" to Penn's interests, although he does not deal with the years before 1687; *David Lloyd: Colonial Lawmaker* (Seattle, 1959), 23-24.

on the simple but effective technique of gradually assuming powers reserved for the proprietor under the Frame of 1683. Thus in 1685 Council quietly absorbed Penn's power of judicial appointment, first by making an *ad hoc* appointment to a county court, a procedure which quickly became the accepted practice, and then by securing passage of a law investing Council with authority to appoint the provincial court as well.[26]

The next attempt to curb Penn's power was even bolder. By Penn's charter from Charles II and by the Frame of 1683, all laws were to be made "by the Governor, with the assent and approbation of the freemen in Provincial Council and Assembly met." The phrase, consonant with constitutional theory of the seventeenth century, implied that no law existed or could be created without the assent of the proprietor or governor, from whom, as the King's beneficiary, legislative authority descended. In 1685, however, the lower house noticed that the laws submitted by Council, under Lloyd's supervision, were presented "by the authority of the President and Council." The innovation was of prime importance for it attributed to Council an independent legislative authority which altered the entire concept of lawmaking expressed in the frame of government. The Assembly objected to this variation not out of any tenderness for the proprietor's privileges but because it had also been ignored. Council conceded the point, although at the General Assembly of 1686 it again introduced bills under the illegal preamble, until challenged again by the lower house.[27]

By the end of 1686, Thomas Lloyd, in league with most of the merchants and an increasing number of the larger

[26] *Minutes of Council,* I, 120, 127, 129, 153; *Laws of Pennsylvania,* 168, 178.
[27] *Minutes of Council,* I, 133-134; *Votes of Assembly,* I, 60.

landowners, had taken the first steps toward dismantling the machinery of proprietary government. The Free Society of Traders was all but defunct except as a land company. Penn's land policy was vocally opposed and frequently ignored. Some of his most trusted appointees were discredited; some had turned against him; others were dead or dying. Provincial and county courts were falling under the domination of Council, where Penn's few remaining supporters were losing their grasp. Proprietary customs, the "public supply" promised in its place, quitrents, and even a public tax for the support of government had all been studiously ignored, leaving Penn in a state of exasperation.[28]

Trapped in England, Penn did what he could to bring his province to account. For two years after his return to England in 1684 he had relied on high-toned advice and appeals to conscience to cure the disunity and insubordination in his colony, promising at the same time to hasten his return to the Delaware. But by early 1687 it was clear that his return must be delayed indefinitely. Settlement of the boundary dispute with Lord Baltimore moved at an agonizingly slow pace; and as Penn wrote Thomas Lloyd, he could not "leave the thing unfixt I came on purpose to obtaine."[29] Perhaps more important, he found his presence in England vitally important in parrying moves for the royalization of his government as a part of current plans for imperial reform; he warned in one letter of "a Storm . . . that is falling upon other Colonys."[30] Unable to assume the leadership of

28 Penn to Thomas Lloyd, Nov. 7, 1686, Parrish Collection, Proud Papers, II, 5 (copy) .

29 Penn to Thomas Lloyd, Sept. 21, 1686, *PMHB*, 80 (1956) , 240. For Penn's struggle with Baltimore in England see Illick, *Penn the Politician*, 52-75.

30 Penn to James Harrison, Sept. 23, 1686, Dreer Collection, William Penn Letters, 17; see also Penn to Thomas Lloyd, Nov. 7, 1686, Par-

his colony, Penn decided to attempt a reorganization of the executive arm of government. He had long been dissatisfied with the Council, which had functioned in this capacity since his departure. "My former deputation [of executive authority]," he wrote, "[was] clogg'd with a long and slow tale, and then with unwillingness, and sometimes reflections even upon me for their pains of hearing one letter read."[31]

The formula Penn struck upon was a commission of five deputies, any three of whom could enact, annul, or vary laws "as if I myself were there present," reserving to the proprietor "the confirmation of what is done, and my peculiar royalties and advantages." Previously there was no "visible" deputy governor when the Council was not in session, noted Penn in justifying the change. "Now they [there] shall be one, Sitt they, or sitt they not."[32]

Penn's instructions to the new Commissioners, like his injunctions to the reconstituted Board of Propriety, were aimed at ending factional struggles and obtaining strict conformity to proprietary policy. The councilors must be diligent in attending meetings; if they neglected their responsibility, Penn would dissolve the frame of government without further ado. Disorders in the Assembly and Council must be suppressed and both bodies permitted no further

---

rish Collection, Proud Papers, II, 5 (copy). The attack on the colonial charters is discussed in Philip S. Haffenden, "The Crown and the Colonial Charters, 1675-1688," *William and Mary Quarterly*, 3rd Ser., 15 (1958), 297-311, 452-466. Penn's maneuvers to defend his charter are best treated in Illick, *Penn the Politician*, 77-102.

[31] Penn to Eckley, Claypoole, More, Turner, and Lloyd, June 6, 1687, Penn Papers, Domestic and Miscellaneous Letters, 85; Penn to Lloyd, Feb. 1, 1686/87, *ibid.*, 84.

[32] Penn to Commissioners of State, Feb. 1, 1686/87, Proud, *History of Pennsylvania*, I, 305-307; Penn to Phineas Pemberton, Feb. 8, 1686/87, Etting Collection, Early Quakers and the Penn Family, 4.

encroachments "upon the powers and privileges remaining yet in me." "Parleys," or "open conferences," between the two legislative bodies, conceded by Council during the past two years, must end. Council must propose bills, the Assembly "consent or dissent, according to charter."[33]

Unfortunately, Penn's choice of commissioners probably eliminated any chance that the new, firmer policy could succeed. Thrown together and charged with mending the deep-rooted political divisions were five strong-willed and virtually incompatible figures. "I chose those about the town and that did not agree, so each shall have a share [of power]," Penn explained. But such a combination was fated from the outset to compound, not cure, the province's ills. Cheek by jowl on the new commission sat Nicholas More, James Claypoole, Thomas Lloyd, John Eckley, and Robert Turner. More was a particularly uninspired choice, since his high-handed and abusive behavior over a period of years had earned him the distrust of almost everyone in the colony. Claypoole was almost as unpopular, as even Penn admitted.[34] Lloyd, increasingly unyielding in his antiproprietary attitudes, was deeply distrusted by More and Turner. Eckley spoke for the Welsh community west of Philadelphia, which even now was troubling the province with claims that Penn had granted its members an autonomous "barony," free of tax obligations and independent of the local courts. Penn's plea to his Commissioners to "draw not several ways, have no cabals apart, nor reserves for one another, [but] treat, with a mutual simplicity, an entire confidence in one another" revealed how little he understood

[33] Penn to Commissioners of State, Feb. 1, 1686/87, Proud, *History of Pennsylvania*, I, 305-307.

[34] Penn to Harrison, Jan. 28, 1686/87, Penn Papers, Domestic and Miscellaneous Letters, 32.

—or was ready to admit—the extent of the rifts in Quaker society.[35]

It was with no great difficulty that the antiproprietary Quaker elite thwarted Penn's plans for stabilizing affairs through the appointment of the Commissioners of State. At first Thomas Lloyd and his supporters charged Penn with an unwarrantable revision of the Frame of 1683, pointing out that such a constitutional change could be made only with the consent of six-sevenths of the General Assembly.[36] More than a year passed, with Penn and the provincial leaders arguing over the legality of the change at a distance of 3,000 miles, before the new form of executive government was accepted.[37] Once installed, the new Commissioners of State, led by Lloyd, made it their guiding principle to enlarge the scope of their power. Before another year was out they had sought and obtained both the right to sit in Council, and hence to dominate that body, and the power to function as the Provincial Court. In a move of equal importance, they disputed Penn's right to approve or veto legislation passed by the General Assembly. As governor, Penn had always reserved this right and had reiterated it in his commission to the new executive body. When the matter was raised in Council, Penn learned from William Markham, its members "stood Stiffly for their Charter" and insisted that Penn's claim to a veto power was a breach of it. Markham disputed the point, reminding the members of the custom-

[35] Penn to Commissioners of State, June 6, 1687, *ibid.*, 85.

[36] Penn to Harrison, Sept. 8, 1687, *ibid.*, 34.

[37] During the course of the debate over the new executive branch of government, two of the Commissioners of State, More and Claypoole, died. Penn commissioned John Simcock and Arthur Cooke in their places. Both men had been among his early supporters but by now had drifted toward the antiproprietary camp. Penn's commission to Simcock and Cooke is in Penn Papers, Domestic and Miscellaneous Letters, 86.

ary right of confirmation possessed by colonial governors in other colonies. But his critics rejoined that in neighboring colonies the lower house proposed laws.[38]

Such a bold and unprecedented statement of provincial autonomy in legislative matters only dramatized the growing split between the proprietor and leaders in the colony. In 1683 Penn's power to veto legislation had been the subject of lengthy debate; but the General Assembly had conceded the point then rather than accept financial liability for the colony's adherence to the Navigation Acts. As recently as September 1686 Penn had written Lloyd threatening to withhold his confirmation of all laws passed since his departure and this had been received by Lloyd without protest, if not with enthusiasm.[39] Now the Council embraced a radically different interpretation of the clause in the Frame of 1683 which required all laws to be passed "by the Governor and the freemen in Council and Assembly met." In delegating executive authority to the Commissioners of State, Council argued, Penn had surrendered every portion of his legislative power.

The doughty resistance exhibited by most of the provincial leaders in response to Penn's new policy revealed the change that had overcome Pennsylvania society. In the early years Penn had projected a kind of joint partnership with his merchant and gentry associates. Now, before the end of the first decade, loyalties to Penn had eroded badly. By 1688 only a small cluster of faithful friends remained to support his cause: Robert Turner, Thomas Holme, William Markham, John Goodson, Phineas Pemberton, and William Clarke. Samuel Richardson, a Jamaican merchant who had been in the colony for a short time, spoke for many when

[38] Markham to Penn, May 2, 1688, *PMHB*, 90 (1966), 510-511.
[39] Penn to Lloyd, Sept. 21, 1686, *PMHB*, 80 (1956), 246.

he asserted that the interests of the people and the proprietor had become incompatible. Many of Penn's former friends agreed. Joseph Growdon, a First Purchaser of 5,000 acres and a leading figure in Bucks County, turned bitterly against Penn's restrictive land policy and became a tireless critic of the proprietor.[40] In 1687, when Penn's Board of Propriety ruled against Growdon in the settlement of a protracted land dispute, the Quaker railed that "he would make a Nationall business of it and Impeach [the members of the Board] for a breach of the Charter." Arthur Cooke, John Simcock, and even David Lloyd, who had recently arrived in the colony bearing Penn's commission as Attorney General, supported Growdon. William Markham's admonishments that Growdon and his friends had "broken the Charter all to peaces already" and would not mend it with further commotions impressed nobody.[41]

By 1688, the Quaker alliance of merchants and prosperous landowners, the former concentrated in Philadelphia, the latter in Bucks and Chester counties, was preeminent at all levels of government. They dominated the Commission of State, made the Council almost wholly their preserve, held most of the proprietary and provincial offices, and monopolized the county courts. Such lesser offices as they did not occupy—county sheriff, court clerk, recorder of wills, constable, and coroner—were filled by their consent or preferment.

Of the Commissioners of State, all merchants, only Robert Turner defended Penn's interest. Among the councilors

[40] The disaffection of Richardson and Growdon is related in Markham to Penn, Aug. 22, 1686 and May 2, 1688, *PMHB*, 90 (1966), 329-330, 508-514; and Growdon to Penn, March 16, 1687/88, Myers Collection, cxlviii, folder 18 (copy) CCHS.

[41] *Ibid.*; Markham to Penn, May 2, 1688, *PMHB*, 90 (1966), 513.

from the upper counties, antiproprietary attitudes prevailed, varying only in degree. Only two, William Yardley, a landowner in Bucks County, and merchant Samuel Carpenter, evinced any sympathy for Penn's designs, and even they lapsed frequently into opposition. In Bucks and Chester counties all the councilors sat concurrently on the benches of quarter sessions and common pleas, joined by other justices who sat in the Assembly. Of the seven Philadelphia County justices, two sat on the Board of Propriety, one on the Commission of State, and one in the Assembly. From the Lower Counties came nine councilors, only two of whom, both Quaker merchants, gave even faint support to proprietary policy. The other seven joined the dominant Quaker party led by Thomas Lloyd whenever a question of proprietary privilege was involved, although they made no secret of their dislike of Quaker domination over the Lower Counties.[42]

The loss of confidence in Penn and the erosion of a sense of community among the Quakers during the first decade in Pennsylvania involved not only the consolidation of a powerful antiproprietary faction, but a coalescing of lesser men into a loose party of opposition against the Philadelphia Quaker merchants and their country allies. Engaged as they were in contesting proprietary authority imposed from above, the leading men of the province found themselves faced with an equally immediate threat from below where

[42] Members of the Council are listed in *Laws of Pennsylvania*, 515, 523; the composition of the county courts is taken from *Records of the Courts of Common Pleas and Quarter Sessions of Bucks County, 1684-1700* (Meadville, Pa., 1943), *Records of the Courts of Chester County, 1681-1697* (Meadville, Pa., 1910), and Samuel W. Pennypacker, *Pennsylvania Colonial Cases* (Philadelphia, 1892). The alignment is based on an analysis of Council votes and information given in letters previously cited in this chapter.

men of the second rank, making the Assembly their forum, grasped for wider power. By and large these men were small merchants and artisan-shopkeepers from Philadelphia or landowners of the middle rank from the outlying counties. At the county level they occupied lesser local positions and sat occasionally with their more powerful neighbors on the county courts. Although they had been skirmishing with the Council since 1683, such men were hardly less inclined to antiproprietary sentiments than their superiors, for they shared with them a growing dissatisfaction with Penn's policies, particularly as they related to land.

Nowhere was the struggle for power between the two social groups—separated by thin and often obscure lines—more directly or dramatically expressed than at the meetings of the General Assembly after Penn's departure. In 1685 the lower house set the tone of things to come by daring Council to prevent them from "reading, debating, and concluding upon the promulgated Bills by vote . . . without any the least Restriction by the Council to hinder them from so doing."[43] This initial thrust was followed by an attempt to impeach two of Penn's proprietary officials, Nicholas More and Patrick Robinson. This attack led to fiery exchanges between the Assembly and the accused, and finally to the forcible removal of Robinson, who in a last gesture of defiance prostrated himself on the floor of the legislative chamber and shouted his denial of the Assembly's authority to challenge his performance as Clerk of the Provincial Court.[44]

These confused elements of strife, evident in the tumultous General Assembly of 1685, crystallized in the following year. The Assembly continued its offensive, raising new challenges to the Council's power. The Council responded

[43] *Votes of Assembly*, I, 59-64.
[44] *Minutes of Council*, I, 135-153; *Votes of Assembly*, I, 65-69.

by attempting to arrest the speaker of the House, John White, for a misdemeanor allegedly committed as sheriff of New Castle County. In an atmosphere of increasing tension, Council and Assembly aired their disagreements. It mattered little whether the issue was the right of the Assembly to impeach proprietary officials or to debate and amend legislative bills initiated by Council, the Council's right to arrest a member of the Assembly, or the Assembly's power to cast all laws into abeyance by withholding its consent from the ambiguous annual bill for "the continuation of former laws."[45] Of prime significance was the fact that during the first decade a consensus could never be found on the proper distribution of political power. Political domination by any group, whether it spoke in the name of the proprietor or the resident merchants and large landowners, was unacceptable to large segments of the society represented in the Assembly. Almost as disturbing were the self-intensifying effects of the quest for power. As the alarmed Markham wrote Penn, further convulsions of the sort that buffeted the General Assembly of 1686 would "hazard the overthrow of Government."[46]

Although the Assembly acquired somewhat broader powers in its struggle with the Council between 1683 and 1687, it lost much of the ground it had gained in 1688 when the Council responded to new demands for wider privileges with a full-scale counterattack. In forceful language the Council rejected the Assembly's demands that it should receive its committees, denied that the lower house could meet in secrecy, ordered the Assembly to conduct no business beyond

[45] *Minutes of Council*, I, 178-184; *Votes Assembly*, I, 73-77. Markham's description of the General Assembly is in his letter to Penn of Aug. 22, 1686, *PMHB*, 90 (1966), 319-321.

[46] Markham to Penn, Aug. 22, 1686, *PMHB*, 90 (1966), 321.

the consideration of bills proposed by the Council, and threatened to dissolve the Assembly if it did not hew to these demands. The Council, in effect, was asking an increasingly restless Assembly not only to curb its instincts for further power but to give up privileges earned piecemeal since 1683. This forceful mood reflected not only the growing solidification of the province's leading figures, but the opportune support of Penn, who viewed the advancing designs of the Assembly as a perversion of the Frame of Government and had recently ordered his Commissioners of State to prevent further encroachments upon the powers of the Governor and Council.[47] The Assembly, he later wrote, had no right to prepare, amend, or even debate laws proposed by the Council, but "only the power of I or no, yea or nay." To claim more or do more was to "overthrow the Charter quite in the very root of the Constitution of it."[48]

Penn's broad attack on the continuous efforts of the Assembly to establish a separate identity and a larger scope of power for itself augmented the strength of the Council, dominated now by his most outspoken critics. Armed with the proprietor's injunctions, the councilors moved to repulse the Assembly in its new demands and to narrow the privileges of its competitor. No joint sessions were permitted at the General Assembly of 1688 and the lower house had to content itself with presenting a bill of grievances, which the Council, with the victory in hand, gladly promised to consider.[49] The triumph of the dominant faction, led by Thomas Lloyd, seemed complete. While brushing aside

[47] *Votes of Assembly*, I, 83-86; *Minutes of Council*, I, 223-226; Penn to the Commissioners of State, Feb. 1, 1686/87, Proud, *History of Pennsylvania*, I, 305-307.

[48] Penn to the Commissioners of State, Sept. 18, 1688, in Hazard, ed., *Register*, 4 (1829), 105.

[49] *Votes of Assembly*, I, 86-93; *Minutes of Council*, I, 225-226.

most of the proprietary reform program promulgated from above, the Lloydians had seized on Penn's complaints about the Assembly to quash the challenge from below.

A Puritan in Pennsylvania

By the spring of 1688 Penn was compelled to admit that his new forceful policies had failed to cure the colony of its twin diseases—opposition to proprietary policies and internal faction. In a last attempt to enlist the support of the provincial leaders and to mend the rifts between them, Penn offered Thomas Lloyd the position of Deputy Governor. He would be aided by two assistants, Penn wrote, and with the support of either could "do all as fully as I myself can do." When Lloyd refused the office, apparently because he was unwilling to accept responsibility for executing the proprietor's long-distasteful policies, Penn gave up his hopes that the Quakers could reform themselves internally and appointed a transplanted Massachusetts Puritan, Captain John Blackwell, as Deputy Governor.[50] It was a radical step filled with risks, for Puritans were cordially hated in Quaker communities, especially in the New World where Friends had been beaten, mutilated and hanged by Puritan magistrates in Massachusetts only a few decades before. But Penn was impressed with Blackwell's record as a man of wide experience in matters of government, finance, and administration. He knew that the restless Puritan's career over the last quarter-century had carried him to far corners of the English empire—as Cromwell's Treasurer at War and Receiver

---

[50] Penn to Lloyd, March 28, 1688, Penn Papers, Domestic and Miscellaneous Letters, 89; Lloyd's refusal is revealed in Penn to [Hugh Roberts?], Dec. 6, 1689, Penn Letters and Ancient Documents, I, 62, American Philosophical Society.

General in Ireland in the 1650's, as one of the original proprietors of the Bahama Islands, and as an officer of government and land-bank promoter in Massachusetts.[51] Here was an individual, stern but devout, who might set affairs to rights in Pennsylvania.

There may have been more to the appointment of Blackwell than Penn intimated, although the proprietor was in obvious need of a deputy who could cure the chronic ills in Pennsylvania. By July 1688, when the commission to Blackwell was drawn, Penn was in a precarious position as a result of his well-known association with James II, whose pro-Catholic policies had already thrown England into advanced stages of revolutionary activity. The imprisonment of seven Anglican bishops on June 8 and the birth of a son to James two days later, auguring a Catholic succession, gave further impetus to the revolutionary movement, a fact of which Penn was well aware. Long suspected as a Jesuit, even by certain Quakers, Penn occupied a distinctly dangerous position. Not only would he be in great personal danger should James be deposed, but his colony too might be sacrificed to the vindictiveness of the impending Protestant government. It is likely that Penn saw the appointment of a Puritan deputy governor as a means of warding off the

---

[51] Blackwell's early career is sketched in John T. Hassan, "The Bahama Islands: Notes on an Early Attempt at Colonization," *Proceedings of the Massachusetts Historical Society*, 2nd Ser., 13 (1900), 20-27; and W.L.F. Nuttall, "Governor John Blackwell: His Life in England and Ireland," *PMHB*, 88 (1964), 121-141. Blackwell's commission, dated July 12, 1688, is noted in Blackwell to Thomas Lloyd, Nov. 11, 1688, *Pennsylvania Archives*, 1st Ser., I, 106-107; and transcribed in Penn Papers, Governor Blackwell's MSS. There is some reason to believe that Blackwell actively sought the governorship himself by sending his treatise on land banks to Penn in 1687. See Joseph Dorfman, "Captain John Blackwell: A Bibliographical Note," *PMHB*, 69 (1945), 233-237.

wrath of the King's successors, of proving that he was not "soft on" Catholicism. In September, with plans for the overthrow of James in full tide, Penn advised his Commissioners of State of Blackwell's appointment and urged them, meaningfully, to use his "not being a Friend to Friends Advantage."[52]

Penn's commission charged Blackwell with formidable tasks: suppress the "animosities" in Pennsylvania, "authoritatively" if no other method works; collect quitrents and other proprietary revenues without further delay; curtail the Assembly in its quest for larger powers and limit it to its single function of approving or disapproving legislation.[53] To the Commissioners of State, whom Blackwell would replace on arrival, Penn wrote to introduce the new deputy. Though not a Quaker, Blackwell was "a grave, sober, wise man," and had his orders to "bear down with a visible authority" on the factious colony. "Let him see what he can doe a while," advised Penn.[54] But at the same time Penn promised the Commissioners of State that if Blackwell did not please them, he would be "layd aside." This crippling proviso put the new Governor at the mercy of the very parties he was commissioned to discipline. Blackwell later observed that some in the Council had said from the beginning that his appointment was only probationary.[55]

[52] Braithwaite, *Second Period of Quakerism*, 143-150; Penn to Commissioners of State, Sept. 18, 1688, in Hazard, ed., *Register*, 4 (1829), 105.

[53] Blackwell to Penn, Jan. 13, 1689/90, Society Miscellaneous Collection; William Penn, "Instructions for Lieutenant Governor Blackwell, or whom else it may Concerne," Sept. 25, 1689, Penn Papers, Forbes Collection, I, 10.

[54] Penn, "Instructions for Lieutenant Governor Blackwell. . ."

[55] *Ibid.*; *Minutes of Council*, I, 312; for a careful account of Blackwell's tenure as governor see Nicholas B. Wainwright, "Governor John Blackwell," *PMHB*, 74 (1950), 457-472.

From the moment of his arrival, in mid-December 1688, it was evident to Blackwell that Thomas Lloyd stood behind a movement to subvert his governorship. The manner of his reception was in itself enough to make this consummately clear. Blackwell had written a flattering letter to Lloyd from Boston a month before his arrival, conveying his regards and asking that a guide meet him in New York to accompany him to Philadelphia. Lloyd ignored the letter, leaving Blackwell to cross the desolate Jerseys alone. Arriving at Pennsbury, the proprietor's estate on the Delaware River north of Philadelphia, Blackwell again sent word ahead announcing his intention to arrive in the city the following Monday to publish his commission and meet with the Council. On the appointed day Blackwell rode into a strangely deserted city. Neither the Secretary nor the President of Council was to be found nor anyone who could explain their whereabouts or the reason for their absence. With his horses and servants, the new Governor stood unattended in the street while a flock of boys gathered to laugh at the grandiose newcomer. When Markham appeared at last, he sheepishly confessed that Blackwell's letter from Pennsbury had arrived but that he was "a servant to many, and could act no otherwise than by their direction."[56]

In the months that followed Blackwell was to learn the ingenuity of the Quaker mind in obstructing unwanted authority. At first, Lloyd refused to recognize the validity of Blackwell's commission because it lacked the Great Seal of the colony of which he was sole custodian. When that failed to keep the Puritan Governor from assuming executive power from the Commissioners of State, a boycott of the

---

[56] Blackwell to Lloyd, Nov. 11, 1688, *Pennsylvania Archives*, 1st Ser., I, 106-107; Blackwell to Penn, Jan. 25, 1688/89, Society Miscellaneous Collection; Wainwright, "John Blackwell," *PMHB*, 74 (1950), 459-461.

Council was organized. The Governor's attempts to reassume the power of judicial appointment, which had been absorbed by the Council, and to enforce proprietary policy by appointing sheriffs and county courts sympathetic to his design were also resisted by Lloyd, who again refused to affix the Great Seal required on all commissions of office. Blackwell's appointees were installed nonetheless, for the Governor refused to have his power of appointment negated by Lloyd's obstructionism. Lloyd countered by encouraging the displaced officeholders to withhold the records and seals of their courts from Blackwell's appointees. Even open defiance was attempted when Samuel Richardson, a member of the Council and one of Lloyd's firm supporters, declared at a meeting of the Council that he did not regard Blackwell as governor nor did he believe that Penn had power to "make a Governor." Blackwell labeled this bald subversion and ordered Richardson to withdraw from the Council; but the Quaker merchant refused to quit his seat, avowing passionately that he "was sent by the people" and would leave only by their command.[57]

By March 1689, after three months of intricate jockeying for position, the wheels of government had all but stopped. Blackwell commanded a thin majority in the Council where he was backed by most of the councilors representing the Lower Counties, by Robert Turner and William Markham (faithful adherents of Penn), and by Griffith Jones, a Philadelphia merchant disenchanted with the dominant Quakers. But his obvious determination to put an end to the power of Lloyd and his Quaker supporters had invigorated the opposition and made any consensus in the Council clearly impossible. There were "two Governors and two

[57] *Ibid.*, 461-465; *Minutes of Council*, I, 230-256; Blackwell to Penn, Jan. 25, 1688/89, Society Miscellaneous Collection.

Councils: One within and another without," Turner charged, and added that Lloyd, through his obstructionism, was coldly denying Penn's authority. Another report reached Penn that the King's authority itself was being opposed and the Lloydians, from all appearances, were "raysing a force to Rebell."[58]

Blackwell's authoritarian conceptions of political control and his military manner only compounded his difficulties in dealing with his wily Quaker adversaries. In lengthy sessions he lectured the Council on the extensive powers to which Penn, as proprietor, and he, as his deputy, were entitled; on the illegal inroads which the Council had made on proprietary prerogatives; and on the multitude of "offences, Crimes, and misdemeanors" which Thomas Lloyd had committed "in the high usurpation of arbitrary and illegal powers." The condition of the body politic in Pennsylvania required radical surgery, Blackwell warned. Thomas Lloyd must be impeached and tried before a special court; the Council must give up its claims of autonomous power and return to the Frame of 1683 and Penn's charter as a basis of government; the proprietor's judicial prerogatives must be restored; and the colony must be cleansed of its factious and insubordinate tendencies.[59]

This catalogue of reforms to be carried out against the independent-minded Quaker merchants and landowners and

[58] *Minutes of Council*, I, 253-257.

[59] *Ibid.*, 268-269. Blackwell's most pungent speech to the Council in defense of Penn's prerogatives is preserved in his hand in Penn Papers, Gov. Blackwell's MSS. Also see his letter to Penn of April 9, 1689, Gratz Collection, Governors, Box 32. Anguished complaints of Blackwell's authoritarian approach to problems of government in Pennsylvania, from such Quaker leaders as Phineas Pemberton, Samuel Carpenter, Joseph Growdon, and John Simcock, can be found in Etting Collection, Pemberton Papers, I, 31-38, and Penn Papers, Official Correspondence, I, 11.

Blackwell's unrestrained indictment of Thomas Lloyd were ill-calculated to stabilize a deteriorating situation. He was asking the most influential men in the province to surrender almost all of the autonomous power wrung piecemeal from Penn over the last six years, to yield up their leader to impeachment proceedings in the hands of a court appointed by the proprietor's militant Puritan deputy, and to return to a state of strict subservience to an absentee landlord whose charter was in dire jeopardy, as was his very life. Although Blackwell was correct in almost every charge he made—the Lloydians had indeed tampered with the frame of government to Penn's disadvantage—his inflexible approach to the crisis only strengthened the determination of his opponents to bring this proud, unbending man to his knees before he eclipsed their power and destroyed them altogether.

The General Assembly of 1689 provided the setting for the final confrontation between Blackwell and the Quaker leaders. Like the Council, the Assembly was split between supporters and opponents of the Puritan governor. Most of the Quakers in the Assembly, who had contested the power of the Lloydian circle since 1683, readily buried old differences to join in the fight against Penn's detested Puritan deputy, for the threat which Blackwell posed far exceeded any that Lloyd had presented. Nonetheless, Blackwell could still count on the support of most of the representatives from the Lower Counties and a few other unflagging opponents of Lloyd, such as Joseph Fisher of Philadelphia and James Sandelands of Chester.[60]

Almost from the outset, it was clear that the General As-

[60] The alignment of Council and Assembly has been established from the votes taken in both houses and from a list of those who boycotted legislative sessions. *Minutes of Council*, I, 274-297; and *Votes of Assembly*, I, 106-108.

sembly of 1689 would be not so much the occasion for legislative business as an opportunity for the two embattled sides to test their mettle against each other. Already the Council sessions were reverberating with what the clerk could only describe in the minutes as "many Intemperate Speeches and passages . . . fitt to be had in oblivion."[61] Proceedings in the Assembly proved equally tempestuous: petitions flew back and forth; legislative boycotts were organized by both camps as angry crowds gathered outside the legislative chambers; and the two main protagonists, Lloyd and Blackwell, distributed to the population at large political broadsides, which vied for honors in abusiveness and in charges of betrayal of the people of the colony. When Blackwell sent the sheriff of Philadelphia County into the Assembly to arrest one of its most prominent members, John White, the last remnants of constituted authority nearly crumbled. Though White was arrested, he escaped later in the day, only to be taken again that night when Blackwell's men forced their way into the house of Benjamin Chambers where several of the Lloydian councilors were spending the night. Though White was dragged from the house, it was not without a struggle, and none of the participants involved could fail to see that Blackwell's hold on the reins of government was perilously insecure. Nothing but the last minute intervention of Lloyd, Penn learned, prevented the outbreak of "the same disorders and confusions our neighbours were in"—an ominous reference to the full-scale rebellions in progress in New York and Maryland.[62]

Such resorts to force, though they represented temporary victories for Blackwell, could not prevent Lloyd and his cir-

[61] *Minutes of Council*, I, 270-271.

[62] *Votes of Assembly*, I, 98-106; Arthur Cooke, Griffith Owen, John Bristow, et al. to Penn, April 11, 1691, Penn Papers, Autograph Petitions, 7.

cle from bringing about an impasse in government—the goal they sought. With legislative proceedings stalemated in the General Assembly, a majority in the Council agreed to continue all laws currently in force, even without the approval of the General Assembly, and to allow the courts appointed by Blackwell to function, even though Lloyd refused to legitimize them with the Great Seal.[63] But Blackwell harbored no illusions about his further usefulness to Penn among the Quakers. Nothing in a lifetime of military and political experience had prepared him for the task of governing the people of Penn's colony. So obstinate and factious were the Quakers and such were the concessions already made to the provincial leaders, he informed Penn, that he was powerless to reestablish proprietary prerogatives. The Quakers, he wrote in a letter of resignation, "have not the principles of government amongst them, nor will [they] be informed," and ended with the quip that the mosquitoes in Philadelphia were worse than armed men, though not nearly so nettlesome as the "men without Armes." To a friend he fumed that the wild animals that filled Penn's forests could govern better than the "witless zealots who make a monkey house of his Assembly." The Quakers were chronically contentious, he added, "each praying with his neighbour on First Days [Sundays], and then preying on him the other six."[64]

Though they had hamstrung Blackwell in his attempts to emasculate their autonomous power in Pennsylvania, the Lloydian faction paid a price for their victory. Because Blackwell maintained a narrow edge in the Council, partic-

[63] *Minutes of Council*, I, 290-297.

[64] Blackwell to Penn, June 24, 1689, Stauffer Collection, Governors of Pennsylvania, 20; Blackwell to Thomas Hartley, ca. August 1689, quoted in Augustus C. Buell, *William Penn* (New York, 1904), 225.

ularly after he had succeeded in ousting Lloyd and two of
his followers, Lloyd was forced to oppose the Puritan Governor through an assertion of the Assembly's rights. In
speeches before that body, in petitions to the Governor, and
in political broadsides the Lloydians invoked the power of
the freemen and the rights of the Assembly, maintaining
rights for the lower house, in their efforts to ineffectualize
Blackwell, that they had long opposed when the Council
had held the upper hand.[65] Included were the right of the
Assembly to sit on its own adjournment and its power to
establish courts of justice—privileges which even the ambitious Assembly had never claimed in the previous years.
Only a year earlier, armed with Penn's ringing protest at the
Assembly's illegal encroachment on the powers of the Governor and Council, Lloyd had led the assault on the privileges of the lower house—a counteroffensive that had
neutralized many of the gains made by the Assembly since
1683. But now, unable to control the Council, Lloyd had
turned to the Assembly as a vehicle of opposition. Cast in
his new role as tribune of the people, as crusader against
Blackwell's allegedly tyrannical designs, Lloyd was obliged
to invoke the very arguments employed against him earlier
by the ambitious Assembly.

Compelled as he was to mobilize public support against
Blackwell, Lloyd succeeded in radicalizing the very nature
of politics in Pennsylvania. Charges in the Assembly that
the "Rights, Freedoms and Liberties of every Freeman [are]
broken down, slighted and trodden under Foot" had an inflammatory effect; so did Lloyd's technique of raising mobs

[65] *Votes of Assembly*, I, 96-110; Thomas Lloyd, *A Seasonable Advertisement to the Freemen of this Province* . . . (Philadelphia, 1689).

to demonstrate in the street outside Council's chambers.[66] Lloyd's organization of the "Charter Club" to oppose Blackwell's defense of Penn's powers, and his use of political propaganda to "stir up the people into comotions," as Blackwell charged, were effective stratagems in the campaign to drive the Puritan Governor out of Pennsylvania.[67] But as the Lloydians later discovered, this stirring of the political consciousness among previously quiescent elements of the population, this mobilizing of public opinion, introduced a style of politics in Pennsylvania that vastly complicated the problem of political control by an upper-stratum alliance of Quaker merchants and large landowners.

Penn needed nothing more than the overwrought letters he received in the summer of 1689 from leaders on both sides of the struggle to convince him that his plan for stabilizing affairs in Pennsylvania was a total failure. Again faced with chaos in his colony, he was forced to choose between the obviously unpopular Blackwell and some alternative plan of government. Compounding the difficulty of the decision was the perilous position in which Penn had been left by the overthrow of James II in December 1688. As an intimate associate of the deposed monarch, Penn found himself under a cloud of suspicion. Many openly accused him of secret ties with the Jesuits and gave currency to rumors that he had taken orders at Rome and said mass at Whitehall. Twice in 1689 Penn was arrested on suspicion of high treason. Although cleared of the charges, he was a marked man, victimized by the anti-Catholic hysteria sweeping the

[66] *Votes of Assembly*, I, 108; Blackwell to Penn, May 1, 1689, Provincial Papers, 1664-1712, Department of Public Records, Harrisburg, Pa.

[67] *Ibid.*; Blackwell's reply to *A Seasonable Advertisement to the Freemen of this Province*, Penn Papers, Forbes Collection, I, 46.

country.[68] Under the circumstances return to Pennsylvania was impossible; the future held only the gravest uncertainties.

Confronted with the possibility of losing Pennsylvania and in great personal danger, Penn answered the crisis on the Delaware by temporizing. He was deeply disillusioned with the conduct of Lloyd and his party, he confided to a friend in England, but at the same time would not have the Quakers "trod under" by Blackwell. As a stop-gap measure Penn asked the Council either to act itself as the executive arm of government or to nominate a slate of candidates from which he could choose a deputy governor. Blackwell was granted his release as requested, but was offered the post of Receiver General, endowed with full power to collect quitrents and manage proprietary revenues.[69]

Penn, in effect, returned power to the very alliance of merchants and landowners which had fought with such determination against his deputies and his interest. Blackwell recognized Penn's decision as tantamount to a vindication of Thomas Lloyd and reacted angrily when Penn chastised him for "unChristian" behavior toward the Quakers, suggesting that "an Evangelicall way of Ruling" might have accomplished more. His orders were to "rule the meek meekly, and those that will not so be ruled, rule with authority," Blackwell reminded the proprietor. Given these instructions, Penn's latest exhortations to govern the Quakers not by command but by love and persuasion seemed

[68] Braithwaite, *Second Period of Quakerism*, 151, 161-162; William Popple to Penn, Oct. 20, 1688, in Janney, *William Penn*, 337-341.

[69] Edward Blackfan to Phineas Pemberton, Sept. 6, 1689, Parrish Collection, Proud Papers, II, 40; Penn to Blackwell, Sept. 25, 1689, Dreer Collection, Penn Letters, 29.

ludicrously inappropriate, especially since the colony was in an advanced stage of insubordination. "When a fire is kindled in a city," Blackwell warned, "we do not say, coldly, Yonder is a great fire: Pray God it do us no harm. And in times of publique defection, we are not to read tame lectures of contemplative divinity, but to oppose growing evills with all earnestnesst."[70]

Penn's gamble with Blackwell had boomeranged. In attempting to stifle antiproprietary passions and to discipline an increasingly autonomous-minded Quaker elite, he had succeeded only in giving the colonists new cause to resist what they now concluded was an unsympathetic and estranged proprietor. Far from composing provincial affairs, the appointment of Blackwell had increased the militancy of the antiproprietary Quakers in the legislature and given new cohesion to the circle of merchants and landowners who followed Thomas Lloyd. Penn had gone halfway toward reasserting authority in Pennsylvania and then turned back. When crisis came, he failed to support Blackwell, most likely because, as his retiring Governor suggested, he "chiefly aymed at their contentment who are of your society." Blackwell warned that this was a fundamental error, for the Quakers were ready to "blaspheme" Penn.[71] Precariously situated in England, unable to believe that his "holy experiment" was foundering on the rocks, Penn was forced to return power to those who had done so much to diminish his privileges and authority.

[70] Blackwell to Penn, Jan. 13, 1689/90, Society Miscellaneous Collection; Penn to Blackwell, Sept. 25, 1689, Penn Papers, Forbes Collection, I, 10.

[71] Blackwell to Penn, Jan. 13, 1689/90, Society Miscellaneous Collection.

CHAPTER 4

Crisis on the Delaware

BY THE SPRING of 1689, colonists in Pennsylvania who looked only on the surface of events might have predicted the end of years of factional disputes and the dawn of a new era of unity and stability. Blackwell, outmaneuvered by Lloyd and his followers, had returned to Boston. Penn, in hiding, was able to exert scant influence over his colony. The Quaker elite, firmly grasping the reins of government, seemed at last ready to govern the colony free of external influence. But outward appearances were deceiving, for the Quaker magistracy, far from restoring Pennsylvania to the original purposes of its founder, was poised on the brink of a controversy so intense, so all-encompassing, so disruptive of the social fabric, that colonial society for two decades would reflect the animosities which it unloosed.

The Quakers Return to Power

Blackwell's resignation, after thirteen months of relentless pressure by the Philadelphia Quaker merchants and their allies in the country, made it transparently clear that the proprietary will, pronounced from afar, could not be forced upon the upper layers of provincial society. In January 1690, when the Council voted to assume the authority of the departing deputy governor and chose Thomas Lloyd as its president, the return of political power to its former location was all but complete. Lloyd quickly consummated the change. John Eckley and Samuel Richardson, whom Blackwell had excluded from the Council, resumed their seats;

127

all charges against Lloyd lapsed without further mention; and the new president, by virtue of his position as Keeper of the Seal, received the Council's approval to sit "ex officio" as a member of any county court. When county courts were reappointed, Blackwell's supporters learned the price which they now had to pay for their allegiance to Penn's deputy. Griffith Jones was excluded from the newly constituted courts in Philadelphia and Sussex counties where he had sat under Blackwell; William Markham was stripped of his office as Clerk of the Philadelphia County Court; John Claypoole, who had carried out arrests of prominent Quakers at Blackwell's command, was ousted as Sheriff of Philadelphia County. To the reconstituted Provincial Court went three other Lloydians from the upper counties—Arthur Cooke, John Simcock, and Joseph Growdon—and two neutral representatives of the Territories, Peter Alricks and Quaker Thomas Wynne. Those who had endorsed Blackwell could only bitterly decry the Lloydians' "lofty" and "revengeful" policy.[1]

The power of the antiproprietary faction had never seemed so encompassing. The Council acted in both executive and legislative capacities and controlled the courts as well. Thomas Lloyd exercised far-reaching powers in every sphere of government. Penn himself was hopelessly trapped in England and lacked means to enforce either his land or revenue policy. Even a majority of the lower house fell into line behind the dominant Quaker party, demonstrating none of the aggressive pursuit of privileges that had been

[1] *Minutes of Council*, I, 321, 329, 343-344. Members of the new county and provincial courts are listed in *ibid.*, 320-321 and 343. For complaints to Penn see Robert Turner's letters to Penn of May 3, 1690 and May 23, 1691, David M. Stauffer, ed., *Westcott's History of Philadelphia, 1609-1829* (32 vols., [scrapbooks], Philadelphia, 1913), II, 179, and Dreer Collection, Penn Letters, 68.

characteristic of the years before Blackwell's arrival. Representatives of the upper counties and the few Quaker delegates from the Territories apparently agreed that the preservation of political autonomy outweighed any internecine rivalries. As if to symbolize the new unity, Joseph Growdon, a central figure in the Lloydian alliance and a former fixture in the Council, was chosen Speaker of the Assembly, while David Lloyd, equally warm in his antiproprietary sentiments, was installed as Clerk.[2]

In May 1691, Penn further reinforced the power of the ruling circle by incorporating the town of Philadelphia, an act long requested by the merchant leaders. Municipal affairs were entrusted thereafter to a closed, self-perpetuating body, patterned after contemporary municipal corporations in England. With the exception of the mayor, who was elected annually by the aldermen and councilmen, Penn made the initial appointments, which carried lifetime tenure. The powers of the new city government were extensive, including almost exclusive jurisdiction in civil and criminal courts and the right to pass municipal laws, erect public buildings, and appoint municipal officers.[3]

Penn's initial appointments placed the reins of power in Philadelphia squarely in the hands of Thomas Lloyd and his partisans. Humphrey Morrey, formerly a Quaker merchant in New York and one of Lloyd's close associates, sat as Mayor. Quaker John Delavall, another merchant and Lloyd's son-in-law, functioned as Recorder. David Lloyd, by now a trusted lieutenant of his kinsman, Thomas Lloyd, was Clerk of the Board of Aldermen and Clerk of the City

[2] *Votes of Assembly*, I, 111.

[3] The incorporation of Philadelphia had been suggested by the city's merchants as early as 1684. *Minutes of Council*, I, 64. The charter is printed in *PMHB*, 18 (1894) , 504-509.

Courts. On the aldermanic board sat four merchants, a physician, and a large landowner—all Quakers but the last. The Common Council was similar in complexion, composed entirely of Quaker merchants and shopkeepers in the town.[4] Conspicuously absent were the recent supporters of Governor Blackwell—Griffith Jones, William Markham, Robert Turner, Patrick Robinson, and Thomas Holme.

In spite of appearances, the consolidation of political power by the Quaker leaders clustered around Thomas Lloyd was not a prelude to a period of political and social calm; in fact, precisely the reverse was true. This could be seen only imperfectly when the Lower Counties, only weeks after John Blackwell left for Boston, rose in resentment against the Quaker leaders to the north. In part, their opposition mirrored old apprehensions concerning the concentration of political power in the hands of prominent Quakers and the economic domination of thriving Philadelphia over its downriver satellites. But the advent of war between France and England in 1689—King William's War in the North American colonies—brought fresh cause for complaint. The long and undefended coastline of the Lower Counties was an open invitation to French privateers who cruised the western Atlantic to prey on merchant shipping and unprotected coastal towns. Merchants and tobacco planters in the Territories, conscious that the war might spread to their very doorsteps, called for river fortifications and a militia as early as April 1689. The Quakers, opposed to military measures out of religious scruples, tended to ignore the situation, seeing no danger "but from the Bears and wolves," as a member of the Council remarked. A year later, non-Quakers throughout the colony petitioned for defensive preparations. At first the Quakers agreed not to

4 The initial appointments were included in the charter itself. *Ibid.*

block such protective measures as the Lower Counties deemed necessary. But the Friends soon reversed themselves, rejecting the notion that danger was imminent and alleging that the Territories threatened the peace and prosperity of the province by "raising men and money and housing a Constant Millitia which in all Likelyhood, in Considering our principles and poverty, might have caused us to leave our half made plantations, our unfinished houses and return poor and with griefe to our Native Country."[5] Though the statement hardly described the generally healthy economic conditions in Pennsylvania, it reflected accurately the wide rift which the military issue was creating between the two geographical areas.

Confronted with a Quaker majority which would countenance no military preparations, the Lower Counties turned to open defiance. The time has come "for us to assert our Right before it be quite lost," read a broadside published by the leading figures of New Castle County in February 1690. The next step was taken in November when the councilors from the Lower Counties, assembling separately, declared themselves the independent government for the Territories. Acting swiftly, they commissioned a Provincial Court for the Lower Counties and resolved that all their county officers should be appointed without interference from Philadelphia.[6]

Thomas Lloyd did what he could to smother this insub-

[5] *Minutes of Council*, I, 302, 306-311, 332, 334; Address to William Penn, May 18, 1691, Penn Papers, Autograph Petitions, 11. The address was signed by councilors Cooke, Simcock, Growdon, Owen, Delavall, Duckett, Bristow, Jenkins, and by 17 Quaker members of the lower house. See also, Robert L. D. Davidson, *War Comes to Quaker Pennsylvania, 1682-1756* (New York, 1957), Chap. 1.

[6] Advertisement of Councilmen and Justices of the Peace of New Castle County, Etting Collection, Provincial Council Papers; *Minutes of Council*, I, 344-345.

ordination, declaring all actions of the separate council illegal and attacking its "clandestine meetings."[7] But words accomplished little. In March 1691, the Lower Counties councilors again resolved to act independently of the Quaker government at Philadelphia. Strengthening their determination was the arrival of word from Penn that the Council was to choose between three forms of deputy governorship: the Council could itself function as the deputy governor, it could accept a commission of five leading figures chosen by Penn from all factions in the colony, or its members could nominate three men from whom Penn would select a governor. When Lloyd swung the majority of Council behind the proposal for a single deputy governor and himself received its endorsement as governor *pro tem*, the dissident members from the Lower Counties, mindful that such a plan meant a further augmentation of Lloyd's already broad powers, promptly seceded.[8]

The earnestness of the secessionists was evident when they continued to meet independently and appointed officers in the Lower Counties.[9] As powerless to coerce as Blackwell had been, the ruling Quakers took what comfort they could in loudly denouncing their opponents to Penn and accusing the leaders of the Lower Counties of loose morals and sedi-

[7] Declaration of the President and Council, April 11, 1690, in Proud, *History of Pennsylvania*, I, 352-354.

[8] Penn to Council, Nov. 11-17, 1690, Society Miscellaneous Collection, MSS Minutes of Council, March 30-31, 1691, Penn Papers, Assembly and Provincial Council. The declaration of secession and a long letter to Penn expressing the grievances of the Lower Counties, both dated April 6, 1691, are in Penn Papers, Three Lower Counties, 65.

[9] MSS Minutes of Council for the Three Lower Counties, April 4, 6, 7, 9, 1691, Penn Papers, Three Lower Counties, 65. The county appointments are given in Sussex County Court Record, 1689-99, Delaware Archives, Dover, Del.

tious spirits.[10] But it was clear that short of force the dis-affected Lower Counties could no longer be kept under Quaker management. Penn himself recognized the futility of the situation and appointed William Markham deputy governor of the Lower Counties in 1691. Acting with their councilors, Markham was granted the same powers of appointment as Thomas Lloyd exercised to the north, including the power to appoint a Provincial Court.[11]

While the Quaker leaders were concerned about insubordination in the Lower Counties which they were powerless to suppress, far greater challenges to their hold on economic and political affairs were developing. Across the Atlantic the English throne was occupied by a man far less sympathetic to the Society of Friends than his predecessor and one whose accession had marked the onset of a war which promised to reach all the way to Pennsylvania. Should the province become a theater of operations—there were many who viewed this as a certainty—the embarrassment, if not the collapse, of Quaker government could be predicted. Even worse, Penn, who had so effectively shielded Pennsylvania during James's reign, no longer exercised the slightest influence at Whitehall and was, in fact, in virtual seclusion. None could say whether his charter would survive the pressure to reorganize the colonies for administrative and defensive purposes. Penn himself seemed a strangely distant figure now, absent for seven years and unknown to many of the newer merchants and landowners in the colony. His return was problematical at best and in addition the at-

[10] Arthur Cooke, Griffith Owen, et al. to Penn, April 11, 1691, Penn Papers, Autograph Petitions, 7; Council and Assembly to Penn, May 18, 1691, *ibid.*, 11; Joseph Growdon to Penn, April 28, 1691, Myers Collection, CXLVIII; folder 23, CCHS.

[11] Proud, *History of Pennsylvania*, I, 357.

titude that the interests of Penn and the colonists were antithetical spread steadily—not a new view but one which now gained wider acceptance. Quakers in the General Assembly of 1691 complained that Penn's denial of the Assembly's right to elect a speaker or clerk and his exercise of proprietary powers encroached upon the rights of freeborn Englishmen—rights which were not canceled by crossing the water. "Certainly," they complained, "the King our Soveraigne Intends not that a subject shall Exercise Greater power over his people in a forraign plantation than he doth himself at home in parliaments."[12] Many whose voices were weighty, Penn heard, claimed that anyone employed in the proprietor's behalf was incapable of representing the public interest. No doubt such men "would if they durst or could, say, Away with the Governor too," he lamented.[13]

There were other reasons for concern. To the south, beyond the recalcitrant Lower Counties, Lionel Copley, royal governor of Maryland, sent emissaries to Pennsylvania "to privately feel the pulses of the inhabitants," and penned damning reports to the Lords of Trade, which recommended royal government as the only antidote to the disorder and lack of defensive preparations in Pennsylvania. From New York came insistent calls for aid in preparing common defenses against the French and Indians.[14] Even to the east, in traditionally Quaker West New Jersey, affairs gave Penn-

12 Address of Council and Assembly to Penn, May 18, 1691, Penn Papers, Autograph Petitions, 11. That Lloyd and his adherents in the Council should employ such arguments was a measure of their change in attitude toward the Assembly. Just three years before Lloyd had eagerly seized upon Penn's attack on the Assembly to quash the ambitions of that body.

13 Penn to Council, Nov. 17, 1690, Society Miscellaneous Collection.

14 Lionel Copley to Earl of Nottingham, 1692, William H. Browne et al., eds., *The Archives of Maryland* (70 vols., Baltimore, 1883—), VIII, 358; *Minutes of Council*, I, 332, 334-335.

sylvanians pause. Since 1687, when the right of government had passed from Edward Byllynge to the Anglican Daniel Coxe, Quaker ascendancy in the colony had been slipping. In 1688, West Jersey had become a part of the Dominion of New England. Worse still, when Coxe recovered the government in 1689, he chose as his governor the Burlington merchant, John Tatham. Hardly a man in West Jersey was more distasteful to the Lloydian leaders. A former Papist who had left England under duress in 1684, Tatham had been involved since his arrival on the Delaware in a rancorous land dispute with the Quaker Joseph Growdon. An outsider, he was cordially disliked by the whole Quaker mercantile circle.[15]

Although Tatham probably never took office, his appointment was a prelude to the further erosion of Quaker influence in West Jersey. In 1692 Coxe sold his interest in the colony to the West Jersey Society, a joint-stock company of English merchants and gentlemen, predominantly Anglican and primarily interested in exploiting the economic possibilities of the Delaware region. The members included Sir Thomas Lane, President of the company and shortly to become Lord Mayor of London; Edward Richier, London merchant and brother of the Governor of Bermuda; Edmund Harrison, Director of the New East India Company, Governor of the Greenland Company, and member of the Levant Company; Sir John Moore, another merchant prince, and earlier Lord Mayor of London; and a battery of other mercantile luminaries. Under the Society's direction all appointive offices—governor, deputy governor, chief agent, surveyor general, and factor-general—went to Anglicans, many of them already residents of the province and

[15] Pomfret, *West Jersey*, 158-163; Henry H. Bisbee, "John Tatham, Alias Gray," *PMHB*, 83 (1959), 256, 260.

the leaders of a growing anti-Quaker faction. An Anglican minister was set to work as a kind of missionary among the Quakers. Shipbuilding, whaling, and a host of other economic activities figured in the Society's plans for the development of West Jersey—schemes which could not help but arouse apprehension among the economic leaders of Pennsylvania.[16]

The Anglican penetration of the Delaware Valley came at a particularly unfortunate time, for it coincided with the economic dislocation which accompanied King William's War. At first the imperial struggle between England and France seemed to offer favorable prospects. When hostilities began in May 1689, Philadelphia was riding the crest of a decade of rapid growth. By one estimate the city could count nearly a thousand houses and the colony a population of 12,000.[17] Pennsylvania's agricultural surpluses now reached markets extending from New England to the southern colonies and throughout the West Indies. Even the recent rebellions in the neighboring colonies of New York and Maryland, side effects of the English Revolution of 1688, had benefited Pennsylvania, for they had induced many to migrate to the Quaker colony.[18]

[16] Pomfret, *West Jersey*, 170-176, 189; original members of the West Jersey Society and appointed officers are listed in John R. Stevenson, "The Great New Jersey Trust, 1691 to 1909," *Proceedings of the New Jersey Historical Society*, 3rd Ser., 6 (1909-10), 130-131. Brief accounts of the Society in the 1690's are in William T. McClure, Jr., "The West Jersey Society, 1692-1736," *ibid.*, 74 (1956), 1-20; and Joseph Payne, *History of the West Jersey Society* (London, 1895).

[17] William Penn, *Some Proposals for a Second Settlement of the Province of Pennsylvania* (London, 1690). Penn may have been lavish in his estimates for promotional purposes. See Greene and Harrington, *American Population*, 114.

[18] For the drain which Pennsylvania was exerting on Maryland and New York, both in terms of trade and population, see Alexander

Even the onset of war caused the merchants no undue concern, for it seemed to offer unique opportunities. The unexpected success of France in disrupting England's trans-Atlantic trade—even control of the English Channel was in question—threatened disaster to the southern colonies, where the tobacco exports to England formed the backbone of trade.[19] But in the middle colonies many expected trade advantages. If English shipments to the West Indies were cut off, the highly profitable provisioning trade would fall into the laps of the mainland colonies, especially those like Pennsylvania, which produced grain and foodstuffs. Penn, quick to note this possibility, wrote the colony in 1689 that the losses inflicted by French privateers had trebled the price of exports from England. It was with great difficulty that a ship cleared English waters, he advised, which "must needs enhance the vallue of all sorts of provisions in the Islands; so that our calamitys here are your market and gain."[20]

It was an illusory advantage; for the French privateers, as the colonists soon learned, were as effective in interrupting trade on the Spanish Main and off the coast of North America as they were in the eastern Atlantic. By September

---

Beardsley to John Tyzack, ca. 1690, *PMHB*, 4 (1880), 196; Governor and Council of New York to the King, Aug. 6, 1691, *N.Y. Colonial Documents*, III, 798-799; Council of New York to William Blathwayt, May 30, 1692, *ibid.*, III, 837; Benjamin Fletcher to the Lords of Trade, Oct. 9, 1693, *ibid.*, IV, 55; Francis Nicholson to the Duke of Shrewsbury, June 14, 1695, *Calendar of State Papers, Colonial Series, 1693-96*, #1897 (cited hereafter as *CSP*); Testimony of Reverend John Miller before the Board of Trade, Sept. 4, 1696, *N.Y. Colonial Documents*, IV, 183.

[19] Ralph Davis, *The Rise of the English Shipping Industry in the Seventeenth and Eighteenth Centuries* (London, 1962), 24-25.

[20] Penn to Robert Turner, Oct. 4, 1689, in Hazard, ed., *Register*, 4 (1829), 135.

CRISIS ON THE DELAWARE

1689, when 80 English merchantmen were reported lost in European waters, 62 vessels had fallen to the French in the American and Caribbean theaters. French marauders hovered off colonial ports, waiting for shipping to emerge.[21] Governor Kendall of Barbados wrote frantically to the Lords of Trade in August 1690 that unless provisions got through the French gauntlet from either "Old or New England," the slaves and poorer whites would starve.[22] Trans-Atlantic trade routes may even have been more secure than West Indian ones after 1689, for the English government instituted effective convoy protection for the former, but never extended this shield to trade between the mainland colonies and the West Indies. In 1692 Penn lamented the decay of Pennsylvania's trade; by 1694 land prices were falling precipitously in Philadelphia.[23] In the last few years of the war, when the French privateering efforts were contained, both Pennsylvania and New York reaped handsome profits from their favored position in the West Indian trade. But until about 1695 the Pennsylvania merchants profited little from the war.[24]

[21] Edward Blackfan to Phineas Pemberton, Sept. 6, 1689, *PMHB*, 40 (1916), 503-504; "Account of Ships Taken Lately by French Privateers," in *CSP 1689-92*, #467; —— to Thomas Brinley, July 7, 1690, *ibid.*, #994.

[22] Governor James Kendall to Lords of Trade, Aug. 22, 1690, *ibid.*, #1034.

[23] Arthur P. Middleton, *Tobacco Coast; A Maritime History of Chesapeake Bay in the Colonial Era* (Newport News, Va., 1954), 301; Penn to Capt. Benjamin Fletcher, Dec. 5, 1692, *CSP 1689-92*, #2667. The economic recession in 1694 is described in *Penn-Logan Correspondence*, II, 157.

[24] For the later benefits of the war see Robert Quary to the Board of Trade, Sept. 22, 1697, *CSP 1696-97*, #1338; Commissioners of Customs to the Lords of the Treasury, Nov. 17, 1698, *Calendar of Treasury Papers, 1697-1701/2* (London, 1871), 244; James Logan to Penn, Aug. 22, 1705, *Penn-Logan Correspondence*, II, 53; and Report of the

Already apprehensive at the wartime stagnation of trade
and the inroads threatened by the West Jersey Society,
Pennsylvania merchants could look to a third unsettling
development by 1693. In London, a group of wealthy merchants laid plans for a New Pennsylvania Company, a joint-
stock venture designed to exploit the growing demand in
Pennsylvania for English goods and to tap the resources of
the colony. Included were some of London's most prosperous merchants: Walter Benthall, a shipper to Barbados and
investor in East Jersey lands; Benjamin Braine, active in the
Chesapeake and Baltic trade; Thomas Byfield, a merchant
prince with a finger in the trade of the East and West Indies, the Carolinas, New York, Pennsylvania, and the Baltic;
William Withers, future alderman of London; and Daniel
Quare, noted clockmaker and mercantile investor of London. In all, 79 men invested in the company, most of them
merchants and tradesmen, perhaps half of them Quakers.
Six were proprietors of East New Jersey; seven had earlier
invested in the now virtually defunct Free Society of Traders. The men who provided the impetus for the company
—Thomas Byfield, Benjamin and James Braine, Richard
Haynes and John Lamb—had all been trading with Pennsylvania since about 1690.[25]

The plans blueprinted by the New Pennsylvania Company were reminiscent of those outlined by the Free Society
of Traders eleven years before. Sixty thousand acres of land
were to be purchased from Penn and £18,000 to £20,000

House of Lords, Jan. 31, 1698/99, Leo F. Stock, ed., *Proceedings and
Debates of the British Parliaments respecting North America* (5 vols.,
Washington, D.C., 1924-41), II, 170-171.

[25] A draft charter of the company with a list of original subscribers
is in CO 5/1233, Public Record Office, London. I have consulted photo-
graphic transcripts in the Library of Congress.

of English commodities shipped on consignment to the province in the first year. A whale fishery and a shipyard would be established, plank exported, and naval stores—pitch, tar, resin, hemp, and flax—produced for the English navy.[26] When the company received provisional approval for its charter from the Privy Council late in 1693, two ships "laden with goods and merchandise of the growth, product, and manufacture of this kingdome" immediately embarked for Philadelphia.[27]

Although the evidence of attitudes in the colony toward the new joint-stock company is meager, it is possible to infer something of merchant reaction. The New Pennsylvania Company was closely patterned in its objectives upon the old Free Society of Traders. Like its predecessor, it sought to control the English export trade to Pennsylvania and to harvest profits from speculation in land. But unlike the Free Society, its stock belonged entirely to English investors; none was offered to settlers in Pennsylvania. Consequently, all profits flowed back to England, a situation which the Free Society had been created to prevent. The New Pennsylvania Company, in short, demonstrated an unpleasant fact of economic life in the province: provincial merchants lacked sufficient capital to control the trans-Atlantic trade and must be content to act as middlemen, merchandising commodities shipped to them on consignment from England.

Although economic subordination to English merchants was probably recognized as an inevitable disadvantage of economic immaturity, the grandiose plans of the New Pennsylvania Company seemed to rankle colonial merchants.

[26] "Proposals of New Pennsylvania Company to Lords of Trade, May 30, 1693," CO 388/343-344, Public Record Office, London.

[27] The progress of the company's charter can be followed in CO 5/1233, Library of Congress transcripts; and CO 388/336-365, Public Record Office, London.

The factors, or commission agents, of the company, Charles Saunders and Joseph Pidgeon, were unpopular among the colonial merchants around Lloyd, just as other Philadelphia merchants who represented English exporters had been since 1688.[28] It is no coincidence that all of the principal Philadelphia factors involved in English trade—Patrick Robinson, Charles Saunders, Joseph Pidgeon, Andrew Robeson, and John Duplovneys—were political opponents of the ruling group and none of them were Quakers except Duplovneys.[29]

By the early 1690's, the dominant Quakers of Pennsylvania, though they had regained the reins of political power, seemed beset by a sense of impending crisis. Pennsylvania had been founded as a Quaker preserve, a corner of the earth where Friends might pursue their millennium unhindered. The first decade had brought unceasing turmoil, capped by the imposition of a rigid and detested Puritan governor on the colony by a distant proprietor who seemed insensitive to the problems and interests of his colonists. Finally quit of Blackwell and returned to power, the Quaker elite found itself challenged anew, this time by a bewildering variety of forces which appeared beyond its ability to control. The Lower Counties had renounced

[28] Articles of Agreement between Charles Saunders and the New Pennsylvania Company, Dec. 21, 1693, Society Miscellaneous Collection. Saunders was to receive the conventional 5 percent commission for his services as factor.

[29] The trade between England and Pennsylvania and the factors involved can be reconstructed in outline form from the various letters of attorney and contractual agreements preserved in the deed books of the period. For the factors noted above see Philadelphia Deed Book C2-3/119-121; Deed Book E2-5/13-20, 140-142, 167-170, 233-234, 287; Exemplification Book 8/24, 42-43. See also the Minutes of the Board of Property, *Pennsylvania Archives*, 2nd Ser., XIX, 114-115, 177-178.

Quaker authority—and gained Penn's endorsement of their actions; a sympathetic monarch had lost his throne and the Quakers, thereby, their influence in English government; Louis XIV's pursuit of glory and the intricacies of European diplomacy had cast England into a global war which made it appear that the Quakers must sacrifice either their principles or their government; West Jersey smoldered under the growing Anglican influence; war disrupted trade; and wealthy men in London launched ambitious programs to exploit the Delaware Valley and channel all profits eastward. Few of these disturbing developments could be combatted, as could an unpopular governor in Philadelphia, for they were essentially external rather than internal attacks on the economic and political power of the ruling Quakers.

Encircled by hostile and unreachable forces, the Quaker magnates responded by working to build impregnable defenses against internal and external threats. Every officeholder who supported Penn's interests was stripped of office, even though the proprietor, after Blackwell's removal, had specifically ordered that all officials be retained. William Markham, Robert Turner, and Francis Rawle were the most important of those who lost important administrative positions in what Turner reported to Penn as an alarming monopolization of power by men who "oppose any power to thyself, concluding [that] while the government [is] in themselves the power [is] gon from thee."[30] Lloyd's extensive power and his zealousness in removing his opponents, Turner charged, caused the entire body of officeholders to array themselves against Penn, for they stood in "awe and

[30] *Minutes of Council,* I, 342-344; Penn to Council, Nov. 11, 1690, Society Miscellaneous Collection, Penn Papers; Turner to Penn, May 23, 1691, Dreer Collection, Penn Letters, 68.

feare" of Lloyd and his subalterns "least they be turned out [*of office*]." Even David Lloyd, who Penn had sent to the colony as Attorney General to prosecute proprietary causes, was "turned as a nose of wax" and now pleaded against Penn in the courts. Judges and juries were so wholly suffused with antiproprietary sentiment that Penn's Receiver General was "affraid to venture a Cause of thine in courtt." The proprietor was much "trodden down" by those in power. Impervious to criticism, Lloyd obtained the election of John White to the Assembly in Philadelphia County and then appointed him county sheriff—an innovation in plural officeholding that the grateful White repaid by using the weight of his office to collect "voluntary" contributions for Lloyd, who had suffered mercantile losses. Many resented such devious means of subordinating the whole apparatus of government to Lloyd's will, Turner warned.[31]

Although the ruling Quakers successfully eliminated dissident elements from government, their garrison mentality had created ugly tensions in Pennsylvania by 1692. In the Lower Counties planters and merchants openly defied what they regarded as oppression by a narrow oligarchy. In the upper counties, non-Quakers, unseated officeholders, the remnant of the proprietor's friends, and elements of the lower and middle classes all rankled at the high-handedness of the dominant party of Quakers.

When Council proposed a general tax on real and personal property in 1692, it unwittingly provided the alienated groups with an issue through which they could express their common discontent. The tax was not prohibitive, only a

[31] Turner to Penn, May 23, 1691 and June 15, 1692, Dreer Collection, Penn Letters, 68-69.

penny in a pound, or less than half of one percent of assessed value; yet it was loudly protested. The source of the dissatisfaction was apparently not the tax itself but its intended use. While no commitments were mentioned in calling for the levy, a salary for Deputy Governor Thomas Lloyd, who was financially embarrassed at the time, was uppermost in the minds of its promoters. When the Assembly met, a petition bearing the names of 261 freemen of Philadelphia County was presented. The tax was not only needless, but, as the remonstrators stated enigmatically, threatened them with "Bondage and Slavery."[32] Prominent among the signators were Lloyd's merchant opponents Robert Turner, Griffith Jones, Joseph Fisher, Andrew Robeson, and Thomas Budd. The rest of the list virtually constituted a directory of the town's lesser merchants, shopkeepers, and master artisans. A large number of names representing the non-Quaker elements in the community—Anglicans, Germans, and Swedes—were also included. The petition accomplished its work and blocked passage of the bill in the lower house—a defeat which the Lloydian Council "highly resented," as it duly informed the Assembly.[33]

An Apostate in Philadelphia

So combustible was the atmosphere in Pennsylvania in 1692 that it took only the spark provided by a single Quaker metaphysician to spread the flames of civil controversy to the religious sphere. The conflagration that ensued, known as the Keithian schism, enveloped Quaker society for almost two years. Before the fires were extinguished, the Quaker community was deeply riven and the power of the Quaker

32 The petition is in *PMHB*, 38 (1914), 495-501.
33 *Votes of Assembly*, I, 126-127.

leaders who gathered around Thomas Lloyd had been shaken to its roots.

George Keith came to America in 1685 as Surveyor General of East New Jersey. He owed his appointment to the reputation he enjoyed among leaders of the Society of Friends in England as the most dynamic and learned of the Quaker itinerant preachers. Educated at Marischal College in Aberdeen, Scotland, Keith was deeply introspective and intellectual, a man for whom the raw wilderness of East Jersey provided few comforts. Those who had journeyed with him in the early days of Quaker proselytizing also knew him as a moody, brooding individual, given to temperamental fits and passionate outbursts. In Keith, the pendulum of human emotions swung in an arc so wide as to suggest an unstable, if not disturbed, personality.

In the New World, Keith was deeply apprehensive of the effects which the wilderness environment might have on the religious commitment of Quakers. By his reckoning, such untutored, ingenuous folk, cast into a disintegrative setting, needed an orderly set of tenets to guide them, some systemization of their primitive Quaker beliefs. But Keith was out of harmony with a majority of the Friends in calling for a more concrete expression of Quaker creed. Less educated, not given to philosophical inquiries, and little able to understand the need for doctrine, they hewed to the simpler and older faith in the sufficiency of the "inner light"—the ability of each Quaker to formulate his own beliefs, building upon spiritual resources within him. Nor could the average Quaker comprehend the doctrine which Keith was preaching of the "two Christs"—the divine, spiritual Christ who was the second part of the Trinity, and the bodily, human Christ who had inhabited the earth.[34]

[34] Ethyn Williams Kirby, *George Keith, 1638-1716* (New York, 1942),

In 1689 Keith accepted an appointment as tutor of the newly established Quaker school in Philadelphia. The following year, even more convinced by the tumultuous events of Blackwell's rule that Quakerism was failing in its new setting, Keith appeared before the Yearly Meeting of Friends—the gathering of all Quaker Monthly Meetings from West Jersey and Pennsylvania—to present a body of rules as a basis of church polity. Included were proposals for a confession of faith to be required of those seeking admission to the Society, for the election of elders and deacons within each meeting, and for the silencing of persons "raw and unseasoned" or unsure in their beliefs. In addition, Keith stressed the need to place more emphasis upon the Bible as a fountain of spiritual growth and less on hidden sources—"the light within" which Quakers taught was residual in every individual.

These were radical proposals. Quakers had always identified the strength of their movement with freedom from dogma and reliance on the individual's capacity to pursue his own salvation, guided by the in-dwelling light. Keith seemed intent on stripping the Quaker faith of one of its most salient characteristics.[35] Not a little shaken by Keith's

---

39-42, 47-53. I have followed Kirby's excellent account in detailing the unfolding of the Keithian controversy. Keith's position on "the two Christs" can be traced as far back as the 1670's when he accompanied Penn and other Quaker leaders on proselytizing trips through England, Scotland, and the Rhineland.

[35] *Ibid.*, 53-57. Keith later wrote that hundreds in Philadelphia agreed with him that there was "too-great laxness of Discipline amongst us, and . . . but little inspection into the good lives and Manners of them that profess Truth amongst us." *An Account of the Great Divisions* . . . (London, 1692). In attempting to formulate a Quaker creed, Keith was heartened by the work of the Newport, Rhode Island Meeting which in 1690 had promulgated a statement of beliefs known as the "Rhode Island Sheet." Kirby, *George Keith*, 56-57.

reforming zeal, the Yearly Meeting utterly rejected his articles as "downright Popery," a phrase heavy with inference in view of the contemporary fears in England of a "Catholic plot." Undismayed, Keith continued his crusade, introducing a year later new proposals for greater order and discipline and less spontaneity in Quaker meetings. Meanwhile, he continued his arguments about the "two Christs." Again he was rebuffed. By now Keith believed that the political unrest which Thomas Lloyd's policies had created within the Quaker community was further evidence of the centrifugal tendencies besetting the Society. What was needed was a definition of doctrine, a crystallization of the Quaker faith, a tightening of the structural relationships of the various meetings, and a greater emphasis on Christian fundamentals. Broadening his attack, Keith suggested that the Quakers' profession of nonresistance rendered them incapable of performing the duties of civil government.[36] This was a particularly discomfiting suggestion in view of the current pressure being exerted by the non-Quaker elements of the province for defensive preparations.

In September 1691, as the spirit of defection coursed through the Lower Counties and tensions in Philadelphia rose over Thomas Lloyd's aggressive pursuit of absolute political control, the Keithian controversy reached a turning point. William Stockdale, prominent in civil and religious affairs, brought a charge of heresy against Keith at the Yearly Meeting. It took nothing more than this to involve the entire Quaker community in controversy, for now it was necessary to determine who was orthodox and who was

[36] *Ibid.*, 56-61. The fullest attack on Quaker participation in government was published by Keith and his followers in 1693. See *A Testimony and Caution to such as do make a Profession of Truth . . . That They should not be concerned in Worldly Government . . .* (Philadelphia, 1693).

heretical. At first, this seemed a way of stopping the dispute before it got out of hand: with both sides claiming to speak the true essence of Quakerism, and each gathering supporters, either Keith or Stockdale must be charged as a deviant and disciplined by the Yearly Meeting. And there seemed little doubt that a condemnation of Keith could be obtained, for control of the Yearly Meeting was firmly in the hands of the orthodox Quakers, led by Thomas Lloyd and the foremost men of the colony.[37]

The Quaker establishment had not, however, calculated what it would do if Keith, after his condemnation as an apostate by the Yearly Meeting, refused to accept their judgment. Precisely this happened; officially charged with heresy, Keith resumed his attacks with redoubled zeal. Carefully, he enlisted the support of Philadelphia's only printer, Quaker William Bradford, and then began to feed the flames of controversy with a steady stream of vitriolic broadsides and pamphlets that elaborated his arguments and lavished abuse on his opponents. In print and from the pulpit Keith labeled the orthodox Quakers "fools, idiots, silly souls, hypocrites, hereticks, heathens, rotten ranters, Tyrants, Popes, Cardinals," and charged them with entertaining "more Doctrines of Devils and Damnable Heresies . . . than any Profession of the Protestants." Keith had not exhausted the vocabulary of abuse, however; his adversaries retaliated with epithets of "Brat of Babylon," "Pope Primate of Pennsylvania," "Father Confessor," "Lyar," "Devil," "Muggletonian," and others.[38] As charges and countercharges flowed, both in and out of meetings, order began to crumble. Meet-

---

[37] Kirby, *George Keith*, 62-70.

[38] *Ibid.*, 70-78; Keith, *An Account of the great Divisions Amongst the Quakers in Pensilvania* (London, 1692) , 6-8; Keith, *An Expostulation with Thomas Lloyd* . . . (Philadelphia, 1692) , 6-7.

inghouse doors were locked against opponents, tensions rose, and the calm dignity of Quaker worship gave way to verbal violence. By June 1692, the Secretary of the Philadelphia Monthly Meeting was obliged to record that devotions were impossible "by reason of a turbulent and unsubdued spirit, which has much disquieted us."[39]

To the already apprehensive Lloydian faction, Keith's incendiary behavior represented the most dangerous of a series of threats to its position. The Quaker magistracy was well aware that apart from what it regarded as his theological errors, Keith's radical stand threatened not only religious unity in Pennsylvania, but civil authority as well. Keith openly accused those who sought his condemnation in church affairs with equal oppressiveness in the civil realm. Thomas Lloyd and his henchmen, he asserted, exercised "usurped authority" over the people. Samuel Jennings, one of Lloyd's close associates, "hath already shown himself too high and imperious both in Friends Meetings and worldly courts."[40] Thomas Lloyd, Arthur Cooke, John Delavall, Samuel Jennings, John Simcock, Samuel Richardson, Anthony Morris, and others of the ruling clique denounced him as heretical, he charged, and then used their power as magistrates to impose their decree on monthly meetings throughout the province "when most of the Friends thereof are great strangers to the Matter in Controversy, not knowing which Party is in the Right." Keith continued: "where

[39] "Philadelphia Monthly Meeting Minutes," *Publications of the Genealogical Society of Pennsylvania*, 4 (1911), 158, as cited in Kirby, *George Keith*, 68-69. In 1692 Keith published nine vituperative pamphlets and broadsides indicting Thomas Lloyd and the orthodox Quakers.

[40] George Keith, *An Appeal from the Twenty Eight Judges . . .* (Philadelphia, 1692), 2; Keith, *The Plea of the Innocent against the False Judgment of the Guilty . . .* (Philadelphia, 1692), 13.

they think their . . . judgement will not readily be swallowed down, they Follow it from Meeting to Meeting, cloathed with their Magistratical Robes, and if any Friends Show their dislike there of having it imposed on them without their own consent, and consideration of the matter, presently threaten to bind them to the good behavior of the Peace, and call out for a Constable, thereby endeavoring to trample us down by their heightened Power and Authority."[41]

Keith did not mistake the determination of the ruling Quakers to suppress through civil action what they could not exorcise within the meeting. Resolved to quiet the inflammatory Scotsman, five adherents of Lloyd, all justices of the Philadelphia County Court, signed a warrant for the arrest of William Bradford and John McComb, printer and distributor of Keith's fiery tracts. Bradford, who supported Keith, had not hesitated to publish literature on both sides of the controversy. But he balked when Lloyd attempted to strong-arm him into refusing Keith's business, even though he knew that his contract as printer for the Philadelphia Quakers would be canceled in retaliation.[42] McComb was an old enemy of the magistrates for his work as Governor Blackwell's messenger. Now, in August 1692, both Bradford and McComb were arrested. Neither man could get a written statement of the indictment brought against him and both therefore refused to recognize the legitimacy of their arrest. Nonetheless, they were confined in the Philadelphia jail for four months. When they were finally

[41] George Keith, *An Expostulation with Thomas Lloyd, Samuel Jennings and the Rest of the Twenty Eight Unjust Judges* . . . (Philadelphia, 1692), 4. See also Keith, *The great Divisions Amongst the Quakers in Pensilvania*, 8-9.

[42] Kirby, *George Keith*, 69; the warrant is reprinted in Keith, *An Appeal from the Twenty Eight Judges*. . .

brought to trial, the Philadelphia Quarter Sessions Court sentenced them to prison for printing books without the name of the printer or place of publication in violation of an obscure and little enforced English law nowhere to be found in the Pennsylvania lawbooks. The Lloydians removed all doubt about their determination to silence their attackers by seizing Bradford's press and type and revoking McComb's license as tailor and victualler.[43]

In a further attempt to stifle dissent the Council met on September 20, 1692 and took the extreme measure of ordering all justices and judges to prevent the publication of any material tending toward sedition, disturbance of the peace, "subversion of the present Frame of Government," "raising of Dislike in the people" of the Government, or "contempt of magistracy." It was a heavy-handed attempt to gag Keith and his partisans and evidence of the deep sense of insecurity overtaking the orthodox Quaker magistracy.[44]

Still Keith could not be muzzled. To the chagrin of the Lloydians he found new ways of distributing his fiery literature. In response, the Philadelphia County Court, composed of six of the city's most important Quaker merchants, issued a proclamation warning Keith and his adherents that further attacks, either by word or print, on Thomas Lloyd and the magistrates would be made "at their Peril."[45] Keith was the wrong man to threaten with such restrictions. He had suffered imprisonment and persecution in Scotland for the faith and was willing, if not eager, to be martyred now. True to their promise, the magistrates met Keith's next public denunciation of their policies by indicting and

[43] Kirby, *George Keith*, 73-74.
[44] MSS Minutes of Council, Sept. 20, 1692, Penn Papers, Assembly and Provincial Council.
[45] The proclamation is in Proud, *History of Pennsylvania*, I, 374-376.

trying him and three of his supporters—Thomas Budd, a merchant; William Bradford; and Peter Boss, a West Jersey critic of the Quaker magistrates. The Quaker justices were wise enough not to martyr Keith by sentencing him to prison; instead they contended themselves with imposing a more or less symbolic fine of £5. Budd and Boss received like fines, and Bradford, acquitted of the charges, was returned to jail to complete the sentence earlier imposed. According to Keith none of the defendants were allowed to appeal the decisions to the Provincial Court or the Privy Council in England.[46]

Yet Keith's voice could not be smothered, despite the Lloydians' control of the apparatus of church and state. The Yearly Meeting in 1692 disowned Keith "for his vile Abuses and ungodly exposing of them in print, and otherwise endeavoring by his misrepresentations of them to make them the Derision of the heathen and scorne of fools." The County Court of Philadelphia denounced him in proclamations and convicted him of slander. But nothing stopped the bitter dispute from raging on. Keith continued to gain supporters, Quaker congregations split, and meetings degenerated into verbal warfare between apparently irreconcilable factions. The climax came in early 1693 at the largest meetinghouse in Philadelphia. On a Saturday night, cloaked by darkness, partisans of Keith worked feverishly at one end of the meetinghouse to erect a gallery from which their leader might exhort the worshippers the next morning. Keith's opponents had long controlled the permanent gallery at the opposite end of the room and denied the apos-

[46] Kirby, *George Keith*, 80-85. Penn, whose charter hung precariously in the balance, expressed concern that the oppressive nature of the trial would arm his critics with another weapon. In 1692 Penn seems to have favored Keith in the dispute raging in Pennsylvania. See Kirby, *George Keith*, 96-97.

tate entrance to it. The next day, as the Quakers filed into the meetinghouse for the weekly devotions, they found themselves caught in the cross fire of two groups of impassioned Friends. Accusations and counteraccusations filled the air as each side struggled to be heard. But the verbal exchanges paled before the physical demonstration that followed. Axes appeared from nowhere as each group sought to destroy the other's gallery. Posts, railings, stairs, seats— all went down before the angry blows of the two opposed camps.[47]

The Anatomy of Religious Controversy

Such violence within the Quaker community stemmed from far more than doctrinal disagreement. If Keith's arguments about the organizational defects and metaphysical shortcomings of Quaker beliefs appealed to some of the best-educated Friends, such subtleties were beyond the ken of most. Not a dozen men with a university education resided in Pennsylvania at the time and few colonists were capable of understanding the complexities of Keith's disquisitions, which as one critic observed were "Tedious, Dry, and Insipid."[48] Most Quakers, as Keith's biographer notes, were "utterly unprepared to become analytical" about the logical consistency or philosophical implications of the Quaker creed, preferring to abide by the simply understood doctrine of the "inner light" and to avoid questions of what was orthodox and what was not.[49] Although it is true that the intensity of religious conviction ran high in the seventeenth century and that the untutored were frequently aroused

[47] *Ibid.*, 76, 85-87.
[48] Samuel Jennings, *The State of the Case . . .* (London, 1694) , 13-15, as cited in Kirby, *George Keith*, 61.
[49] Kirby, *George Keith*, 62.

against real or supposed enemies of the faith, this explains only Keith's opponents, not his adherents. That so many would give unqualified support to his recondite views must be explained in other terms.

Keith's appeal, in all likelihood, was rooted not in the intellectual or religious realm but in the far more mundane area of economic and political affairs. Most of his adherents in Pennsylvania were not particularly attracted by his proposals for doctrinal and administrative reforms, which were conservative in nature, but they were driven to his camp by the domineering behavior of the Lloydian elite and its rapid accumulation of power in the early 1690's. As Robert Turner had explained to Penn, Lloyd's efforts to remove from office all who had opposed him and his attempts to raise a tax for his own salary antagonized more than a few. Many of the participants in the controversy admitted as much. One of his supporters, Samuel Jennings, wrote that the Quakers in Pennsylvania were "ripe" for conflict. Turner pointed to the interlocking nature of religious and civil conflict: "Alls a fire spiritual and temporal," he wrote to Penn in explaining the oligarchical thrust of Thomas Lloyd's governorship. Penn himself believed that "Thomas Lloyd's height had administered occasion for a difference in spirit between Geo. Keith and him from the first," and stated his impression that people were drawn to the fiery Scotsman more by personal than philosophical considerations.[50] By all appearances, the Keithian movement provided a popular means of expressing opposition to an upper layer of Quakers whose political domination was becoming brittle and overbearing. By and large Keith's supporters did not

[50] Jennings, *State of the Case*, 40; Turner to Penn, June 15, 1692, Dreer Collection, Penn Letters, 69; Penn to Turner, Nov. 29, 1692, Penn Papers, J. Francis Fisher Copies, 31.

intellectualize their position; they were reacting, probably semiconsciously in some cases, against a faction of men who seemed insensitive rather than responsive to their notions of equitable government.

An analysis of the political orientation and the socio-economic composition of the two camps offers confirmation of this view. Leading the orthodox Quakers against Keith was Thomas Lloyd. Among his most active supporters were merchants Arthur Cooke, Samuel Jennings, John Delavall, Samuel Richardson, Anthony Morris, and Robert Ewer, and such long-standing political adherents from Chester and Bucks counties as John Blunston, John Simcock, George Maris, Nicholas Waln, William Yardley, and Phineas Pemberton. Other merchants who had followed Lloyd in politics also took his side in the religious controversy: Samuel Carpenter, Humphrey Morrey, John Day, James Fox, and John Jones.[51] Most of these men were probably convinced that Keith expounded false tenets. Others probably knew only that the Scotsman stirred already unsettled minds with his unorthodox beliefs and appealed to the same class of people that chafed under the present political management. Among the several hundred Quakers who publicly avowed their opposition to Keith, not one was known as a political opponent of Thomas Lloyd. Conversely, among the county and provincial officeholders—by 1692 almost all of

[51] Keith identified many of the leaders of Quaker orthodoxy in his many polemical pamphlets of the period. Some of his major critics are listed in the declaration of the "Twenty Eight Judges" at the Quarterly Meeting of June, 1692. The signators are listed in Charles P. Keith, *Chronicles of Pennsylvania, 1688-1748* (2 vols., Philadelphia, 1917), I, 221-222; a far longer list of anti-Keithians is found in the "Testimony against Geo Keith signed at the Yearly Meeting, September 7, 1692," Yearly Meeting Minutes, 1681-1746, Department of Records, Friends Bookstore, 310 Arch Street, Philadelphia. Thirty-nine anti-Keithians endorsed Samuel Jennings' *State of the Case*, 79-80.

155

them were a part of Lloyd's network of influence—the denunciation of Keith was almost unanimous. In the Council, for example, all nine Quakers opposed Keith. So did the entire membership of the Provincial Court. On the benches of the Bucks and Chester county courts not a man could be found who did not condemn Keith. On the Philadelphia Court only one of eight Quakers supported Keith, and that was Robert Turner, who had been an avowed political opponent of Lloyd for years.

An examination of Keith's followers shows a similar congruence between political and religious positions. The most prominent Keithians were precisely those men who led the political opposition against Thomas Lloyd. Most of them had supported Governor Blackwell and had lost their voice in public affairs when Lloyd returned to power. Merchants Robert Turner, Griffith Jones, and Andrew Robeson were the most substantial of them. They were joined by lesser traders such as Charles Pickering, George Hutcheson, and Joseph Fisher. Keith also found considerable support among the shopkeepers and master artisans of Philadelphia.[52] It is striking to note how consistently these men had also petitioned against the Council-sponsored tax of 1692. Of 87 known Keithians in Philadelphia, 71 had opposed the tax. In marked contrast, among 204 Quakers who had signed

[52] Twenty-one of Keith's followers signed his tract *Some Reasons and Causes of the Late Separation* . . . (Philadelphia, 1692); the names of twenty-eight adherents who signed a defense of Keith dated July 3, 1692 are given in Keith, *Chronicles of Pennsylvania*, I, 223. Sixty-six Keithians signed another paper entitled "Declaration from the Yearly Meeting at Burlington, the 4th, 5th, 6th, & 7th Days of the seventh Month, Anno 1692," in Parrish Collection, Proud Papers, II, 42; other partisans are identifiable in a variety of sources listed in *Inventory of Church Archives, Society of Friends in Pennsylvania* (Philadelphia, 1941), 198-201.

condemnations of Keith's doctrines, only 12 joined the tax protest.

It is equally illuminating to trace the pattern of religious dissension within social classes in Philadelphia, at the same time noting the correlation between religious and political estrangement. John Goodson, a Philadelphia Quaker merchant, had described the "business community" of the town to Friends in England on the eve of the Keithian schism, listing some 35 occupational categories and the number of men engaged in each. Though Goodson supplied no names, a recent attempt has been made to reconstruct the city's mercantile and artisan classes with such success that virtually all the merchants, shopkeepers, and artisans have been identified.[53] Making necessary changes to reflect new arrivals and deaths within the community after the time of Goodson's description, one can obtain a reasonably accurate profile of the town's occupational structure as the fires of religious controversy broke out.

Among twenty merchants in Philadelphia, the anti-Keithians enjoyed the support of eight men, none of whom signed the tax protest. All who had been in Philadelphia in Blackwell's time had arrayed themselves against the Governor. Nine merchants were Keithians; of these all but two petitioned against the tax. Of the six who had been in Philadelphia during Blackwell's tenure, five had given him their support. Of the three remaining merchants, two were Anglicans, both opponents of Lloyd, and one left no trace of his position on the religious issue. Shopkeepers numbered sixteen. Frequently they were merchant aspirants, often engaging in mercantile ventures when the opportunity presented

[53] Hannah B. Roach, "Philadelphia Business Directory, 1690," *Pennsylvania Genealogical Magazine*, 23 (1963), 95-129.

itself; many denoted themselves "merchants" in deeds and other legal documents. Three condemned Keith, but did not oppose the tax. Nine followed the apostate, six of them signing the tax petition. The position of the remaining four is unknown on the religious question, but three protested the tax. Eighty-nine artisans—brewers, bakers, butchers, carpenters, cordwainers, brickmakers, smiths, coopers, and the like—are identifiable. Only fifteen, or about 19 percent of the Quakers involved, signified their rejection of Keith. Of these, four signed the tax protest. By contrast, forty-four, or about 55 percent of the Quaker artisans in Philadelphia, backed Keith, and thirty-four of these protested the tax. Thirty artisans took no known position on the religious dispute, at least ten of them because they were not Quakers and others, no doubt, because they preferred to remain neutral. Fifteen of these individuals protested the tax.

Both Keith and the orthodox Quakers drew support from the outlying districts and from other counties. The anti-Keithians were strongest in Bucks and Chester counties where Lloyd had long commanded the fealty of the principal landowners such as Pemberton, Growdon, Simcock, Blunston, Yardley, Waln, and Bristow. The Keithians commanded a considerable allegiance in the northern parts of Philadelphia County where the yeomanry and non-Quaker elements also actively opposed the tax measure of 1692.

A final indication of the interrelated nature of religious, economic, and political positions came in 1693. In the previous year, as the Keithian schism was reaching its climax, Penn's right to government was suspended and his colony placed under Benjamin Fletcher, governor of New York. Fletcher's arrival in 1693, eclipsing the power of Thomas Lloyd and his party, was not wholly unwelcome. Shortly after his arrival, a petition of welcome and support signed by 117 inhabitants of the city and county of Philadelphia was presented to the new Governor. The signators expressed the hope that "the Confusions and Disorders under which we have labored for some time past, will . . . be stopt and extinguished," and praised Fletcher for his unblemished reputation in New York.[54] Of the 204 Quakers who had signified their rejection of Keith only one signed the declaration. Among known partisans of Keith, by contrast, thirty-five signed the greeting, including almost every prominent member of the Keithian camp: Griffith Jones, Robert Turner, Joseph Wilcox, Thomas Tresse, James Stanfield, Charles Saunders, Patrick Robinson, Francis Rawle, Joseph Pidgeon, Charles Pickering, William Lee, Thomas Harris, John Duplovneys, and Francis Cooke—practically a catalogue of deposed officeholders, factors of English merchants, faithful supporters of Penn, and lesser merchants (in short, of Thomas Lloyd's political enemies). A few may have been trimming sails, but the composition of the pro-Fletcher element bears more than coincidental resemblance to the political and religious malcontents of the period from 1688 to 1693. The Lloydian party admitted as much, writing Penn after Fletcher's arrival that the "contrary faction" readily supported the new Governor.[55]

Though the evidence is incomplete, there are strong grounds for concluding that Keithianism, though it originated as a highly intellectual attempt to reform the Society of Friends in Pennsylvania and West Jersey, took on a far broader meaning for elements of Quaker society. What be-

[54] *The Address of some of the Peaceable and Well Affected Freeholders and Inhabitants of the Town and County of Philadelphia* (New York, 1693).

[55] Cooke, Simcock, Richardson, Fox, Carpenter, and George Murrie to Penn, Jan. 18, 1693/94, Parrish Collection, Proud Papers, II, 28-30 (copy).

gan as a doctrinal protest became a formula for expressing far more down-to-earth resentments. A whole stratum of lesser merchants, shopkeepers, and master artisans—upward moving individuals, not a few of whom would enter the circle of mercantile leadership in the next decade—found that Keith's program provided a means of challenging the Lloydian "greats," who were resented for their narrow control of provincial life. The texture of the debates, the scurrilous language used by Quakers against each other, and the abstruseness of the theological issues at stake all suggest that participation in the movement was for the most part emblematic of deep-rooted political and economic grievances felt by many within the Quaker community. In many cases those who joined Keith were innocent of opinions on the theological hairsplitting in progress. But they had been highly politicized by nearly a decade of political acrimony —and particularly by the inflammatory techniques employed by Thomas Lloyd in his struggle against Blackwell. Many had remained neutral in the initial stages of the controversy. But the attempts of the Lloydians to pressure the Quaker meetings into endorsing their condemnation of Keith and the subsequent jailing of Bradford and McComb doubtless swayed many who harbored political or economic resentments against Lloyd and his faction. Keith was not far from the truth when he wrote that "all sober People did resent their Proceedings very ill, and as proceeding from a cruel Spirit of Persecution."[56] At the height of the crisis, the Council unwisely attempted to pass an unprecedented provincial tax. Coming during a period of wartime insecurity and economic dislocation, the measure only roused further opposition. Anxiety-ridden at the tenuousness of their po-

[56] George Keith, *New England's Spirit of Persecution Transmitted to Pennsylvania* (New York, 1693) , 4.

sition, the dominant Quakers became brittle, insensitive, and inclined to pursue their adversaries as they themselves had been pursued in England only a few decades before.

The Dynamics of Instability

No more dramatic symbol of the failure of the Quaker polity in Pennsylvania could be found than the Keithian schism. For more than a decade, since their first arrival in 1682, Quakers had wrestled with the problem of political disunity and social instability. Now the fires of contention had spread to the religious community itself.

For historians this decay of Quaker solidarity has proved a thorny problem. Why should the Quakers, released from persecution in England and given a government of their own in a fertile, strategically located river valley, fall prey to political and religious guerrilla warfare? Why should the shared values, the common outlook, the sense of community which had solidified Quakers in England, provide so little cohesive force in Pennsylvania? Most historians have skirted the issue, either taking little account of the chronic friction of the early years or passing it off as a kind of prodromal sign of eighteenth-century revolutionary democracy.

The answer in all likelihood lies elsewhere. In part the problem of factionalism among people who were supposedly bound together by common purpose was the effect which promotional literature had in raising the expectations of immigrants to a height that probably could never have been realized in Pennsylvania. There had always been a strong prophetic strain in Quakerism, and Penn's promotional pamphlets, though he was more cautious than many colonial promoters in his promises, fed these utopian anticipations all too well. Pennsylvania, by all accounts, was to be an approximation of Zion. According to Penn it lay "600 miles nearer the Sun than England" and thus enjoyed a mild climate not unlike that of Naples or the southern parts of France. The woods abounded with game and wild fruit, the streams with fish, the fields with Indian corn, wild hay, and berries. Penn, what is more, promised to reside in the country as a protective father, guarding the Quakers against outside interference and internal dissension.[57]

Exposed to Penn's propaganda and released from the burdens of persecution in the Old World, it is not surprising that the early settlers were psychologically conditioned to expect a New Jerusalem on the banks of the Delaware. "More and not less [liberty] seems the Reasons . . . to Plant this Wilderness," Penn would later reflect. Or, he would write, "are wee come 3000 miles into a Desart of orig[inal] wild people as well as wild Beasts . . . to have only the same priviledges wee had at home?"[58] Penn at the time was objecting to the attack on provincial autonomy by the government in London, but his words point precisely to the sense of anticipation felt in Pennsylvania from the outset. People whose religion and humble positions in English society had made any lofty aspirations unthinkable, acquired almost overnight in Pennsylvania an enlarged sense of self-importance and a limitless vision of what was attainable in the New World. That the immigrating society included so few genuinely upper-class individuals only made the notion of access to high places all the more common. Bit by bit, alien-

<hr>

[57] Penn, *Some Account of Pennsylvania* . . . , Meyers, ed., *Narratives*, 207-208; Penn, *Letter* . . . *to the Free Society of Traders, ibid.*, 225-229, 240-242; Penn, *A Further Account of Pennsylvania, ibid.*, 259-278.

[58] Penn to the Board of Trade, April 22, 1700, Penn Letter Book (1699-1703), 27; Penn to Charlewood Lawton, Aug. 18, 1701, *ibid.*, 111.

ation set in when individuals found Pennsylvania, as good as it was, less than they expected.

The failure of Pennsylvania society to coalesce in the early years is also attributable in minor degree to the effects of the wilderness environment. In England, a relative orderliness, at least in public affairs, was assured by the long development of prescriptive authority, which operated in every sphere of life. This did not mean that there was no scrambling for place and position in England, but merely that such competition was conducted within prescribed channels. But in Pennsylvania inchoate institutions and unfixed patterns of political recruitment led to a pursuit of position which bordered at times on anarchy. What was true in public life, moreover, was hardly less true in private. Penn, who fully recognized this disintegrative effect of the expansive wilderness, cautioned the Provincial Council in 1686 to cultivate sobriety, suppress "clandestine looseness," and set a high example for those in lower stations. "For since people are less under Notice and so more left to themselves in the wilderness of America, then in thes[e] more planted and crowded parts of the world," he warned, "so they have more need to watch over themselves and become a law to themselves."[59] Later he described those who opposed his authority as "those *sturdies* [who] will never leave off till they catch a *Tartar* and must come hither to be lost in the crowd of taller folks, to be humbled and made more pliable; for what with the distance and the scarcity of mankind there, they opine too much."[60]

Other colonies also felt the atomizing effects of the wilderness. In England a person who harbored resentments against a member of the magistracy was likely to keep silent

[59] Penn to Council, 1686, *PMHB*, 33 (1909), 310.
[60] Penn to Logan, July 12, 1704, *Penn-Logan Correspondence*, I, 305.

or oppose authority indirectly; for there were no uninhabited river valleys or vast tracts of land to which he could repair if the fires of contention grew too hot. But America was filled with Roger Williamses, Anne Hutchinsons, and Samuel Mavericks—defiant spirits for whom even banishment from the mother colony presented no particular problem. As one historian of New England has written: "The New World, with a three-thousand mile moat on the one hand and boundless free land on the other, offered strong temptation to adventurous spirits to kick over the traces and defy every kind of authority."[61]

Still another problem, which was really cause and effect, was the failure of institutions in Pennsylvania. Penn, who gave much thought to institutions of government, had founded his colony with the idyllic hope that Quakers in America, freed from the corrosive effects of Restoration England, would build a new, regenerated society. Pennsylvania would become an "example to the Nations." In the government, as in the Friends meeting, controverted issues would be resolved through quiet deliberation. Penn expected a deep spirituality to pervade every aspect of life in Pennsylvania, especially government, which he regarded as "a part of religion itself, a thing sacred in its institution and end."[62] His would be a society of freedom but not license, a place where liberties flourished but within an ordered, stable setting.

In spite of these utopian visions, Penn was not so idealis-

[61] Edmund S. Morgan, *The Puritan Dilemma* (Boston, 1958), 96.
[62] Preface to the Frame of 1682 in *Laws of Pennsylvania*, 92. Penn advised his Commissioners of State in 1687 to "retire" to God so that "he may give you a good understanding, and government of your selves, in the management thereof; which is what truly crowns public actions, and dignifies those, that perform them." Penn Papers, Domestic and Miscellaneous Letters, 84.

tic as to think that people transplanted from one side of the Atlantic to the other would be cleansed of antisocial tendencies at one stroke. Laws were carefully drafted to control the baser human instincts, for as Penn remarked in the preface to the Frame of 1682, the first end of government was to "terrify Evil-doers." Characteristically Penn wrote, "Where the Reins of Government are too slack, there the Manners of the People are corrupted; and that destroys Industry, begets Effiminacy, and provokes Heaven against it."[63] In the political sphere, elections would be held by secret ballot, political bribery severely punished, and chicanery strictly guarded against. In the economic sphere laws would guarantee the close regulation of the community's commercial life. Inspection of exports, public supervision of markets, strict regulation of the fur trade, and wage and price controls were only a few of the devices by which the watchful eye of government would aid the functioning of the economy. As for social relationships, Penn relied on ingrained concepts of rank and order and upon the traditional function of the Quaker Monthly Meeting to seek out and restrain "wayward walkers" so as to maintain discipline within the community. Over all would preside the resident proprietor, who would gently urge disquieted souls to moderation and who would be universally accepted as a kind of final arbiter due to his wisdom and strength of character.[64]

In spite of Penn's carefully drafted plans, the institutional framework of his colony never materialized. Proprietary oversight never had the stabilizing effects expected of it because it was resented and contested almost from the beginning. After Penn's return to England, his colony gathered

[63] *Laws of Pennsylvania*, 92; William Penn, *Some Fruits of Solitude* (London, 1901), 72.
[64] *Laws of Pennsylvania*, 115-123, 130-155; Beatty, *William Penn*, 239-243.

economic strength with every passing year and appeared to have less and less need of its creator and benefactor. Sentiment steadily grew that proprietary government was a hindrance to the successful development of Pennsylvania, an apparatus out of place and out of date on the Delaware. Penn's subalterns found cooperation with others difficult, sometimes impossible. As one of Penn's chief advisors was to inform him, unity in the church "makes [it] not so in Civil Government."[65]

Particularly damaging to the infant society was the absence of visible government. The General Assembly met only nine or ten days a year, while months often passed without a session of the Council. From October 1684 to March 1685, for example, the latter body was not once convened. Even at scheduled sessions attendance was dismally poor. "I will no more endure their most slothful and dishonorable attendance," Penn wrote in disgust in 1687; but little heed was taken of his complaints.[66]

The courts were little better. Because of their exclusion from civil government in England, Quakers sorely lacked experience on the bench. Irregular sessions, disputes over the jurisdictional rights of the various courts, and the tendency of leading men in the colony to refuse judicial appointment when the course of public affairs did not suit them, all contributed to confusion in government. Those who served, far from imparting dignity and composure to public affairs, added to the disquiet with heated controversies that plagued judicial proceedings. The first chief justice, Nicholas More, was entirely discredited by impeachment proceedings brought against him in 1685 for misuse of office. Disorder and confusion in the courts and a "want of venera-

[65] Thomas Holme to Penn, Nov. 25, 1686, *PMHB*, 90 (1966), 350.
[66] Cited in Proud, *History of Pennsylvania*, I, 305.

tion to magistracy" was common, wrote one of Penn's advisors, and another marveled at the "clashing there is amongst the Magistrates Even upon the Bench."[67] Even physical violence was not unknown in the highest courts. In 1686 Penn learned that two of his appointees, harboring ancient grudges, had resorted to fisticuffs. When assault charges were subsequently brought to court, tempers flared again, throwing the court "into an Uproare" which lasted until nightfall. "How can offences be well punished by offenders?" Penn asked in despair, "or the Quarrelsome be Reconcilers? . . . If Magistrates draw themselves into Contempt by a mean Behaviour, they can never exercise Power honourably nor successfully."[68]

It is possible, though conjectural, that the humane criminal code may also have contributed to the social confusion in the new colony. Victims of harsh persecution in England, Quakers, not surprisingly, enacted penal laws extraordinarily lenient by the standards of neighboring colonies. Many exploited the new benevolence, however, when released from the close restraints of English life. Hardly a letter reached Penn in England that did not carry accounts of licentiousness and disorder. "Mutch robrey in City and Countrey, Breaking of houses, and stealing of Hoggs," bemoaned one informant. "Vices creepe in like the old Serpent and are now almost to strong for them."[69] Penn, dis-

[67] *Votes of Assembly*, I, 65-67; Holme to Penn, Nov. 25, 1686, *PMHB*, 90 (1966), 350. Markham to Penn, Aug. 22, 1686, *ibid.*, 326. Also see Lawrence Lewis, Jr., "The Courts of Pennsylvania in the Seventeenth Century," *PMHB*, 5 (1881), 141-190.

[68] Nicholas More to Penn, Dec. 1, 1684, Myers Collection, Box 2, #6, CCHS; Markham to Penn, Oct. 5, 1686, *PMHB*, 90 (1966), 337-340; Penn to Thomas Lloyd, Feb. 1, 1686/87, Penn Papers, Domestic and Miscellaneous Letters, 84.

[69] Nicholas More to Penn, Dec. 1, 1684, Myers Collection, Box 2, #6, CCHS.

heartened, could only express his dismay at the lack of discipline in Pennsylvania and preface each letter with a call for more Christian behavior. Later the provincial leaders would enact a more repressive body of laws, expressing the conviction that the original ones were "so easie that they have not answered the good end proposed in making thereof."[70]

Some of these problems were, of course, common to almost all the American colonies in the seventeenth century, but they were probably secondary factors in the chronic instability of early Pennsylvania. Far more important was the crippling effect which the Quaker attitude toward established authority had on attempts at self-government. Though the relationship between social outlook and political behavior is not easy to define, some correlation between the two factors clearly exists.[71] Quakers, like others who sought a new life in America, brought with them not only material possessions, high aspirations, and inherited political ideas, but also a constellation of values, a way of looking at the world, and, stemming from this, a behavioral pattern that carried over into political and social relations.

No strain in the Quaker personality was more visible to his enemies than that of his antiauthoritarianism. Though outsiders' views were colored by a hostility toward the Society of Friends, there was much truth in what they claimed to see. The tendency to balk at constituted authority, to respond hostilely to the surrounding society, was almost a daily part of the average Quaker's life, especially in the early stages of the

70 The question of a humane criminal code is fully discussed in Herbert W. K. Fitzroy, "The Punishment of Crime in Provincial Pennsylvania," *PMHB*, 60 (1936), 242-269.

71 Correlations between behavioral patterns and the functioning of political systems are perceptively discussed by Gabriel A. Almond and Sidney Verba, *Civic Culture* (Princeton, 1963), especially 3-43.

movement. Whether it was a refusal to bear arms, a systematic violation of the Clarendon Code (which made it illegal for Quakers to congregate for religious meetings), a denial of the importance of scriptural revelation, a refusal to take an oath, or a rejection of the normal signs of deference required by seventeenth-century English society, the Quaker was constantly in the business of setting himself or herself in defiance of authority.[72]

The rejection of conventional authority and a militantly negative response to existing norms was, of course, inherent in English Protestantism. As Edmund Burke would later observe, the Protestant dissenters rose "in direct opposition to all the ordinary powers of the world."[73] But nowhere was the dissent more vocal and uncompromising than among the Society of Friends—the extreme "left wing" of the Protestant movement, as it has been called. As incipiently particularistic and antiauthoritarian as were the Puritans, the Quakers were even more so. Arising out of the "bitter background of the north of England" and driven by "the ruthless morality of Puritanism and, most of all, by the intensity of their own inner fight," they set themselves implacably against civil and ecclesiastical authority. Even in social matters the Quakers were "thoroughly radical in their instinctive reactions to all the claims of the highborn and mighty."[74] Women were allowed to play a disturbingly large role in the movement, in the view of Quaker critics,

[72] The most penetrating discussion of the Quaker experience in mid-seventeenth-century England is Hugh Barbour, *The Quakers in Puritan England* (New Haven, 1964).

[73] Quoted in Clinton Rossiter, *Seedtime of the Republic* (New York, 1953), 39-40. Burke went on to note that Puritanism in the American colonies was "a refinement on the principle of resistance; . . . the dissidence of dissent, and the Protestantism of the Protestant religion."

[74] Barbour, *Quakers in Puritan England*, 84, 125-126.

and even servants were exposed to the Society's radical doctrines. Rarely could there be found in the English-speaking world of the seventeenth century a more apocalyptic view of the world, a more intense evangelicalism, or a greater bent for martyrdom. To their enemies the Quakers threatened to cast all society backward to a primitive state with their dedication to a priesthood of all believers and their vow to return to a "primitive Christianity."[75] The Quaker, it might be said, was the epitomization of the revolutionary dynamic contained in English Protestantism. In modern sociological parlance, the Quaker was the supremely "inner-directed man."

The insurrectionary tendencies, which were so evident in the first flush of Quaker enthusiasm, abated after the first two decades of the movement in England. No longer was "going naked for a sign," or disrupting Anglican church services, or intentional civil disobedience regarded with favor by Quaker leaders.[76] But given the continued enforcement of the Clarendon Code and the Friends' uncompromising opposition to many social conventions, antiauthoritarianism could by no means be rooted out of Quaker life. Most of the leaders of the colony on the Delaware, men such as Robert Turner, Arthur Cooke, James Claypoole, James Harrison, Phineas Pemberton, Caleb Pusey, and John Simcock, had long experience in nonconformity—in both the seventeenth-century and twentieth-century senses of the word. Familiarity with English gaols was more the rule than the exception among Quaker colonists in the New World. A list of English emigrants from Bristol in the second half

75 The general view of the Quaker as a social revolutionary was capsulized, as Tolles remarks, in an anti-Quaker tract of 1660 entitled *Hell Broke Loose; or, An History of the Quakers*. Frederick B. Tolles, *Quakers and the Atlantic Culture* (New York, 1960), 21.

76 Barbour, *Quakers in Puritan England*, 65-66, 234-256.

of the seventeenth century reveals the names of some 500 Quakers who had suffered fines or imprisonment for practicing their faith. Of the early Quaker purchasers of land in Pennsylvania, more than half are known to have undergone persecution in England.[77] Pennsylvania, in short, was populated in the early years by people steeped in a tradition of opposing prescriptive authority.

While Quakers were instinctively negative in their opposition to authority, especially civil authority, they were not unrestrained individualists. There was much in the Quaker code of values which implied just the opposite. In his emphasis on simplicity of dress and plainness of language, for example, the Quaker practiced a self-control rare in the seventeenth century. The refusal to bear arms and the eschewal of all forms of violent social control were also exercises in restraint. But most of all, Quakers showed their group orientation in a strongly developed sense of community. For the Quaker this began with a common belief in the "inner light." It was also strengthened by decades of persecution, which forced Friends to band together, thus offsetting, as Frederick Tolles has pointed out, "the centrifugal tendencies inherent in the doctrine of the 'inner light' and substituting an organic social theory for one that might otherwise have been wholly atomistic."[78] Despite their emphasis on the individual, the leaders of the Quaker movement recognized the need for a hierarchy of Monthly, Quarterly, and Yearly Meetings and for disciplinary machinery within the Society.[79]

[77] N. Dermot Harding, *Bristol and America* . . . (London, [1929]) ; Pomfret, "First Purchasers of Pennsylvania," *PMHB*, 80 (1956) , 139.
[78] Tolles, *Meeting House*, 7.
[79] The growth of a disciplinary and administrative apparatus within the Society of Friends is traced in Arnold Lloyd's *Quaker Social His-*

In the social as well as religious sphere Quakers recognized the necessity of structure. "The compliance of a society to such methods of order as the elders thereof have exhorted to, and the generality . . . have embraced," wrote Penn, are "expedients of order, and methods of rule about things universally agreed upon." In society as in the church each had his place and function. Penn opposed luxurious living because it represented an attempt to live above one's station and thus to confound "all reasonable distinction and those civil degrees that are amongst people."[80] Robert Barclay summed up the Quaker affirmation of an ordered society: "I would not have any judge, that . . . we intend to destroy the *mutual* Relation, that either is betwixt *Prince* and *People, Master* and *Servants, Parents* and *Children*; nay not at all: We shall evidence, that our Principle in these things hath no such tendency, and that these Natural Relations are rather better established than any ways hurt by it."[81]

Nowhere is the seeming ambivalence in the Quaker system of values more apparent than in the Quaker attitude toward deference. Quakers steadfastly refuse to observe the customary seventeenth-century signs by which one acknowledged social superiors—uncovering of the head, bowing and genuflecting, and the use of flattering titles of address or of the pronoun "you." Such scruples did not signify a belief in an equalitarian society, however. For Quakers, while rejecting the usual signs of social deference, felt no urge to build a society devoid of rank and distinction. They held the usual seventeenth-century view that society, by the

tory, 1669-1738 (London, 1950) , and in Braithwaite, *Second Period of Quakerism*, Chaps. 9, 10, 12.

80 Penn, *"Just Measures," 1692*, and *An Address to Protestants, 1679*, quoted in Dorfman, *Economic Mind in American Civilization*, I, 80.

81 Quoted by Tolles in *Meeting House*, 110-111.

nature of things, should be stratified. Neither did they have misgivings in singling out particular men to hold the reins of political and religious leadership. Members of Council in Pennsylvania, for example, were to be selected as those "of most note for their wisdom, virtue, and ability."[82] Even the councilors, drawn from the upper stratum of provincial society, were unashamed to refer to Penn as "an affectionate & tender father whose children wee know wee are." To such men, Penn's request some years later that "some particular mark of respect . . . be continued to his family, for distinguishing them above the rank of those who have planted under him" must have come as a perfectly reasonable demand.[83] Quakers did not object to an ordered society where rank and privilege was conferred upon those whose stake in the community was the largest. Their equalitarianism, if that word can be used at all, was confined to a sense of the equal worth of each individual in the sight of God and the capacity of every man to find God within himself apart from scriptural revelation or external authority. Unlike the Leveller complaints of the Cromwellian interlude, Quaker protests regarding equality, as Hugh Barbour has written, were "meant fundamentally as an assault on pride . . . not as a social reform." Wrote John Whitehead, a leading Quaker spokesman: "We design to level nothing but Sin."[84] Quakers opposed social deference but not a deferential society. Their quarrel was not with the structure of society but with its social conventions.

There were, then, two sides to the Quaker personality.

[82] *Laws of Pennsylvania*, 94. An earlier draft of the Frame of Government had been worded "wisdom, virtue, and substance."

[83] Council to Penn, April 9, 1689, Penn Papers, Official Correspondence, I, 11.

[84] Barbour, *Quakers in Puritan England*, 163; Whitehead, *Written Gospel-Labours*, cited by Barbour, *ibid.*, 167.

On the one hand, Quakers were wont to emphasize restraint, control, community, hierarchy, organicism. On the other hand, they were apt to celebrate equality, individualism, freedom, nonconformity. The one set of tendencies was centripetal in its effects, the other centrifugal; the one, collective, the other, atomistic.

In Pennsylvania, given their own government and free of persecution, Quakers might have been expected to sublimate their individualistic and antiauthoritarian tendencies and to join hands in the work of building a reconstructed society. Certainly Penn expected no less. Theoretically at least, the act of immigration would represent the ultimate rejection of English authority, the final breaking away from an unredeemed society. Yet Quakers in the New World seemed instinctively to act like Quakers in the Old, even though the magistrates were of their own choice and religious persuasion. Penn's letters to the colony in the 1680's are filled with dismay at a people so "governmentish," so "brutish," so susceptible to "scurvy quarrels that break out to the disgrace of the Province," so wont to question civil authority and eager to deny the legitimacy of proprietarial policies.[85] Surviving court records confirm this view of a people suffused with litigiousness and antisocial tendencies. One of Penn's confidants despaired at "the surging waves of pestiferous apostates and runagadoes" which threatened to overrun the infant government.[86] Another con-

[85] Penn to James Harrison, Nov. 20, 1686, Penn Papers, Domestic and Miscellaneous Letters, 31; Penn to Commissioners of State, Feb. 1, 1686/87, *ibid.*, 84. For similar remarks see also Penn to Harrison, Dec. 4, 1685, *ibid.*, 22; Penn to Thomas Lloyd, Aug. 15, 1685, *ibid.*, 81; Penn to Friends and Counsellors, Aug. 19, 1685, Logan Papers, I, 8 (copy).

[86] Phineas Pemberton to Penn, April 3, 1687, Etting Collection, Pemberton Papers, I, 20. On the contentiousness of the early settlers see

cluded that the Quakers were not "fitted to rule themselves or to be ruled by a Friend thats a Governor." Similarly, Blackwell concluded that the Quaker personality was unsuited for government, that something in their makeup led them to indulge almost compulsively in oppositional politics.[87] Quantification is scarcely possible in such subjective matters, but one suspects that Penn's advisors had correctly identified a kind of residual antiauthoritarianism carried by Quakers to the Delaware. Penn himself would write in frustration that there was "nothing but good said of the place, and little thats good said of the people."[88]

Utopian propaganda, frail institutions, the effects of the environment, and the antiauthoritarian instincts of the Quakers—all contributed to the breakdown of a sense of community in early Pennsylvania. But perhaps the highest position in the hierarchy of causes should be reserved for the structure of immigrant society itself. It is of no small importance that the spectrum of wealth was so narrow in the first few decades, that mobility—upward and downward —was so extensive, and that economic power was never stabilized in the hands of a small cohesive group. It was the wrong kind of environment for establishing a political elite, proprietary or otherwise.

This telescoped and mobile society of the early years is not apparent at first glance, especially when one finds that

---

Herbert W. K. Fitzroy, "Richard Crosby Goes to Court; Some Realities of Colonial Litigation," *PMHB*, 62 (1938), 12-19.

[87] Thomas Holme to Penn, Nov. 25, 1686, *PMHB*, 90 (1966), 350. John Blackwell to Penn, May 1, 1689, Provincial Papers, Dept. of Public Records, Harrisburg; Blackwell to Penn, June 24, 1689, Stauffer Collection, Governors of Pennsylvania, 20; Blackwell to Thomas Hartley, ca. Aug. 1689, in Augustus C. Buell, *William Penn* (New York, 1904), 225.

[88] Penn to James Harrison, Nov. 20, 1686, Penn Papers, Domestic and Miscellaneous Letters, 31.

about half of the adult males arriving in the first half-dozen years were indentured servants. But that was less important, as it turned out, than the fact that the other half of the immigrant population was composed primarily of people only a step or two above the servant level—men of the yeoman and artisan class. Of even greater significance is the fact that those who formed the uppermost stratum of immigrant society were so singularly unimpressive. Rarely could Penn attract immigrants who could base their claim to status on education or familiarity with public affairs. There were only a handful of university trained men in Pennsylvania in the first two decades, and only one or two of them chose to enter the political arena. Those upon whom Penn conferred power at the outset of his "holy experiment" were innocent of experience in matters of government.

Penn, of course, would have preferred it otherwise. But he was forced to rely upon the best of what was available to him. In Chester County, for example, he entrusted power to John Simcock, John Blunston, and Caleb Pusey. The first two were yeoman farmers from Cheshire, England, the latter was a lastmaker by trade. All three had been able to invest £100 or so in Pennsylvania land, but more important all had been traveling ministers for the Society of Friends and thus were able to influence Quakers in their area to pull up roots in England and join them in the pilgrimage to Pennsylvania. In 1693, at the time of the first provincial tax, Simcock, Blunston, and Pusey were among the highest taxpayers in their county, paying between ten and twelve shillings each.[89] But this was no indication of accumulated wealth.

[89] Biographical sketches of Blunston, Pusey, and Simcock are given in George Smith, *History of Delaware County, Pennsylvania* (Philadelphia, 1862) , 447, 494-495, 501. The tax list of 1693 is in Chester County Miscellaneous Papers, 1684-1847.

Many of their farmer neighbors paid as much, and the average taxpayer contributed only a few shillings less. In Philadelphia, to take another example, Penn vested power in a small group of men who called themselves either gentlemen or merchants. Most of them had invested in at least 5,000 acres of Pennsylvania land, which would have cost them £100. Their titles, however, signified mainly an attempt to confer dignity upon themselves; in reality, they lived much like their neighbors. A few had military backgrounds which Penn presumed would qualify them as leaders and administrators. Several had been shopkeepers and small-time traders in England, though some of them seem to have fallen upon hard times and come to Pennsylvania to escape their creditors and start afresh; several men had the simple advantage of minor bookkeeping knowledge or had been schoolteachers, which enabled them to keep records legibly. Taken together they were an unimpressive lot, hardly calculated to overawe the lesser immigrants. Too many of their fellow settlers, as it would emerge, knew of the insignificant and, in a few cases, questionable roles they had played in English society. The founding elite, then, was distinguished chiefly for its rough-hewn style of life. A generation or more would be required for members of the upper stratum to build estates and reputations which would clearly differentiate them from those lower on the social scale.

This concentration of sturdy and ambitious yeomen and artisans, together with the absence of a moneyed upper class, probably contributed materially to Pennsylvania's phenomenally rapid growth. But in political affairs the effects were the opposite. Since the political elite was composed of men only a step or two ahead of the rest of the population, traditional patterns of social and political deference were subjected to severe strains. It was a dysfunctional system, with various parts of the social organization working at cross-purposes. The structure of the society and the fluid economic system thrust people upwards and bred propulsive ambitions within the middle and lower ranks, while the political system was designed to rest upon the rule of a dual elite—proprietary and provincial—which the people at large accepted. As economic and social differentiation increased during the eighteenth century, political elites would function with far less difficulty because their superiority reflected the actual structure of society in Pennsylvania. But in the seventeenth century ordinary people chafed at any barrier blocking their way. Individuals who had never owned more than 10 or 20 acres of land in England grew resentful of paying an annual quitrent of one shilling for 100 acres of fertile New World soil and were easily stirred to oppose those in positions of power. As Penn, with his characteristic insight, wrote, "the Great fault is, that thos who are there, loose their authority, one way or other in the Spirits of the people and then they can do little with their outward powrs."[90]

In the end, no fruitful attempt can be made to rank precisely the factors which contributed to Quaker instability in Pennsylvania. The antiauthoritarian strain in the Quaker makeup and the unstructured nature of the society seem of particular importance. But it is more significant that all of these factors interpenetrated so that no single thread in the cloth of Quaker experience can be entirely separated from the others. The crucial point is that almost all of the elements which distinguished the Quaker's existence in Pennsylvania from his life in England seemed to promote rather than restrain the atomistic component in his cultural pattern. The vastness of the wilderness and the availability

[90] Penn to Thomas Lloyd, Sept. 21, 1686, *PMHB*, 80 (1956), 243.

of cheap land tended to break down the sense of corporate-
ness while at the same time complicating the disciplinary
functions of the Monthly Meeting. The utopian hopes
raised by Penn led to spreading disillusionment, for
they elevated expectations to a level that could never be
fulfilled. The unprecedented access to office which the
Quakers enjoyed led to a scramble for position and place
as men sought to achieve what had been beyond their
remotest hopes in England. And, ironically, the absence of
persecution deprived the Quakers in Pennsylvania of an
important annealing force which had operated in England.
In the Old World the Quakers' insularity was a form of self-
protection and a source of unity. But in Pennsylvania, where
they represented the dominant culture, Quakers had no
need to cling together in mutual defense. In England a side-
effect of persecution was fusion; in Pennsylvania the absence
of persecution contributed to fission. In England Quakers
looked inward; in Pennsylvania they looked outward. Antiauthoritarian tendencies and the psychological effects of
the wilderness put insupportable burdens on institutions
which were inherently frail, and fragile institutions encouraged resistance to authority.

Religious values, though of great importance in sustaining the Quaker community, could never overcome entirely
the atomizing tendencies of life in Pennsylvania or stifle the
immoderate quest for political and economic advantage.
Just as the leading Quakers who gathered around Thomas
Lloyd had initially opposed Penn's proprietary circle and
later overpowered his deputy governor, the lesser men in
the colony, as if forgetful of the Old World concept of an
ordered society, now sought to curb the power of the ruling
group. Ultimately, controversy in the secular sphere spilled
over into the inner sanctum of the Society of Friends—the
last preserve of unity in Pennsylvania. Keith's doctrinal

crusade against the Quaker leaders was deeply intellectual in its origins; but for his followers it came to represent a means of responding to unfavorable economic and political conditions which seemed to them to stem from self-interest in the Lloydian circle. The composition of Keith's following signified better than anything else the unsettled nature of colonial society: the Quaker leaders, who had so recently gained power at the expense of the proprietor's supporters, were now themselves challenged from below.

These same problems arose in the other American colonies but not in such an acute form as they did in Pennsylvania. The Quaker as a social type was simply an exaggerated form of the Puritan as a social type. The effect of the wilderness in Pennsylvania was not much different than in New England or in the colonies on the Chesapeake. The proprietary system of land management only added a further dimension to the governmental and social problems which everywhere embroiled English colonists in the seventeenth century. Pennsylvania, however, differed from New England in its failure, in the first few decades, to develop a mechanism for ridding itself of its more strenuous malcontents. Though John Winthrop saw the splintering of the Massachusetts Bay Colony into "a hundred earnest little Utopias" as the most crucial problem he faced,[91] he unwittingly succeeded in maintaining a semblance of stability in the colony because he failed to keep the dissident elements within his fold. Pennsylvania, on the other hand, developed no art of casting out its malcontents or encouraging them to stake out settlements of their own farther to the west. Instead antagonistic factions within Pennsylvania society were allowed to remain in the colony and to resolve their differences as best they could.

[91] Morgan, *Puritan Dilemma*, 75.

CHAPTER 5

The Quest for Provincial Autonomy

WHILE political turbulence and religious disunity reached a climax on the Delaware, the Privy Council in London rescinded Penn's rights of government in Pennsylvania. For years Penn had warded off the blow, at first capitalizing on his influence at the Stuart court and later benefiting from the preoccupation of William III's government with the more pressing concerns of internal stability and foreign war. But the mushrooming conflict with France soon provided not only the incentive, but the necessity, of reorganizing colonial defenses—a process which had as its logical beginning the elimination of private charters. For the Quaker leaders of Pennsylvania, buffeted as they were by the internal struggles against Blackwell and Keith, the abrogation of Penn's charter represented an even greater danger, for it promised to obliterate Quaker polity—however strife-ridden—altogether. It was only after Pennsylvania fell under royal rule that the provincial leaders recognized that their fate was interwoven with the vicissitudes of English politics and that they badly needed the influence of William Penn at the center of English government. It was this precariousness of their position in a period of imperial reorganization and international war that created a new proprietary faction in Pennsylvania at the end of the seventeenth century. But at the same time, the backwash of two decades of civil and religious controversy, as well as new patterns of immigration, kept Pennsylvania in a state of political disequilibrium which even Penn's return to the colony in 1699 could not cure.

Imperial Reform

The desire at Whitehall to systematize and rationalize the imperial apparatus was far from new in the 1690's.[1] The grant of Penn's charter in 1681 had been in itself almost a contradiction of a colonial policy which had sought spasmodically since 1675 to bind the overseas possessions more firmly and profitably to England. But under proprietary government Pennsylvania had hardly been touched by attempts of the English government to modernize her colonial system. Laws seldom reached the Privy Council for approval as required by charter; the Navigation Acts were frequently ignored; and instructions in the early 1690's to put the colony on a wartime footing and to contribute to Fletcher's intercolonial military command centered at New York were met with a bland noncompliance which suggests how well the Quaker government knew the limits of the English government's ability to enforce her overseas policies. Imperial designs, like those of an absentee proprietor, commanded scant respect when the means of enforcement were barely visible.

By 1691 the situation had changed markedly. The global war with France convinced virtually everyone in London concerned with affairs of empire that the colonies, in both economic and strategic terms, were crucially important in the competition with France for trade and empire. Heretofore, a concern for regularity and discipline had inspired colonial reform; now nothing less than the fate of England's overseas possessions was at stake. Inspired by the critical nature of the colonial defense problem and also by recent reports from the Governor of Maryland that Pennsylvania

[1] A general treatment of imperial reform in the late seventeenth century is found in Andrews, *Colonial Period*, IV, 144-429.

merchants were trafficking with the French and with pro-French Indians, the Lords of Trade recommended on October 12, 1691 that Pennsylvania be placed under royal government and annexed to either New York or Maryland.[2] A full year passed before Captain Benjamin Fletcher, royal governor of New York, was commissioned to assume the government of Pennsylvania, and another six months elapsed before Fletcher arrived in Philadelphia to promulgate his commission—painful evidence of how slowly the wheels of empire turned in the seventeenth century.[3]

Fletcher's arrival in Philadelphia on April 26, 1693 was reminiscent of Blackwell's entrance little more than three years before. Although the Governor of New York came under the King's commission, not Penn's, he represented the same fundamental challenge to the power of the ruling Quakers. Fletcher was an Anglican and like Blackwell a military man, reason enough for immediate resentment among Quakers. But unlike Blackwell, Fletcher carried with him the full weight of royal authority, including the power to appoint a lieutenant governor and a council; to veto legislation passed by an elective assembly; to adjourn, prorogue, or dissolve legislative sessions; to appoint justices of the peace and provincial officers; and, with the "advice and consent" of his appointed council, to establish county and provincial courts. His letters of instruction, in effect, re-

[2] Gov. Francis Nicholson to the Lords of Trade, Jan. 26, 1690/91 and June 10, 1691, *CSP 1689-92*, #1302, 1583; Journal of the Lords of Trade, Oct. 12, 1691, extract in *ibid.*, #1820.

[3] Fletcher's commission and instructions from the Crown are in *Minutes of Council*, I, 345-364. The Privy Council's decision to put Pennsylvania under his governorship is recorded in W. L. Grant, ed., *Acts of the Privy Council of England, Colonial Series* (London, 1908-11), II, #437. The passage of Fletcher's commission through the bureaucratic machinery may be followed in *CSP 1689-92*, #2179, 2214, 2227, 2296, 2573.

placed Penn's Frame of Government, fashioned just ten years before. Additional powers permitted him to "levy, arme, muster, Command, and employ" all persons whatsoever for military duty, to build fortifications or defensive installations deemed necessary, and to exercise vice-admiralty jurisdiction in the colony.[4]

Fletcher did not come to Philadelphia unacquainted with the situation there or with a completely open mind about the Society of Friends. His military and Anglican background was enough to prejudice him against Quakers even before his arrival in New York and his attitudes could hardly have changed thereafter. His closest advisers in New York were Anglican merchants, who for years had been exhorting the Crown to stop illegal trade on the Delaware and to annex Pennsylvania to New York. Fletcher merely echoed such sentiments when he wrote to England in April 1693 that Pennsylvania was the bane of New York's existence, harboring her deserters, robbing her of trade, and paying not the slightest heed to the Acts of Navigation. Even as he wrote, Thomas Lloyd was politely informing the New York Governor that Pennsylvania could contribute neither men nor money to the intercolonial defense preparations going forward under Fletcher's direction.[5]

Once in Philadelphia, Fletcher moved swiftly to establish his authority. Thomas Lloyd was offered the first place in the Council. When he declined—a forewarning of the obstructionist policies which the ruling group was to follow—Fletcher set diplomacy aside and appointed nine opponents

[4] *Minutes of Council*, I, 352-357.

[5] Fletcher to Earl of Nottingham, as mentioned in minutes of the Committee of Trade and Plantations, June 12, 1693, in *N.Y. Colonial Documents*, IV, 31; Thomas Lloyd to Fletcher, March 27, 1693, *ibid.*, 35.

of Lloyd, five of them non-Quakers, to the Council.[6] Utilizing his appointive power, Fletcher completed the political upheaval by commissioning William Markham lieutenant governor, reinstalling John Claypoole, Lloyd's old opponent, as sheriff of Philadelphia County, and appointing in other counties wholly new slates of officers and justices, composed generally of men acceptable to the new anti-Lloydian councilors. On the new provincial bench sat Andrew Robeson, William Clarke, John Cann, William Salway, and Edward Blake—all merchant opponents of the dominant Quaker faction except Clarke.[7] A circle of officials more disaffected from the policies of Thomas Lloyd and Quakers of the upper echelon could hardly have been found.

The turnover of power, however objectionable to the Quaker leaders, gratified many. Those who endorsed the printed declaration of support for Fletcher represented about one-sixth of the freeholders of Philadelphia County. The Lower Counties, as might have been expected, warmly welcomed the Anglican governor when he journeyed downriver with William Markham to publish their commissions at New Castle. The ceremony, which marked a formal end

[6] *Minutes of Council*, I, 364-370, 378. Fletcher's account of Thomas Lloyd's obstructionism is in his letter to William Blathwayt, Aug. 18, 1693 (photostat), Manuscript Collection, New York Historical Society. The new councilors were Markham, George Foreman, John Cann, Patrick Robinson, Lasse Cock, William Salway, Andrew Robeson, William Clarke, and Robert Turner. Later, three other opponents of Lloyd were added: Griffith Jones, Charles Saunders, and John Donaldson.

[7] All appointments are in "A List of Officers appointed and Commissionated by His Excellency Ben: Fletcher Captain Generall and Governor in Chiefe of the Province of New Yorke . . . at Philadelphia, 26 April 1693," CO 5:1038/16v, Library of Congress transcripts. The religion of each appointee is given. Of 62 appointments, 17 went to Quakers. Lloyd's supporters were limited to 9 places, all on the county courts.

to what had long been construed as a domineering and self-interested Quaker regime, brought forth the "fireing of guns, great Shouting and joy."[8]

The ousted Quakers, old hands by now at oppositional politics, did not passively accept the new regime. Seven of the unseated councilors petitioned Fletcher to allow an elective Council as prescribed by the Frame of 1683. When this failed—it was in direct conflict with Fletcher's instructions from the Crown—the Lloydians embarked on a program of obstruction. Previous Quaker officeholders shunned such places as Fletcher offered them on the new county courts, unseated county clerks refused to yield up the court records to their successors, and the Quaker leaders, displaced in the Council, quickly moved to obtain seats in the new Assembly.[9]

Thereafter the game was the familiar one played against Blackwell: refuse to admit the governor's power until threatened with treason; stall for time; bargain for laws investing the Assembly with wider powers; narrow the scope of appointed officials and county courts; and word legislative acts so ambiguously that their meaning would be open to endless questioning. After two weeks of maneuvering with the wily Quaker Assembly, Fletcher had little to show for his efforts other than a modest money bill which was rendered harmless by the provisions that the lower house should supervise the assessment and collection of the tax in each county.[10] Returning to New York, Fletcher wrote to London that the Quaker leaders of Pennsylvania were doing "as much as in theire [power] . . . to baffell my endeaviors

[8] *The Address of Some of the Peaceable and Well Affected Freeholders* . . . (New York, 1693) ; *Minutes of Council,* I, 369.

[9] *Minutes of Council,* I, 371-372, 374-375, 378, 382, 387-388.

[10] *Minutes of Council,* I, 400-431; *Votes of Assembly,* I, 134-154; *Laws of Pennsylvania,* 222.

QUEST FOR PROVINCIAL AUTONOMY

... for theire Majesties service."[11] A year later, when he returned with fresh demands for money and men to support the war effort, Fletcher was thwarted again, though he promised that money granted by the Quaker Assembly would not be "dipt in blood" but used to feed and clothe destitute Indian allies.[12]

Aided by important connections at Whitehall and by his return to favor at the court of William III, Penn was able to obtain a restoration of his charter in 1694.[13] The decision was not entirely inconsistent with the new imperial thrust, for it was based on the recognition that Quaker cooperation in the defense of the middle colonies had failed dismally under the unpopular Fletcher and might better be obtained through a bargain with Penn. Thus Penn's rights of government were restored on the condition that he obtain full compliance with future requests for men and money and, if necessary, take personal charge in the colony.

Though rid of Governor Fletcher, the Quakers were by no means free of the incursions of imperial authority. In fact, the colony was only in the first stages of a struggle with Crown officials that would last for more than a decade. Prominent among their royal antagonists were two ambitious and determined colonial servants, Edward Randolph and Francis Nicholson, who for years had been matching wits with independent-minded English subjects in North America.

Neither Randolph nor Nicholson was destined for greatness in England. Both might have served out their lives

[11] Fletcher to the Secretary of State, Aug. 18, 1693, *N.Y. Colonial Documents*, IV, 52-53.

[12] *Votes of Assembly*, I, 157; *Minutes of Council*, I, 456-463.

[13] Letters patent restoring the government of Pennsylvania to Penn are in *ibid.*, 473-474. Penn's campaign to regain his government may be followed in *CSP 1693-96*, #1138, 1144, 1152, 1164, 1181, 1186-1188, 1213, 1238, 1251-1252.

187

there at some subsidiary level of government, blocked on the bureaucratic ladder for want of family connections or a high-placed patron. Restless and ambitious, both had sought appointments in the colonies—the field of opportunity for those willing to sacrifice the amenities of the more cultivated life in England. Since 1676 Randolph had functioned in the colonies as a sort of troubleshooter for the Crown. In 1691 his years of service were rewarded with appointment as Surveyor General of the Customs for North America. Nicholson came to America in command of a company of foot troops, assigned to Sir Edmund Andros, Governor of the Dominion of New England. Thereafter he had served as lieutenant governor in both New York and Virginia and in 1693 had obtained the governorship of Maryland.[14] Both men were Anglicans with little sympathy for nonconformity, religious or otherwise, and both pursued their jobs with a compulsive vigor that suggested their chronic resentment of the disobedient colonial subjects among whom they were forced to live for the sake of professional advancement. Randolph boasted "that he had lived five and twenty years on the curses of the people," wrote the Governor of Maryland in 1692.[15]

Throughout the 1690's Randolph and Nicholson made periodic trips through Pennsylvania, gathering evidence

[14] Randolph's role in imperial reorganization is perceptively studied by Michael G. Hall, *Edward Randolph and the American Colonies, 1676-1703* (Chapel Hill, N.C., 1960). Nicholson's early career is detailed by Bruce T. McCully, "From the North Riding to Morocco: The Early Years of Governor Francis Nicholson," *William and Mary Quarterly*, 3rd Ser., 19 (1962), 534-556. An excellent analysis of Nicholson's approach to colonial government is given by Stephen S. Webb, "The Strange Career of Francis Nicholson," *William and Mary Quarterly*, 3rd Ser., 23 (1966), 513-548.

[15] Gov. Lionel Copley to the Lords of Trade, July 29, 1692, *CSP 1689-92*, #2370.

for reports to London. Little they saw pleased them. Philadelphia and New Castle, they charged, were centers of illegal trade and notorious refuges for pirates. Maryland tobacco streamed into the colony where it evaded the King's customs, and was then illegally shipped to Scotland. European vessels traded freely on the Delaware. And when a seizure for violation of the Navigation Acts was made—a rarity—colonial judges and juries refused to convict.[16]

By early 1696 the efforts of Randolph, Nicholson, and others concerned with colonial administration began to bear fruit. Awakened to the cost of illegal trade—the Customs Commissioners estimated it robbed the Crown of £50,000 in 1694—and to the necessity of securing colonial compliance with laws of the realm, Parliament passed a new Navigation Act designed to extend and coordinate the authority of the Crown in the colonies. The heart of the act provided for the establishment of vice-admiralty courts in the colonies which would have jurisdiction over legal actions involving violations of the trade acts. By another provision, appointment of governors in proprietary colonies would require endorsement by Whitehall—an attempt, as Randolph later wrote, "to bring the Governments of Proprietys to a dependence on the Crown."[17]

16 Randolph to the Commissioners of Customs, June 27, 1692, Robert N. Toppan and A.T.S. Goodrick, *Edward Randolph: Including His Letters and Official Papers . . . 1676-1703* (Boston, 1898-1909), VII, 356-372; Randolph to William Blathwayt, Aug. 16, 1692 and May 18, 1694, *ibid.*, VII, 398-399, 462; "Account of severall things whereby illegall Trade is encouraged in Virginia Maryland and Pennsylvania . . . ," *ibid.*, V, 117-124; Nicholson to the Duke of Shrewsbury, June 14, 1695, *CSP 1693-96*, #1897; same to Lords of Trade, June 14, 1695, CO 5/713, Library of Congress transcripts.

17 Randolph to William Blathwayt, Aug. 25, 1698, quoted in Hall, *Randolph*, 165; see *ibid.*, 156-165, for a thorough discussion of the evolution of the Navigation Act of 1696. The establishment of the vice-

Protracted debate over the issue of illegal trade and the establishment of vice-admiralty courts, involving the colonial proprietors, the Commissioners of Customs, the newly established Board of Trade, the Attorney General of England, and the House of Lords, awakened many to the degree of autonomy which proprietary and charter colonies in North America had gained. Randolph's crusade had opened Pandora's box. By February 1697, the House of Lords had decided to take up the whole issue of colonial trade. Unfortunately for Penn and the merchants of Pennsylvania, the discussion centered on the Quaker colony, perhaps through the design of Randolph or possibly because of the general concern with governmental instability there.[18]

With Randolph acting as chief informant, the Lords' examination of Pennsylvania "took on the aspect of a trial at law."[19] Aided by detailed letters from Governor Nicholson, Randolph presented massive evidence of Pennsylvania's complicity in illegal trade: the Navigation Acts were continually flaunted; hostile juries refused to convict illicit traders; Penn's attorney general, far from prosecuting the King's cause, pled against the Crown; pirates streamed into Pennsylvania from South Carolina and received pardons or papers of naturalization from the governor, who, with his two merchant assistants, did all in his power to thwart the enforcement of the acts of trade; Patrick Robinson, a Scots-

admiralty courts is treated in Helen J. Crump, *Colonial Admiralty Jurisdiction in the Seventeenth Century* (London, 1931).

[18] Hall, *Randolph*, 166-173; Peter Laslett adds new details on the establishment of the Board of Trade in "John Locke, the Great Recoinage Act, and the Origins of the Board of Trade, 1695-1698," *William and Mary Quarterly*, 3rd Ser., 14 (1957), 370-402.

[19] Hall, *Randolph*, 173.

man and Secretary of Council, aided the Scottish merchants, who were notorious offenders of the trade acts.[20]

Penn made a spirited defense in the face of Randolph's carefully collected evidence, denying some of the charges, upholding the integrity of his government, and attempting to shift the blame by suggesting that incompetence within the customs service was at the root of colonial evasion of the Navigation Acts.[21] Penn, of course, was simply putting the best possible face on a plainly difficult situation. It was Pennsylvania's misfortune to be examined for an irregular trade that flourished in every colony, both on the mainland and in the West Indies. As evidence of his own attachment to the interests of England, Penn offered the Lords his own program for more effective regulation of trade.[22]

By promising immediate reform, Penn was able to stave off further action against his government for the moment. But the Lords reminded him that further complaints against proprietary governments would cause Parliament to take "another course in this matter, which will be less pleasing

[20] Minutes of the Lords' hearings are in *The Manuscripts of the House of Lords, 1698-1714*, New Series (London, 1900-62), II, 410-414 (cited hereafter as *H. of L.*). The evidence presented by Randolph and Penn's defense is in *ibid.*, 446-472, 501-504. Many of the charges made by Randolph are elaborated in his letters to various agencies of government concerned with colonial affairs; see Toppan, *Randolph*, V, 125-130, 135-136, 143, 151-160; BT Plantations, IV, Pt. 2, 123 i.

[21] "Mr. Penn's Answer to Mr. Randolph . . . ," Toppan, *Randolph*, VII, 508-510.

[22] "An Expedient against Fraud . . . ," *H. of L.*, II, 490-491; Penn's plan involved what he considered a foolproof system of certificates of lading backed by security bonds. As the Commissioners of Customs indicated, his proposals differed only in detail from the system already in use. The enforcement of the Navigation Acts proved impossible, as the Commissioners pointed out, not because of mechanical flaws in the system, but because common law juries, attorneys general, and even colonial governors shirked their duty in supporting the Crown. See *ibid.*, 491-494.

to them."[23] Penn lost no time after this rebuke in chastising the colonial merchants; the reports of Randolph and Nicholson, he warned, had done great damage to Pennsylvania and the Quakers. Steps must be taken immediately or the colony would again be placed under royal government.[24]

In the closing years of the seventeenth century the English movement to bring the American colonies within the pale of a coordinated and disciplined imperial system continued to threaten Quaker autonomy. Edward Randolph returned to the colonies in December 1697 to direct a revitalized and remanned customs service backed by vice-admiralty courts; and within a few months he set out for Philadelphia "spoiling for a fight," as his biographer relates. Penn had cautioned him that at any further "dust and malice" raised against Pennsylvania he would "fling away [his] scabbard" and use his influence at court to undermine Randolph's position.[25] But Randolph had not forgotten the unhospitable receptions which Philadelphia Quakers had provided for him on earlier trips through Pennsylvania and he was eager now to repay the Quakers.[26]

When Randolph arrived in Philadelphia, he found noth-

[23] Minutes of the Committee hearings, March 11, 1696/97, *ibid.*, 414.

[24] Penn to Council, Sept. 5, 1697, *Minutes of Council*, I, 527; Penn to Carpenter, Simcock, Lloyd, et al., Dec. 1, 1697, Quaker Collection, Haverford College Library, Haverford, Pa.

[25] Hall, *Randolph*, 179; Penn to Randolph, Oct. 16, 1697, Ellesmere MSS, Henry E. Huntington Library, San Marino, Calif.

[26] In 1695 the Quaker magistrates had arrested Randolph and jailed him in Philadelphia. Toppan, *Randolph*, v, 114-116. For two months prior to his arrival in Philadelphia, Randolph had sojourned in Annapolis, Maryland with Governor Nicholson, who welcomed the opportunity to join in an attack on the Quaker colony. For indications of the close coordination between the two men see Nicholson to Earl of Bridgewater, June 30, 1697 and Penn to Nicholson, Nov. 22, 1697, Huntington Library, San Marino, Calif.

ing to convince him that Pennsylvania had changed during his absence in England. There were widespread reports that Markham and the merchants of Philadelphia harbored members of the piratical crew of Henry Avery, one of the most notorious and widely sought buccaneers in North American waters. The legislature virtually asserted its independence from the Crown by omitting from colonial laws the customary preface acknowledging the English monarch as "their sovereign Lord and King." Both Attorney General David Lloyd and Governor Markham refused to cooperate in prosecuting plantation bonds of Pennsylvania merchants forfeited for failure to deliver cargoes in England as pledged. In his determination to thwart the enforcement of the trade acts, the Governor had adjourned the courts for six months, Randolph reported, and refused to replace Lloyd with an attorney general who would prosecute for the King.[27]

Among merchants and those dependent upon them, the arrival of Randolph as the chief agent of the new, more forceful colonial policy caused grave concern. It was only a question of time until the vice-admiralty court would be established at Philadelphia to implement the Navigation Acts. And the "huffing and bouncing" Randolph, as Markham described him, was obviously impatient to bring business to the new prerogative court as soon as it was established. Even more alarming, the Surveyor General had re-

[27] Randolph to the Board of Trade, April 26, 1698, and to William Popple, April 25, 1698, Toppan, *Randolph*, v, 173-174, 169-171; Randolph to Popple, May 12, 1698, *CSP 1697-98*, #451; Randolph, "Narrative of his Survey in the Plantations . . . of America . . . ," Nov. 5, 1700, Toppan, *Randolph*, v, 213-219. For the complicity of the Pennsylvania government in harboring pirates see *Maryland Archives*, xxv, 553-594; Robert Turner to Penn, June 26, 1697, Dreer Collection, Penn Letters, 72; Penn to Samuel Carpenter, John Simcock, et al., Dec. 1, 1697, Quaker Collection, Haverford College Library.

fused to accept the Quakers' attestation of allegiance to the Crown in lieu of an oath of loyalty required by all ship owners under the new Navigation Act. If Randolph should be upheld in this decision, Quaker merchants would be ruined overnight.[28]

Although they faced no less a power than the English government, the provincial leaders accepted Randolph's challenge with as little hesitation as they had shown in battling Penn, Blackwell, Fletcher, or Markham. At first the Quakers attempted to deflect Randolph's charges by indicating Pennsylvania's faithful adherence to English laws. The Council issued a report blandly denying any knowledge of illegal trade. A proclamation against illicit trade and the harboring of pirates was promulgated.[29] And at Markham's urging, the General Assembly passed "An Act for Preventing Frauds and Regulating Abuses in Trade" which, under the guise of implementing the Navigation Act of 1696, provided for the trial of all alleged violations of the trade acts "according to the course of the Common Law . . . within this government by twelve lawful men of the neighborhood, where the offence is Committed."[30] The effect of this provision, however, was to authorize precisely what the Navigation Act of 1696 had been devised to prevent—the trial of illegal traders before local common law juries. Ingeniously, the Pennsylvanians had found a loophole in the loosely written English law, which, as one of the vice-admiralty judges admitted, was a "dark contradictory Act."[31]

28 Markham to Penn, April 24, 1697, *CSP 1697-98*, #76xiv; Randolph to Popple, April 25, 1698, Toppan, *Randolph*, v, 169-171.

29 *Minutes of Council*, I, 528-530.

30 *Laws of Pennsylvania*, 272; another provision permitted Quaker shipowners to sign an attestation or affirmation of allegiance in place of the objectionable oath required by the English Act of 1696.

31 Robert Quary to Lords of Admiralty, March 6, 1699/1700, *H. of L.*, IV, 326.

There is little doubt that it was David Lloyd, a trained law-yer, who noticed the provision that trade violations could be heard in any "Colony province County precinct or Divi-sion of any of the plantations at the pleasure of the officer or informer." Lloyd and the leading merchants of Phila-delphia asserted that this justified a supplementary pro-vincial law allowing the trial of such cases before local com-mon law juries.[32]

Two months after the Pennsylvania trade act was passed, Randolph was back in Philadelphia, this time joined by a man who would plague the Quaker merchants for more than a decade to come—Robert Quary. A staunch Anglican, Quary had served as Secretary of Council and briefly as Dep-uty Governor in South Carolina in the 1680's. Randolph had encountered him during his previous service as Surveyor General of Customs and in 1697 had proposed the Carolin-ian as judge of the vice-admiralty court for Maryland, Penn-sylvania, and West Jersey. Like so many others in the colonies, Quary had mixed his trade with politics. The mer-chants prominent in the New Pennsylvania Company were among his contacts in London, and when he arrived in Phil-adelphia in July 1698, he came not only as vice-admiralty judge but also as factor for the Company. Possibly Penn had helped in procuring the position for Quary in the hope of building up credit with a man whose judicial appointment would be of great consequence to the merchants of his col-

[32] Lokken, *David Lloyd*, 79-82. Lloyd, Samuel Carpenter, and Ed-ward Shippen defended the common law trials authorized by the Pennsylvania Act of Trade in a letter to Penn dated July 4, 1698 in Norris Papers, Family Letters, I, 112. The General Assembly also justi-fied the act in a message to the King, May 1698, BT, Proprieties, II, B. 18.1.

ony. If that was so, Penn was soon to be sorely disappointed.[33]

Neither Quary nor Randolph, upon arrival in Philadelphia, failed to see the implications of the Pennsylvania trade act. Quary hesitated to establish his court at all since he deemed his authority, in effect, already superseded. "My hands are tied," he wrote to Governor Nicholson, "for I cannot allow trial by jury, nor by this law [the Pennsylvania trade act] can they suffer the Court to try without a jury."[34] Randolph wrote heatedly that the "sham law had utterly destroyed the design and intent of the Act for Preventing Frauds" and pointed out that by another clause, which made customs collectors who detained a ship more than one tide liable for triple damages if they lost their case in court, the collectors' work was made all but impossible.[35] Governor Nicholson, who exercised overall vice-admiralty jurisdiction for the Chesapeake and Delaware bays, echoed Randolph's complaints that the Pennsylvania Act of Trade was only a pretense "of securing the King's interest." The provision for imposing provincial fines on illegal traders was only "grass to hide their snake," for a common law jury would rarely, if ever, render a conviction. "I have observed," concluded Nicholson revealingly, "that a great many people in

[33] For Quary's career in the Carolinas see M. Eugene Sirmans, "Politics in Colonial South Carolina: The Failure of Proprietary Reform, 1682-1694," *William and Mary Quarterly*, 3rd Ser., 23 (1966), 33-55.

[34] Quary to Nicholson, July 9, 1698, *CSP 1697-98*, #760v; see also Quary to the Board of Trade, Aug. 25, and Sept. 6, 1698, *ibid.*, #772, #796. Quary was doubly hindered by the ineffectiveness of the other officers of the court. The Register, as he wrote, lived a hundred miles away; the Marshall was all but crippled; and the advocate—"the Essential Officer of the Court"—had no intention of emigrating from England where he had procured the position as a sinecure. See Quary to Board of Trade, Aug. 25, 1698, *ibid.*, #772.

[35] Randolph to the Board of Trade, Aug. 25, 1698, Toppan, *Randolph*, v, 189-191.

these Colonies, especially under proprietors and in Connecticut and Rhode Island, think that no law of England ought to bind them without their own consent; for they foolishly say that they have no representative sent from themselves to the Parliament in England, and they look upon all laws made in England, that put any restraint upon them, as great hardships."[36]

Though the Quaker leaders could parry royal officials in Pennsylvania blow for blow, they could not stop the damaging flow of reports to London. Quary complained angrily that "the King's interest was never so much abused" and reported that even Edward Shippen, a former Speaker of the Assembly, was engaged in illegal trade, while at New Castle the King's collector connived openly with merchants. "They doe what they please, and your officers must take what the Merchants will give them," wrote the exasperated Randolph.[37] Casting caution to the wind, David Lloyd, the Attorney General of the colony, had argued that the vice-admiralty court being established at Philadelphia was illegal, and railed before the Council that anyone who aided or encouraged the court was a greater enemy to the "liberties and priviledges of the people than those that established and promoted ship monie in King Charles the first's time."[38] Emboldened by this kind of defiant bluster and by the conviction that Penn's return to a place of favor at the court of William III would shield them from royal interference, leading merchants in Pennsylvania went so far as to claim that the King's only function on the Delaware was "to re-

[36] Nicholson to the Board of Trade, Aug. 20, 1698, *Maryland Archives*, XXIII, 488-503.

[37] Quary to Nicholson, July 21, 1698, *CSP 1697-98*, #760v; Randolph to the Commissioners of Customs, Aug. 8, 1698, BT, Proprieties, III, C.26 #2.

[38] *Minutes of Council*, I, 603-604.

ceive a bear skin or two yearly" and that the laws of England reached no farther than the boundaries of the mother country.[39]

By the summer of 1699 the torrent of complaints about insubordination and noncompliance in Pennsylvania, penned by Quary, Randolph, Nicholson, and officers of the vice-admiralty court at Philadelphia, began to take effect. The Board of Trade sent a detailed report to the Lord Justices, cataloguing abuses of imperial policy in Pennsylvania.[40] The Privy Council responded promptly by voiding the Pennsylvania Act of Trade and ordering Penn to remove William Markham and David Lloyd from office.[41] Even more important Penn was brought to believe that only by returning to his colony and personally implementing Crown policy could he preserve his charter.

Penn's Return

While servants of the Crown denounced Pennsylvania following the restoration of Penn's charter in 1694, the old Quaker alliance quickly reassumed control of the levers of government. The task was no longer complicated by a reassertion of proprietary authority, for Penn's letters of previous years, alternately conciliatory and threatening, came no more. By now the proprietor was a changed man. Years and events had crowded in on him, dulling his earlier optimism, tempering his utopian zeal. For four years, from

[39] Robert Suder to Governor [Nicholson?], Nov. 20, 1698, in William S. Perry, ed., *Papers Relating to the History of the Church in Pennsylvania, 1680-1778* (n.p., 1871), 11; Quary to the Board of Trade, May 18, 1699, *CSP 1699*, #426.

[40] Board of Trade to the Lord Justices, Aug. 4, 1699, *CSP 1699*, #694.

[41] Privy Council to Penn, Sept. 12, 1699, Penn Papers, Official Correspondence, I, 17.

1690 to 1694, he had suffered harassment at the hands of a government whose suspicions of him were reawakened at every new Jacobite threat. War brought chaos and depression to his Irish estates on which he depended for income. His wife died in February 1694. Philip Ford, his secretary for twenty years, began a notorious campaign to collect staggering debts which he claimed Penn owed him. His decade-long effort to achieve stability in Pennsylvania and to obtain compliance with proprietary policy had failed dismally. And finally, beset by political and religious fragmentation, the government of Pennsylvania had been taken from him altogether. "I am a man of sorrows," he wrote poignantly in 1694.[42]

A realist through bitter experience, Penn now conceded the colony virtual autonomy and refrained from mentioning quitrents, customs, the settling of land, or perversions of the Frame of 1683. A decade of frustration had convinced him that reform, if possible at all, must await his return to Pennsylvania. For the moment his concern was only to ensure adherence to the conditions upon which his rights of government had been restored.

Penn's commission to William Markham as lieutenant governor and the Crown instructions ending Fletcher's authority arrived in Philadelphia in late March 1695. Markham was to govern with the "advice and consent" of two assistants, Samuel Carpenter and John Goodson. Presumably Penn intended his colonists to return to the Frame of 1683 when he commanded that "the charter be strictly observed." Unfortunately, whether "charter" referred to the King's initial charter to Penn or to the Frame of Govern-

---

[42] Peare, *William Penn*, 313-332; Braithwaite, *Second Period of Quakerism*, 151-175.

ment, frequently spoken of as the "charter," nobody could say with certainty.[43]

The ambiguity of Penn's instructions deprived Markham of the unequivocal authority he so badly needed to reconstitute the government on the basis of the Frame of 1683, as he discovered when new elections for the Council and Assembly were held in March 1695. David Lloyd, who had become the Quakers' chief spokesman following the death of Thomas Lloyd in 1694, warned that there was no special virtue in returning to the Frame of 1683 and called for a "new modelling" of government. What Lloyd and his followers projected was a charter which guaranteed the Assembly a controlling role in political affairs. At a minimum the rights of the Assembly would include sole power to initiate legislation and the right to sit on its own adjournment, judge the qualifications of its members, regulate its own affairs, and meet in closed session.[44]

This effort to shift the center of political gravity from the Council to the Assembly was strikingly different from earlier quests by the lower house for a larger role in the political process. The struggles of the 1680's had involved the ambitious attempts of a coterie of lesser landowners, merchants, and shopkeepers to challenge their political superiors. The movement of the mid-1690's by contrast, was the work of

[43] The commissions to Markham, Carpenter, and Goodson are in *Minutes of Council*, I, 474-475; Penn to Friends and Brethern, Nov. 24, 1694, *HSP Memoirs*, III, Pt. 1, 288.

[44] *Minutes of Council*, I, 482-484. In 1693 Quaker leaders had drafted proposals for a new constitutional system. Although David Lloyd and three other Quakers were commissioned by the Quaker community to confer directly with Penn, the danger of an ocean crossing during time of war apparently postponed the mission. The 1693 proposals are in Norris Papers, Family Letters, I, 122. Gov. Fletcher reported the intended mission to William Blathwayt in a letter of Aug. 18, 1693 (photostat), Manuscript Collection, New York Historical Society.

the ranking Quakers of the province, the very men who had controlled the Council a decade before, just as they did now. Deliberately they sought to diminish the power of the Council and to deliver control of the legislative process to the stronghold of their former competitors. Such tactics, so contradictory at first glance, were closely reasoned. The governments of Blackwell and Fletcher had convinced men at the top of provincial society that the lower house was far less susceptible to proprietary or royal control than the Council, and was a far more defensible bastion of provincial autonomy. Whereas the Council might be appointed under a royal governor—and some said under Penn as well, if he chose—the Assembly would always be elected. Leading Pennsylvanians understood that with Penn's charter under heavy attack by neighboring governors and Crown officials, the reestablishment of royal government was highly possible —even probable. Far better that the lower house be invested with the widest possible powers in advance of such a change. If the Council remained elective, the leading Quakers had little reason to doubt that they could dominate both houses; if it did not, they could operate from the Assembly, which they had controlled since the governorship of John Blackwell.

Lieutenant Governor Markham was far from receptive to the proposed change in government. Neither were the delegates from the Lower Counties, who had rejoined the province in legislative matters after the reinstatement of Penn's rights of government. To both Markham and the Lower Counties the need to comply with Governor Fletcher's repeated requests for military assistance dwarfed the necessity of reorganizing government. The orders from London to contribute to defensive preparations, if ignored,

Markham warned, "may prove verie fatall to us all."[45] At the same time, recognizing the Quakers' scruples against appropriating money for military preparations, Markham sweetened the cake by hinting that once the money bill was passed a discussion of constitutional revision would not be inappropriate.[46] The Assembly responded cagily by passing two bills, neatly linked, for Markham's approval. The first appropriated funds for both the war effort and his salary, although the Crown's call for the contribution of a militia unit was ignored. The second bill, entitled "An Act of Settlement," was nothing less than a wholly new frame of government.[47] By its provisions the Council would be pared to two members per county and the Assembly to four, thus reducing the overall representation by half. The franchise was altered to exclude those not resident in the colony for a year, suggesting an attempt to diminish the strength of the sizable number of non-Quakers migrating to the colony from New York and Maryland. In addition, the rural qualification for the vote was relaxed to include all freeholders with 50 acres rather than 100 acres as before. But the urban requirement was stiffened to exclude anyone without a £50 estate free of debts, whereas before only the payment of scot and lot (a municipal householder's tax paid by virtually

45 *Minutes of Council*, I, 485-488; among the Council members who pressed for a transfer of legislative power were Samuel Carpenter, Samuel Richardson, Anthony Morris, Joseph Growdon, Phineas Pemberton, William Biles, David Lloyd, Caleb Pusey, and George Maris— all prominent leaders of Quaker society.

46 *Votes of Assembly*, I, 178-181; *Minutes of Council*, I, 489, 505.

47 *Ibid.*, 489-491; *Votes of Assembly*, I, 181. A draft of the Act of Settlement is in CO 5/1233, Library of Congress transcripts. According to the Council minutes, the appropriation was simply "for the support of government." But in a letter to Fletcher, dated May 26, 1696, Markham revealed that the Quakers would contribute £200 to the war effort if their new form of government was approved. Letter in *CSP 1696-97*, #27xi.

every free white adult male) had been required. Like the residency requirement, the new property qualifications were apparently designed to swell the rural Quaker vote while cutting back the urban—and increasingly non-Quaker—vote.[48] No less important, the act conferred upon the Assembly the power to initiate legislation, sit on its own adjournment, and judge the qualifications of its members.

The ease with which the two bills passed both houses of the General Assembly indicated the sway which the leading Quakers now held in both the Council and Assembly. But Markham was far from satisfied with the dual bill. "You have delivered mee these two bills together," he charged, "as if you want to tack them soe the one to the other, as that I must pass both or neither." When the Assembly failed to pass the money bill separately, Markham adjourned the legislature for the year.[49]

Although Pennsylvania was not alone in defying royal instructions to contribute to defensive efforts—Fletcher had as much difficulty with Connecticut, Massachusetts, and Rhode Island—the Quaker leaders were playing a dangerous game. Even Penn was convinced that they were invoking religious principles simply to protect their pocketbooks. Aware how precariously his charter hung in the balance, he adjured the Council to "stand up" to the colony's obliga-

[48] Quakers composed a decreasing proportion of Philadelphia society in the 1690's. Isaac Norris, writing in November 1699, estimated that of 220 persons who had recently succumbed to a yellow fever epidemic, about eighty to ninety were Quakers—suggesting a population about 40 percent Quaker. See Isaac Norris to John ———, Nov. 22, 1699, Norris Letter Book (1699-1701). Of 511 deaths recorded in Philadelphia between 1692 and 1700, 216 (42.3 percent) were Quakers. See also Quaker deaths given in Hinshaw, ed., *Encyclopedia of Quaker Genealogy*, II, 331-440, and "An Account of the Burialls of such as not Friends within this town of Philadelphia . . . ," *ibid.*, 441-449.

[49] *Minutes of Council*, I, 494-495.

[50] The proprietor's fears were well grounded, for Gov-Fletcher, in vehement letters home, was complaining that Pennsylvania sent "neither one man nor one penny" for his use. In 1696, after Markham informed him that nothing could be obtained from the General Assembly without a concurrent change of government, Fletcher wrote the Lords of Trade that it was manifestly clear that the Quakers had "as little regard for the interest of their proprietor Mr. Penn as they have for His Majesty's service."[51]

A fifteen-year veteran of the political wars in Pennsylvania, Markham recognized that it was Penn who was most immediately endangered by the standoff with the General Assembly, for his charter had been restored on the condition that his colony comply with the requirements of empire. Convinced that the raising of men and money was vital to the protection of Penn's rights of government, Markham yielded in 1696 to the bargain he had scorned a year before. If the Assembly would pass a military appropriations bill, he promised, a new frame of government would be allowed.[52]

The compromise was quickly effected. The Assembly passed a new model of government, known as the Frame of 1696, which differed only in detail from the proposals of a year before. Coupled with it was a bill raising £300 for

[50] Penn to Council, Nov. 5, 1695, Parrish Collection, Proud Papers, I, 39. Fletcher's difficulties in raising intercolonial forces are described in James S. Leamon, "Governor Fletcher's Recall," *William and Mary Quarterly*, 3rd Ser., 20 (1963), 527-542.

[51] Fletcher to Lords of Trade, May 30, 1696; to William Blathwayt, May 30, 1696; and to Lords of Trade, June 10, 1696, *N.Y. Colonial Documents*, IV, 150, 157-159.

[52] *Minutes of Council*, I, 505-507. Markham even attempted for a few months to assume powers of government equivalent to those exercised by the royal governor in New York, but he gave up this expedient in the face of stiff opposition from the Quaker leaders. *Ibid.*, I, 495-505.

Governor Fletcher's use.[53] It was a victory not only for colonial autonomy but for the Quaker elite as well. Hereafter, each county elected only two representatives to the Council and four to the Assembly, a more manageable number than before. The new property requirements did much to pare the political influence of the swelling non-Quaker population, as did the revised residency provision, now raised to two years. The power to initiate legislation and to sit on its own adjournment belonged at last to the Assembly. Far from representing "the complete recognition of the supremacy of the popular will," as one historian has described it, the Frame of 1696 represented a conscious tightening of the reins of power by the most affluent and powerful segment of provincial society.[54]

Although the dominant Quakers had outmatched Markham, they could never really unify Pennsylvania society in the closing years of the seventeenth century. Time had not yet erased the rancor within Keith's circle, though Keith himself had returned to England in 1694; the merchant-planters of the Lower Counties remained chronically alienated from their northern neighbors; and, if Governor Nicholson can be believed, "great heat and animosities" still kept the Quaker community off balance.[55] Even more threatening to the Quakers in power was the steady drift of Anglicans into Pennsylvania in the 1690's. In 1695 Christ Church rose proudly in the heart of bustling Philadelphia—an in-

[53] Ibid., I, 507-509; Votes of Assembly, I, 185-194.

[54] Shepherd, Proprietary Government in Pennsylvania, 284. The Frame of 1696 and the money bill are in Laws of Pennsylvania, 245-256. The new articles of government, as first submitted to Markham, included a residency requirement of three years. At the Governor's insistence this was reduced to two years. Minutes of Council, I, 508.

[55] Nicholson to the Duke of Shrewsbury, June 14, 1695, CSP 1693-96, #1897. The after-effects of the Keithian schism are considered in Kirby, George Keith, 91-94.

eradicable reminder to Friends of the changes overtaking their colony. For the Anglicans it was the fulfillment of visions dating back to 1681, when, through the influence of the Bishop of London, a clause had been included in Penn's charter providing for an Anglican chaplain in the colony whenever settlers there requested one. For years Quakers had anxiously watched the growth of the Anglican and non-Quaker community, a trend accelerated when the end of Anglo-French hostilities in 1697 freed the seas and consequently swelled the flow of immigration to Pennsylvania. The fact that the new settlers were preponderantly non-Quaker seemed to indicate that among the Friends in England, who had never amounted to more than a tiny fraction of the population, the inclination to leave the Old World had been virtually exhausted. By 1698 more than a few of the important merchants supported the Anglican Church, as did Robert Quary and John Moore of the vice-admiralty court and Governor Markham, a life-long Anglican.[56] Though still outnumbered, the Anglicans seemed to be gaining disproportionate influence in the province.

The character of the new immigration made Quaker leaders tremble at the prospect of engulfment by a church that for decades had persecuted Friends in England. The Anglicans were not altogether mistaken when they charged that Quakers did everything in their power to emasculate them politically. The Frame of 1696, with its stricter property requirements for city dwellers and two-year residency qualification, was an obvious attempt to keep the new immi-

[56] The general background of the Restoration policy of the Anglican Church in the colonies is described by Philip S. Haffenden, "The Anglican Church in Restoration Colonial Policy," Smith, ed., *Seventeenth-Century America*, 166-191. For the early history of the Anglican Church in Philadelphia see Keith, *Chronicles of Pennsylvania* I, 327-366.

grants, who congregated in Philadelphia, from the polls. Angered by this, the Anglicans joined Robert Turner's faction in 1697 to protest this alteration of government without the required consent of the proprietor and six-sevenths of the General Assembly. As Quakers went to the polls in March of that year to elect representatives under the new articles of government, Turner and the Anglicans staged elections of their own in the city and county of Philadelphia under the provisions of the superseded Frame of 1683.[57]

Hypersensitive to the attacks of neighboring governors and Crown agents, the leading Friends, according to their critics, became intolerant and tyrannical in their use of office. They maligned their former colleague, Arthur Cooke, who had joined Turner's opposition faction in 1696; they intercepted mail to Turner and his supporters; they concealed Penn's letters of instruction when they ran counter to their designs; and, instead of unifying the various interests of an increasingly pluralistic society, they excluded all non-Quakers from political office.[58] Even the right of petition was denied the Anglicans in 1698 when a remonstrance to the King for the "free exercise of our Religion and Arms for our Defense" was suppressed by Quaker magistrates on the grounds that it violated a law prohibiting inflammatory

[57] An account of the separate election engineered by the Turnerian faction is given in Turner, Francis Rawle, Arthur Cooke, Griffith Jones, and Joseph Wilcox to Penn, April 9, 1697, Hazard, ed., *Register*, 6 (1830), 257. Elected to the Council were Cooke, Joshua Carpenter (an Anglican), and Samuel Carpenter, his brother; elected to the Assembly were Turner, Joseph Fisher, Joseph Wilcox, Joseph Ashton (all Quakers but also Keithians and previous political opponents of Thomas Lloyd); Toby Leech (an Anglican); and Andreas Bankson (a Swede). A remonstrance to Penn decrying the Frame of 1696 is in Society Miscellaneous Collection, Petitions.

[58] Turner, Cooke, Rawle, Wilcox, and Jones to Penn, April 9, 1697, Hazard, ed., *Register*, 6 (1830), 257; Turner to Penn, April 15, 1697, Society Miscellaneous Collection.

criticism of the government. In Quaker courts, the Church-men avowed, the word of an African slave was more acceptable than that of an Anglican.[59] "Oh, that ever it should be written, if not printed," Robert Turner wrote Penn, "the loud Cry of Oppression from Philadelphia . . . the love of the brethren now persecuting . . . one the other, which is beyond the persecution in New England. . . . Let the Quakery in Pensil-vania and Philadelphia have a care lest custom harden them also. . . . Persecution is the hate of a falling Church."[60]

The colony to which Penn returned in December 1699 bore but slight resemblance to the infant society he had left in 1684. The population had increased almost fourfold, now numbering about 15,000. Philadelphia, the colony's empo-rium, had already overtaken New York as the second largest city in British North America.[61] Throughout the 1690's a steady stream of families—the laments of the governors of New York and Maryland testified to this—had drifted into Pennsylvania from neighboring colonies, seeking relief from militia duty and high taxes. And following the Peace of Ryswick, which ended King William's War in 1697, nearly every outgoing ship from England bound for Pennsylvania brought its human cargo. Provincial merchants and plant-ers still knew little of the cultivated country estates, polished coaches, and imported luxuries that a later generation would display, but there was an air of moderate if unspec-

[59] Robert Suder to Francis Nicholson, Nov. 20, 1698, in Perry, ed., *History of the Church in Pennsylvania*, 9-12.

[60] Turner to Penn, April 15, 1697, Society Miscellaneous Collection; Turner to Penn, June 26, 1697, Dreer Collection, Penn Letters, 72.

[61] Greene and Harrington, *American Population*, 114, 117; Carl Bridenbaugh, *Cities in the Wilderness; the First Century of Urban Life in America, 1625-1742* (2nd edn., New York, 1955), 6; Robert Quary's estimate of "upwards of 7000 men" capable of bearing arms in 1699, suggesting a population of 35,000, is clearly excessive. See Quary to the Board of Trade, June 1, 1699, *CSP 1699*, #483.

tacular prosperity that struck all who visited the province. Benjamin Bullivant, a prominent Anglican from Massachusetts, recorded his impression in 1697 of "a very magnificent City," with some stately dwellings belonging to the most affluent merchants and a building boom in progress. "If anyone were to see Philadelphia who had not been there [before]," wrote the city's Swedish minister in 1700, "he would be astonished beyond measure that it was founded less than twenty years ago." A newly arrived merchant from Jamaica, Jonathan Dickinson, noted in the same year that Philadelphia was "so thronged with people that there is hardly a house Empty and rents grow high."[62]

But in its political affairs, Penn found the colony as divided as when he had departed in 1684. In both city and country the majority of Quakers were content to follow the entrenched Quaker leaders, foremost of whom was David Lloyd—the "chief Director in the Government" by

[62] For the magnetic influence of the Delaware Valley on New York and Maryland, see Fletcher to Col. Lodwick, June 13, 1693 and to the Lords of Trade, Oct. 9, 1693, *N.Y. Colonial Documents*, IV, 32, 55; also Gov. Francis Nicholson to the Duke of Shrewsbury, June 14, 1695, *CSP 1693-96*, #1897, and Gov. Fletcher to the Lords of Trade, June 10, 1696, *CSP 1696-97*, #25. The postwar tide of immigration is noted in Jonathan Dickinson's letters of May 14 and July 5, 1698 and June 25, 1700, Dickinson Letter Book, Library Company of Philadelphia; and Isaac Norris's letters of July 21, Aug. 24, Nov. 19, and Dec. 4, 1699, Norris Letter Book (1699-1701). In 1701 Penn estimated the arrival of about 1,500 persons, Penn to Robert Harley, ———, 1701, Duke of Portland MSS, *HMC, 15th Annual Report*, Appendix, Pt. IV (London, 1897), 32. See also Wayne Andrews, "A Glance at New York in 1697: The Travel Diary of Dr. Benjamin Bullivant," New York Historical Society *Quarterly Bulletin*, 40 (1956), 69-70; Andreas Rudman to ———, 1700, in Ruth L. Springer and Louise Wallman, "Two Swedish Pastors Describe Philadelphia, 1700 and 1702," *PMHB*, 84 (1960), 207; Bronner, *Penn's "Holy Experiment,"* 224-225, citing Dickinson Letter Book.

Edward Randolph's account.[63] Enjoying the support of the Quaker merchants of Philadelphia and most of the country Quakers, Lloyd's party clearly controlled affairs at all levels of government. Both the Council and Assembly were under its sway, as were the provincial and county courts and the municipal government of Philadelphia. But inveterately opposed to the Quaker leaders were the former Keithians, led by Robert Turner, and a growing Anglican minority; together they had kept alive the tradition of opposing as well as denying the legality of constituted authority. "What I have met with here is without Example," Penn wrote his agent in London shortly after arriving, "and what a Diadem could not tempt [a man] to undergoe . . . seventeen years faction in Government and almost indissolvable knots in Property."[64] It was also a colony habituated to self-rule, as turbulent as that might be. Proprietary prerogatives, so long as Penn remained in England, had been systematically disregarded.

Yet Penn was not without hope that his return might set matters to rights and possibly even return the colony to its founding principles. He still retained some of his old charisma which had worked so effectively in the recruitment of settlers in the early 1680's and which had always made him a venerated figure at Quaker meetings. Moreover, as an English aristocrat, a leader of the English Quaker movement, and a confidant of kings, his personal influence was still considerable. His connections at Whitehall were of particular importance to the colonial merchants who were attempting to outskirt Randolph, Quary, and the new vice-admiralty court.

[63] Randolph to Board of Trade, April 26, 1698, Toppan, *Randolph*, v, 178.
[64] Penn to Lawton, 1700, *Pennsylvania Archives*, 1st Ser., I, 139.

Penn's arrival in the colony with his family and a retinue of servants and associates was by all accounts a gala affair, with large crowds lining the shore as his ship passed Chester and half of Philadelphia at the waterfront to witness his debarkation two days later. For a few months old grievances seem to have faded away as a renewed sense of common purpose overtook the colony. "Things in Church and Government," wrote Isaac Norris, "seem to goe well."[65]

But Penn's long-anticipated return, though it temporarily reconciled opposing Quaker interests and quieted Anglican fears, had no lasting effects. At a special session of the General Assembly called shortly after his arrival, Penn succeeded in pushing through a bill condemning illegal trade in terms strong and unambiguous enough to satisfy the colonial authorities in London.[66] But barely five months later the General Assembly was opposing Penn at every turn. Two bills of overriding importance dominated debate: a revision of the Frame of 1696 and a proprietary tax. Neither measure passed. The levy for Penn, noted Isaac Norris, a rising young Quaker merchant, was voted down "verry unhansomly," although an impost upon liquors, promising a far smaller income, was conceded to the proprietor.[67] Plans for a new charter also foundered, principally because the Lower Counties refused to accept any constitutional arrangement under which their affairs would be subject to

[65] Isaac Norris to Thomas Lloyd, Jr., Dec. 29, 1699, Norris Letter Book (1699-1701). Penn's return is described in Frederick B. Tolles, *James Logan and the Culture of Provincial America* (Boston, 1957), 15-16.

[66] The proceedings of the General Assembly can be followed in *Minutes of Council*, I, 589-595, and *Votes of Assembly*, I, 221-233.

[67] Norris to Philip Ford, June 13, 1700, Norris Letter Book (1699-1701). The proceedings of the General Assembly are in *Minutes of Council*, I, 605-613, and *Votes of Assembly*, I, 233-242.

Quaker control. Deadlocked, the legislators agreed to defer further attempts at settlement until a special session scheduled for October 1700. Penn was asked in the interim to govern under the King's patent alone. In the face of such failures and with the sudden decline of his influence, Penn's optimism for salvaging the "holy experiment" rapidly evaporated. By the end of the year his letters to England spoke no more of plans to reunify his colony, but referred instead to "this licentious wilderness."[68]

In part the disillusionment with Penn originated in resentment of some of the men whom the proprietor had brought with him from England to assist in the work of reestablishing proprietary authority and political equilibrium in Pennsylvania. John Guest and Robert Assheton, both Anglicans and trained lawyers, can be taken as examples. Penn appointed Guest Chief Justice of the Provincial Court and Assheton Attorney General in a move designated to strengthen the courts while offsetting charges that justice was unobtainable in Pennsylvania except for Quakers. But to the local Quaker magnates, who had dominated the judiciary for years, the prospect of yielding their positions to the new Anglican placemen was not easy to swallow.[69]

The man whom Penn brought with him as his secretary and chief factotum in 1699, James Logan, was hardly more acceptable. He was only twenty-five when he arrived in the colony and displayed erudition beyond his years. What was worse, he quickly proved his ability to administer proprietary policy. It was apparent that he had caught the proprietor's eye as a person of unusual promise. Inclined toward ostentation, disdainful of the provincial atmosphere of

[68] Penn to Charlewood Lawton, Dec. 21, 1700, Penn Letter Book (1699-1701), 75.
[69] Isaac Norris to Daniel Zachary, Sept. 26, 1701, *Penn-Logan Correspondence*, I, 57.

Philadelphia, cold and unbending, Logan did little to win the confidence of anyone in the colony, even though he was a Quaker. Even Isaac Norris, who was sympathetic to Penn, sniffed that he would avoid Logan's company, being himself but "a meer Pennsilvanian."[70]

The appointment of men such as Guest, Assheton, and Logan, who were soon joined by other new associates of Penn, was widely interpreted as an attempt by the founder to turn back the clock in Pennsylvania. People had not forgotten an earlier proprietary circle, which, with Penn, had attempted to function as a political and economic directorate in the early period of settlement.

No less disillusioning to the Quaker community was Penn's determined offensive against illegal trade and his attack on David Lloyd. Penn, of course, was under strict orders from the Privy Council to remove Markham and Lloyd from office for their bold flaunting of Crown authority. But in the case of Lloyd, Penn moved with a special vengeance, which was not unrelated to the fact that Lloyd had stood at the front of the antiproprietary, as well as the anti-imperial, campaigns of the last decade. Not content to strip Lloyd of his offices, both public and proprietary, Penn disclosed his determination to prosecute him before the spring meeting of the quarter sessions court in 1700. Ironically, it was only the plea of Robert Quary, Lloyd's old antagonist, that restrained Penn from pressing his animus. Quary argued that because of Lloyd's wide popularity and unusual legal abilities, the latter at such a premium in the

[70] Isaac Norris to Thomas Lloyd, Jr., Dec. 29, 1699, Norris Letter Book (1699-1701); on Logan see Tolles, *James Logan*, and the careful study by Joseph E. Johnson: "A Statesman of Colonial Pennsylvania: A Study of the Private Life and Public Career of James Logan to the Year 1726" (unpublished Ph.D. dissertation, Harvard University, 1942).

colony, legal proceedings might produce a backlash of anti-proprietary sentiment. Though the case was dropped, Penn's prestige sagged because of his attack on Lloyd, whom many still regarded as the "most active enemy" of the Anglican faction and the most vocal and dedicated defender of the colonists' rights against external authority.[71]

Penn's campaign against illegal trade and piracy had similar effects in eroding his popularity. Penn's charter, to be sure, was in distinct jeopardy, and he was obliged to do all in his power to meet the Privy Council's demand that he cleanse the colony of pirates and illegal traders. The special session of the General Assembly, which Penn called after arriving in Pennsylvania, had little choice but to pass measures sufficient to meet such criticisms. But Penn was greatly resented for his insistence. In several letters to prominent English officials Penn wrote that sentiment was turning against him, in the Lower Counties because of the disruption of the illegal tobacco trade to Scotland, and in the upper counties because he had discharged popular officeholders who had earlier aided pirates seeking refuge in Philadelphia.[72] Penn informed the Board of Trade that he labored under the greatest difficulties: "The people here are soured to see their accusers believed, and think themselves both Innocent, and meritorious." He paid the reckoning, for the Assembly would not pass proprietary money bills to compensate him for years of expense.[73]

[71] Penn to the Board of Trade, April 22, 1700, Penn Letter Book (1699-1701), 24-29. Logan to William Penn, Jr., Sept. 25, 1700, *Penn-Logan Correspondence*, I, 17-18.

[72] *Minutes of Council*, I, 596; Penn to Robert Harley, 1701, Duke of Portland MSS, *HMC, 15th Annual Report*, Appendix, Pt. IV, 31; Penn to Lord Sommers, Oct. 22, 1700, Penn Letter Book (1699-1701), 68-71.

[73] Quary to the Board of Trade, March 6, 1699/1700, *CSP 1700*, #189; Penn to the Board of Trade, April 22, 1700, Penn Letter Book

Interacting with the resentments caused by the formation of a proprietary clique, the attack on Lloyd, and Penn's energetic attempts to placate authorities in London was widespread dissatisfaction with the proprietary land system. Because there was no centralized land office, colonists taking up land were obliged to deal separately with a bewildering variety of officers—the Board of Propriety, Surveyor General, County Surveyor, Registrar General and Keeper of the Seal. Furthermore, a decade of slovenly record keeping and careless surveying had left a morass of unrecorded patents, faulty surveys, and overlapping claims.[74] Penn's determination to put the colony on a paying basis worsened matters. He had returned to Pennsylvania deeply in debt, the victim of his unscrupulous secretary, Philip Ford, who clamored for payment of personal loans which he claimed now totaled £11,000. The Crown also threatened to move against his right of government in the Lower Counties if he did not discharge an obligation of £6000.[75] Additional income was needed to represent his interests in England, to maintain him in a style befitting a proprietor, and to refurbish his weed-grown Pennsbury estate. More-

(1699-1701), 24-29. Penn also informed Secretary of State Vernon and the Commissioners of Customs in the spring of 1700 of his efforts to cleanse the colony. See Penn Letter Book (1699-1701), 7-10, 15-16.

74 The grievances over land matters were summarized in a letter from David Lloyd, Edward Shippen, and Samuel Carpenter to Penn, July 4, 1698, Norris Papers, Family Letters, I, 122; and Benjamin Chambers to Penn, Feb. 1, 1699/1700, Penn-Physick Papers, I, 11.

75 Penn's financial entanglement with the wily Ford is discussed in Shepherd, Proprietary Government in Pennsylvania, 184-198. The Crown debt pertained to the full moiety of "Rents, Issues and Profitts," which Penn had agreed to pay the King when the Lower Counties were ceded by the Duke of York. See Conveyance of Delaware from the Duke of York to William Penn, Aug. 24, 1682, in BT, Proprieties, v, 1699-1701, F. 71.

over, he had long harbored resentments at the niggardliness of his colonists, who had returned virtually nothing to him by way of proprietary customs or quitrents while leeching his fortunes, according to his reckoning, of some £20,000.[76] Penn had founded the colony not only out of utopian zeal but in the expectation, as he later wrote, that his services to so many hundreds of people would be rewarded with "a solid Comfort."[77] Determined to collect payment for land already taken up and to gather in long overdue quitrents, Penn established a "Court of Inquiry" in December 1700. Its members were to entertain complaints over the mismanagement of land titles, inspect all patents, and examine the state of quitrents to determine what was due.

The quality of the response which the court aroused must have startled Penn. Philadelphians petitioned that a prerogative court with such investigatory power was "a great Agrievance" and "contrary to their Rights and Priviledges as free born English Subjects And not Warranted by any Law Custom or Usage of this Province." When it became apparent that few would even answer the summonses issued by the court, Penn commissioned James Logan to undertake an inspection, county by county, of land titles and claims. Logan was empowered to order resurveys, issue patents, sell surplus and vacant lands, ascertain overdue quitrents, collect them along with any other outstanding proprietary debts, and, if necessary, sue debtors. Logan met nothing but resentment and obdurant refusals wherever he went. The proprietor, he later wrote, "had hopes on his Arrival of rais-

[76] Bronner, *Penn's "Holy Experiment,"* 231, citing Penn to Lord Romney, Sept. 6, 1701, Penn Papers, Granville Penn Book. Penn's estimated losses were only calculated guesses and usually exaggerated. See Shepherd, *Proprietory Government in Pennsylvania*, 183.

[77] Penn to "My Ould Friends in Pennsylvania," June 29, 1710, Gratz Collection, Governors of Pennsylvania, Box 33a.

ing a considerable Sum here, which was not then easily practicable; therefor during the first year here, to the great dissatisfaction of his friends who had received him with transports of joy he was hard to the People; and thereby lost the affection of many who had almost ador'd him."[78]

During the summer of 1700 Penn's policies underwent a striking change. Upon arriving in the province six months earlier he had set himself a triple task: to establish conformity with English commercial regulations, to stabilize and harmonize government, and to rejuvenate long-neglected proprietary prerogatives. But now he shifted ground; he abandoned his attempt to force Pennsylvania to comply with imperial policy and turned openly on Quary and Randolph.

If Quary is to be believed, Penn changed direction to win the support of Quaker merchants for a proprietary money bill which had been defeated by the previous Assembly but was scheduled for reconsideration at the forthcoming special session in October.[79] Quary, however, was hardly an objective commentator; it is clear that Penn's reversal was far more complicated. One factor was the growing strength and determination of the Anglicans and Penn's inability to mediate the differences between Churchmen and Quakers. Although the Anglicans maintained that Penn never intended his negotiations to succeed, there is little reason to doubt the sincerity of the proprietor's efforts. More stock should be put in Penn's complaint that the Anglicans were

[78] For the heated opposition to the Court of Inquiry see "Report on petition of inhabitants of Philadelphia to the Assembly," Sept. 18, 1701, Logan Papers, Provincial Council, III, 24; Logan's commission is in Society Miscellaneous Collection, Penn Papers. His later comment is in a letter to John, Thomas, and Richard Penn, Nov. 14, 1731, Penn Papers, Official Correspondence, II, 213.

[79] Quary to the Lords of Admiralty, Nov. 14, 1700, *CSP 1700*, #932i.

content to reject any overtures of reconciliation because they thought they saw the end of Quaker government in sight. By shunning places on the Philadelphia County bench unless oaths of allegiance and the swearing of witnesses was allowed in accordance with English court procedure, the Anglicans confronted the Quakers with a dilemma: either they must compromise their religious principles by allowing the detested oath in their courts, or face charges that they excluded Anglicans from the judiciary because of their insistence that the courts be conducted consistent with English practice.[80]

Met with this kind of response to his conciliatory overtures, Penn appointed an all-Quaker court in Philadelphia and took his stand against the Anglicans. Quary, Nicholson, and the Bishop of London, he charged, were conspiring to subvert proprietary government in Pennsylvania. "Church is their Cry, and to disturb us is their Merit . . . they misrepresent all we doe, and would make us dissenters in our own Country."[81] The Anglican "interlopers" left no stone unturned in their efforts to obstruct Penn's government.

Penn was equally disturbed by the dishonesty and incompetence of Crown officials in Pennsylvania. Many were themselves engaged in evading the laws they were paid to enforce, even as they indicted their provincial competitors. Robert Webb, formerly Collector of the Customs and now Marshall of the vice-admiralty court, declined to appoint a

[80] Penn to Robert Harley, 1701, Duke of Portland MSS, *HMC, 15th Annual Report*, Appendix, Pt. IV, 31-32.

[81] Penn to Charlewood Lawton, 1700, *Pennsylvania Archives*, 1st Ser., I, 141-142, and Dec. 21, 1700, Penn Letter Book (1699-1701), 74-81; also see Penn to Lord Sommers, Oct. 22, 1700, *ibid.*, 68-71. A statement of the Anglicans' position is given in "A Brief Narrative of the Proceedings of William Penn, 1700," in Perry, ed., *History of the Church in Pennsylvania*, 304; Vestrymen of Christ Church to Board of Trade, Jan. 28, 1700/01, *CSP 1701*, #101.

deputy at the very location on Delaware Bay, the Dover River, where tobacco was most often brought from Maryland for illegal export to Scotland. Webb's negligence, Penn hinted, was not unconnected with the fact that he was among the largest tobacco merchants in the Lower Counties. Quary, agent of the New Pennsylvania Company, imported and exported goods as he pleased, while "all others must be Racked by all the Severities he shall think fitt for their Discouragement in Rival Trade to put upon them."[82] As for Randolph, "my one-eyed Friend," as Penn was wont to call him, it was well known that he boosted his own fortunes as a tobacco exporter by paying duty on 400 pound hogsheads into which 800 or 900 pounds of leaf was pressed. Quary was gone eight months a year on trading voyages to the southern colonies for the New Pennsylvania Company and freely admitted his "unacquaintance" with civil and maritime law. And though he preyed on all, Anglicans brought before the court knew they had little to fear. Such arbitrary and unskilled proceedings dampened trade. If there must be vice-admiralty courts in America, Penn exclaimed, they should be staffed with experienced officers, "for as these manage, great Discouragement is given to trade." Already ships were being diverted to other ports rather than risk the vagaries of the vice-admiralty gauntlet at Philadelphia.[83]

Apart from the unfitness of Crown officers, Penn complained that the vice-admiralty court was devouring privi-

[82] Penn to Commissioners of Customs, May 7, 1700 and Aug. 27, 1701, Penn Letter Book (1699-1701), 31-36, 141-143.

[83] Penn to Commissioners of Customs, May 7, 1700, *ibid.*, 31-36; Penn to Robert Harley, 1701, Duke of Portland MSS, *HMC, 15th Annual Report*, Appendix, Pt. IV, 31; Penn to Board of Trade, Dec. 8, 1700, Penn Letter Book (1699-1701), 47-53; same to Charlewood Lawton, 1700, *Pennsylvania Archives*, 1st Ser., I, 139-140. Penn's arguments against the vice-admiralty courts are summarized in Beatty, *William Penn*, 228-230.

leges inhering in the colonies—liberties that belonged to Englishmen on either side of the water. Every private suit that related to provincial waters, such as disputes between ship captains and crew members, or even those concerned with victualling and shipbuilding contracts, was claimed by the vice-admiralty court. The mayor of New York, Penn pointed out, was allowed jurisdiction over inland waters; by his charter from Charles II he possessed equivalent vice-admiralty jurisdiction. "What is the right of the English subject at home should be allowed here," he adjured, "since more and not less [liberty] seems the Reasons . . . to Plant this Wilderness." That property could be condemned without a jury trial was an abridgement of fundamental English rights, Penn wrote, ignoring the fact that he had attempted to institute prerogative courts of his own to deal with property owners who balked at proprietary land policy.[84]

By the summer of 1700, indignant in his own right and spurred on by the colonial merchants, Penn decided to contest Quary's powers by commissioning water bailiffs for the ports of Philadelphia and New Castle. The officers were specifically empowered in local maritime disputes to issue writs which could only be served in the civil and criminal courts of the province. Quary immediately protested the appointments as a direct encroachment on his jurisdiction and an attempt to undermine his office.[85] Penn, in mock surprise, contended that nothing could be more unreasonable. He had appointed a local official that most mayors in English ports, indeed the mayor of New York, could commission. He had no intention of denying the authority of

[84] Penn to Board of Trade, April 22, 1700, Penn Letter Book (1699-1701), 24-29; Penn to Lords of Admiralty, Dec. 10, 1700, *ibid.*, 58-59; Penn to Charlewood Lawton, 1700, *Pennsylvania Archives*, 1st Ser., I, 140-141.

[85] Quary to Lords of Admiralty, Nov. 14, 1700, *CSP 1700*, #932i.

the admiralty court in cases relating to the King's revenue, unlawful trade, or piracy. But the idea that the proprietary authority ended at the water's edge, at Front Street in Philadelphia, was absurd. What would be the consequences if a criminal or debtor, fleeing from civil officers, should step from the wharf to a vessel moored at the quay and there defy the magistracy?[86] Penn alleged that Quary had badly confused the boundaries of civil and maritime law when he claimed that "we can do nothing of Search, Arrest, Attachment, suppression of Riots, &c on the Water before our very doors." The admiralty court met with as much "deference and Compliance" in Pennsylvania as anywhere in the King's dominions. He had even appointed the Advocate of the vice-admiralty court as Attorney General of the province and the Marshall of the court as the Under-Sheriff of Philadelphia. But it was highly objectionable to the provincial merchants that matters of civil record in other colonies should be cast into prerogative courts in Pennsylvania.[87] It was trade that made the wheels of empire turn, Penn warned Robert Harley, Speaker of the House of Commons; and Quary, by his unconscionable extension of power, was greatly inhibiting trade. "They have swallowed up a great part of the Government here," Penn asserted, "[giving] our people the greatest discontent, looking upon themselves as less free here than at home, instead of greater privileges, which were promised."[88]

[86] Penn to Lords of Admiralty, Dec. 10, 1700, Penn Letter Book (1699-1701) , 54-58.

[87] Penn to Charlewood Lawton, 1700, *Pennsylvania Archives*, 1st Ser., I, 140-142; Penn to Lords of Admiralty, Dec. 10, 1700, Penn Letter Book (1699-1701) , 54-58; Penn to Board of Trade, Aug. 26, 1701, *ibid.*, 136-140.

[88] Penn to Robert Harley, 1701, Duke of Portland MSS, *HMC, 15th Annual Report*, Appendix, Pt. IV, 31-33.

The battle over the limits of admiralty jurisdiction was only part of a mushrooming struggle between Quary and Penn, a conflict that would ultimately take the Quaker back to England to defend his charter. Quary, who in March 1700 had assured the Board of Trade that Penn scrupulously enforced the Navigation Acts, now assured his superiors that he had "never laboured under more difficulty than at present," suffering threats and insults from the Philadelphia merchants, while Penn boldly defied the authority of the vice-admiralty court.[89]

Although Penn's claim that Quary's court had overreached its authority was ultimately upheld, he was losing the battle of influence in London. Nicholson, Quary, and Randolph all inveighed against proprietary governments, the latter in person after his return to London in the summer of 1700. Penn advised his agent in England to employ every possible stratagem, bribery included, in order to postpone proceedings against his charter; he instructed him to "Damp, Clogg, and Delay," if Parliament took up the question of superseding proprietary governments. At the same time Penn kept a steady stream of letters flowing to men of high position in London—members of the Board of Trade, Commissioners of Customs, Lords of Admiralty, the Secretary of State, and powerful friends in the House of Lords.[90]

By 1701 letters from England convinced Penn that the annulment of his charter was imminent. In a desperate attempt to forestall *quo warranto* proceedings he exhausted

[89] Quary to Board of Trade, Nov. 14, 1700, *CSP 1700*, #932; Quary to Lords of Admiralty, Nov. 14, 1700, *ibid.*, #932i; Randolph to ———, March 24, 1700/01, Toppan, *Randolph*, v, 266.

[90] Hall, *Randolph*, 201-204; Penn to Lawton, Dec. 21, 1700 and July, 1701, Penn Letter Book (1699-1701), 78-79, 106-107. Ten letters to the Secretary of State, Board of Trade, Commissioners of Customs, and Lords of Admiralty, all written in 1700, are in the Penn Letter Book (1699-1701), passim.

every scrap of influence at his disposal, writing letters to all his connections in and out of government.[91] In each case Penn offered the same defense of proprietary charters: initially they had been erected and maintained to spare the English government the expense and trouble of planting colonies; even now they could be made to conform to the Navigation Acts far more readily than their royal counterparts. Admittedly there was illegal trade in Pennsylvania— it would never be completely stopped until patrol vessels policed the network of streams flowing into Delaware Bay —but in neighboring Maryland, despite the vigilance of the royal governor and the prodigious effort of Edward Randolph, illegal traffic was "twenty seven times" worse. The prosperity of his colony, Penn reminded the government, was based primarily on provisioning the West Indian islands—a trade which necessitated no illicit traffic. Penn closed his defense by asserting that any abrogation of his rights of government, as the result of charges made by opportunistic critics, would be an act of "downright Parliamentary omnipotency."[92]

Despite his influence at Court, Penn could not deter the Board of Trade. Randolph's constant theme, that colonial reform was impossible while proprietary and charter governments existed, had begun to penetrate to high places. By April 1700, a bill annulling all such charters had been introduced in the House of Lords. In the protracted debate that followed, Quary's stinging reports on defiance of Eng-

[91] The letters, dated between Aug. 25 and 27, are in Penn Letter Book (1699-1701), 118-143.

[92] Penn to Robert Harley, Aug. 27, 1701, Duke of Portland MSS, *HMC, 15th Annual Report*, Appendix, Pt. IV, 19-21; Penn to Board of Trade, Aug. 26, 1701, Penn Letter Book (1699-1701), 136-140. Also see Penn to Lord Romney, Sept. 6, 1701, Penn Papers, Granville Penn Book, 6; and Illick, *Penn the Politician*, 195-202.

lish law in Pennsylvania figured prominently. By October 1701, the Board of Trade declared that they could find no evidence that Penn was entitled to rights of government in the Lower Counties.[93] And though the bill against the charters did not pass—"by reason of the shortness of time and the multiplicity of other affairs," according to the minutes of the Board of Trade—there was general agreement that it would be approved during the next session. Faced with this prospect, Penn announced in August 1701 that he must return immediately to England to neutralize the assault on proprietary government being made, as he charged, by those "gaping for Preferments under the Specious pretence of Serving the king's Interest."[94]

A Constitutional Chess Game

Penn's spirited defense of provincial rights, initiated in the summer of 1700, did much to rally the most influential elements of the Quaker community behind him. In June the principal merchants of Philadelphia, shamefaced as one disclosed at the refusal of the last Assembly to vote a tax for Penn's support, proposed to raise money privately for the proprietor.[95] By October, when a special session of the General Assembly was called to draft new articles of government,

93 For a thorough discussion of the new attack on proprietary charters see Winfred T. Root, *The Relations of Pennsylvania with the British Government, 1696-1765* (New York, 1912), 342-349; and Hall, *Randolph*, 201-208. The attack on Penn's right of government in the Lower Counties is in Journal of the Board of Trade, Oct. 28, 1701, *CSP 1701*, #973.

94 *Minutes of Council*, II, 32; Penn's comment on the motives of his critics is quoted in Root, *The Relations of Pennsylvania*, 348-349.

95 Isaac Norris to Philip Ford, July 10, 1700, Norris Letter Book (1699-1701); letter from Philadelphia merchants to Joseph Growdon, William Biles, and Phineas Pemberton, June 29, 1700, Etting Collection; Pemberton Papers, I, 92.

Friends were acting with a semblance of unity. The fact that so many of the Quaker leaders were elected to the lower house—Shippen, Owen, Story, Morrey, Pusey, Growdon, Norris—was a measure of how effectively that body had been transformed into a center of Quaker political power. In fact six of the elected assemblymen were members of Penn's Council, commissioned by the proprietor barely four months before. All six of these men requested that Penn accept their resignations so that they might sit in the lower house where more important work was to be done.[96]

Never in nineteen years had a General Assembly deliberated at such length as did the legislature at New Castle from October 14 to November 27. In spite of the protracted debates, however, a new frame of government did not emerge. Delegates from the Lower Counties, apprehensive that the swelling population to the north would soon lead to the creation of new counties, insisted that the only basis for a continued legislative union was an equality of representation from upper and lower counties. As in the previous May, attempts at compromise proved fruitless and the entire matter of a new frame was postponed again, this time until the next year. Similar geographical conflicts, compounded by religious ones, plagued negotiations for a tax to recompense Penn for the expense of supporting the colony's cause in England over the years. "Much tensing and Sometimes of[f] the Hinges," reported Isaac Norris of the proceedings. Two thousand pounds were ultimately voted—essentially the same measure that had failed five months before—but only after the upper counties consented to raise more than three-quarters of the total.[97] It was a sign not only of the

[96] *Minutes of Council*, I, 614.
[97] *Votes of Assembly*, I, 257-260, 274-275; Isaac Norris to Daniel Zachary, Dec. 8, 1700, Norris Letter Book (1699-1701).

relative growth of the counties around Philadelphia, but of the new favor which Penn had won for his recent efforts against Quary and the vice-admiralty court.

Though basic differences still existed within the Quaker community over proprietary land policy and the proper form of government, there was a growing belief by 1701 that most of the issues between Penn and his colonists could be successfully compromised. However, when Penn announced in August 1701 that the antiproprietary bill before the House of Lords made his return to England imperative, the situation changed. For Penn's impending departure necessitated an immediate solution to the whole knotty question of governmental reorganization, as well as to all other outstanding issues relating to proprietary powers. Who could predict when Penn would return to his colony, if ever? Reports from England indicated that in all likelihood the colony would fall again under royal control. Clearly this might be the last opportunity to negotiate the questions of autonomous powers.

In the immediacy of the situation lay the roots of a new political division. The colony faced a period of uncertainty which led many to conclude that a large degree of self-government must now be sought as a hedge against the reestablishment of royal government or the possibility that Penn might not return. Issues that might otherwise have been settled at a leisurely pace now demanded immediate solutions. Others, on which compromise was acceptable so long as Penn's residency in Pennsylvania made renegotiation possible, required permanent answers—and answers favoring the colonists. Outside of the Anglicans there were probably few who did not prefer proprietary to royal government; but almost everyone in Pennsylvania agreed that the colony should be shielded in every way possible from authority exercised from afar, whether proprietary or royal in origin.

The announcement of Penn's plans for departure was a signal for negotiations over a new form of government to begin. There was little doubt that David Lloyd would lead the movement for a new frame of government, not only because of his reputation as the most articulate and energetic defender of provincial liberties but also because of his skill as a lawyer and legislative draughtsman. Sensitive to the advantage of staying in the background as the unassuming proprietor, Penn remained at his country estate above Philadelphia, leaving the negotiations to James Logan. When rumors reached him that Lloyd denounced his powers as proprietor, he directed Logan to rally his supporters. Already Penn was sure of the allegiance of a circle of placemen —Griffith Owen, James Logan, Robert Assheton, Isaac Pennington, Thomas Story, and others. In addition some of the most influential merchants and landholders seemed sympathetic to his position.[98]

But Lloyd, too, had been recruiting support. When the General Assembly met on September 15, he was ready with a petition signed by sixty-eight Philadelphians asking that the Assembly act to preserve provincial rights before Penn's departure. Specifically, a charter of property was demanded to "absolutely secure and Defend us in our Estates and Propertyes from himself [Penn] his heirs and assignes forever." Other clauses called for a reform of land-granting procedures, the abolition of quitrents and groundrents for the entire town of Philadelphia, and the transfer of all disputes relating to property from Penn's Board of Propriety to the ordinary courts of justice. Lastly, a new frame of govern-

[98] Lokken, *David Lloyd*, 87-88, 96-98; Penn to Logan, Aug. 13 and Sept. 6, and Sept. 8, 1701, *Penn-Logan Correspondence*, I, 52-53, 56-58.

227

ment was demanded, the particulars of which the petitioners were ready to supply.[99]

If Penn detected an undercurrent of hostility in the tone of the remonstrance, he was not mistaken, although even his supporters, as property-conscious as others, would have endorsed many of the demands. The names of those who signed the petition were perhaps even more significant than their demands since they revealed the radical shift in tactics which David Lloyd had undertaken. A few were merchants: Griffith Jones, Joseph Wilcox, Francis Rawle, Samuel Holt, and Thomas Harris. But the majority were shopkeepers and artisans. As a group, they represented precisely that element which in the 1690's had gathered first around George Keith and then Robert Turner in resisting the Quaker magnates. The determined Welshman, in search of support, had allied himself with the ambitious middle-class Philadelphians and malcontented merchants whom, as a spokesman for the dominant Quaker leaders, he had resisted for years.

The Assembly's general acceptance of the remonstrance to Penn indicated that even among Penn's friends there was a general desire to dismantle the proprietary land system. Seven of the nine articles in Lloyd's petition were adopted almost verbatim by the lower house for presentation to Penn. To these were added nine additional articles, all relating to property, including demands that Penn make all land in the Lower Counties available at the "old rent" of one bushel of wheat per 100 acres and that every landholder be granted a 10 percent bonus on his estate.[100]

[99] Petition of the Inhabitants of Philadelphia to the Assembly, Sept. 17, 1701, Logan Papers, Provincial Council, III, 20.

[100] *Votes of Assembly*, I, 287-289. In 1700 Penn had agreed that when resurveys indicated that a landowner had received more land than

Penn reacted forcefully. Some of the articles, he pointed out, were not properly the business of the legislature; he would never allow the Assembly "to intermeddle with his Property." Nine days later he delivered a point-by-point reply. To certain administrative changes he consented. But on every substantive issue—the repeal of Philadelphia rents, the dissolution of the Board of Propriety, and the sale of land in the Lower Counties at a reduced quitrent—Penn refused to budge.[101]

Penn was not without support in the lower house, but a majority, including almost all the members from the Lower Counties, opposed his land policy. Disagreement in this area prejudiced compromise on a new plan of government. The Assembly was stalemated on the matter of a new constitutional arrangement, revealed one of Penn's supporters in the lower house, "for the Philistines be upon us still." Confident that the proprietor must yield substantial power in granting a new form of government, members from the Lower Counties and Lloydian "malcontents" opposed anything offered by Penn's friends. Penn, it was reported, was "much Grieved at this parting Carriage of the people" and highly resented the petition made to the Assembly and endorsed by that body.[102]

With debate stalled on the charter of property and a new frame of government, Penn offered a bill for the reorganization of the courts. The essence of the bill, prepared by John Guest, Penn's newly appointed Chief Justice and a man

---

stipulated in his deed, he should be allowed 10 percent of the overage. Using this as a lever, the Assembly argued that all landowners be granted a bonus.

[101] *Votes of Assembly*, I, 291, 303-305; *Minutes of Council*, II, 40-45, 54.

[102] Isaac Norris to Thomas Lloyd, Jr., Sept. 16, 1701, Norris to Daniel Zachary, Oct. 3, 1701, Norris Letter Book (1699-1701).

little favored in the colony, was the preservation of the proprietor's powers in the judicial system. Receiving the bill from the Council, where Penn's supporters had endorsed it, the lower house debated only briefly before rejecting the bill and returning it unceremoniously to its author.[103] A week later, David Lloyd offered the Assembly his own "Bill for Regulating Courts." In contrast to the proprietary measure, it greatly enlarged the power of the county courts in cases of equity and in maritime cases which were "by the laws and usage of the Kingdom of England, not within the Cognizance and proper jurisdiction of the Admiralty." The first innovation bit deeply into the traditional jurisdiction of the provincial court in equity cases, and the provision on maritime cases was an obvious challenge to the authority of Quary's vice-admiralty court. In both cases a decentralization of judicial authority was involved. Moreover, appellate jurisdiction was given solely to the provincial court, eliminating Penn's Council as a court of appeals. Other elaborate provisions of the bill concerning court procedures, the use of writs, the dates of sessions, and other details, indicated that Lloyd intended to place the judiciary, though nominally appointed by the proprietor, under the control of the Assembly.[104]

The Assembly approved Lloyd's bill as promptly as it had rejected Guest's and displayed its gratitude by voting the author £50. Penn was far from pleased, but three days before his ship sailed he approved it; he was probably convinced that he could win nothing better from what was clearly a determined Assembly.[105]

[103] *Votes of Assembly*, I, 300-301; *Minutes of Council*, II, 45.

[104] *Votes of Assembly*, I, 314; *Minutes of Council*, II, 52. Lloyd's bill is in *Laws of Pennsylvania*, 311-319, and is analyzed in detail in Lokken, *David Lloyd*, 103-107.

[105] *Votes of Assembly*, I, 316-318; Lokken, *David Lloyd*, 108.

With time running out, Penn now yielded to a plan of government that differed only in detail from the Frame of 1696, which he had harshly criticized when he returned to the colony in 1699. On the eve of departure, his alternatives were few. The Frame hardly signaled "the final triumph of radical democratic principles," as one historian has written, though it did provide the basis for an apparent change in the allocation of political power.[106] The Council was not even mentioned in the legislative process, a notable structural change since it made the Assembly the only unicameral legislature in the English empire. That this would alter the balance of political power was not yet evident; influential Quakers as members of the Council had for a decade worked toward the enlargement of the Assembly's role as a means of protecting provincial autonomy from proprietary or royal incursions. These influential men had encountered as little difficulty in obtaining seats in the supposedly more democratic body as in the more selective Council. In fact, since the end of Fletcher's tenure, the speakership of the lower house had gone to men whose estates and influence placed them in the uppermost stratum of society—David Lloyd, Edward Shippen, John Blunston, Phineas Pemberton, and Joseph Growdon.

Nonetheless, the Charter of Privileges, as the Frame of 1701 was called, conferred on the Assembly many of the parliamentary privileges which Penn had steadfastly denied that body for years: the right to prepare legislative bills, elect its own officers, appoint committees, sit on its own adjournment, judge the qualifications of its own members, and impeach officers of government. On the other hand, Penn gained the right to appoint a Council, even if it was

[106] Isaac Sharpless, *A Quaker Experiment in Government* (Philadelphia, 1898), 64. The Frame of 1701 is given in *Minutes of Council*, II, 56-58.

assigned no role in the legislative process. Another concession was made when all matters or complaints relating to property were assigned to ordinary courts of justice. This was of special significance since it neutralized the power of Penn's Board of Propriety, the center of proprietary land administration, and gave life to a measure which the proprietor had adamantly refused to endorse only weeks before when it was presented as a part of Lloyd's Charter of Property.

Like the other measures rushed through in the waning days of Penn's residence, the Charter of Privileges was approved under duress. Penn later wrote that he had not favored the measure and approved it only when he saw that Lloyd had convinced a majority that it was a form of government "nearer to English methods, which they called for so often." This was probably true. But Penn, as he later admitted, also consented to the Frame of 1701 because he fully expected Parliament to strip him of his rights of government and hoped that the wide autonomous powers granted the colonists by the new frame of government would shelter Quakers from an arbitrary royal governor. On this point Penn and his later critics agreed.[107]

Only a day before sealing the Charter of Privileges Penn conferred a new charter on the city of Philadelphia. It differed from the city charter of 1691 in increasing the powers of the municipal government and tightening the qualifications for freemanship. Under the new document the jurisdiction of the Philadelphia City Court was broadened to include all criminal and civil actions in both the city and

[107] Penn to Logan, Jan. 16, 1704/05 and May 10, 1705; and Roger Mompesson, Feb. 17, 1704/05, *Penn-Logan Correspondence*, I, 356, 373; II, 16; Jasper Yeates to Robert Quary, Jan. 10, 1701/02, CO 5/1261, #139iii, Public Record Office, London.

county of Philadelphia. Only men resident in the city for two years and possessed of a £50 estate were eligible for freemanship—an innovation that would have excluded about 30 percent of those on the tax list of 1697.[108]

In the appointment of municipal officers Penn made further attempts at compromise. The principal officers—mayor, recorder, sheriff, and clerk—were drawn from his circle of supporters. But in appointing councilmen and aldermen, who with the mayor and recorder controlled the city government and constituted the city courts, Penn yielded almost entirely to Lloyd's new constituency. Among the eight aldermen and twelve councilmen, all merchants or rising shopkeepers, only six had not signed the petition which Lloyd had presented to the Assembly. Why Penn installed so many of Lloyd's supporters, who enjoyed rights of "perpetual succession" thereafter, is not altogether clear. One surmises that he was bowing reluctantly to the considerable strength which Lloyd had demonstrated among the vocal middle class, while at the same time symbolizing his parting plea that Quakers bury their differences and work together in the capital city of his "holy experiment." Three days after the city charter was signed, Penn commissioned a council to advise his deputy governor during his absence. In his choice of members—Edward Shippen, Samuel Carpenter, John Guest, William Clarke, Thomas Story, Griffith Owen, Phineas Pemberton, Caleb Pusey, John Blunston, and Samuel Finney—Penn gave notice that he would rely on the wealthiest merchants and a few close friends to uphold his interests in Pennsylvania.[109]

[108] The Philadelphia Charter of 1701 is given in *Votes of Assembly*, I, 393-401. The effect on voting eligibility is based on an analysis of the 1697 tax list in Philadelphia County Miscellaneous Papers, I, 24½-28.

[109] The charter included Penn's appointments: Edward Shippen, Mayor; Thomas Story, Recorder; Thomas Farmer, Sheriff; and Robert

Not until Penn was aboard the *Dolmahoy* at New Castle, awaiting a favorable wind to weigh anchor, was the property issue forced to a conclusion. Aboard the ship, Lloyd's supporters presented a draft charter of property, unmistakably the Welshman's handiwork, and urged Penn to sign it. Penn hastily scanned the document and gave it his provisional approval, probably because he sensed the danger of leaving the colony in an unrelenting posture.[110] If no dissenting word arrived within six months, he promised, the charter would take effect.

When Penn had time to examine the charter at length, he found that Lloyd had written far more than a bill to secure the property interests of the colonists. The document, in fact, went far toward superseding Penn's role as a land proprietor. According to its provisions, the probating of wills, the settlement of estates, and all legal suits relating to land were to fall under the direction of a General Court, composed of Penn's lieutenant governor, four commissioners of property appointed by Penn, ten members elected annually by the freeholders, and six assistants, of whom half were named by the proprietor and half by the General Court itself. The powers of the court were not limited to property affairs. They included the power to create both courts of record and equity as well as "all other such

Assheton, Clerk. The appointments to the Council are in *Minutes of Council*, II, 61. Unlike the Councilmen and Aldermen, the Mayor sat for one year only. His successor was selected by the other members of the corporate government, who enjoyed lifetime tenure. Thus the mayorship went to a staunch supporter of Lloyd just a year after Penn's departure.

110 "The Proprietor's Agreement about the Charter for the Lower Counties," Oct. 31, 1701, *Penn-Logan Correspondence*, I, 58-59. Lloyd's Charter of Property, a fragment of which is missing, is transcribed with an introduction by Edwin B. Bronner in *Pennsylvania History*, 24 (1957), 267-292.

Courts as may be requisite and necessary for the administration of justice." Since elected members of the court would outnumber those appointed by the proprietor by thirteen to eight, the whole judiciary power, as well as control of property affairs, was to be transferred, in effect, to the representatives of the freemen. It was an innovation that struck at the heart of the concept of feudal overlordship— and a scheme which Penn promptly disavowed when he arrived in England.[111]

Penn was forced to make one final concession before leaving Pennsylvania—the promise of legislative independence to the Lower Counties. His grasp on the region had always been weak, since the Duke of York's title was questionable when he granted the area to Penn in 1681. Penn's possession of the right of government there was uncertain, although the proprietor argued that the Act of Union, signed by the representatives of the Lower Counties and the province in 1682, governmentally bound that area to his province by its own consent. Never reconciled to a union with the Quakers, the Lower Counties over two decades had grown more convinced that only political separation would emancipate them from the heavy hand of their Quaker neighbors. By the time Penn returned in 1699, sentiment had hardened; the leading merchants and planters agreed that the Act of Union was a dead letter since it had never been reenacted after Fletcher had rescinded all provincial laws in 1693. They had been "great sufferers" by the union, they told Penn, and could no longer bear the burden of such disadvantageous ties. Penn attempted a reconciliation; but the antagonisms displayed in the General Assemblies of 1700 and 1701 convinced him that further attempts at peacemaking, no matter how desirable from his point of view,

[111] *Minutes of Council*, ii, 62.

would be fruitless. "Our people are much dissatisfied and in great disorder," his principal confidant in the Territories had written in February 1701.[112] To bind a chronically disaffected people to the Quaker province promised far greater difficulties than a separation of governments. For while the Lower Counties were always the less powerful of the two regions, their voice in the lower house was sufficient, as had been demonstrated more than once, to block a quorum. Yielding to the inevitable, Penn attached to the Charter of Privileges, six days before he left the province, a provision for the political separation of the Lower Counties when they or the Quaker counties around Philadelphia should so choose.

Penn's sojourn in the colony, lasting only twenty-three months, was a disheartening failure if his avowed aims in returning to Pennsylvania are taken as criteria. At first successful in pacifying the Crown officers, he reversed field by mid-1700 and launched a vigorous defense of provincial and proprietary liberties. But while his turnabout won him support in the colony, at least for the moment, it also provided the justification for a new attack on proprietary charters by the determined bureaucrats of imperial reform. As a result, Penn was compelled to return to England to defend his charter. Proprietary government, though it would last another three-quarters of a century in Pennsylvania, had lost its most prestigious advocate in the New World.

Nor could Penn prevent the population shifts which so alarmed the Quakers, for he was powerless to block the influx of non-Quaker immigrants, even if financial embar-

112 William Clarke to Penn, Feb. 27, 1700/01, Penn Papers, Friends House, London. The efforts of the representatives of the Lower Counties to complete a separation while Penn was in the colony can be followed in *Votes of Assembly*, I, 306-311; and *Minutes of Council*, II, 49-52.

rassment had not made him welcome every possible purchaser, regardless of religion. It was, in part, this growing
pluralism that thwarted Penn's attempts to unify his colony.
Anglicans and Quakers, passionate enemies in a century
brimming over with religious controversy, seemed incapable of coexistence. This was especially true in Pennsylvania
where one group saw the colony as the long-promised fulfillment of sectarian visions, while the other, gaining in relative numbers and enjoying support from England, refused
to concede the permanence of Quaker control. Other religious groups were also proliferating—Pietists, Presbyterians,
Baptists. These conditions were a foretaste of the religious
diversity that later gave the colony renown as the crossroads
of New World sectarianism. The "holy experiment," as conceived by Penn and his early backers, was never really possible.

But even more basic to Penn's failure to establish a stable,
proprietary government was his inability to appreciate that
semifeudal privileges seemed anachronistic to a majority of
the colonists in the Delaware Valley. "Can it Enter the head
of any man of Common Sence," he wrote just before his departure, "knowing any thing of America, that wee came
hither to be under a Kings Governour that is Mercenary
and that has no interest in the Country but [is] changeable
every three years perhaps . . . are wee come 3000 miles into a
Desart of orig[inal] wild people as well as wild Beasts . . . to
have only the same priviledges wee had at home?"[113] Penn
was railing against the incursions of royal authority when
he wrote, but it was indicative of the blind spots in his
thinking that he could not perceive the widespread hostility
to proprietary as well as royal power. To men like David

[113] Penn to Charlewood Lawton, Aug. 18, 1701, Penn Letter Book,
(1699-1701) , 111.

Lloyd they were equally to be resisted. "More [rights], and not less, seems the Reasons of the grant to Plant this wilderness," wrote Penn to the Board of Trade. But, again, he never allowed himself to believe that the argument applied to proprietary powers as well.[114] In matters of land, and to a lesser degree in affairs of government, Penn found it difficult to bend to colonial conditions, to circumstances that bore scant resemblance to what had been expected two decades before when initial plans for Pennsylvania lay on the drawing board in London. Penn knew the realities of economic life in Pennsylvania—the shortage of specie, the everlasting search for exports marketable in England, the reliance on land speculation as a major source of profits. But confronted with financial problems of his own, he would not give up the hope of large profits in his venture. Unwilling to adopt original plans to unforeseen conditions, he watched his outdated land policy erode the affections of large numbers of colonists. Penn never succeeded in enforcing his will, whether it related to the collection of quitrents, settling of land, reservation of land for proprietary manors, or collection of proprietary customs. Yet at the time of his departure for England, he instructed James Logan to pursue quitrents and "look carefully" after such medieval privileges as fines, forfeitures, escheats, deodands, and strays—evidence that he had conceded little to the extensive antiproprietary sentiment which such prerogatives had evoked.[115]

In contrast, Penn conceded much in the realm of government, although in reality he was only giving his consent to what had been accomplished without it during the years of

[114] Penn to Board of Trade, April 22, 1700, Penn Letter Book (1699-1701), 24-29. The same grievance was expressed by Penn to Robert Harley in 1701. Duke of Portland MSS, HMC, *15th Annual Report*, Appendix, Pt. IV, 31-33.

[115] "Instructions to J. Logan, my Receiver and Secretary," Nov. 3, 1701, *Penn-Logan Correspondence*, I, 59-60.

his absence. The privileges of the Assembly, accumulated piecemeal over more than a decade, were legitimatized; his control of the judiciary was to be shared with the Assembly; and the city government was turned over to the popular element. But Penn had by no means conceded political autonomy to the colony. He still hoped that his powerful circle of place holders could accomplish during his absence what he himself had been unable to do while in residence. He placed his principal confidence in James Logan. "I have left thee an uncommon trust," he wrote. This was no exaggeration, for Penn had appointed the young Scotsman Provincial Secretary, Clerk of Council, Receiver General, Commissioner of Propriety, and Proprietary Secretary.

Others upon whom Penn relied included John Guest, Chief Justice of the Provincial Court, Presiding Judge of the Philadelphia Courts, and member of the Council; Robert Assheton, Town Clerk, Clerk of the Peace, and Clerk of the Philadelphia Courts; Thomas Story, Recorder of Philadelphia, Master of the Rolls, Keeper of the Seal, Commissioner of Proprietary, and member of the Council; Edward Shippen, Mayor of Philadelphia, Commissioner of Proprietary, and member of the Council; Griffith Owen, Commissioner of Proprietary and member of the Council; Samuel Carpenter, Provincial Treasurer and councilor; John Moore, Register General and Attorney General; and his brother-in-law, Edward Pennington, Surveyor General. As Deputy Governor, Penn chose Andrew Hamilton, already the Governor of East and West New Jersey, and, although an Anglican, a man who commanded respect among Friends and Churchmen alike.

This small group of men, holding among them most of the strategic offices, both provincial and proprietary, represented a formidable power in Pennsylvania. Many of Penn's initial appointees had died or defected after his first return to England; now, however, his potential influence was greater than at any time since the earliest days of the settlement. Penn may have left behind a phalanx of carefully placed supporters, but they would have to vie for political supremacy with those who dominated the county courts, the legislature, and the Philadelphia city government. It was in these sectors that the strength of David Lloyd and his partisans bulked largest. Lloyd already commanded the allegiance of the middle class in Philadelphia as well as that of many landowners in Chester County. Whether Lloyd could attain the allegiance of influential merchants and landowners—men such as Caleb Pusey, John Blunston, John Simcock, Joseph Growdon, Isaac Norris, Jonathan Dickinson, Samuel Richardson, and Anthony Morris—was a question which would go far in determining the nature of political control in the early eighteenth century.

Whether their support could be won was dependent, in turn, upon the execution of proprietary policy. As long as Penn lobbied against the institution of royal government the upper members of colonial society were not likely to follow the demagogic Lloyd, unless in their view the proprietary machinery was the greater of the two evils. At the same time, having enjoyed power so long, such men were not inclined to surrender it to a Lloydian coalition exerting pressure from below. These were men who had wrested control of provincial politics from a proprietary clique in the early 1680's and had defended it since against the thrusts of Penn's lieutenant governors, leaders in the Lower Counties, lesser Quakers, Anglicans, and English bureaucrats. Their efforts signified the continuous effort required of provincial aristocracies, fluid and bucolic as they were, in establishing and maintaining political superiority in the colonial environment.

240

CHAPTER 6

The Politics of Disaffection

FOR TEN YEARS after Penn's departure from his colony, the future of Pennsylvania remained dismally uncertain. In many respects the situation recalled the time of troubles from 1689 to 1694. In England, Parliament renewed moves to abrogate the independent charters; in Pennsylvania the authority of Penn's deputy government underwent repeated challenges. The Council met infrequently, payment of quit-rents stopped, land sales withered, and the Lower Counties, virtually independent of Pennsylvania now, lacked visible signs of government. Among Friends internal divisions, fed by conflicts of personality and aggravated by economic distress, kept the colony in a state of chronic disequilibrium. All the centrifugal forces at work during the first two decades seemed to have ripened in the opening years of the eighteenth century. This left James Logan, who was foremost among those who wished to protect Penn's interests and who cherished an ordered, stable, community-oriented society, at the brink of despair. It seemed, wrote Logan, that the "Powers had brake loose from their center" in Pennsylvania and that "Hell itself is transplanted hither." Penn, by 1705, saw himself as "a crucified man between Injustice and Ingratitude" in Pennsylvania and "Extortion and Oppression" in England.[1]

Defending the Charter

The Board of Trade, by the time of Penn's arrival in England in December 1701, was already deep in deliberation

[1] Logan to Penn, July 25, 1706, Logan Letter Book (1702-09), 232; Penn to Logan, Sept. 14, 1705, *Penn-Logan Correspondence*, II, 71.

concerning the "unification" of the North American colonies. Hearings continued in the early months of 1702, as colonial bureaucrats attempted to steer through Parliament their bill for annulling the proprietary and corporate charters. As before, they made Pennsylvania a focal point of their attack, for the Quaker colony—a seat of non-Conformity, a region of contentious political factions, a province slow in matters of colonial defense, and allegedly a locale addicted to illegal trade—seemed to present the most convincing case for imperial reorganization.[2]

Ostensibly, the attack against Pennsylvania was led by the Board of Trade. But it was an open secret in England and the colonies that Henry Compton, the ambitious Bishop of London, and other important Anglicans such as Doctor Thomas Bray had as active an interest in the proceedings as the Whitehall bureaucrats. Since 1701, when the Society for the Propagation of the Gospel in Foreign Parts had been founded to pump blood into the lifestream of the Anglican Church in America, a circle of middle-Atlantic Churchmen, in contact with the Bishop, had been the prime agents in the war against independent charters. Compton had been a member of the Board of Trade since 1696; and, as Penn noted, Quary's recall in 1701 "to prejudice us & the government" was not the work of William Blathwayt alone, but bore the stamp of the Bishop of London as well.[3] Bray in 1701 had published a tract decrying "the deplorable State of the English Colonies where they have been in a manner

2 The best accounts of the new attempt to pass a Unification Bill are in Hall, *Randolph*, 202-218; and Alison G. Olson, "William Penn, Parliament and Proprietary Government," *William and Mary Quarterly*, 3rd Ser., 18 (1961), 176-195.

3 Penn to Logan, July 28, 1702, Penn Papers, Penn Family to Logan, I, 6. For Compton's career see Edward F. Carpenter, *The Protestant Bishop* (London, 1956).

abandoned to Atheism; or, which is much at one, to Quakerism, for want of a clergy settled among them."[4]

While the Anglican establishment in London mounted its offensive, its chief representatives in the colonies joined in the attack. Lord Cornbury and Chief Justice John Bridges of New York, Jeremiah Basse, former governor of East and West Jersey, Quary and John Moore in Pennsylvania, and Nicholson and Sir Thomas Lawrence in Maryland all fed grist into the propaganda mill of imperial reorganization through appearances before Parliament and the Board of Trade and by a steady stream of reports discrediting proprietary governments.[5] More than pride of empire or love of church animated these men; although those factors were undoubtedly important, they were interwoven with thoughts of career advancement, which almost certainly could be expected in the event of colonial unification. Penn resented the fact that private governments should suffer attacks by "knaves" and "beggars" so that "some people may have more Governments to exercise, & Governors to goe halves with—a corruption that has been thought to raigne too long already."[6]

It was Quary who took up the advocacy of colonial reform before the Board of Trade in March 1702, replacing the

[4] Cited in I. K. Steele, "The Board of Trade, the Quakers, and Resumption of Colonial Charters, 1699-1702," *William and Mary Quarterly*, 23 (1966), 613.

[5] The letters of these officials to various agencies of the English government are in *CSP 1702* and *CSP 1702-03*, passim; for their testimony before the Board of Trade and Parliament, see Stock, ed., *Proceedings*, II, 424-443; III, 1-6; and *H. of L.*, VI, 81-92. For the comments of Penn and Logan on the concerted Anglican efforts see *Penn-Logan Correspondence*, I, 202, 225-226, 228, 278, 354; II, 32; and Penn to Robert Harley, 1701 and Feb. 9, 1703/04, Duke of Portland MSS, *HMC, 15th Annual Report*, Appendix, Pt. IV, 30-32, 80.

[6] Penn to Lord Romney, Sept. 6, 1701, Penn Papers, Granville Penn Book, 6.

aging Randolph, whose irascibility and failing health had at last impelled the Board to ease him out to pasture. Reciting a litany of charges against the Quaker government, Quary argued that England would never achieve a disciplined, organic empire until the proprietary charters were extinguished.[7]

But Quary had a formidable opponent in Penn; for the Quaker proprietor was probably the most persuasive lobbyist for independent charters to be found on either side of the Atlantic. For each of Quary's accusations, Penn unleashed a rejoinder or counteraccusation: Quary himself had chided him, the Quaker proprietor related, for pursuing illegal traders too vigorously; Quary had overextended the authority of the vice-admiralty court in Pennsylvania, as the most eminent lawyers of England conceded; Quary, not Penn, was guilty of debauching the Pennsylvania Indians and driving them away from friendship with the English; Quary manipulated the evidence to discredit the administration of justice and made reckless, false charges concerning the denial of appeals. Furthermore, Penn pointed out that Governor Hamilton served without approbation only because Penn could not await the confirmation of a deputy before returning to England, and this stopgap measure had the approval of one of the Crown's ranking lawyers in the colonies, Chief Justice William Attwood of New York. The English government, Penn charged, had vested vice-admiralty authority in a man, who by his own admission was unacquainted with the civil law and whose activities as the

[7] Hall, *Randolph*, 213-217, details Randolph's loss of influence; Quary's report is in *CSP 1702*, #342i, supplemented by additional evidence in *ibid.*, #260, 356.

largest merchant and factor in the colony made a shambles of disinterested enforcement of the laws of trade.[8]

For two months in 1702, from mid-April to mid-June, Quary and Penn hurled charges and countercharges at each other before the Board of Trade. The net effect was negligible; Quary, while he could demonstrate irregularities in trade and government in Pennsylvania, could never prove that Penn's colony was much different than other provinces —royal, charter, or proprietary—in this respect.

Ultimately, the issue was decided not by the Board of Trade, where Quary's voice carried the most weight, but by Parliament, where Penn commanded an influence which the colonial bureaucrat could never hope to match. Utilizing contacts built up over the years, Penn and other Quaker lobbyists recruited both Whig and Tory support in opposing the Unification Bill which, as recent historians have pointed out, was at best a blurred political issue with far too many implications to split Parliament on strictly political lines.[9] Three times between 1702 and 1705 bills for vacating the proprietary charters came before committees of the Privy Council or before the House of Lords. Each time new reports from imperial officials told of malfeasance and maladministration in the colonies. And each time Penn was the most influential of those who rose to defend the private charters. Both in 1702 and later Penn made numerous appearances before the Board of Trade, the Privy Council, and the House of Lords and wrote letter after letter to high-placed friends. Would "the heat of a few churchmen, headed by a Flanders camp parson, under the protection

[8] The seemingly endless effusion of charges and countercharges between Quary and Penn can be followed in *ibid.*, #260, 305, 356, 391, 462, 498, 563, 568, 580, 612, 638, 648.

[9] Olson, "Penn, Parliament, and Proprietary Government," 183; Steele, "Board of Trade, Quakers, and Colonial Charters," 596-619.

of the Bishop of London," he wrote, be sufficient to abrogate a charter granted two decades before to insure that the Quakers might "enjoy their conscience more quietly?" Would a handful of "officious and turbulent persons" be allowed to bring down proprietary charters? "How much better the colonies thrive in proprietary hands than under the immediate government of the Crown," Penn pleaded with Robert Harley. What had the Crown done with Virginia in eight decades that could compare with Pennsylvania's improvement in less than three? Which was the better yardstick of a colony's value to the mother country: its growth and trade with England or the particular form of its charter?[10] In the end Quary lost not only his campaign to rescind the private charters but his job as judge of the vice-admiralty court at Philadelphia as well. The opposition of the Board of Trade bothered Penn little, he wrote bitterly, since the Quaker proprietor could afford to ignore its members, "having a greater Interest then all of them."[11]

While Penn beat back Quary's charges, lobbying intensively in Parliament for support, he shrewdly divulged that if the English government felt its control of Pennsylvania essential to the symmetry of empire, he would sell his rights to Pennsylvania for the £30,000 he had invested so far in the province and the guarantee that Quakers be allowed free exercise of their religion. Throughout the years when the Unification Bill remained under parliamentary consideration, Penn continued this tactic of leavening his defense of proprietary charters with offers to sell his government.[12]

10 Penn to Harley, Feb. 9, 1703/04, Duke of Portland MSS, *HMC, 15th Annual Report*, Pt. IV, 79-81.

11 Quary to Board of Trade, July 25, and Oct. 15, 1703, *CSP 1702-03*, #950, 1150.

12 Penn first indicated his plan to offer Pennsylvania to the Crown in a letter to Logan dated June 21, 1702, Janney, *William Penn*, 457-

It was a radical turnabout from his position in 1700 when he insisted that the land of the Delaware River Valley, stripped of the rights of government, was like the ring without the jewel.

In offering to relinquish his government, Penn had not turned his back on the colonists in Pennsylvania. Most of the Pennsylvanians, particularly the merchants, were convinced that the outbreak of war again between England and France in 1702 would bring the enemy to Delaware Bay, where the Quaker government, because of religious scruples, was impotent to deal with the threat. Nor could the colony count on the English government for support; the mother country, it was thought, "will rather leave us to tug for ourselves . . . for there are no succors to be expected to a colony, especially a step-child as we are, from her principles."[13] Only as a royal colony could the exposed Pennsylvanians expect the Crown to shield them.

Penn ultimately prevailed, almost to his and the merchants' chagrin. Too many in Parliament were either unconvinced by the arguments of the imperial reformers or not yet ready to challenge the Crown for control of the colonies. Much, after all, had been done since 1696 to regularize relationships between the colonies and the mother country, including the formation of the Board of Trade, tightening of the laws of trade, revamping of the customs

---

458. For his negotiations with the English government in 1702 see *CSP 1702-03*, #677, 684, 705, 728, 802-803, 823, 825, 837.

[13] Logan to Penn, May 2, 1702, *Penn-Logan Correspondence*, I, 88-89; eight days later Samuel Carpenter wrote Penn that the situation of Pennsylvania justified a surrender of government to the Crown. Quaker Scrapbook (Am. #12780), I, 213. Logan's later reports that the principal Quakers agreed upon the necessity of selling the government are given in *Penn-Logan Correspondence*, I, 147, 226-228, 284; II, 156.

service, standardization of colonial money, and creation of an agency for the promotion of the colonial Anglican Church. Given time, these measures might achieve what the abrogation of private charters could not. Almost as important was the press of international events, which pushed problems of bureaucratic efficiency into the background after 1702. All matters relating to the colonies moved "with an unspeakable delatoriness" because of the preeminent importance of "forraign affaires," Penn wrote after the outbreak of war.[14]

Disruption of Government

While Penn waged his campaign in London to fend off the colonial administrators—or, in the last resort, to surrender his government on his own terms—the nature and allocation of political power in Pennsylvania remained an unsettled question, a subject for continual and sometimes violent debate. Despite passage of the Charter of Liberties in 1701, which had presumably redefined the structure of government in accordance with the desires of a majority of the colonists, many in the colony were unwilling to accept the arrangement as permanent. In fact the sentiment for increasing provincial autonomy beyond the present limits was so great that annual sessions of the Assembly almost always turned into heated debates between the lower house and the governor over constitutional rather than legislative issues. Only twice in the decade after Penn's departure was it possible to pass legislation; the tendency was to descend into the thickets of argument over the rights and privileges of the people as opposed to the proprietor.

Apart from the desire for greater autonomous power, the

14 Penn to Logan, July 28, 1702, *PMHB*, 36 (1912), 305.

problem of continued political unrest was magnified by the peculiar fact that several important factions in the colony regarded the disruption of government as a positive good, an end in itself. For the Anglicans nothing was more important than keeping Quaker polity in a state of chronic confusion, for it was thought that the return of royal government, so ardently desired, could be hastened by proving the ineptitude of Friends in matters of state. Henceforth the Anglicans capitalized on every opportunity to disrupt the legislative, judicial, and administrative processes. The three Anglicans designated by the English government to administer official oaths in Pennsylvania, for example, refused to swear Governor Hamilton into office unless the legal instrument used for such occasions, the *dedimus potestatum*, was put in their possession for safekeeping. This was a concession which Hamilton, on the advice of the Chief Justice of New York and other legal authorities, felt he could not make, for the *dedimus* was traditionally preserved by the government itself.[15] Another ploy was to spread rumors: after Hamilton ordered the formation of a militia in 1702, it was said that those who answered the call to arms would begin their training with a forced march to Canada. No stone was left unturned, Penn learned, to thwart attempts to raise a militia, since the Anglicans "would have nothing done that may look with a good countenance at home."[16] Hamilton, himself an Anglican, concurred: "Noebody can imagine what ungentle-like practices are set afoot by those who to the scandal of their profession call themselves Churchmen to discourage those who have inlisted

15 Hamilton to Penn, May 7, 1702, Penn Papers, Official Correspondence, I, 30-31.

16 Logan to Penn, July 29, 1702, *Penn-Logan Correspondence*, I, 124; also see Logan's letters of Aug. 13 and Dec. 1, 1702, *ibid.*, 127-128, 152.

themselves."[17] Similar attempts to obstruct the government
were pursued in 1703. When Hamilton died and the executive functions of government devolved upon the Council,
the Anglicans commissioned to administer the oath of allegiance, or affirmation of loyalty, again invoked technicali-
ties to cripple the government. Unless a quorum of the
Council would subscribe to the oath, the Anglicans argued,
the *dedimus* could not be served. Since the Council included eight Quakers and two Anglicans, this was clearly
impossible. One of the Anglicans named in the commission
reportedly exclaimed that the government, lacking an executive arm, had been "laid on its back, and left . . . sprawling,
unable to move hand or foot."[18] In the courts, the Anglicans also moved to paralyze the machinery of government.
Producing an order of the Queen, which commanded that
anyone wishing to take an oath before a court must be allowed to do so, Quary promised to disqualify all Quaker
magistrates, who could neither take nor administer an oath
from the bench. When Hamilton appointed *ad hoc* courts
composed of Anglican judges to hear a backlog of cases in
Philadelphia, Anglican jury members refused to serve, convinced by Quary and Attorney General John Moore that
the special courts were extralegal. "Their plot," reported
the frustrated Council, "is to have the whole ministry . . .
in confusion, and that thereupon it will be absolutely necessary to be taken into the Queen's more immediate care."[19]

17 Hamilton to Penn, Sept. 19, 1702, *CSP 1702-03*, #24i.

18 *Minutes of Council*, II, 92-96; Council to Penn, Aug. 26, 1703, *CSP
1702-03*, #1407i; also Logan's reports to Penn on the incident in *Penn-
Logan Correspondence*, I, 192-196, 229-230, 239, 242-244. Quary gave his
version of the problem in a letter to the Board of Trade, June 30,
1703, *CSP 1702-03*, #858.

19 *Minutes of Council*, II, 89-90; Council to Penn, Aug. 26, 1703, *CSP
1702-03*, #1407i; the problem is discussed at length in Root, *Relations*

In the Lower Counties the leading planters and merchants applauded the tactics of Quary and the Philadelphia Anglicans. Embittered by proprietary policies and long years of rancorous dispute with their Quaker neighbors, fully exposed to attack from the sea, and disgruntled at a higher quitrent which Penn had recently imposed on newly purchased land in the Territories, the legislators of the Lower Counties welcomed the demise of proprietary government. To press their case in England they engaged the services of Robert Quary.[20] Logan reported that the Lower Counties were entirely disaffected; if they remained quiet, it was only because they fully expected the intervention of Crown government.[21]

More injurious to the proprietary cause than the opposition of the Lower Counties or the Philadelphia Anglicans was the tireless campaigning of David Lloyd. Penn's ship had scarcely cleared the Delaware Capes on the return voyage to England before Lloyd took up the cudgels of the antiproprietary struggle which was to preoccupy him for the next ten years—and to some degree for the rest of his life. From the outset, he emphasized that government must exist not as an extension of proprietary authority but as the instrument of the people's will, expressed by the Provincial

---

of Pennsylvania, 239-248, and in Logan's letter to Penn of June 24, 1703, Penn-Logan Correspondence, I, 193-196.

[20] William Rodney, John Brinkloe, John Walker, et al. to the Board of Trade, Oct. 25, 1701, Miscellaneous Papers, Three Lower Counties, 99; Assembly of Lower Counties to Board of Trade, Nov. 21, 1702, CSP 1702-03, #17v; Quary to Board of Trade, April 7, 1702, CSP 1702, #305; Logan to Penn, March 3, 1702/03, Penn-Logan Correspondence, I, 176.

[21] Logan to Penn, May 11, June 18, and Sept. 2, 1702, Penn-Logan Correspondence, I, 102, 107, 235; Logan and Commissioners of Property to William Clarke, ca. March 1703, Logan Letter Book (1702-1716), 20.

POLITICS OF DISAFFECTION

Assembly and the municipal government of Philadelphia. Lloyd's arguments represented no departure from the familiar antiproprietary themes which by now were more than a decade old. What was new was the state of receptivity to such ideas. For in the decade after Penn's departure a concatenation of events in Pennsylvania created an atmosphere which gave new resonance to Lloyd's appeal for further insulation from external authority.

At the most basic level was the question of Penn's charter. Most men in the colony believed that the English government would soon annul all remaining private charters; many welcomed such a move. Agreement with Lloyd was general that considering the likelihood of royal intervention prudence required that Pennsylvania seek the greatest possible degree of self-government. If Penn's interests suffered as a result, that was unfortunate but unavoidable.[22]

Apart from the logic of Lloyd's arguments, economic setbacks conditioned the colony for the spread of antiproprietary sentiment. Beginning in late 1701, the West Indian grain market, the underpinning of the economy, slumped badly. The following spring brought only further distress. With the outbreak of war, French privateers infested the Caribbean waters, making all mercantile ventures to the islands extremely hazardous. By September 1702, trade prospects were bleak. "Wheat, that when you left us was our best commodity," Logan wrote Penn, "goes begging from door to door, and can rarely find a buyer." With Philadelphia merchants buying no grain, the farmers were utterly without money. Trade was further disrupted by the fallen state of the tobacco market, which left bankrupt the Maryland merchants upon whom Pennsylvanians relied for

[22] Logan to Penn, May 2 and Dec. 1, 1702, *Penn-Logan Correspondence*, I, 87, 147-148.

bills of exchange on English creditors. Trade was "a Lottery," despaired Logan in 1703.[23]

Although the West Indian grain trade revived briefly in the fall of 1703, even greater economic reverses lay ahead. By February 1704, wheat, flour, and bread were a drug on the market again. Disheartening losses were suffered throughout the colony. Samuel Carpenter, whose mercantile success in the seventeenth century had been unequaled, went bankrupt. William Trent and Isaac Norris, Philadelphia's largest traders after Carpenter's retirement, lost one-third of their estates in 1704.[24] A side effect of the war was the drying up of immigration; few dared to make the trans-Atlantic voyage when French privateers roamed the approaches of both the eastern and western Atlantic. With the decline of incoming settlers, the colony lost an important source of specie; land sales ground to a halt; real estate values plummeted. Even Robert Quary admitted that the economic condition of the middle colonies was so dismal that appropriations for defense by their legislatures were out of the question. Although the economy rallied briefly

[23] Penn to Logan, Dec. 1, 1702, *ibid.*, I, 146-147; the downward economic trend can be followed in Logan's letters to Penn, Logan Letter Book (1702-1709); in Logan's letters to various English and West Indian merchants, Logan Letter Book (1702-1726); and in the numerous letters of Isaac Norris to merchant friends in England, the West Indies, and other mainland colonies, Norris Letter Books (1702-1704) and (1704-1706). The disruption of colonial trade with the West Indies is considered in Ruth Bourne, *Queen Anne's Navy in the West Indies* (New Haven, 1939), 58-130. For the effect of Maryland's bankrupt merchants see Gary B. Nash, "Maryland's Economic War with Pennsylvania," *Maryland Historical Magazine*, 60 (1965), 231-244.

[24] Carpenter to Jonathan Dickinson, Dec. 31, 1705, Edward and Louis H. Carpenter, *Samuel Carpenter and his Descendants* (Philadelphia, 1912), 22-23; Logan to Penn, Feb. 11, 1704/05, *Penn-Logan Correspondence*, I, 363. A clear picture of the economic dislocation that prevailed in 1704 and 1705 is given in Logan's letter to Penn, Aug. 22, 1705, *ibid.*, II, 40-58.

in 1705, economic stability did not really return until 1710, when the virtual end of hostilities between England and France restored foreign markets and reopened trade routes to southern Europe and the West Indies.[25]

With the economic fortunes of the colony at a nadir, it was essential that landowners be given at least temporary relief from quitrents and proprietary taxes. Penn, however, hopelessly trapped in debt by the ruthless Philip Ford and unable to negotiate the sale of his colony, kept pressure on James Logan to dun for back rents and arrearages on the £2,000 proprietary tax passed in 1701. Eager to please his patron and more than a little inflated by his extensive responsibilities, Logan attempted to glean taxes and rents from the colonists. His letters to Penn reveal the hostility which he met at every turn. In long outpourings, which testify to his loneliness and sense of alienation in Pennyslvania, Logan spelled out the difficulty of his position. The scarcity of money made the collection of rents and taxes, both payable in specie, virtually impossible. Hard money seemed "to have almost taken its leave of this Continent"; so severe was the shortage that some landowners rumored that Penn himself had carried great sums of gold and silver out of the colony in 1701. Many of the better farmers hardly saw "a piece of eight" from January to December.[26]

Despite the illogic of Penn's policy, Logan roamed the

[25] See Logan's letters to Penn in *ibid.*, I, 66-67, 94-95, 105, 146-147, 269; II, 54; and Logan to Penn, May 17, 1705, *Pennsylvania Archives*, 2nd Ser., VII, 21; Quary to Board of Trade, May 30, 1704, *CSP 1704-05*, #353. A study of the economic impact of the war on the colonies is badly needed. G. N. Clark suggests that English commerce as a whole reached a nadir in 1705. "War Trade and Trade War, 1701-1713," *Economic History Review*, 1 (1927-28), 262-280.

[26] Logan to Penn, June 14, 1703, Logan Letter Book (1702-09), 93; Logan to Penn, May 7, 1702 and Oct. 3, 1704, *Penn-Logan Correspondence*, I, 94, 325.

countryside, county by county, in his fruitless attempts to bring in the taxes and back rents. It was a self-defeating exercise. Hardly a man remained in the colony by 1703 who would aid him in representing Penn's interest, Logan complained. All of the old proprietary stalwarts turned their heads or pleaded the difficulties of the time. Edward Shippen concentrated on his own affairs; Thomas Story disliked "to give any offence" and stood ready to resign his offices; Griffith Owen hesitated to uphold the proprietary interest; Nicholas Waln was wavering; Samuel Carpenter was bankrupt and in retirement at Bristol. "There is generally so great a disregard of thy affairs among the people that to carry them on vigorously is to sail against wind and tide," Logan wrote Penn.[27]

While economic conditions and ill-calculated attempts to collect proprietary taxes and rents played into the hands of Lloyd and his party, renewed religious controversy in Philadelphia added a further dimension to the undercurrent of disaffection. George Keith, the Quaker's old nemesis, and since 1699 a convert to Anglicanism, returned to Pennsylvania in 1702, just when economic dislocation and governmental confusion were at their peak. Ranging up and down the seaboard as the itinerant agent of the Society for the Promotion of Christian Knowledge, the evangelical arm of the Church of England, Keith clashed with Cotton Mather and the Congregational fathers in Boston, scourged the Quakers at Newport and Long Island, and then moved south into the Jerseys and Pennsylvania. For two winters, in 1702-1703 and 1703-1704, Keith trekked over his old battlegrounds, assailing Friends at public gatherings and distributing anti-Quaker tracts printed in New York by his old

[27] Logan to Penn, May 7, July 9, Oct. 2, 1702, and March 3, 1702/03, *ibid.*, I, 94-95, 102-121, 139-141, 174.

friend William Bradford.[28] Though he converted few Quakers to Anglicanism, Keith added fuel to the fires of Quaker-Anglican hostility and increased the combustibility of the atmosphere. Former Keithians were reminded of old wounds inflicted by the leading Quakers in the tempestuous days of the great schism. Old issues in the Keithian controversy of 1692 were re-argued and old doctrinal and civil disputes exhumed.

Also contributing to the success of David Lloyd's anti-proprietary campaign was the ineptitude of Penn's deputy governors. John Evans, who held the office from 1704 to 1709, was only twenty-six years old when he reached the colony and was handicapped by an unstable personality. Though Penn could advertise him to the Board of Trade as liberally educated, well-traveled, sober, judicious, encumbered neither by debt nor aristocratic temperament, and "a known zealous member of the Church of England," the truth of the matter was that Evans had done nothing but play the gentleman since reaching adulthood, was ut-

28 Kirby, *George Keith*, 114-116, 125-147; Norris to Jonathan Dickinson, Nov. 8, 1702, and to Thomas Lloyd, March 17, 1702/03, Norris Letter Book (1702-1704), 11, 39. Quakers and Anglicans had been exchanging blows in print since 1700, when Daniel Leeds, a West Jersey Anglican, published his scurrilous anti-Quaker tract, *News of a Strumpet Co-habitating in the Wilderness: a brief Abstract of the Spiritual and Carnal Whoredoms & Adulteries of the Quakers in America Delineated in a Cage of Twenty Unclean Birds* (Philadelphia, 1701). Leeds indicted Quaker leaders, including Samuel Jennings, Thomas Lloyd, Robert Ewer, Thomas Fitzwater, and Arthur Cooke, with a catalogue of sins ranging from adultery and drunkenness to money-clipping and venality. Leeds was answered by Caleb Pusey, a Quaker leader in Chester County. The literary war, which lasted until 1706, can be followed in Charles Evans, *American Bibliography* (14 vols., Chicago, 1903-59), I, #916, 948, 982-83, 1055, 1094, 1110, 1113, 1143-44, 1163, 1192, 1230-31, 1235, 1248, 1277. Keith's account of his mission, edited by Edgar L. Pennington, is in *The Historical Magazine of the Protestant Episcopal Church*, 20 (1951), 346-479.

terly without experience in government, and had only his father's friendship with Penn to recommend him.[29] That Penn would send such a stripling into the political jungles of Pennsylvania at a time when his colony lay politically paralyzed testified both to the proprietor's financial inability to employ a man with real qualifications and to the low regard which men of talent in England had for the job of governing the Pennsylvania Quakers.

At first Evans was perceptive enough of the forces lying in wait for him to rely on the advice of the Council in his attempts to carry out Penn's instructions to "keep up the Powers of my Graunt . . . and in no wise suffer them to be broaken in upon by any refractory or factious Persons whatever."[30] But his sense of self-importance and his close association with Penn's impetuous son, who had accompanied him to the colony, soon led Evans to seek his own solutions to problems of government.

In two particular cases his attempts at independent action played directly into the hands of David Lloyd and those who measured success in provincial politics by their ability to invest all power in the Assembly and the municipal Corporation of Philadelphia. The first occurred in 1706, just after Penn's supporters were able to discredit Lloyd for independently sending an abusive remonstrance to Penn in the name of the Assembly. In May a member of the lower house, William Biles, had risen before the legislature to

[29] Penn to Board of Trade, July 8, 1703, Penn Letter Book (1699-1701), 153; Edward D. Neill, "Memoir of John Evans, Deputy Governor of Pennsylvania," *New England Historical and Genealogical Register*, 1st Ser., 26 (1872), 421-425.

[30] Penn to Evans, Sept. 5, 1704 and Nov. 6, 1704, *New England Historical and Genealogical Register*, 26 (1872), 425-426; Penn to Evans, March 5, 1704/05, Macalester College, St. Paul, Minn. (photostat in Howland Collection, Haverford College Library). Penn's commission to Evans is in Peters Papers, I, 9 (copy).

criticize Evans's performance as governor and ended his speech on a nearly treasonous note, urging his legislative colleagues to "kick out" the Governor, who was "but a boy" and "not fit to Govern us."[31] Outraged, Evans brought suit against Biles for £1000. A jury of enquiry found damages in the amount of £300; Biles was also brought before the Quaker Yearly Meeting and condemned for his intemperate attack. This much done to the Governor's satisfaction, the Assembly and some of Philadelphia's leading Quakers urged Evans to forego the damages awarded, since Biles, a Bucks County farmer, could never be expected to pay the fine without auctioning half his estate. Instead, Evans issued a writ for his arrest and held Biles in close confinement for more than a month. Leading Quakers pleaded in vain with Evans that "he had stabbed his own interest." Remonstrances and solicitations from all sides failed to move the Governor. By the end of March, when Evans finally released Biles from prison, the tide of public opinion was surging again in Lloyd's favor.[32]

In the wake of the Biles incident came a second blunder, equally damaging to the proprietary cause. Word reached Philadelphia in the spring of 1706 that French naval successes in the West Indies had made the Caribbean all but a French sea. St. Christopher and Nevis lay in ruins and a fleet of 27 warships, bolstered by a swarm of privateers and small craft, had brought colonial trade with the islands virtually to a standstill. New York and Philadelphia trembled at the prospect of a French invasion. Never had there been such fortifying in America, Logan wrote Penn, with shops

---

[31] Logan to Penn, June 12, 1706, *Penn-Logan Correspondence*, II, 131. Lloyd's temporary loss of popularity is discussed by Lokken, *David Lloyd*, 151-161.

[32] Logan to Penn, June 12, 1706, *Penn-Logan Correspondence*, II, 131-133; *Votes of Assembly*, I, 572.

shut in New York and "all hands taken to the mattock and shovel and spade to keep him [the Frenchman] out when he comes."[33] For Evans, who had struggled long and unsuccessfully to establish a militia in Pennsylvania, the situation seemed to provide a golden opportunity. Exasperated at Quaker scruples concerning the militia—many suspected that Friends' objections had economic as well as religious origins—and disgusted at Anglican attempts to obstruct the militia as a means of discrediting Quaker government, Evans vowed to teach all sides a lesson.

On the morning of May 16, 1706, the sheriff and clerk of New Castle County rode breathlessly into town and poured out the news that six French brigantines were pushing upstream to take Philadelphia. The Frenchmen, he reported, had passed New Castle at two that morning, tarrying only long enough to batter the town with forty or fifty guns. Lewes, downstream from New Castle, lay in smoking ruins.[34] Evans sounded the alarm and galloped about town, sword drawn, directing all who could bear arms to a hill overlooking the river in the southern part of the city. The wildest disorder followed: powder was dealt out, two apprentices blew themselves up in their eagerness to initiate action, women miscarried, shopkeepers threw their goods into wells or hastily buried them in the ground, younger Quakers inexplicably found themselves shouldering arms and digging in for the fight, while other Friends, fleeing town, trembled at the shouts of Anglicans, who flung out warnings that under the circumstances Quakers and Frenchmen would make equally attractive targets. By nightfall, with the enemy not

[33] Logan to Penn, May 28, 1706, *Penn-Logan Correspondence,* II, 123-124; Logan to Edward Hackett, Aug. 13, 1706, Logan Letter Book (1702-16), 80.

[34] Logan to Penn, May 28, 1706 and June 12, 1706, *Penn-Logan Correspondence,* II, 123-126, 133-135.

yet in sight, the Philadelphians realized that they had been duped by their wily Governor who had concocted the canard with his New Castle friends to show the Quakers of Philadelphia how "naked and defenceless" their city would be in case of a real French attack. Though it did that, the more lasting effect was to convince many "well-wishers to the Government" that William Biles was right in labeling the Governor an incompetent and hotheaded youth.[35]

By June 1706, Logan recognized the full extent of the damage caused by Evans's impulsive behavior. For the first time since Penn's departure the Assembly included a strong element of upper-class moderates sympathetic to Penn's interest; but they showed their disgust for the Governor's war games by vowing not to run for reelection in October. Logan reported that Lloyd now "carries fair with our weak country" and predicted correctly that the next Assembly would be hostile beyond comparison. To make matters worse, Evans, who had previously consulted with Penn's friends on the Council, now closed his ears to advice, taking up residence out of town and brooding on the inadequate salary provided by the close-fisted Assembly.[36]

Economic dislocation, the threat of French attack, the portent of royal government, hostility in the Lower Counties, tension between Quakers and Anglicans, unwise attempts to enforce collection of proprietary taxes and rents, the timidity of the proprietor's supporters, an enfeebled executive government—all mingled to create conditions favorable to David Lloyd and to his design to fashion an all-

[35] The scene was described in *Minutes of Council*, II, 240-244, 249-250; Samuel Preston to Jonathan Dickinson, May 19, 1706, *Penn-Logan Correspondence*, II, 123-126, 133-135; and Logan to Edward Hackett, Aug. 13, 1706, Logan Letter Book (1702-16), 80.

[36] Logan to Penn, ca. June 1706, July 25, 1706, July 27, 1706, *Penn-Logan Correspondence*, II, 118-119, 137-141, 143-146.

powerful antiproprietary party from the dissident and disillusioned elements of Pennsylvania society.

Lloyd concentrated on two primary objectives in his pursuit of power: domination of the Corporation of Philadelphia and control of the Provincial Assembly. The allegiance of the Corporation was virtually assured, since the city government was self-perpetuating and securely in the control of Lloyd's supporters. Reports reached Penn that the Corporation—an "imperium in imperio" in Logan's view—openly opposed his interests. When the Philadelphia County Court authorized Logan's collectors to put liens on the property of tax evaders, for example, the City Court asserted its authority in such matters and annulled the decision. Though the Governor and Chief Justice of the colony ruled this illegal, the Lloydian city government "carried it . . . by force, declaring thou hadst given a charter, that was their expectation of it, and none whatever should hinder them." Penn's interests were further subverted when the Mayor's City Court claimed all fines which had formerly accrued to the proprietor. "Destroy or humble the Corporation, thy most backward friends in government," begged Logan.[37] But Penn was hoist with his own petard. He agreed with those who complained that the "extravagant Charters" granted in 1701 "destroyed the very being of Government." But having earlier conceded such extensive powers as a hedge against royal government, there was little he could do.[38] Penn threatened to revoke the city charter, but he must have known that even if such a decision could be enforced, which was doubtful, it would only be

[37] Logan to Penn, Oct. 2, 1702; Penn to Logan, Feb. 24, 1702/03; Logan to Penn, ca. April and Aug. 10, 1706, *ibid.*, I, 137-139, 169; II, 119, 146.

[38] Quary to Board of Trade, Dec. 7, 1702, *CSP 1702-03*, #16.

employed by David Lloyd to prove the despotic tendencies of proprietary government.[39]

The Assembly was somewhat more difficult for Lloyd to control, although he was able to carry every election in the decade after Penn's departure except in 1706 and 1710. In five of these years he was elected Speaker and at one point assumed the Clerkship of the House concurrently. When the Corporation of Philadelphia chose Lloyd to replace Thomas Story as City Recorder in 1704, Penn's most determined critic completed his personal occupation of the strategic positions of power.[40] As Recorder, Lloyd ranked second only to the Mayor in city government and sat as president of the city courts and a member of the Philadelphia County Court.

Vested with multiple powers, Lloyd continued his campaign to neutralize proprietary influence in Pennsylvania. The first step was to thwart any continuing legislative union of the northern section of the colony and the Lower Counties. Since 1701, when Penn had provided for the legislative separation of the two areas, leading men in the Lower Counties had wavered on the question of breaking ties. But now Lloyd insisted that the refusal of the Lower Counties to send representatives to the Assembly in 1702 had permanently broken the legislative link between the province and the Territories.[41] That done, Lloyd introduced three bills ingeniously constructed to shield colonial institutions almost entirely from external influence. The first, "The Bill for Confirmation of the Charter of Privileges," was more

39 Penn to Logan, Feb. 24, 1702/03 and Jan. 16, 1704/05, *Penn-Logan Correspondence*, I, 169, 351-359.

40 Lokken, *David Lloyd*, 134-135, 142; Logan to Penn, July 14, 1704, *Penn-Logan Correspondence*, I, 304.

41 *Votes of Assembly*, I, 407-410; *Minutes of Council*, II, 123-140; Shepherd, *Proprietary Government in Pennsylvania*, 338-341.

than its title implied. Apart from confirming the Frame of 1701 by legislative act, its ostensible purpose, it broadened the parliamentary privileges of the Assembly to include not only the right to sit on its own adjournment, but to dissolve or prorogue itself—powers previously reserved for the executive as his only remaining means of restraining the legislature.[42] Lloyd's second bill, "for Confirmation of the Charter of the City of Philadelphia . . . ," was likewise promoted simply as a legislative confirmation of powers granted by Penn in 1701. It was no secret, however, that the bill, if passed, would insure the supremacy of the city of Philadelphia over Philadelphia County. The County Courts would lose all jurisdiction over the city except in cases of capital crimes, while two seats on the county courts would be reserved for aldermen of the city. Other functions which were now under the jurisdiction of the proprietor or the Assembly would be transferred to the municipal government: the power to establish an orphans' court, to raise money for municipal improvements, to appoint all city officers except sheriff and coroner, to remove officers of the city government, to set fees and salaries within the municipality, and to record and enroll all deeds and legal documents pertaining to property transactions, mercantile transactions, wills, administration of estates, and indentures.[43] In short, the act put the city of Philadelphia beyond proprietary reach. Greater autonomy could scarcely have been granted if the city had been reconstituted by royal patent as an independent colony within the boundaries of Penn's grant. So many "extravagant privileges and new grants"

---

[42] *Minutes of Council*, II, 149-150; Logan to Penn, July 14, 1704, *Penn-Logan Correspondence*, I, 298-299.

[43] *Minutes of Council*, II, 155-156; a rough draft of the bill is in Provincial Papers, 1664-1712, Dept. of Public Records, Harrisburg.

were crowded into the bill, wrote Logan, that Judge Mompesson, one of the ablest legal minds in the colonies, concluded that even London's charter of incorporation paled by comparison.[44]

The third bill, "An Act for the Regulation of Courts," represented only a new version of the judiciary reform bill of 1701 which Penn had disallowed after his arrival in England when he realized that it transferred his power to establish and regulate the courts to the Assembly. Tied to the bill, for the purpose of sweetening, was a clause favored by Quakers of all political tendencies—the substitution of the affirmation, to which Quakers could subscribe, for the detested oath. Though the bill contradicted an order of the Queen-in-Council, which made the oath mandatory for all officers of government, it had Penn's endorsement, for the proprietor insisted that the Queen's dictum on oaths conflicted with his charter rights.[45]

Taken together, Lloyd's legislative proposals promised to confer remarkable powers upon the Assembly and the Corporation of Philadelphia—powers far beyond those enjoyed by provincial assemblies and municipal governments in other colonies and in some ways greater even than those possessed by Parliament and city corporations in England.

Although Lloyd could not enact this kind of legislative program as long as Penn or his deputy in Pennsylvania possessed a veto power, he could keep the proprietary faction off balance and maintain his own popularity by insuring that the annual meetings of the Assembly focused on bills of this nature—proposals which involved, essentially, the division of power between the people as represented in the

[44] Logan to Penn, Sept. 28, 1704, *Penn-Logan Correspondence*, I, 317.
[45] *Votes of Assembly*, I, 415-420; *Minutes of Council*, II, 155-156; Lokken, *David Lloyd*, 135-136.

Assembly and the absentee proprietor or his representatives in residence. Nothing dramatized this confrontation better than the controversy over the courts. Word had been received in 1705 that the Queen-in-Council had rejected the Judiciary Act of 1701 under which the courts functioned, but the Assembly in that year had been unable to agree with the Governor on a new bill. With the courts disabled, debts went uncollected, wills unproven, and criminals untried. Then in 1706, assisted by the Council, Evans submitted a new court bill to the Assembly. It provided for the concentration of appointive power in the deputy governor and, most importantly, for the transfer of equity jurisdiction to a special court appointed by Penn's deputy and sitting in Philadelphia. The court, it was clear, would be controlled by the merchants of Philadelphia and since most suits for debt found their way into equity court, there was little doubt that indebted country farmers had much to fear. The Assembly countered with a wholly different bill which not only retained equity jurisdiction in the county courts, where country debtors could expect a sympathetic hearing from their neighbors, but gave the Assembly power to remove judges whose performance was deemed unfit, strengthened the powers of the Philadelphia City Court, reserved fines assessed by county and city courts for judicial salaries instead of for the proprietor's coffers, prohibited imprisonment for debt except under unusual circumstances, and transferred final authority over land titles from the proprietor to the county courts instead.[46]

When Evans perceived that Lloyd and the Assembly would not yield to his court bill, which in many respects allowed the proprietor or his deputy greater power than

[46] *Minutes of Council*, II, 258-266; *Votes of Assembly*, I, 586-600. The fullest explanation of the issues involved is in Lokken, *David Lloyd*, 166-176.

provided in 1701, he threatened to establish the courts by ordinance. This assertion of the prerogative power only further antagonized the Lloydians and ultimately changed a debate over judicial organization into a question of constitutional rights. Since 1684, courts had been established by the legislature in Pennsylvania except in the city of Philadelphia. There were few now, in a time when Penn's government was in obvious peril, who wished to reestablish the precedent of the prerogative power over the courts, whether Penn's charter allowed it or not. And there were few, in a period of economic slump, who wanted to turn the equity courts over to the Governor and his merchant allies in Philadelphia.[47]

From November through January, the Council and Assembly hurled messages back and forth in the battle over the courts. Gradually, both sides withdrew some of their more extravagant demands. The Governor agreed to forego his appointive court of equity and the Assembly yielded on the right of the courts to use fines for judicial salaries. But another month of heated debate made it apparent that the judiciary issue had become secondary to the question of Evans's right to establish the courts by decree—the threat to which he always resorted in his debates with the Assembly.[48] Both sides cited the English constitution. The Assembly, charged Evans, took measures "that no people in the world ever attempted before under an English Constitution." Lloyd and the Assembly argued that they strove for only those powers "agreeable to an English Constitution," but if Penn's charter rights, issued twenty-four years before, blocked the attainment of privileges enjoyed else-

---

[47] *Minutes of Council*, II, 267-275; Logan to Penn, Nov. 26, 1706, *Penn-Logan Correspondence*, II, 180.
[48] *Minutes of Council*, II, 276-343; *Votes of Assembly*, I, 599-725.

where in the English colonies, then it was time to discard the charter.[49]

Personal bitterness on both sides added to the inflammatory atmosphere. Logan had the bad sense to stride into a Philadelphia coffeehouse, which had become the Assembly's political club, and tear from the wall the Assembly's minutes, which were now regularly posted there in the form of battle communiqués. Outraged at this, the Assembly, on Christmas Eve of 1706, ordered articles of impeachment drawn up against Logan. Lloyd was equally provocative. At joint conferences between the Council and Assembly he resorted to intentional breaches of conduct, finally refusing to stand when addressing the Governor as if to assert symbolically the legislature's equality with the executive. When Evans refused to tolerate this calculated insult, Lloyd stalked out of the conference room followed by the members of the whole House in single file.[50]

It was symptomatic of the need on each side to project the appearance of victory that even when compromises were reached on the major issues posed by Lloyd's court bill, the measure failed to pass because of disagreement over far less important matters—the county courts' right to grant licenses to public houses and the power of the Assembly to remove clerks of court for misbehavior. Evans finally established the courts by ordinance on February 22. But it was a hollow victory. Never again could the Governor expect the Assembly, whose members now complained darkly of a government by decree, not law, to appropriate money for his salary. Deeply depressed, Logan warned that the proceedings, which in the final stages had become more an exercise in

[49] *Minutes of Council,* II, 309-310, 293.
[50] *Votes of Assembly,* I, 652; *Minutes of Council,* II, 310-315; Logan to Penn, March 2, 1706/07, *Penn-Logan Correspondence,* II, 194.

verbal violence than in parliamentary government, could only presage the "Approaching Destruction" of Pennsylvania.[51]

By 1708 Penn's discouragement with his colony was nearly complete. "What Proprietor and Governour would care one jot what becomes of such foolish, if not wicked people," he wrote, while condemning David Lloyd as "a traitorous person, . . . a delinquent and a vile ingrate." Penn wrote these lines from the confinement of debtors' prison where he had languished, his health failing, since January 1708. Not until the autumn of that year, when £6,600 was raised by English Quakers for the discharge of his debt to the heirs of Philip Ford, was Penn released.[52]

For Lloyd and his followers Penn was no longer much of a threat. But James Logan was another matter. Intellectual, imperious by nature, vested with a multitude of powers and titles, and inflexibly opposed to all innovations that diminished proprietary power, Logan was clearly the chief remaining obstacle in the quest to emasculate Penn's power in Pennsylvania. Nothing was of greater importance to Lloyd, once it became apparent that the legislative impasse over the

[51] *Minutes of Council*, II, 339-342, 356, 361; Logan to William Penn, Jr., April 4, 1707, Logan Papers, X, 9. Governor Evans's ordinance for establishing the courts is in Miscellaneous Manuscript Collection, 1701-1742, American Philosophical Society.

[52] Penn to Logan, May 18, 1708, *Penn-Logan Correspondence*, II, 271. A small group of Quaker merchants is historically given credit for providing the funds which obtained Penn's release from prison. See, for example, Shepherd, *Proprietary Government in Pennsylvania*, 197; Peare, *William Penn*, 404; Keith, *Chronicles of Pennsylvania*, II, 483-484. Actually the money was subscribed by almost sixty Quaker merchants, shopkeepers, artisans and widows in Bristol and London. See the "Declaration by Henry Gouldney, Joshua Gee, Silvanus Grove, and John Woods . . . ," Oct. 7, 1708, Bedfordshire County Record Office, as cited in Catalogue of Wynne Collection Relating to William Penn at Bedfordshire County Record Office, Friends House, London.

court bill could not be broken, than to oust Penn's omnipresent agent on horseback, who dunned for rents, cried unendingly for the collection of taxes, and stubbornly upheld the privileges of his patron as proprietary overlord. That Lloyd was Welsh and Logan Scotch-Irish also contributed to their mutual antagonism, as did the fact that Lloyd saw Logan, his junior by eighteen years, as his chief rival for power in Pennsylvania politics.

After Lloyd regained control of the Assembly in 1706, the removal of Logan became a fixed object of antiproprietary policy. Immediately after convening, the House cited Penn's secretary for contempt and in the following year impeachment proceedings were instituted for "divers Crimes and high misdemeanors." The charges, which were highly unspecific, included tampering with public documents, the maladministration of proprietary land policy, violations of the Frame of 1701, and employment of tactics by which Logan had allegedly "Endeavored to deprive the Queens Subjects . . . of the priviledges and benefits which they ought to Enjoy by the fundamental Laws of England & Establisht Constitutions of this Government and instead thereof to Introduce an arbitrary Government against Law."[53]

Logan was in no real danger. For while Lloyd could assert the right of the Assembly to impeach officers of government, Evans could refer to English constitutional precedent, which Lloyd so frequently invoked, to point out that only the upper house of the legislature could try impeached officials. Since the Council in Pennsylvania no longer exercised a legislative role, no legally qualified body existed to hear and judge articles of impeachment.[54]

[53] Articles of Impeachment against James Logan, Feb. 25, 1706/07, Logan Papers, IV, 21. Logan's "Answers to the Assembly's Articles of Impeachment" of March 4, 1706/07 is in Logan Papers, IV, 35.
[54] *Minutes of Council*, II, 364-379.

Though Lloyd was temporarily stymied in his vendetta against Logan, the arrival of Evans's successor, Colonel Charles Gookin, in January 1709 seemed to provide a new opportunity for unseating the proprietor's secretary. Hoping to find a more pliant governor, Lloyd reactivated the charges against Logan. Like his predecessor, Gookin boasted no experience in government or statecraft, and had only an undistinguished military career to commend him. At Gookin's inaugural meeting with the Assembly, Lloyd delivered a withering attack on Logan, charging the Secretary with the political perversion of Governor Evans, the initiation of great oppressions in the colony, and responsibility for the present "Miseries & Confusion of the State & Divisions in this Government." The return of political stability could only come, Lloyd argued, after the removal of this proprietary satrap from the Council.[55]

Gookin had no intention of purging Logan from his Council, for Penn had emphatically instructed him to seek the Secretary's counsel in political and proprietary affairs.[56] This left Lloyd to fall back on the old issues of the Assembly's privileges, the judiciary reform bill, and the limitation of proprietary powers. For half a year after Gookin's arrival, the Governor and Assembly parried, each seeking weaknesses in the other's armor. While the Assembly resurrected all the old issues for which no solution had been found under Hamilton's or Evans's governorships, Gookin pressed strongly for money to raise and equip a troop of men for the intercolonial expedition to be launched shortly against Canada. To Gookin's request for 150 men or £4,000 (the equivalent in money) the Assembly responded with an of-

55 *Ibid.*, II, 427-434.
56 Penn's instructions to Gookin are in Penn Papers, Assembly and Provincial Council, 25.

fer of £500—and even this bill passed only by a majority
of one. Gookin regarded so paltry a sum as a calculated af-
front, especially since every other colony had met or exceeded the Queen's requests. Even West New Jersey, Pennsylvania's poorer Quaker sister, had granted £3,000 in lieu
of her quota of militiamen.[57]

All the venom born of a decade of political conflict, all
the grievances arising from the extended economic slump,
as well as all the insecurities stemming from the threat of
French attack, the precariousness of Penn's hold on his colony, and the opposition between the upper and Lower
Counties came to a head in November 1709. On the first
day of that month Logan appeared before the Assembly
to announce his impending departure for London on proprietary business. It was well known that Logan had been
planning a return to England in order to discredit the
Lloydians and to confer with the trustees of Pennsylvania
to whom Penn had mortgaged the colony. Now he asked
the Assembly either to prove or dismiss the charges against
him.[58]

The Assembly replied by attempting to shift the burden
of proof to Logan. Having depicted the House as the enemy
of the proprietor and its Speaker as corrupt, Logan must
now present his evidence. Logan refused, arguing that some
of the principal witnesses had left the colony, making it impossible for him to substantiate his charges. The Assembly

[57] *Minutes of Council*, II, 435-476; *Votes of Assembly*, I, 825-881.
Gookin to Gov. Francis Nicholson, June 17, 1709, *CSP 1708-09*, #580;
Gookin to Penn, July 25, 1709, Blumhaven Foundation Library, Phila-
delphia; Logan to Penn, June 9, 1709, *Penn-Logan Correspondence*,
II, 349-351. For the expedition against Canada, see George M. Waller,
Samuel Vetch, Colonial Enterpriser (Chapel Hill, 1960).

[58] Petition of James Logan to the Assembly, Nov. 1, 1709, *Penn-
Logan Correspondence*, II, 396-399; Logan to the Assembly, Sept. 19,
1709, *ibid.*, 395-396.

insisted, however, that Logan put his proofs before the House prior to his departure and that he provide an account of all money which had come to his hands, whether in the form of proprietary fines, forfeitures, rents, taxes, or imposts. Logan answered that he had never received taxes or imposts and that he was in no way accountable to the Assembly for proprietary fines and forfeitures. As to his charges against Lloyd, he retorted, their truth was common knowledge.[59]

It was apparent that in their eagerness to destroy each other politically, both Lloyd and Logan had made vague and extravagant charges in the culminating months of their struggle. Neither man could document his allegations, which depended upon definitions of such words as "rights," "powers," "prerogatives," and "privileges"—terms upon whose meaning there had never been agreement in Pennsylvania and which had been in a process of change for almost two decades. Thus, each antagonist found it necessary to shift the burden of proof to the other rather than substantiate his own charges.

Frustrated by their inability to impeach Logan, but determined that he should not depart unscathed, the Assembly declared the proprietor's secretary ineligible for any public office and ordered the Sheriff of Philadelphia to confine him until he should "willingly make his Submission to the Satisfaction of this House."[60] The Council promptly countermanded the Assembly's orders, asserting that the House had no authority to apprehend any person except its own members. Determined to have the last word, but incapable of overpowering the Governor and Council, the Assembly retorted that the Governor had exceeded his own

[59] *Votes of Assembly*, II, 925-927.
[60] *Ibid.*, II, 926-929.

authority in denying the Assembly the right to punish "Contempts and Abuses offered them." Remonstrances and heated language followed, culminating in a final disagreement over whether the Assembly, having earlier adjourned itself, could legally reassemble. It was a fitting conclusion to a decade of governmental strife that the opposing elements of government could no longer agree even on the existence of the Assembly.[61]

On December 3, 1709, ten years to the day after he had arrived in Philadelphia, James Logan boarded the *Hope Galley*, bound for Lisbon and England.[62] Behind him he left a government which had all but ceased to function and a proprietary apparatus which could only occasionally command the loyalty of the Quakers in Pennsylvania and almost never the acquiescence of other groups. Ahead lay only uncertainties: a disillusioned, bitter proprietor; the English mortgagers of the colony; and a battery of Crown administrators in London whose worst suspicions about Pennsylvania seemed to have been borne out by the chronic instability which had gripped the Quaker colony for almost a decade.

"The Rattle of Rights and Privileges"

For eight years, from late 1701 when Penn left his colony until December 1709 when James Logan embarked for England, Pennsylvania was caught in the crucible of political controversy. No element of government, whether Assembly, Council, governor, county court, provincial court, or pro-

---

[61] *Minutes of Council*, II, 507-508; *Votes of Assembly*, II, 933-936. Logan gave his version of the dispute in "The Secretary's Justification to the Assembly's Remonstrance," Sept. 28, 1709, *Penn-Logan Correspondence*, II, 360-390. Lloyd presented his case in "The Speaker's Vindication against James Logan's Invectives . . . ," *ibid.*, II, 402-415.

[62] Logan's journal of his voyage to England is in the Howland Collection, Haverford College.

prietary agency, escaped unscathed in the cross fire of factional politics. Every component of constituted authority was challenged, deprecated, or called into question. Almost every institution of political and proprietary authority was scrutinized, found wanting, and, if it could not be altered, condemned. At moments—such as in 1703 and 1708—government virtually ceased to function. Governors Hamilton and Evans gave up residency in Philadelphia, the courts lapsed for want of legislative backing, and the Council was reduced to a cypher.

In some measure this decade of strife was a response to particular developments in the early eighteenth century —Penn's tangled affairs in England, the economic dislocation caused by war, the rash behavior of Governor John Evans, and the personal feud between James Logan and David Lloyd. But at a more fundamental level, the political paralysis was simply the epitomization of tendencies imbedded in the Quaker experience in Pennsylvania since 1682. The embroidery of the early eighteenth-century political fabric depicted a variety of individual discontents, parochial issues, and emergent constitutional questions; but the warp and woof of the carpet was woven of strands tracing back to the previous decades. In this sense, the period from 1701 to 1710 represented no new departure in provincial politics, no embryonic drive to democratize political institutions anticipating the American Revolution, but the culmination of the response of first-generation Quakers to political responsibility.

Continued reluctance to accept constituted authority figured most prominently among the tendencies toward political instability in the colony. The aberrant behavior of many of the Quaker leaders in the 1680's, the open warfare against Blackwell, the Keithian controversy, and David

274

Lloyd's campaigns of the eighteenth century were all a part of the pattern of defiance. Other colonies, it is true, were not free of the strife that gripped Pennsylvania; political faction and social disruption almost inevitably attended the rerooting and adaptation of English institutions in a wilderness environment. Robert Quary reported from Virginia in 1705 that he had never seen "such a soure temper'd people" in an assembly and warned that a "factious uneasy spirit" was common to all the plantations. Other governors sent home similar reports of churlish, disputatious persons, both in and out of power.[63] Though comparative quantification is hardly possible, one concludes that a behavior pattern common to all of the colonies was seen in Pennsylvania in somewhat magnified form. If antiauthoritarianism was residual in dissenting Englishmen transplanted to a frontier which in the early stages lacked well-established political institutions and social controls, it was seen in its most extreme form in Quaker Pennsylvania.

Conditions in Pennsylvania only intensified the antiauthoritarian cast of Quakerism. Penn, who alone possessed the charisma to stabilize the Quaker community, if it could be unified at all, was absent for all but a few years during the first three decades of the colony's existence. Ill-advised policies regarding land and proprietary revenues tended to split Pennsylvania society into contending and antagonistic

[63] Quary to the Board of Trade, Oct. 15, 1705, *CSP 1704-05*, #605. The colonial series of the *Calendar of State Papers* is filled with similar reports from royal officials and governors, which of course reflect something of the viewer as well as the viewed. Gov. Evans of Pennsylvania reported typically to the Board of Trade that "it is the great unhappiness of these parts of the world in Generall, to be too much divided in Opinions." Much skill would be required to "take off the Edge of some Men's unreasonable Anger," Evans concluded. Evans to the Board of Trade, May 30, 1704, *CSP 1704-05*, #359.

groups, and, finally, to alienate even the closest of Penn's friends. Moreover, life in the "howling wilderness," as some called it, had a peculiar effect on the humor of people. Many, as they looked out from a modest farm in Bucks County or from an artisan's bench or merchant's wharf in Philadelphia, took a fierce pride in their accomplishments. They saw themselves as people who had endured for years the persecutions of petty authorities in England, suffered a long and hazardous ocean passage, toiled through droughts, epidemics, and fluctuating economic conditions, weathered religious controversy, and resisted Puritan governors, Anglican imperialists, and proprietary placemen. But withal, they had carved out a niche in the New World where people of humble station, as even the least optimistic would admit, had greater opportunity than England had ever promised. Pennsylvania was no place, William Markham said, for a person to learn breeding or polite language. "Conversation runs low," Logan complained in 1712; a learned person could hardly be found "for every 1000 miles of the Queen's Dominions."[64] But the average settler, if less educated and not so well read as his English counterpart, had more to show for his efforts.

Pride of this sort—a kind of crude nationalism—had as a corollary a hypersensitivity to criticism which sometimes bordered on cultural paranoia. People were thin-skinned, quick to anger, and inclined to magnify the smallest issue which aroused their resentment. John Evans found Pennsylvanians touchy beyond reason, given to enlarging the smallest issues into matters of great moment. Pride was "the national Infirmity," asserted James Logan, who on another occasion found "a general Infatuation gott amongst us, as

64 Markham to Penn, April 27, 1697, *CSP 1697-98*, #76xiv; Logan to Thomas Goldney, July 3, 1712, Logan Letter Book (1712-1715), 27.

if we were preparing for Destruction," and deemed that "we are generally in these parts too full of ourselves, and empty of sence to manage affairs of Importance."[65] Isaac Norris, one of those in Pennsylvania least given to hyperbole, found "a strange, unaccountable humour (almost a custom now) of straining and resenting everything, of creating monsters and then combating them."[66]

From easily aroused resentment, it was only a step to intractability. What Evans, Logan, and Norris noted in the early eighteenth century differed only in degree from what John Blackwell had described in the late 1680's when he concluded that the Pennsylvanians were temperamentally unfit for government. Nobody appreciated the colonial syndrome better than Penn himself. "There is an Excess of vanity," he wrote in 1705, "that is Apt to Creep in upon the people in power in America, who having got out of the Crowd, in which they were lost here . . . think nothing taller than themselves, but the Trees, and as if there were no After Superior Judgment to which they should be accountable." As an antidote to such self-importance, Penn suggested that the colonists take turns in revisiting England where they might "lose themselves again amongst the Crowds of so much more Considerable people." Their sense of proportion restored, Pennsylvanians might return to America "much more Discreet and Tractable and fit for Government."[67]

Also of great importance in the political dynamics of the early eighteenth century was the relatively unstructured

[65] Evans to the Board of Trade, May 30, 1704, *CSP 1704-05*, #359; Logan to Hannah Penn, Oct. 28, 1715, Logan Letter Book (1712-1715), 352; Logan to Penn, Nov. 22, 1704, *Pennsylvania Archives*, 2nd Ser., VII, 15-16.

[66] Norris to Penn, Dec. 2, 1709, Norris Letter Book (1709-1716), 112.

[67] Penn to William Mompesson, Feb. 17, 1704/05, *Penn-Logan Correspondence*, I, 374-375.

character of the young society which made Penn's proprietary form of government seem painfully out of place and gave David Lloyd an ideal social milieu in which to make his appeals to the people. A rough profile of colonial society, which helps to illustrate this point, can be drawn from the provincial tax list of 1693 and the wills and inventories of estates for this era.[68]

Although they were not enumerated in the tax lists, Africans, of course, occupied the lowest position in the social hierarchy. Since 1684, when a ship with 150 slaves had reached the colony, Africans had arrived at Philadelphia and New Castle in small numbers. That 68 Africans belonged to 19 individuals listed in the 198 inventories of estate probated at Philadelphia between 1683 and 1700 suggests that between 5 and 10 percent of the colonists owned slaves at this time. By the early 1700's African slaves could be found on many of the larger farms in the colony and were numerous enough in Philadelphia to cause concern about their congregating in the streets.[69]

[68] The tax list for the city and county of Philadelphia is in *PMHB*, 8 (1884), 85-105; for Bucks County in Bucks County Miscellaneous Papers, 1682-1772, foll. 17-23; for Chester County in Chester County Miscellaneous Papers, 1684-1847, fol. 17; for the Lower Counties in Miscellaneous Papers, Three Lower Counties, 1655-1805, foll. 25-33.

[69] Edward R. Turner, *The Negro in Pennsylvania* (Washington, 1911), 1-3; Thomas E. Drake, *Quakers and Slavery in America* (New Haven, 1950), 1-33; Darold D. Wax, "Quaker Merchants and the Slave Trade in Colonial Pennsylvania," *PMHB*, 86 (1962), 143-159. The arrival of slaves in 1684 is recounted by Nicholas More in a letter to Penn, Dec. 1, 1684, Myers Collection, Box 2, #6, CCHS. The extent of slave ownership is based upon an analysis of wills given in Philadelphia Wills and Inventories, Book A (1682-1699); Book B (1699-1705), photostats at Genealogical Society of Pennsylvania. If inventories of estate were more commonly made for men of high economic standing, then the degree of slaveholding would be inflated. Fear of the sizable Negro population was expressed in 1702 when the Grand

The indentured servants stood above the African slaves on the social ladder. In the early years of settlement such persons probably constituted about one-third of the population. But by 1700 almost all of those who had signed indentures as a means of obtaining passage to the New World had gained their freedom. Though other servants trickled into the colony during the 1680's and 1690's, it is likely that by the end of the century the proportion of indentured persons in the population had fallen considerably, possibly as low as 10 percent.[70]

Free, white males who possessed little or no taxable property, either real or personal, composed a much larger group. In the country, these were men recently released from indentures, grown sons living at home, and agricultural laborers. In Philadelphia, they were often seamen and workers. As indicated in Table A, more than half of the adult male population in the Lower Counties, where tobacco was cultivated on sizable farms, had no rateable estate. Land ownership was far more prevalent in the upper counties. Roughly four-fifths of the adult males in Chester County owned land; and for the upper counties as a whole only about one man in four paid only the head tax.

The generally roughhewn caste of rural society is further revealed by the predominance on the tax lists of men with modest estates. This was particularly noticeable in Bucks, Chester, and Philadelphia counties. Almost two-thirds of

---

Jury of Philadelphia charged "the great abuse & The Ill Consiquence of the great multitude of Negroes who commonly meete togeither in a Riott & Tumultios manner on the first days of the weeke [Sundays]." Grand Jury Presentment, Sept. 18, 1702, Wallace Collection, Ancient Documents of Philadelphia, 11.

[70] Cheesman A. Herrick, *White Servitude in Pennsylvania* (Philadelphia, 1926), passim. The trend would be reversed with the great influx of Scotch-Irish and Germans after 1714.

TABLE A

DISTRIBUTION OF TAXABLE WEALTH IN 1693

Total Value of Taxable Wealth	Number of Taxpayers in Each Bracket				Percentage of Taxpayers in Each Bracket			
Pounds	Bucks County	Chester County	Phila. County	Phila. City	Bucks County	Chester County	Phila. County	Phila. City
Unrated	63	52	109	75	42.0	18.5	32.4	21.4
1-50	37	179	99	80	24.6	63.7	29.5	22.9
51-100	35	42	92	109	24.2	15.0	27.4	31.2
101-200	12	6	30	43	7.8	2.1	8.9	12.2
201-500	2	2	6	31	1.4	.7	1.8	7.7
501-1,000	—	—	—	12	—	—	—	3.5
	149	281	336	350	100.0	100.0	100.0	100.0

	Kent County	Sussex County	New Castle County	Kent County	Sussex County	New Castle County
Unrated	67	107	167	42.6	56.3	62.5
1-50	—	—	2	—	—	.7
51-100	40	33	56	25.4	17.4	21.0
101-200	32	31	22	20.5	16.3	8.3
201-500	16	19	20	10.2	10.0	7.5
501-750	2	—	—	1.3	—	—
	157	190	267	100.0	100.0	100.0

the men with taxable wealth in Chester County, for example, had estates rated no higher than £50. Even more striking, only about one man in ten in the upper counties (excluding the city of Philadelphia) was assessed for more than £100. All such figures, of course, must be inflated somewhat to compensate for the common practice of undervaluing property for tax purposes. Even so, it is clear that the spectrum of wealth in the countryside was narrow. It appears that in the Lower Counties more accurate valuations were made. Again, however, the concentration of planters in the middle range of wealth is striking. Of 272 men with taxable estates, 214 (78.4 percent) paid taxes on estates valued between £51 and £200. Even the wealthiest colonists boasted estates valued only a few hundred pounds higher than their middling neighbors. The estate of the richest man in the Lower Counties was rated at £750.

Added evidence of the colony's social structure can be gained by examining the wills and inventories of estate probated at Philadelphia between 1683 and 1702. Inventories of estate, which are extant for almost 60 percent of the wills probated in the first two decades of settlement, as a rule reflect the true value of the deceased's real and personal property.[71] Generally, they may be taken as a more accurate gauge of individual wealth than the tax assessments. Even so, the inventories do not reveal a markedly different pattern of stratification. Again, one sees in the countryside a society of simple farmers struggling to make the transition from subsistence to commercial farming. In Chester County, where landholding was most prevalent, 70 percent of the inventories described assets worth no more than £250, including real property. In Bucks County the pattern was much the same. Typically, an inventory of £250 or less

[71] The following discussion is based on an analysis of the inventories given in Philadelphia Wills and Inventories, Book A (1682-1699) and Book B (1699-1705). All values are given in Pennsylvania money, which, by 1700, could be converted to English sterling by subtracting one-third. It is difficult to determine whether the inventories are cross-sectional. Wills of laborers, husbandmen, and yeomen frequently lack inventories, but the same is true of some of the wealthiest merchants and landowners—Andrew Robeson, Thomas Holme, Thomas Brassey, and Arthur Cooke, to cite just a few examples from this period. One suspects that the estates of lower-class individuals were less frequently inventoried. Abstracts of all wills included in Books A and B are given in *Pennsylvania Genealogical Magazine*, 1 (1895), 45-84; 2 (1900), 7-33; 3 (1906), 12-37, 144-152, 245-254.

reveals a man who worked about a quarter of the 100 or 200 acres he had purchased, who lived in a crude two or three-room house worth no more than £25 or £30, and who owned, in addition, only an outbuilding or two, a dozen farm animals, and a meager assortment of implements and household goods. Richard Few, a Chester County yeoman, who left an estate worth £256, may be taken as an example. All but about £60 of his estate was accounted for by his farm buildings and 197 acres of land of which only a part was under cultivation. Other than that, he possessed only some wearing apparel (£8), beds and bedding (£9), crude furniture and old lumber (£2), tools, utensils, and kitchenware (£4), two pair of oxen (£18), eleven swine and one bull (£9), and two cows and a calf (£9). Dozens of inventories tell a similar story.

Though the great majority of settlers owned a little more than the bare essentials of life, there were some whose standard of living was on the rise. In both Bucks and Chester counties, about one-fifth of the estates inventoried were valued between £251 and £500. People in this category typically owned more land, usually 500 acres or more. But their inventories still portray a roughly textured life. More farm animals, a horse or two, some finished chairs, tables, and chests in the house, a bit of pewter or brassware in the kitchen, and an occasional piece of linen on the table was all that differentiated their existence from that of their poorer neighbors. Usually it was the greater acreage they had under cultivation, not their style of life, that set them apart from men of lesser estates.

Only about 10 percent of the country people could boast of estates worth £500 or more. In seventeenth-century Pennsylvania this signified a modest prosperity. Only at this level of wealth does one begin to find evidence in the inventories of occasional luxuries—the East India pillow case, fire dogs with brass heads, chair cushions, spice boxes, walnut chairs, silver buckles, and the like. That the mode of living began to change at about this level is also made apparent through the frequent mention of African slaves in inventories of £500 or more.

Because the city of Philadelphia had undergone commercial development, its social structure was somewhat different from that of the countryside. Numerous skilled craftsmen, shopkeepers, and even workers engaged in the rougher trades of a mercantile society swelled the middle class of society. One-quarter of the city dwellers were taxed for assets valued above £100, as opposed to about 10 percent of the country folk (Table A). Roughly one-fifth of the estates inventoried for residents of the city were valued between £250 and £500, and another fifth between £500 and £1,000 (Table B). At the same time, a lesser number of shopkeepers and merchants attained a level of affluence rarely matched in the country. Men whose taxable assets exceeded £200 were uncommon outside of Philadelphia, while in the capital city 12.3 percent of the white adult males fell into this category. In the upper counties not a single estate outside of Philadelphia was taxed at more than £400. But in the city, twenty-two individuals had property valued above £400 and four boasted estates assessed at £1,000 or more (Table A). Similarly, the inventories of estate show that in the first two decades almost one Philadelphian in ten left an estate worth more than £1,000, whereas in the country such men were rarities (Table B).

Among the prosperous, merchants predominated. Thomas Budd left an estate of £1,676. Philip Richards's estate was valued at £1,813, including three African slaves and land worth £1,260. James Claypoole left property worth

TABLE B

DISTRIBUTION OF INVENTORIED ESTATES, 1683-1702

Inventoried Value of Real and Personal Property	Number of Inventoried Estates in Each Wealth Bracket			Percentage of Inventoried Estates in Each Wealth Bracket		
Pounds	Bucks County	Chester County	Phila. City	Bucks County	Chester County	Phila. City
1-50	5	7	12	18.5	18.9	12.3
51-250	15	19	35	55.6	51.4	35.7
251-500	5	7	22	18.5	18.9	22.5
501-1,000	2	2	20	7.4	5.4	20.4
1,001-2,000	—	2	7	—	5.4	7.1
2,000 plus	—	—	2	—	—	2.0
	27	37	98	100.0	100.0	100.0

Inventoried Value of Real and Personal Property	Total Value of Inventoried Estates in Each Wealth Bracket			Percentage of Total Inventoried Wealth in Each Wealth Bracket		
Pounds	Bucks County	Chester County	Phila. City	Bucks County	Chester County	Phila. City
1-50	192	263	277	3.5	2.7	.7
51-250	1,864	2,536	4,756	33.9	25.7	11.2
251-500	2,316	2,456	7,664	42.1	24.9	18.1
501-1,000	1,132	1,688	13,471	20.5	17.2	31.7
1,001-2,000	—	2,905	10,899	—	29.5	25.7
2,000 plus	—	—	5,316	—	—	12.6
	5,504	9,848	42,383	100.0	100.0	100.0
Average Value of Inventoried Estates	204	266	427			

£1,468, William Frampton, assets of £812, Robert Ewer, £865, and Arthur Cooke, £2,570. Well-to-do artisans were by no means uncommon. William Alloway, a tallow chandler, left an estate valued at £602; Nathaniel Harding, a basketmaker, left £696; and there were many others like them. It was indicative of the high degree of mobility in Philadelphia that no man in the first twenty years of settlement died with a larger fortune than James Fox. Immigrating to Pennsylvania in 1686, Fox attempted to launch an enterprise for manufacturing woolens. When this failed, he moved to Philadelphia and started a bakery. Fox's operations flourished and by the time of his death in 1699 he was one of the largest grain merchants and land speculators in the colony. His estate, valued at £2,746, included three white indentured servants, four Negro slaves, and real estate valued at £1,500.

Pennsylvania at the beginning of the eighteenth century, then, was still a society in the early stages of development. In the country many of the farms were beginning to produce surpluses for the Philadelphia export market. But the small subsistence farm was still typical, as was the unpretentious yeoman farmer. Everywhere outside of Philadelphia one saw a relatively undifferentiated society with only a handful of individuals standing above the common farmers and landless rural workers. In Philadelphia rapid growth had brought about a somewhat more complex social structure. Slowly, as the city took her place in the world of Atlantic commerce, the distance between rich and poor widened. As the city grew, it became more diverse and more stratified.[72] And yet even in Philadelphia clearly defined lines between economic classes were badly blurred and a distinctive upper class had not yet formed. The top and bottom layers of society, as they existed in England, were still largely unrepresented. Few could parade aristocratic pretensions. Even those merchants in the city who were later

[72] The absence of tax lists for Philadelphia for more than fifty years after 1693 makes precise analysis of the changing social structure impossible. My conclusions are based on an analysis of wills for the first half of the eighteenth century and the incomplete tax lists of 1754 and 1756, given respectively in *Pennsylvania Genealogical Magazine*, 21 (1959), 161ff, and 22 (1961), 10ff.

"Quaker grandees" were still a generation away from that status. James Logan warned a friend in 1713 that Pennsylvania was barren of "men of Parts & Learning," and cautioned that anyone who thought to take up a position of importance in Philadelphia should be "furnished with an Exterior suited to take with the common humours of the Crowd."[73] Furthermore, mobility up and down the ladder of success was far greater than in the countryside. One observer in Philadelphia remarked that there were many who had come to the city penniless and were now "richer by several hundred pounds." Another citizen testified that some who had hardly been able to earn a living in England were well-to-do in Philadelphia.[74] Pennsylvania was a good place for a workingman "to gett a good living in," one commentator noted, but hardly a country in which to accumulate a great estate.[75]

Such a social setting offered David Lloyd ideal conditions in which to advertise his appeals against proprietary privilege and the authoritarian tactics employed by Penn's placemen. Conversely, this rough equality of condition made the work of James Logan and Penn's deputy governors far more difficult, for they were attempting to gain acceptance of proprietary prerogatives and to promote deferential attitudes in an environment where governors and governed lived much alike.

One further element in the political equation was the role played by individual eccentricities, the clash of per-

73 Logan to Josiah Martin, Aug. 4, 1713, Logan Letter Book (1712-1715), 131.

74 Andreas Rudman to ———, 1700, *PMHB*, 84 (1960), 207; Gabriel Thomas, *An Historical and Geographical Account of Pensilvania and of West-Jersey*, 1698, in Myers, ed., *Narratives*, 327. See also Tolles, *Meeting House*, 114-115.

75 Logan to Daniel Flexney, May 4, 1715, Logan Letter Book (1712-1715), 286.

sonalities, and occasionally the intervention of sheer mis-chance. The importance of personalities in Pennsylvania may, in fact, have been amplified simply because men like Lloyd and Logan operated within a system where the respective powers of the various agencies of government were not precisely defined—a system which had been in flux since the initial Frame of 1682 was rejected by the first representative body convened in Pennsylvania.

It was Pennsylvania's peculiar fate that in the early eighteenth century the man best qualified to assume the role of political leader was also the one who took an almost perverse delight in battling prescriptive authority. David Lloyd was a gifted man, a brilliant orator and student of the law, a skilled advocate, and an unequaled legislative draughtsman and parliamentarian. But he was also proud, volatile, vindictive, and highly ambitious. After 1699, when Penn removed him from his public and proprietary offices at the demand of the Crown, he lapsed into a deeply revengeful mood and thereafter his resentment of Penn and all who supported him was boundless. All of the passion which in the mid-1690's he had directed against the King's officials in Pennsylvania, now found vent in an assault on the machinery of proprietary management. When his only child died in June 1701, a victim of shock or suffocation at the hands of a house servant who had locked the boy in a small closet, Lloyd sunk into a slough of despair which seems to have reinforced his view that the world was a hostile and unremitting place.[76] Embittered by his dismissal from office, shunned by the wealthier Quakers as a dangerous firebrand, and wounded by personal misfortune, Lloyd became the archetypical New World malcontent—fulminating against constituted authority, translating personal

[76] Lokken, *David Lloyd*, 95-96.

grievances into public causes, and conjuring up visions of encroaching and threatening forces which lay in wait of unwary and defenseless settlers.

Whether Lloyd's politics were personal rather than ideological is not an easy question to answer. Historians who look for tribunes of the people in the pre-Revolutionary period tend to stress Lloyd's unyielding commitment to democratic principles and his abiding faith in the people. Unwilling to probe the less accessible recesses of his mind, they have taken his political jeremiads at face value.[77] People of the time, who did not know what epic events lay over the horizon, and whose problems were immediate and real rather than distant and historiographical, took a colder view of Lloyd. Evans, Gookin, and Logan frequently noted Lloyd's vindictiveness and believed that the Welshman was motivated far less by political principles than by the spirit of revenge and desire for power. Despite his smooth language and pretenses, Logan reported in 1704, Lloyd "cannot sometimes conceal his resentment of thy taking, as he calls it, his bread from him, this expression he has several times dropped, overlooking his politics through the heat of his indignation."[78]

[77] See, for example, Lokken, *David Lloyd*; H. Frank Eshelman, "The Constructive Genius of David Lloyd in Early Colonial Pennsylvania Legislation and Jurisprudence, 1686 to 1731," Pennsylvania Bar Association *Reports*, 16 (1910) , 406-461; Burton A. Konkle, "David Lloyd and the First Half Century of Pennsylvania," unpublished manuscript at Friends Historical Library, Swarthmore College, Swarthmore, Pa.

[78] Logan to Penn, Oct. 3, 1704, *Penn-Logan Correspondence*, I, 323. For similar descriptions of Lloyd's vengefulness and emotionalism see Logan to William Penn, Jr., Sept. 25, 1700, Logan to Penn, Oct. 27, 1704 and July 27, 1706, *ibid.*, I, 18, 339-340, II, 142; Gov. Charles Gookin to Secretary of the Society for the Propagation of the Gospel, Aug. 27, 1709, Perry, ed., *History of the Church in Pennsylvania*, 50-52; Gov. John Evans to Council, April 12, 1709, *Minutes of Council*, II, 436.

The objectivity of Logan and Penn's deputy governors is suspect, of course, since Lloyd was systematically attempting to reduce their power. But there is little in Lloyd's behavior during the early eighteenth century to discredit Logan's view. So intense was Lloyd's animosity toward Penn that he saw the proprietor's policies as premeditated attempts, dating back to the origins of settlement, to curtail colonial rights. To cast Penn in this light was to misunderstand the whole nature of proprietary politics. For although Penn often offended colonial sensibilities, he was neither vindictive, autocratic, nor hungry for power. It was stability and unity, he hungered for, along with a proprietary revenue. "There is some," Isaac Norris wrote aptly in a thinly veiled reference to Lloyd, "who by Linking [the] imaginery with the true Intrest of the Country therewith Couch & Cover their own Interests & disguise & do so perplex affairs as to . . . almost give the Honest and Undesigning to Dispair of any Reconciliation or progress to a Settlement."[79]

Lloyd's willingness to form almost any alliance which would further his ends provides another insight into the nature of his politics. After 1700, Lloyd openly recruited support among precisely the groups in Pennsylvania which he had so strenuously opposed in the 1690's—the King's officers in Pennsylvania, the Anglicans of Philadelphia and Chester, and the dissident Quakers who had followed Keith. Lloyd amazed Philadelphians in 1702 by accepting an appointment as deputy advocate of the vice-admiralty court at Philadelphia over which Robert Quary presided as judge.[80] It was Lloyd's mocking attack on Quary's court which had caused his removal from public office just three

---

[79] Norris to Penn, Feb. 13, 1704/05, Norris Letter Book (1704-1706), 21-22.
[80] Lokken, *David Lloyd*, 119.

years before. Equally surprising was his alliance with John Moore, the Anglican advocate of Quary's court, for the purpose of enlarging the power of the Corporation of Philadelphia.

In the last analysis, there was no particular inconsistency between Lloyd's vendetta against Penn and his apparent promotion of "democratic" principles. Lloyd promoted the powers of the Assembly and the Corporation of Philadelphia because, as it happened, they were the only centers of power in Pennsylvania beyond the reach of the proprietor —or the Crown if Penn should lose or sell his government. It was only good politics to dress his arguments in acceptable constitutional garb. Thus Lloyd took pains to invoke precedent whenever he could in arguing for the Assembly's privileges. If he sought a privilege for the legislature which Parliament enjoyed in England, he made much of the necessity of modeling colonial assemblies after the House of Commons.[81] Penn's deputies could play the same game, citing parliamentary precedent whenever Lloyd sought powers for the Assembly which were unknown in England.[82] It was precisely because antiproprietary rhetoric and constitutional arguments were mutually reinforcing that Lloyd could play the patriot in Pennsylvania while quenching his thirst for revenge and feeding his appetite for power.

[81] *Minutes of Council*, II, 371; Lloyd, "The Speaker's Vindication . . . ," *Penn-Logan Correspondence*, II, 411. In 1709 the Assembly, again under Lloyd's leadership, gave its unanimous opinion "that 'twill be our great Happiness to follow the Queen's good example, and that of her Parliament, in the Administration at Home." *Votes of Assembly*, II, 832.

[82] Gov. John Evans accused Lloyd and his followers in the Assembly of attempting to "reverse the method of Govmt. according to our English Constitution, and Establish one more nearly resembling a republick in its stead." *Minutes of Council*, II, 325. See also, *ibid.*, II, 305-307, 309-310.

Locked as they were in a struggle for power, it was almost inevitable that Lloyd and Logan should caricature each other's views. In Lloyd's mind, Logan took his rules of government from "Machiavel and those high flown statesmen." His "inclination to a despotic power" would lead to the oppression of the people, the violation of their charters, the denial of their rights, and, finally, to the elimination of all means of redress.[83] Logan, in short, was represented as a threat to all that Quakers had left England to escape. Conversely, Logan charged Lloyd with following a policy calculated to maim government in Pennsylvania permanently. It was Lloyd who, for all his lectures on English constitutional history, would have the Assembly invested with complete legislative power while reducing the Council to insignificance. What kind of constitutional precedent did that follow, asked Logan. Councils were deemed necessary in all governments, "from the most barbarous to the politest," especially in the crucial business of legislation. But Lloyd seemed to believe that England "never so truly knew liberty" as when the monarchy was overthrown more than a half century before. Logan, however, believed that those who now disturbed the equilibrium of government in Pennsylvania, like their predecessors in England during the Civil Wars, would perpetrate "the greatest grievance the nation had ever known."[84]

In actuality Logan was no lover of despotism and Lloyd no advocate of popular rule. Logan's political thought was consistent with the conventional Whig faith of the day in a balanced government which combined popular and aristocratic elements. As Penn's chief supporter and confi-

[83] Lloyd, "The Speaker's Vindication . . . ," *Penn-Logan Correspondence*, II, 408.
[84] Logan, "The Secretary's Justification . . . ," *ibid.*, II, 365.

dant in Pennsylvania, he sought to maximize the power of the Council, where Penn's conservative friends congregated, and to minimize the strength of the Assembly, where the proprietor's enemies held sway. By the same token, Lloyd worked to enlarge the powers of that element of government which he controlled, while chipping away at instruments of government dominated by his opponents. In later, less vexed times, Lloyd too would acknowledge the wisdom of a government of counterbalancing powers. But in the confused and disorderly years of the early eighteenth century, circumstances required that both Logan and Lloyd act as if their political ideologies were poles apart. Obscured was the fact that both men were inheritors of the same political tradition. What passed for constitutional questions were in reality reflections of real and immediate problems. Both men might ransack the law books and historical texts in order to ground their position upon abstract theory and ancient precedent. But the problems over which they fought were not theoretical or philosophical but visible and palpable—issues which arose from particular conditions in Pennsylvania, from Penn's position in England, from bureaucratic activity at Whitehall, and from the international wars of Louis XIV. No amount of citing precedent and invoking ancient rights could obscure the fact that what both Logan and Lloyd sought in Pennsylvania was political supremacy.

Ironically, the interminable battle of words, the endless process of assertion and counterassertion, the taking of extreme positions for purposes of bargaining led both antagonists further afield than they wished to go. Logan grew increasingly distrustful of the people and came at last to doubt that they were capable of self-government.[85] By 1709

85 The Quakers, Logan wrote in 1704, were "unfit for Government by

his misanthropy had hardened to the extent that he was inclined to question the good faith of any popular leader who opposed him. Pessimism distorted all his views. At the same time he came to believe that he alone could discern what was best for Pennsylvania. Lloyd followed a similar pattern, seeing only the worst in Logan, impugning the Secretary's motives at every turn, and convincing himself that Logan and Penn intended the destruction of representative government in Pennsylvania. As Isaac Norris noted, government in Pennsylvania seemed incapable of reaching any middle ground "between arbitrary power and licentious popularity."[86]

In such a make-believe world, where hyperbole was the customary mode of argument and distrust the nearly universal attitude, words became more important than actions and points of ceremonial propriety took precedent over legislative proposals. Thus the Assembly of 1707 broke up over a question of whether or not the legislature was obliged to assemble when the Governor chose to address it. In 1709 a dispute over the Speaker's refusal to stand when addressing the Governor brought legislative proceedings to a halt. The Assembly, noted one of its members, showed less concern for considering "solids and substantials" than for indulging in windy debates "upon Everything that is said or done . . . always remonstrating, and valluing the last word highly." There was little hope of conducting business, given

themselves, and not much better with others." Logan to Penn, Nov. 22, 1704, *Pennsylvania Archives*, 2nd Ser., VII, 16. Even twenty years later Logan thought that the main source of trouble in Pennsylvania had been "in heaping things called Privileges (which no English subject ever had) on a People that neither knows how to use them nor how to be grateful for them." Logan to Hannah Penn, Jan. 1, 1725/26, Logan Letter Book (1702-1726), 288.

[86] Norris to Penn, Oct. 11, 1704, Norris Letter Book (1704-1706), 2.

"the air of grandure and sacred care for the honor and Dignity of the house . . . and the Secret pride thereof . . . in the great pretenses to any professions of mean and Despicable thoughts of themselves."[87]

Though David Lloyd was more interested in shielding Pennsylvania from proprietary authority than in shifting the center of political gravity downward in the colony, his campaign against Penn and Logan had the latter rather than the former effect. In this sense, historians who have seen in Lloyd the spokesman of the people, and in his politics the democratization of Pennsylvania society, have fastened on an important truth, even if they have misunderstood its causes and significance. For a radical shift in political power did occur in Pennsylvania after Penn's departure in 1701. It came neither as the planned result of Lloyd's policies nor as the fulfillment of his political beliefs, but rather as a side effect of the techniques he employed in battling traditional authority.

At the root of this inadvertent democratization was Lloyd's necessity to turn for political support to a segment of society which in England had been politically quiescent and in Pennsylvania had gradually been acquiring political awareness. To some extent, Pennsylvania had always had a high potential for "middle-class democracy." Society was relatively fluid and the incidence of land ownership among the humble was far greater in the New World than in the Old; expectations were higher and the distance between gentleman and husbandman was relatively slight.

Although Pennsylvanians crowded the middle of the economic and social spectrum in the period before 1720, the inherited traditions of deference and political acquiescence had not altogether disappeared. In the early years, county

87 Norris to Penn, Dec. 2, 1709, Norris Letter Book (1709-1716), 112.

elections had usually served only to confirm such candidates for the Council or Assembly as the leading men saw fit to propose. Poor roads, bad weather, and a general readiness to concede political power to the wealthier and better educated men in the province seems to have been the general rule. The comments of Phineas Pemberton to Penn in 1687 illustrate the point. Pemberton, a leading figure in Bucks County, related that one of the lesser county officeholders had "miscarried in several respects." The offender had been "dealt with" for his misdemeanors and would be excluded from the county court that year. So would another landowner, formerly a justice of the peace, but now out of favor. "William Beakes out [of office] last [year]," wrote Pemberton, "and intend [to] keep him so til he be better in our Country."[88] Even in 1700, though by that time the pattern had begun to change, only thirty freemen took the trouble to participate in the Bucks County election for the legislature.[89]

The importance of Lloyd's activities was that in his search for support he expanded the politically relevant strata of Pennsylvania society and drastically altered the social bases of political leadership.[90] As Lloyd was quick to see, the configuration of colonial values, which reflected English precedents in the early years, denied him the constituency he needed to wage his war against proprietary privilege. George

[88] Pemberton to Penn, April 3, 1687, Etting Collection, Pemberton Papers, I, 20.

[89] Penn to Logan, Sept. 8, 1701, *Penn-Logan Correspondence*, I, 54. This amounted to a turnout of between one-fourth and one-third of the electorate. The 1693 county tax list indicates 86 eligible voters; it is probable that by 1701 the number had increased to 100 or more.

[90] For a suggestive study of the functional relationship between social change and increased political participation see Karl Deutsch, "Social Mobilization and Political Development," *American Political Science Review*, 55 (1961), 493-514.

Keith had faced the same problem a decade before. His answer had been to activate a part of the community that in a deferential society had rarely been heard from. Lloyd followed Keith's lead and carried his techniques a step farther. Like the Quaker apostate whom he had bitterly opposed, Lloyd pitched his appeal to the smaller country farmer, the city artisan, and the disaffected freeman—men whose economic or social expectations had not always been met under the existing leadership. Logan, for one, was well aware that Lloyd's success had much to do with his ability to capitalize on Keith's earlier work. By raking up the ashes of the Quaker controversy, Lloyd garnered the support of the common people who had joined the apostate in significant numbers in the 1690's.[91]

Aiding Lloyd in his quest to arouse the political consciousness of the lower classes were the election laws passed in 1700 and 1706 and the provisions of the Frame of 1701. Although none of these statutes altered the electoral qualifications, which remained lenient, the manner of election underwent considerable revision. The 1700 election law initiated the practice of publicizing writs of election—authorizations by the governor for the holding of elections. Magistrates were required to read the writs in "the capital town or most public place within their respective bailiwicks" and post election notices upon a tree or house along the roads leading from every precinct to the principal towns of each county. The call to the polls was also to be displayed on every county courthouse, church, and meetinghouse in the province. Though seemingly innocuous, it was an important encouragement to those, who, because of poor roads, distant polling places, or an ingrained sense of def-

---

[91] Logan to Penn, Dec. 20, 1706, *Penn-Logan Correspondence*, II, 186-187; Logan, "The Secretary's Justification . . . ," *ibid.*, II, 381-382.

erence, had ordinarily acquiesced to the political wisdom of the more experienced members of the community. A second step was taken in 1701, when the secret ballot, one of the Harringtonian devices incorporated in the Frame of 1683, was abandoned. In its place, much to Penn's dismay, a complicated system of oral voting was substituted. Both these measures were reenacted in the election law passed in 1706. In Logan's judgment, both election laws aided Lloyd in mobilizing the support of lesser men in Pennsylvania against merchants and large landowners sympathetic to Penn. "We will never obtain a good election," the Secretary wrote in 1709, "until the recent voting law be replaced."[92]

The significance of David Lloyd's style of politics is clear if his supporters are compared with those of Thomas Lloyd, his seventeenth-century predecessor in the cause of antiproprietary reform. In terms of broad objectives the two men differed little: both opposed Penn's control of the judiciary, both viewed his land policy as inequitable and venal, both resented the power enjoyed by proprietary officeholders, both sought a delimitation of proprietary prerogatives and an increase in provincial autonomy. But whereas Thomas Lloyd had sought in the seventeenth century to fashion an antiproprietary party from among the wealthier Quakers—shopkeepers, merchants, and large landowners— David Lloyd worked in the eighteenth century to politicize a mass of individuals who were mixed in ethnic and religious background and who, with significant exceptions, occupied lesser positions on the economic and social ladder.[93]

[92] Logan to Penn, Feb. 3, 1708/09, *ibid.*, II, 313. The election laws are in *Statutes of Pennsylvania*, II, 24-27, 212-221 (See Bibliographical Note on this source) ; and *Votes of Assembly*, I, 389-390.

[93] Members of Lloyd's faction in the Assembly, though they owed their election mainly to their leader's mobilization of the colony's lower ranks, were themselves often men of considerable wealth. This

Thomas Lloyd's had been a revolt of the emerging Quaker Establishment—or at least a sizable portion of it. David Lloyd's was a revolt of all those who resisted these uppermost Quakers: Anglicans, former Keithians, the Welsh, many of the younger Quakers, and farmers and city artisans of all descriptions who had suffered from wartime economic dislocation, resented proprietary taxes and quitrents, and suspected that Penn had left them insecure in their property rights.

The pervasive feeling of alienation which distinguished David Lloyd's followers is evident in James Logan's description of the "irretrievably disaffected" Assembly of 1706.[94] In a letter to the proprietor, Logan gave a group portrait of the incoming legislature: David Lloyd was "thy Inveterate Revengefull Enemy"; Griffith Jones was "out of unity and when he Traded, of a scandalous Character"; Joseph Wilcox and Francis Rawle were leading Keithians; John Roberts and Robert Jones were "the two most disaffected to thee that Cou'd be found among all the Welsh being intirely D. Loyd's Creatures"; Joshua Carpenter was "A Churchman and thy sworne Enemy"; Samuel Levis had recently disavowed the Society of Friends; John Swift, though formerly a Quaker, was now "an obstinate Baptist"; William Paxton was "tolerably sensible but much disaffected ever since 1701"; and Samuel Dark, though honest, was "much

---

was especially true of those elected from the city and county of Philadelphia. Lloyd owned vast acreage in all three counties of the province and lived handsomely on his fees as Pennsylvania's most sought after lawyer. Griffith Jones and Joshua Carpenter were among the largest property owners in Philadelphia; Joseph Wilcox and Francis Rawle did not lag far behind them. The leading Lloydians in Chester and Bucks counties were less prosperous, but could still be considered substantial farmers.

94 Logan to Penn, ca. Oct. 1706 and June 12, 1706, *Penn-Logan Correspondence*, II, 119, 131.

disaffected since the reign of j[ohn] B[lackwell]." Others Logan described as "simple honest weake men."

Though Logan could hardly be relied upon for total objectivity in describing the Assembly, his analysis was accurate in important respects. As in other years during this era, the House was largely composed of Anglicans, former Keithians, other disillusioned Quakers, disaffected Welshmen who represented a resentful ethnic minority, and Quakers who were convinced by Lloyd's oratory and the depressing effects of the war that Logan and those who inclined toward elitist politics in Pennsylvania served only the proprietor and themselves. Isaac Norris, whose neutrality in the political warfare of the period made him a more reliable commentator than either Lloyd or Logan, concluded that the political distemper after 1701 was "fermented and Managed" by those who were "Either professt or secritt enemies of the proprietor" and agreed with Logan that "most of those Sticklers in assembly are Either Keithians or such as Stand Loose from Friends."[95] Though he may not have known it, Norris was describing a society in which social and religious leadership was no longer coincident with political leadership. In the 1680's and 1690's, the politics of discontent had involved staunch Quakers at the top of the social ladder who sought to clog the machinery of proprietary management so that they might themselves gain control of the "holy experiment." By contrast, the politics of discontent after Penn's departure in 1701 exemplified the reaction of various resentment-laden groups against all forms of authority, whether originating in proprietary policies, imperial regulation, or the attempt of Quaker worthies to monopolize political power.

[95] Norris to Joseph Pike, Feb. 18, 1709/10, Norris Letter Book (1709-1716), 132-133.

One further characteristic distinguished the disaffected: on the whole they represented a second generation of Pennsylvanians. If one considers the ages of Logan and Lloyd, the two leading antagonists in the early eighteenth century, this fact would appear to be false: in 1705 Logan was thirty-one and Lloyd was forty-nine. But by and large the men who gathered in opposition to Lloyd were either Penn's personal friends or the last survivors of the first generation of Quakers who had joined the proprietor two decades before in the work of building a New Zion on the Delaware. Among them were Samuel Carpenter, John Goodson, Caleb Pusey, John Blunston, Samuel Finney, John Guest, Robert Assheton, Griffith Owen, Thomas Story, Joseph Growdon, William Mompesson, Nathaniel Newlin, Jeremiah Langhorne, and Edward Shippen. Many of them had followed Thomas Lloyd in the 1680's in attempting to limit Penn's power. But the Keithian schism and Penn's return in 1699 had reunited them with the proprietor. Clustered around Lloyd, by contrast, were many sons of First Purchasers—second generation Pennsylvanians such as John Roberts, Joseph Wilcox, Francis Rawle, Joseph Wood, William Hudson, and Robert Jones. Some of the old malcontents of the early days—William Biles and Griffith Jones, for example—also joined their ranks, as did Anglicans, Welshmen, and former Keithians of various ages. But it was the younger men to whom Logan referred when he wrote Penn of "that corrupted Generation here" which gave Lloyd such political strength. Similarly Logan complained that the "young forward novices and a few partisans of D. Lloyd" drowned out "the more sound and ancient Friends" at business meetings of the Society of Friends.[96]

[96] Logan to Penn, Aug. 10, 1706, and June 28, 1707, *Penn-Logan Correspondence*, II, 147, 230.

Over this mixed lot of malcontents—a "Gallimaco fry," as Logan called it—David Lloyd held unchallengeable sway for almost a decade. He alone had the legal grasp, the legislative skill, the verbal capacity, and the fixity of purpose to lead a decade-long campaign against proprietary authority. Other men in Pennsylvania possessed legislative or legal skills during this period—Mompesson, Assheton, Guest, Logan, Carpenter, Pusey, Growdon, and others—but they rarely ran for seats in the Assembly. Unchallenged in the House, Lloyd found it easy to overawe those whose allegiance he did not already enjoy. The Welshman had a faculty of leading the assemblymen "out of their depth," Logan asserted in 1704; when this did not suffice, "his accomplices in the house drown all others with their noise."[97] Governors Evans and Gookin were both impressed with Lloyd's powers of persuasion. Honest men of good intentions were quickly won over by his arguments, wrote Evans, so that the whole Assembly vibrated with an "implacable & base malice" which really reflected the attitude only of Lloyd and his hard core of followers. The Assembly, wrote Gookin, was entirely governed by Lloyd—"one of those lawyers styled cunning," who did Penn all the harm in his power "under the pretence of reforming abuses."[98] The Council noted that many of the assemblymen could not fathom the complexities of Lloyd's bills for establishing courts, his arguments in behalf of legislative privileges, or his references to English law and parliamentary precedent. But Lloyd, using the difficult times to good advantage, convinced them of the necessity and legality of his program. The Lloydian

[97] Logan to Penn, Oct. 3, and Oct. 27, 1704, *ibid.*, I, 323, 339.
[98] Evans to Gov. Charles Gookin and the Council, Apr. 12, 1709, *Minutes of Council*, II, 436; Gookin to Secretary of the Society for the Propagation of the Gospel, Aug. 27, 1709, Perry, ed., *History of the Church in Pennsylvania*, 50-52.

leaders, concluded Isaac Norris, had "other Ends than what Is penetrated into by some pretty honest but not knowing men."[99]

In his more heated moments, Logan was wont to charge that Lloyd purposely induced "Knaves and fools" to run for the Assembly "that they might the easier be led by the Rattle of Rights and Privileges." But in calmer moods he recognized that most of the assemblymen were honest if plain men, who deferred to Lloyd's parliamentary knowledge, skill in drafting laws, and political fluency because they were untutored in the arts of government. It was the middle-class landowner or city artisan—hard hit by economic depression, apprehensive of the security of his land title, harassed by debts to city merchants, and disgusted by the impulsive actions of Governors Evans and Gookin— who was misled by the "artifices and smooth language" of David Lloyd.[100]

In expanding the politically relevant sector of society and in encouraging the common people to participate in government, Lloyd had introduced a style of politics in Pennsylvania which Penn and the original promoters of the colony had never anticipated. The proprietor had envisioned an annual gathering of the colony's most substantial men, who for eight or ten days would deliberate, much in the manner of the Quaker meeting, and pass such laws as were required for the common interest. Instead, government now seemed to consist of long verbal battles between the Assembly and the governor, extended legislative sessions which

[99] Council to Gookin, April 7, 1709, *Minutes of Council*, II, 439-441; Norris to Joseph Pike, Dec. 18, 1709/10, Norris Letter Book (1709-1716), 132-133.

[100] Logan to Penn, Nov. 22, 1704, *Pennsylvania Archives*, 2nd Ser., VII, 15; Logan to Penn, Oct. 3, 1704, *Penn-Logan Correspondence*, I, 323.

sometimes ran to seventy or eighty days a year, published remonstrances and accusatory letters to Penn, invective and recrimination, and long harangues on the rights of the people and legislative bodies. Lloyd's ten year outcry against proprietary prerogatives and upper-class privilege had infected the whole community, imparting a chronic feeling of resentment against authority of any kind.

Reminded repeatedly of their rights and encouraged to stand firm against unjust and oppressive external authorities, both proprietary and imperial, many colonists developed a deeply suspicious view of the world. People who had been drawn together by ties of religion and background now looked warily at each other. The old sense of community had been lost. Penn could expect no support or affection from his colonists, Logan lamented, for "every man is for himself."[101] David Lloyd's supporters in the Assembly mirrored the changing popular attitude all too well. Determined to resist traditional sources of authority, they "filled a volume," as Robert Quary observed, with their remonstrances, resolutions, and votes on the rights and privileges of the people. "The infatuated people of this province," warned Logan, would scandalize the Society of Friends by their "ridiculous contending" for rights unknown to "others of the Queen's subjects." "In privileges," wrote Logan on another occasion, "they are for straining the strings till they break."[102]

Logan and Quary were not the only ones who thought the contagion of rights and privileges had become epidemic by dint of Lloyd's efforts. Governor Evans repeatedly complained that Lloyd had beguiled the Assembly into demand-

[101] Logan to Penn, May 28, 1706, *ibid.*, II, 129.
[102] Quary to the Board of Trade, June 28, 1707, *CSP 1706-08*, #1016; Logan to Penn, March 3, 1706/07, April 5, 1705, *Penn-Logan Correspondence*, II, 196, 11.

ing privileges unheard of elsewhere in the English realm. "Through the Skill and artifice of Some Male Contents," wrote a Philadelphia Quaker, "Many narrow Tempers . . . have bin Greatly Enamored with the Name of priviledge and Affected with the Sound of Oppression."[103] When Evans denounced the "ill-grounded fury of a people drunk with wide notions of privileges," and warned that "the severest checks and reproofs from the authority att home" were necessary to tame the Pennsylvanians, he was only echoing sentiments frequently expressed by Penn over the years.[104]

To some extent, of course, the demand for wider privileges was grounded in the nature of colonial settlement. Penn had often admitted that the colonists rightly expected greater freedom in Pennsylvania than in England, that people did not uproot themselves, leave friends and relatives behind, and hazard a journey of 3,000 miles into a wilderness in order to enjoy only the same privileges allowed in England.[105] But now, deftly led by David Lloyd and spurred on by the unfavorable conditions prevailing after Penn's return to England, the colonists had all but declared their independence from proprietary prerogatives and parliamentary restrictions. In their petitions and remonstrances, in their attempts to impeach proprietary officeholders, in their defiance of Penn's deputy governors, and in their refusal to pay taxes in support of either intercolonial defense or the proprietor in England, the colonists had reached a

103 Evans to the Board of Trade, Sept. 29, 1707, *CSP 1706-08*, #1126; *Minutes of Council*, II, 323-325; Samuel Preston to Penn, Nov. 28, 1710, Myers Collection, Box 2, #38, CCHS.

104 Evans to the Board of Trade, Sept. 29, 1707, *CSP 1706-08*, #1126.

105 Penn to Charlewood Lawton, Aug. 18, 1701, Penn Letter Book (1699-1701), 111; also Penn to Robert Harley, 1701, Duke of Portland MSS, *HMC, 15th Annual Report*, Pt. IV, 31; and Penn to Board of Trade, April 22, 1700, Penn Letter Book (1699-1701), 24-29.

new proficiency in the science of antiauthoritarianism. Perhaps never in the first eighty years of colonial settlement in Pennsylvania was the spirit of defiance and alienation from established authority more visible and audible than during the decade of Lloyd's ascendancy. Even more certain is the fact that never in the colonial period were the uppermost members of society, to whom it was expected the generality would defer out of an inbred sense of the "natural degrees among men," less in control of the political process than in the years from 1701 to 1710. The balance of forces between the governor and Council on the one hand and the Assembly on the other, between the proprietary and popular interest, was never more badly out of line. David Lloyd was no democrat in the modern sense of the word. Nevertheless his awakening of previously quiescent elements in Pennsylvania society, and his "Rattle of rights and Privileges" brought Pennsylvania as close to "middle-class democracy" in the first decade of the eighteenth century as it ever would be before the American Revolution.

CHAPTER 7

The Maturing of Pennsylvania

NEARLY three decades of disequilibrium, culminating in the political dominance of David Lloyd and his attempts to impeach James Logan in 1709, seemed to signify the triumph of the strong middle and lower classes of Pennsylvania society. The social underpinnings of political power had been rudely shaken as men who were preeminent in every other sector of colonial life lost control of provincial government. It was not the would-be aristocrat but the sturdy country farmer and the city shopkeeper, whose voice proved to have the greatest resonance in the political arena. Favored by the structure of the still immature society, sensitized by the rhetoric of David Lloyd, and spurred on by unstable economic conditions, these men became the dynamic element in Pennsylvania politics for more than a decade.

But rather than flowering into middle-class democracy of the kind believed by some historians to have flourished before and during the era of the American Revolution, this spirited radicalism lost its appeal in Pennsylvania early in the eighteenth century. David Lloyd's star was setting even before James Logan reached England in 1710. Slowly, tentatively, in the next decade society began to crystallize, to assume a more structured appearance. Hesitantly, and not without interruptions, the wheels of government began to turn again as the management of politics became once more the concern of select groups whose members did not welcome the participation of the lower or middle classes in public affairs. Opposition to political power exercised from above was by no means dead in Pennsylvania, however. A strong tradition of dissent to prescriptive authority remained. But only under special circumstances did it manifest itself, usually during periods of economic difficulties or external threats.

Stabilization of Government

As James Logan arrived in England in 1710, a pamphlet appeared in Philadelphia which, as it was later apparent, signified the trend which events in Pennsylvania would take during the next decade. Entitled *Friendly Advice to the Inhabitants of Pensilvania,* the tract had been written by the Quaker merchant Isaac Norris in preparation for the forthcoming Assembly elections and published by order of the Quaker Yearly Meeting. The fact that Norris, a political moderate who preferred the countinghouse to the assembly room, would enter the political arena so actively was significant in itself, for it indicated a new determination on the part of the leading merchants and landowners to put an end, once and for all, to the politically disruptive activities of David Lloyd.

For years, Norris argued, the Assembly had arrayed itself against traditional forms of government, deliberating endlessly and raising the "Popular & Plausible Cry of Standing for liberties & Priviledges." But little, withal, had been done to serve the country. Instead, government languished and at times seemed at the point of extinction. The time had come to stop disputing and attacking government and to start using it. Pennsylvania needed laws to replace those abrogated in England by the Privy Council. Taxes were needed to settle the chaotic state of finances. Only the fanciful believed that the country could avoid taxes indefinitely. Far better to pay a penny now in the support of proprietary government than six later in behalf of royal government. The support of government, argued Norris, did not imply the destruction of liberties. Let men of property—city merchants and proprietary supporters in the country—be elected "to see whether liberties and proper support of government cannot be both provided for." Divest the legislature of those who "play with words, Combat every thing 'tho never so well designed, start unnecessary Questions & Disputes about *Powers & Dignities,* Create Quarrels & then Remonstrate only," Norris pleaded.[1]

So successful were the exertions of Norris and those who rallied around him that not a single member of the previous Assembly, David Lloyd included, was returned to office in October 1710. Chosen to represent the city of Philadelphia were Norris and Richard Hill, both Quakers and two of the colony's leading merchants. In Philadelphia County merchants William Trent, Thomas Masters, Thomas Jones, Samuel Cart, Jonathan Dickinson, and David Giffing won seats. In Chester and Bucks counties men of the first generation of immigrants—Nicholas Pyle, Nathaniel Newlin, William Biles, Caleb Pusey, and Jeremiah Langhorne—joined younger Quakers who emphasized stable, effective government rather than restrictions of proprietary power.[2]

Adding to the favorable prospects for the stabilization of government was the arrival in November 1710 of an open letter from William Penn to the people of the colony.[3] Conservative Quakers immediately saw its usefulness, for it was

[1] Isaac Norris, *Friendly Advice to the Inhabitants of Pensilvania* (Philadelphia, 1710).

[2] *Votes of Assembly,* II, 937.

[3] Penn to My old Friends, June 29, 1710, Proud, *History of Pennsylvania,* II, 45-53. A manuscript copy of the letter, most of it in the hand of James Logan, is in the Gratz Collection, Governors of Pennsylvania, Box 33.

written in a spirit of conciliation, but asked some pointed questions. Why had the colony become a land of freedom and economic opportunity for its inhabitants but for Penn only "the Cause of Grief, Trouble, and Poverty?" Why must government be carried on with "Divisions and Contentions" and men set against him as if he were an enemy? Privileges, to be sure, should be carefully preserved: allow the Assembly such powers as existed in other colonies; let all privileges enjoyed by Englishmen at home be allowed in Pennsylvania. But for the Assembly to arrogate the executive role of government, to claim the right to meet at any time during the year without the governor's consent, to appoint judges, or to license public houses was "to disturb Government, to break the due proportion of the parts of it, to establish confusion in the place of necessary Order." To remonstrate so unceasingly about "Matters so inconsiderable" was proof, Penn charged, that the colonists were "strangers to oppression, and know Nothing but the Name." Let the Assembly of 1710, he concluded, indicate whether Pennsylvania preferred to recognize the proprietor's rightful interests or call royal government down upon itself.

Although Penn's letter arrived too late to influence the elections of 1710 (as Logan had intended) , it was given wide publicity and apparently had a sobering effect on the colony and the legislature.[4] The Assembly presented a picture of unity and efficiency which contrasted sharply with the previous five years. Fifteen bills were drafted and passed into law, among them an act for establishing courts—a measure upon which agreement could not be found in any of the years when Lloyd was Speaker. A general consolidation of

[4] Samuel Preston to Penn, Nov. 28, 1710, Myers Collection, Box 2, #38, CCHS. Penn's letter had arrived on November 24, nearly two months after the elections.

governmental debts, some of which reached back to 1696, was undertaken. A money bill, the first in five years, was passed for support of government and the intercolonial defense efforts being coordinated at New York.[5] With a sense of satisfaction the Assembly addressed Penn and the Queen at the close of the session, announcing its accomplishments.[6]

Penn took no small pleasure in commending the leading Quakers in Pennsylvania for recapturing the initiative from "those unruly spirits" who had plagued government for so long.[7] In the colony, many seemed ready to concede that the proprietor's sympathizers, against whom David Lloyd had railed so long, could, after all, govern effectively while guarding "rights and privileges." By the time James Logan returned to Pennsylvania in March 1712, the electorate had demonstrated its confidence in the colony's leading men by electing a new Assembly which resembled its predecessor.[8] By this time, in fact, there was little to distinguish those who sat in the Assembly from those who occupied the Council. If the Council could claim such Quaker worthies as Edward Shippen, Griffith Owen, Samuel Carpenter, Thomas Story, James Logan, and Joseph Growdon, the Assembly could boast of men of equal standing and like temperament— figures such as Samuel Preston, Richard Hill, Caleb Pusey,

[5] *Minutes of Council*, II, 518-539; *Votes of Assembly*, II, 937-983.

[6] Assembly to William Penn and Queen Anne, Feb. 28, 1710/11, Pennsylvania Miscellaneous Papers, Penn and Baltimore, 75. Also see Richard Hill, Samuel Preston, Jonathan Dickinson, et al. to Penn, April 10, 1711, Penn Papers, Official Correspondence, I, 44-45.

[7] Penn to Edward Shippen, Samuel Carpenter, Richard Hill, et al., Feb. 10, 1710/11, Penn Papers, Private Correspondence, I, 37.

[8] *Votes of Assembly*, II, 1003. Isaac Norris explained that the proprietor's supporters had lost three Assembly seats in Philadelphia County, partly because of the heavy tax passed by the previous legislature and partly because of insufficient campaigning. Norris to Logan, Aug. 28, 1711 and Oct. 13, 1711, Norris Letter Book (1709-1716), 286, 295-297.

Isaac Norris, Clement Plumstead, Jonathan Dickinson, and Thomas Masters. The similarity of the two previously antagonistic groups is evident in the ease and frequency with which the leading merchants and landowners moved from the Council to the Assembly and back again. A few important figures, men such as Norris, Hill, Preston, and Dickinson, maintained seats simultaneously in both bodies. The Speakership of the Assembly was another indication of the changing political mood. Whereas David Lloyd had been chosen Speaker on all but one occasion between 1702 and 1709, he was elected to the position only once from 1710 to 1720. In every other year of the latter decade a political conservative and proprietary stalwart—either Norris, Hill, Trent, Growdon, or Dickinson—led the legislature.

Even the Corporation of Philadelphia began to lose its antiproprietary character after 1710. Since 1708 additions to the board of aldermen had come from the uppermost stratum of the Philadelphia mercantile community. In that year, for example, Richard Hill and Samuel Preston joined the Corporation. In 1712 Jonathan Dickinson's name was added. George Roche and Pentacost Teague, both rising merchant figures, took their places in 1713. Three years later Abraham Bickley and Joseph Redman, also successful traders, were elected. Progressively the ties between the Corporation and the Council tightened, until the membership of the two bodies had become virtually indistinguishable by the 1720's.[9]

By 1711 the long cry of privileges and liberties was dying. With control of the Corporation of Philadelphia and the Assembly transferred to the Quaker leaders in city and coun-

[9] *Minutes of the Common Council of the City of Philadelphia* (Philadelphia, 1847), 55-94; Judith M. Diamondstone, "Philadelphia's Municipal Corporation, 1701-1776," *PMHB*, 90 (1966), 196-197.

try, and with the Council and the Assembly in close harmony, legislative sessions carried out their work with unprecedented calm. Even money bills passed without undue
difficulty.[10] In 1714 Logan reported that all antiproprietary
factions had withered to insignificance, and in the following
year provincial leaders avowed what had been repeatedly
questioned for three decades—that the public and proprietary interests were "most intimately interwoven."[11] Indicative of the new trend in politics was the atmosphere of calm
in 1714 when the word arrived that the Judiciary Law of
1711 had been annulled in England. Although agreement
could not be reached immediately on a new bill, the Assembly consented to the temporary establishment of the courts
by executive ordinance. In 1707 a similar move to erect
courts by governor's proclamation had brought anguished
cries of constitutional perversion from the Assembly. Now,
recognizing the need to keep the courts functioning, the
Assembly deferred to Governor Gookin after delivering a
short, symbolic protest.[12]

Such friction in government as did remain after 1710 related primarily to disagreements between Quakers and Anglicans or the governor and his council. Anglicanism had
been growing steadily in Pennsylvania in the years after
1700, and Churchmen were much heartened at the prospect
of royal government, which by 1710 they took to be a certainty. "They are full of Envie & bitterness," complained
one Quaker, "and studie all the wayes they can to get the
Government, thinking it too mean for them to be under a

10 *Votes of Assembly*, II, 1036-1065.
11 Logan to Hannah Penn, April 8, 1714, Logan Letter Book (1712-
1715), 185; Joseph Growdon, Griffith Owen, Richard Hill, et al. to
Penn, Aug. 12, 1715, Penn Papers, Autograph Petitions, 17-19.
12 *Minutes of Council*, II, 571-573.

Quaker's Government."[13] Logan complained that the Anglicans treated Friends "little better than Rebels" and bombarded the English government with letters maligning the Quakers.[14]

The Anglicans derived further encouragement from the wave of High Church feeling which had set in during Queen Anne's reign. The Occasional Conformity Act of 1711, designed to eliminate evasion of the Test Act by dissenters, gave Anglicans in Philadelphia all the excuse they needed to oppose the Pennsylvania Affirmation Acts by which Quaker officeholders and judges avoided the distasteful oath of allegiance. In July 1712, when a newsletter from New York brought word that Penn had surrendered his government, Anglicans in Philadelphia grew insolent and abusive, according to Logan. In the Jerseys, Quakers were excluded from the bench and the jury and, according to the Quaker view, deprived of justice. If the Anglicans gained control of the courts in Pennsylvania, Logan warned, Quakers would be reduced to "a real slavery."[15]

Had Pennsylvania enjoyed an experienced and equitable governor at the time, the Anglican-Quaker hostility might have been minimized. Charles Gookin, unfortunately, was not such a man. He had seen much of the barracks and parade ground as a career officer in the regiment of Lieutenant General Thomas Erle, but knew virtually nothing of the council room and assembly house. Upon assuming office in February 1709, Gookin faithfully followed Penn's instruc-

[13] Griffith Owen to Penn, June 11, 1711, Myers Collection, Box 2, #40, CCHS; also see Isaac Norris to Joseph Wyeth, Aug. 26, 1709, Norris Letter Book (1709-1716), 62. For general accounts of Anglican-Quaker hostility see Root, *Relations of Pennsylvania*, 227-255.

[14] Logan to Penn, June 29, 1712, Logan Letter Book (1712-1715), 16.

[15] Logan to Henry Goldney, July 7, 1712, *ibid.*, 43; Logan to Penn, March 31, 1711/12, *ibid.*, 2.

tions, which referred him for advice to Logan and the leading Quaker merchants who sat in the Council. But Gookin
was temperamentally unfit to adjust to the Quaker style of
civil government. Dissenting views expressed in the Council
struck him as a form of insubordination. When councilors
persisted in argument, he tended to ignore them as ill-mean-
ing opponents and sought their advice no longer. Though
he was honorable and intended well, one of his councilors
reported, it was clear that government was not his calling.[16]

By 1712, many leading Quakers began to question even
Gookin's good intentions. Whether he wished to uphold the
proprietary interest any longer was doubtful, for he had
strong reasons to believe that Penn would shortly cease to
be his employer. It was an open secret that James Logan,
while he was in England in 1710 and 1711, had promoted
the sale of Penn's government to the Crown. Though attempts were made to conceal the negotiations, word reached
Pennsylvania in 1712 that Penn had relinquished the rights
of government in his colony for £12,000. What was not
known was that shortly after the arrangements had been
concluded Penn suffered a severe stroke which led to the
postponement of any final settlement.[17] By 1712 all signs
pointed toward the advent of royal government in Pennsylvania. Playing the odds, Gookin acted to advance his can-

[16] Samuel Preston to Penn, Nov. 28, 1710, Myers Collection, Box 2,
#38, CCHS. The best sketch of Gookin and his governorship is in
Keith, *Chronicles of Pennsylvania*, II, 487-510.

[17] Charles H. Smith, "Why Pennsylvania Never Became a Royal
Province," *PMHB*, 53 (1929), 147-149. Smith argues that the sale of
Penn's government was dealt an irreparable blow by the death of
Queen Anne and the dismissal of Robert Harley, the Lord Treasurer,
in the summer of 1714. In the political realignments that followed,
Penn lost most of his influence in high places. For the arrival of word
concerning the sale of Penn's government see Logan to Henry Gold-
ney, July 7, 1712, Logan Letter Book (1712-1715), 43.

didacy as the colony's royal governor. This involved ingra-
tiating himself with prominent Anglicans in Philadelphia,
while at the same time disregarding Penn's Quaker supporters in the Council and Assembly. Logan was well aware of
Gookin's ambitions and hoped to head off the proprietor's
faithless deputy by recommending John Evans as the first
royal governor in Pennsylvania, should Penn's surrender
of the government be concluded.[18] Knowledge that Logan
was promoting Evans, whose record as Gookin's predecessor
was hardly distinguished, only increased the Governor's
hostility toward the Quaker elite. Gookin kept himself "at a
great Distance" from all whom he imagined to hold "so
much as common friendship for Coll. Evans," Logan reported in September 1713. The Governor rarely convened
the Council and made no secret of his low regard for the
Philadelphia Quakers.[19] When the Assembly failed to muster a quorum on the first day of a session scheduled for February 1714, Gookin arbitrarily dissolved the body and refused to allow it to meet thereafter. The Assembly's protests
were met by Gookin's warning to "be gone about their Business" lest he order the sheriff and constables to turn them
out of the Assembly house.[20]

Gookin was openly at war with the Council and Assembly
by 1714. The Governor acted entirely without the Council's
advice, Logan warned, even in matters of the highest importance. More and more of his time was spent at his New Castle plantation. Government is "soe far sunk amongst us that
we scarce have an appearance of it," Logan informed Han-

[18] Logan to Thomas Grey, Nov. 25, 1712; Logan to John Evans, July
5, 1712; Logan to Hannah Penn, April 8, 1714, *ibid.*, 57, 40-41, 185.
[19] Logan to Penn, Sept. 8, 1713, *Pennsylvania Archives*, 2nd Ser., VII,
36-39; Logan to Thomas Grey, March 5, 1713/14, Logan Letter Book
(1712-1715), 177.
[20] *Votes of Assembly*, II, 1087-1089.

315

nah Penn, who by now had assumed the burdens of proprietorship from her failing husband.[21] Some in Pennsylvania were even ready to promote Robert Hunter, the royal governor of New York, as interim governor. Both Logan and the Council petitioned that Gookin be removed. Dissatisfied with the salary voted him by the Assembly, they charged, the Governor pawned offices to the highest bidder; he ignored advice from all men of substance, and showed the greatest ineptitude in matters of government ever known in Pennsylvania.[22] "Few men ever stood more in need of Counsel & as few perhaps have been more difficult to be persuaded by it," advised the Council.[23] All attempts at reconciliation by the leading Quakers failed. Suspicious of everyone around him, willing to trust only his brother-in-law, Richard Birmingham, who acted as his deputy in the Lower Counties, Gookin branded all those who opposed him or who offered advice as "Jacobites, Socinians and Enemies to the King."[24]

Gookin's failure was nowhere more evident than in his handling of the Lower Counties' Assembly of 1715. For five years or more property owners there, convinced of the defects in Penn's title to the Territories and certain of the eventual advent of royal government, had refused to pay quitrents to Penn's agents. Though Assemblies were occasionally held, only a shadow government existed. Nonethe-

21 Logan to Hannah Penn, April 8, 1714, Logan Letter Book (1712-1715), 185.

22 Logan to Hannah Penn, Oct. 4, 1714, *Pennsylvania Archives*, 2nd Ser., VII, 46-47; Logan to Hannah Penn, Oct. 20, 1714, Nov. 1, 1714, Logan Letter Book (1712-1715), 262, 265.

23 Council to Penn, Aug. 12, 1715, Penn Papers, Autograph Petitions, 17-19; Council to Hannah Penn, Oct. 8, 1715, *ibid.*, 13.

24 Logan to Hannah Penn, Aug. 17, 1715, Logan to Henry Goldney, Nov. 24, 1715, Logan Letter Book (1712-1715), 302, 356; Council to Penn, Oct. 8, 1715, Penn Papers, Autograph Petitions, 13.

less, Logan had done what he could to support a few leading men such as John French and Jasper Yeates, who, though unsympathetic to the proprietary cause, at least wished to preserve some semblance of order and stability.[25]

The Assembly of 1715, which in Logan's view was composed of "the best hands I have seen for these many Years," convened at New Castle in October of that year.[26] But Gookin, who apparently resented the challenge which the Assembly seemed to present to his interests, refused to admit the legality of the legislature and after several days of vociferous debate he charged the Assembly as "an unlawful Riot" and ordered its members to disband. Undaunted, the Assembly continued to meet and pointedly ordered an investigation of Gookin's recent dismissal of the popularly elected sheriff of New Castle County. Determined to resist the Governor, who by now was suspected of temporary insanity, the Assembly ordered their sheriff reinstated and commanded him to take possession of the New Castle jail. A scene of wild disorder followed with the Governor and his henchmen attempting to chop down the jail house door while the entire Assembly and half the town of New Castle assembled to witness the proceedings. After a struggle and "a great Deal of bitter cursing and . . . many violent oaths," Gookin recognized that he was stymied. As he rode out of town with his small group of supporters, the Assembly

[25] For affairs in the Lower Counties during this period see the letters of George Dakayne and Jonas Greenwood to Logan in Provincial Papers, 1664-1712 and 1712-1724, Dept. of Public Records, Harrisburg. Dakayne and Greenwood were Logan's agents in the Territories. Logan himself was convinced of the defectiveness of Penn's title to the Lower Counties, as he explained in a letter to Penn, Sept. 15, 1715, Logan Letter Book (1712-1715), 320.

[26] Logan to Hannah Penn, Oct. 28, 1715, ibid., 350-353. The following account is taken from his letter.

promptly reconvened to draft a petition to Penn. Reviling Gookin for his violent acts, his oppression of county officers, and the "miserable Condition" to which they had been reduced by his intemperate rule, the Assembly begged for his dismissal.[27]

The Restructuring of Colonial Society

By 1716 Penn lay close to death. Since 1711, when he had first been disabled by a stroke, he had remained in semiretirement at Ruscombe in Berkshire. Only occasionally did he bestir himself in proprietary matters or in negotiations with the English government. A second stroke in 1712 left him almost entirely incapacitated. Though unable to converse or write and hardly able to recognize old friends, Penn hung to life by a slender thread until July 1718.[28]

Almost the last act to transpire in Penn's name was the appointment as deputy governor of Sir William Keith, son of a Scottish baronet, courtier, and ex-Jacobite. Upon Robert Quary's death in 1714, Keith had been commissioned Surveyor General of Customs for the southern colonies. He was well known to Philadelphia merchants since he had made an official inspection of the customs service in Philadelphia in 1714, and was widely esteemed for his equitable, moderate conduct.[29] In 1716, both Logan and the Council

27 Assembly of the Lower Counties to Penn, Oct. 14, 1715, Penn Papers, Three Lower Counties, 79.

28 Peare, *William Penn*, 411-414.

29 Keith's commission is in Miscellaneous Manuscript Collection, 1701-1742, American Philosophical Society; for sketches of Keith see Charles P. Keith, "Sir William Keith," *PMHB*, 12 (1888), 1-33; and Winfred T. Root, "Sir William Keith," *Dictionary of American Biography* (New York, 1928-58), X, 292-293.

had urged Hannah Penn to appoint Keith in place of Governor Gookin, who by this time was being described by his indignant councilors as a man "to an uncommon degree Stupid, Wilful, Jealous & Irreconciliable," and "the weakest Animal that was ever call'd a Governor."[30] Doubtless the proprietary family was relieved to find a man of Keith's ability and background who was willing to assume the unenviable task of managing the government of Pennsylvania. Returning to England, Keith was commissioned in November 1716; on the last day of May in the following year he arrived at Philadelphia and was promptly sworn into office.[31]

Though he was able to sign Keith's commission and still made a half-hearted effort to keep abreast of events in his colony, Penn probably had little sense of the changes taking place in Pennsylvania in the waning years of his life. Even had his health been restored, the founder might not have realized that Pennsylvania, after three decades, was emerging from the political wilderness. For the letters, petitions, and remonstrances, which begged for relief from the almost irrational behavior of Gookin, concealed the fact that Pennsylvania had entered a new stage of development.

The most apparent changes were physical. Philadelphia was the fastest growing city in the British Empire. From approximately 5,000 inhabitants in 1700, the Quaker capital grew to 6,500 in 1710 and 10,000 in 1720, almost attaining the size of Boston.[32] Population in the countryside showed equally significant increases. Following the Peace of Utrecht,

[30] Logan to Hannah Penn, April 27, 1716, *Pennsylvania Archives,* 2nd Ser., VII, 49-50; Council to Hannah Penn, April 25, 1716, Penn Papers, Autograph Petitions, 15; Logan to William Penn, Jr., Sept. 29, 1715, Logan Letter Book (1712-1715), 320-321.
[31] *Minutes of Council,* III, 13-14.
[32] Bridenbaugh, *Cities in the Wilderness,* 143n.

which ended Queen Anne's War in 1713, Scotch-Irish and German immigrants flowed into Pennsylvania, first at a trickle, but by 1718 in a flood.[33]

Economic development paralleled population growth. Trade emerged from a decade-long slump in 1710, and enterprising Philadelphia merchants, who worked to open new markets, were soon challenging the supremacy of Boston. Further profits flowed from the Iroquois fur trade, which after years of dispute had finally been wrested from the exclusive control of New York.[34] Shipbuilding flourished in Philadelphia; in 1718 no less than ten shipyards lined the Delaware.[35] Although the grain market—still the foundation of Pennsylvania's trade—fluctuated in the years after 1710, the colony enjoyed a level of prosperity unknown since the closing years of the seventeenth century. The value of imports from England, which from 1701 to 1710 had averaged £9,687, more than doubled in the next decade to an average of £19,568 per year.[36]

[33] F.J.F. Schantz, Frank R. Diffenderffer, et al., *Pennsylvania—The German Influence in Its Settlement and Development*, Pt. 7, *Proceedings of the Pennsylvania-German Society*, 10 (1900), 32-37; Wayland F. Dunaway, *The Scotch-Irish of Colonial Pennsylvania* (Chapel Hill, 1944), 50-51.

[34] The letter books of Isaac Norris, James Logan, and Jonathan Dickinson, as previously cited, may be quarried for a mass of information relative to the economic progress of Pennsylvania after 1710. For general treatments see Arthur L. Jensen, *The Maritime Commerce of Colonial Philadelphia* (Madison, Wis., 1963), and John W. Weidman, "The Economic Development of Pennsylvania until 1723," (unpublished Ph.D. dissertation, University of Wisconsin, 1935). The rise of the fur trade is traced in Francis Jennings, "The Indian Trade of the Susquehanna Valley," *Proceedings of the American Philosophical Society*, 110 (1966), 406-424.

[35] Bridenbaugh, *Cities in the Wilderness*, 184.

[36] Figures derived from annual value of goods imported and exported from Pennsylvania to England, as given in Charles Whitworth, *State of the Trade of Great Britain, in its Imports and Exports . . . 1697 to 1773 . . .* (London, 1776), Pt. 2, 67.

James Logan and Isaac Norris may be taken as examples
of the new spirit of enterprise that manifested itself in Pennsylvania at the close of Queen Anne's War. Whereas Philadelphia merchants in earlier years had concentrated on the
West Indian provisioning trade and the tobacco trade with
England, Logan and Norris pursued new mercantile connections. In 1710 Norris moved quickly to take advantage
of a grain shortage in Lisbon. For a year every bushel of
wheat that he and his partners could procure was shipped
to the Iberian peninsula. It was "the best opportunity for
making Returns from here to England . . . that has ever been
known here," he wrote in retrospect.[37] In 1712 Logan and
Norris sent ships laden with provisions to Carolina with the
hope of obtaining a cargo of rice for England. A shipment
of rum to Newfoundland to be bartered for fish for the
Portuguese or Spanish markets represented another attempt
to establish fresh trade connections. In 1714 Logan even
undertook the shipment of lumber to Leghorn in the hope
of opening up Mediterranean trade routes. Both merchants
reaped profits from their mercantile ventures which made
prewar successes, such as they were, pale by comparison.[38]

Less obvious than the physical alterations in colonial society were the social and political changes in progress.
Though an absence of tax lists and land records for the first
half of the eighteenth century makes quantitative analysis
difficult, it is clear that a restructuring of Pennsylvania society was in process, particularly after the Peace of Utrecht.
A major cause of this was the nature of postwar immigration. To a large extent the influx consisted of indentured

[37] Edward Shippen, Samuel Carpenter, Isaac Norris et al. to the Trustees of Pennsylvania, May 24, 1712, Logan Letter Book (1712-1715) , 7.
[38] *Ibid.* (1702-1726) and (1712-1715) , passim; Norris Letter Book
(1709-1716) , passim; Albright G. Zimmerman, "James Logan, Proprietary Agent," *PMHB*, 78 (1954) , 172-176.

servants, depressed and politically inert individuals who crowded the bottom rungs of the social ladder. Indentured servants had never been lacking in Pennsylvania, of course, but not since the first years of settlement had they composed so large a percentage of the population. "Great numbers of People are crowded in upon us" James Logan wrote to England as early as 1713, "but they are mostly Servants, & very few of Estates." Two years later, Jonathan Dickinson noted the large number of servants being brought to Philadelphia by enterprising merchants, who sold them for "ready money."[39] By the second quarter of the eighteenth century Logan was marveling at the German invasion of Pennsylvania and predicting that the exodus to Pennsylvania would parallel the Saxon inundation of Britain in the fifth century. So great was the flow of poor Irish to the Quaker colony that Logan queried if all of Ireland was "to be transplanted hither."[40]

At the opposite end of the social spectrum a class of colonial aristocrats was in the process of formation in the years after 1713. Overseas trade, land speculation, and to a lesser extent the fur trade were the main sources of wealth which helped to create these Quaker grandees and Anglican gentlemen. The end of almost a quarter-century of war, the influx of land-hungry immigrants, and the long-delayed establishment of trading agreements with the Iroquois tribes all helped to produce a stratum of men whose wealth was unmatched in earlier periods.[41] Inevitably, the commercial

[39] James Logan to Penn, Sept. 8, 1713, *Pennsylvania Archives*, 2nd Ser., vII, 39; Dickinson to Jonathan Barnett, Dec. 13, 1715, Dickinson Letter Book (1715-1721), 58, Library Company of Philadelphia.

[40] Quoted in Tolles, *James Logan*, 159-160.

[41] In 1710 and 1711, for example, Logan had shrewdly bought up the "Old Rights" of many of the early land purchasers, who had never immigrated to Pennsylvania. By this means he acquired claims to vast

development of Philadelphia engendered a wider gap between rich and poor and a far greater differentiation in classes.[42]

Any precise definition of this newly wealthy class is hindered by lack of data. After 1712, inventories of estate no longer included real property, which for most men represented a considerable part of their total wealth. Nonetheless, the more opulent style of living among the leading families of Philadelphia—the Norrises, Pembertons, Shippens, Hills, Trents, Dickinsons, Masters, Fishbournes, Plumsteads, and Hamiltons, to mention only the most prominent—gives convincing evidence of the emergence of a colonial elite. Emblematic of the change was the trend among wealthy Quakers toward more fashionable apparel and the careful attention given to the furnishing of houses in the style of contemporary upperclass Englishmen. "According to appearances," wrote one observer in 1724, "plainness is vanishing pretty much."[43] The greater prevalence of slave owning, despite efforts by the Society of Friends to limit the importation of Africans, is another evidence of the more aristocratic tenor of life among the leading representatives of Philadelphia society. Almost every substantial merchant in the city,

---

acreage in Pennsylvania at a time when land was little in demand and just a few years before the great Scotch-Irish and German immigration began. By 1715, Logan was shipping at least £1,000 of furs to England yearly. Tolles, *James Logan*, 86-91; Johnson, "A Statesman of Colonial Pennsylvania," 462-483.

[42] For an instructive parallel in the case of Boston see James A. Henretta, "Economic Development and Social Structure in Colonial Boston," *William and Mary Quarterly*, 3rd Ser., 22 (1965), 75-92.

[43] R. W. Kelsey, "An Early Description of Pennsylvania: Letter of Christopher Sower . . . ," *PMHB*, 45 (1921), 252-253; Carl and Jessica Bridenbaugh, *Rebels and Gentlemen* (New York, 1942), 13-14; Tolles, *Meeting House*, 125-127.

whether Quaker or Anglican, owned slaves; one Quaker owned as many as thirty.[44]

Jonathan Dickinson, a leading merchant of Philadelphia in the early eighteenth century, might stand as an example of the crystallization of a colonial elite. Dickinson had come to the Quaker colony from Jamaica at the end of the seventeenth century, but he maintained property in the West Indies and frequently returned to the islands on trading voyages of particular importance. For a quarter of a century his name in Philadelphia was synonymous with mercantile success. After his death in 1722, the inventory of his estate detailed household goods valued at more than a thousand pounds. Almost every room of his handsome city house contained mahogany furniture of the finest quality. Tea tables, satin-cushioned easy chairs, caned elbowchairs, expensive clocks, and occasional pieces graced his parlors. In the bedrooms were featherbeds with "Inside and outside Curtains, Vailings, head & Tester Clothes." His table displayed elaborate settings of china and silver, Oznabrigg napkins, and expensive glassware. In the stable stood horses and a four-wheeled carriage—perhaps the first to be seen in Philadelphia. No one in the colony had enjoyed such a standard of living in the first three decades of settlement.[45]

Isaac Norris provides another example of the emergence of a genuine colonial aristocracy. Norris had made notable progress in his mercantile affairs since his arrival in Philadelphia from Jamaica in 1697. But wealthy men were not made during the extended period of war that followed.

[44] Darold D. Wax, "The Negro Slave Trade in Colonial Pennsylvania," (unpublished Ph.D. dissertation, University of Washington, 1962), 49; Edward R. Turner, "Slavery in Colonial Pennsylvania," *PMHB*, 35 (1911), 148.

[45] Harrold E. Gillingham, "The Estate of Jonathan Dickinson (1663-1722)," *PMHB*, 59 (1935), 420-429.

"Few if any here can pretend" to the status of "Rich Quakers," wrote Norris in 1711.[46] The next eight years worked great changes in the merchant community, however. By 1713 Norris was inquiring about the price of a coach in London and sending instructions about the family escutcheon, which was to ornament its sides. Feeling pangs of guilt at such ostentation, Norris decided to have only his initials on the carriage door and to leave the rest "all plaine." Later, wrestling with his conscience, he put aside all plans for the coach. But by 1714, Norris was ordering expensive marble from England to grace his fireplaces. Two years later work was begun on Fairhill, his country mansion. By 1720 he not only had his coach, but servants in livery who, as his wife wished, were thereby distinguished from the other family servants.[47]

The trend toward a redistribution of wealth may be further illustrated in Chester County. The landless, who had been proportionately few in the early decades of settlement, increased markedly after 1715. By the 1760's more than 60 percent of the white adult males in the town of Chester held no property and even outside the towns probably about one-third of the adult males were propertyless. Moreover, a gradual concentration of wealth was occurring, though the rate of change was much less rapid than in Philadelphia. In 1693, the lowest 30 percent of the taxpayers in Chester County commanded almost as much of the community's wealth as the next 30 percent, while the upper tenth of the population held less than 25 percent of the county's taxable

[46] Norris to Joseph Pike, Nov. 29, 1711, Norris Letter Book (1709-1716), 265.

[47] Norris to John Askew, May 30, 1713, June 26, 1713, March 3, 1713/14, July 3, 1714, Norris Letter Book (1709-1716), 389, 393, 428, 455; Tolles, *Meeting House*, 130-131.

assets (Table A).[48] But by 1730 the economic strength of
the lower ranks had declined relative to other strata of the
social order while the upper tenth of the population con-
solidated its grip on the community's wealth. This trend
toward a less even distribution of wealth continued throughout the eighteenth century as a rural elite of mill and forge
owners, large farmers, and shopkeepers established their
economic and social distinctiveness, while at the same time
the ranks of the agricultural laborer swelled.

TABLE A

VERTICAL DISTRIBUTION OF ASSESSED WEALTH IN CHESTER COUNTY,
1693-1760

Percentage of Taxpayers	1693	1715	1730	1748	1760
Lowest 30	17.4	13.1	9.8	13.1	6.3
Lower middle 30	21.1	22.9	21.7	21.7	20.5
Upper middle 30	37.7	38.1	39.8	36.4	43.3
Upper 10	23.8	25.9	28.6	28.7	29.9

It is not surprising that the restructuring of colonial society had political effects. Pennsylvania politics in the early
decades had been a kaleidoscope of shifting factions. An
enormous potential for factional conflict had existed in a
society where the opportunities to acquire land, economic
advantage, and political office were far greater than in England, especially for Quakers who had been disabled from
civil government in the Old World. Where the distance
between large and small landowners, artisan and merchant,
rich and poor, was narrow by English standards, patterns

[48] Jackson T. Main, *The Social Structure of Revolutionary America*
(Princeton, 1965), 33-34, 37. The emergence of a distinctive Quaker
social elite is also treated in Tolles, *Meeting House*, 109-143. A more
extensive analysis of the changing distribution of wealth in Chester
County from 1693 to 1802 appears in James T. Lemon and Gary B.
Nash "The Distribution of Wealth in Eighteenth-Century America,"
Journal of Social History 2 (1968).

of elitism, hierarchy, and deference had tended to decay. Simply stated, inherited modes of political behavior found no support from the prevailing social and economic situation; the composition of the initial waves of immigrants and later the extended period of war allowed only a slow evolution toward a more traditional, more structured society. Only with the greatest difficulty could the rough-hewn Quaker elite, having initially outmatched Penn's proprietary circle, maintain itself in power in the first two decades. And in the third decade, from 1701 to 1710, the leading merchants and landowners had lost control altogether to an unlikely coalition of Quaker apostates, Anglicans, Welsh, and second-generation Friends—all bound together by the persuasive rhetoric and political wiles of the ambitious and embittered David Lloyd.

But with the return of economic prosperity to Pennsylvania and the subsequent exhaustion of the politics of discontent, governmental control began to return to a relatively narrow group of merchants and prosperous landowners. As society became more layered, as the consolidation of wealth at the top increased, as social elaborations grew, the nature of politics began to assume a more conventional eighteenth-century look. The thousands of Scotch-Irish and German immigrants, most of whom took up land to the west of the original Quaker settlements, played no immediate role in politics. For a decade or so they remained politically inert, leaving government to those who had risen to prominence in the areas of initial settlement. More and more it was the select few, preeminent in economic, social, and religious affairs, who came to dominate politics. In part this tendency is observable in the changing recruitment of the members of the Council. In the first seventeen years of settlement, 46 men occupied Council seats. During the next period, from 1700 to 1716, the number narrowed to 27, though the population increased. From 1717 to 1733, only 22 men claimed membership in the Council.[49] By the time of Penn's death, a seat in the Council had become symbolic of membership in a select circle of merchant leaders and their landed country friends.

Evidence of the new domination of colonial politics by a distinct upper class is also seen in the control which prominent councilors exerted over the Assembly. From 1710 to 1720, the leaders in the lower house were hardly distinguishable from the leaders in the Council. Isaac Norris sat in the Assembly during eight of these years and held the Speakership twice; Jonathan Dickinson was elected six times to the Assembly and was Speaker once. Richard Hill, appointed to the Council in 1705, sat in the Assembly during every year of the decade but one and was three times Speaker. William Trent sat five times in Assembly and twice held the Speakership. Thomas Masters sat for three years, Samuel Preston for three, William Fishbourne for four, Caleb Pusey for three, and George Roche for two. Other councilors, such as James Logan, Robert Assheton, and Griffith Owen never held seats in the Assembly, just as many assemblymen never sat in the Council. But it is clear that in striking contrast to the years during which David Lloyd dominated the Assembly, the leading merchants of Philadelphia and their clients in the country had finally succeeded in gaining control of the apparatus of government.

The Provincial Court of Chancery—or Equity Court—established in 1720 may serve as a symbol of the resumption of political power by the colonial elite. Equity jurisdiction had always been a controversial issue in Pennsylvania, for

[49] Based on the lists of councilors in *Minutes of Council*, I-III, passim.

opinion was deeply divided as to whether the seat of judgment in equity cases should be the county courts or the governor and his Council. Country farmers, often in debt to
city merchants, favored the county court, composed of their
peers.[50] Merchants and city shopkeepers, on the other hand,
preferred an equity court composed of the city merchants
who sat in the Council. Initially the proprietor and his
Council had functioned as a court of equity. But even in the
1680's pressure had been brought to transfer the administration of equity to the county courts. By 1693 county courts
exercised equity jurisdiction in cases involving less than
£10. David Lloyd's Judiciary Bill of 1701 made the administration of equity the exclusive right of the county courts.
In 1707, when repeal of the Judiciary Act of 1701 again
raised the whole question of judicial procedures, the Lloydians in the Assembly and the principal merchants of Governor Evans's Council argued bitterly over the establishment of courts of equity. Evans finally yielded on the
point, and in 1708 allowed the county courts to function
as original courts of equity.[51]

Although the Judiciary Act of 1711 continued this pattern
of equity jurisdiction, a reorganization of the courts four
years later transferred cases in equity to a Provincial Supreme Court.[52] That the Assembly would promote and pass
such a measure signalized the more conservative temperament of the lower house. In 1720, the Assembly further proposed that Governor Keith establish a Court of Chancery
endowed with exclusive jurisdiction in equity cases. The

[50] Lloyd and his followers had attempted as early as 1704 to provide
greater legal protection for debtors. Lokken, *David Lloyd*, 143-144, 167.
[51] Spencer R. Liverant and Walter H. Hitchler, "A History of Equity
in Pennsylvania," *Dickinson Law Review*, 37 (1933), 156-183; William
H. Loyd, *The Early Courts of Pennsylvania* (Boston, 1910), 159-174.
[52] *Statutes of Pennsylvania*, II, 327-329; III, 67.

governor and the six eldest councilors would compose the court, which was to be modeled on the English High Court of Chancery. Governor William Keith doubted his power to establish the Court except by command of the King, but the Assembly, which in the past had resolutely fought for the right of county courts to exercise equity jurisdiction, pressed him to comply. It was no coincidence that the Assembly included many of Philadelphia's most prosperous merchants—Samuel Carpenter, Isaac Norris, Clement Plumstead, William Trent, Richard Hill, William Fishbourne, and Jonathan Dickinson. Some believed that the Chancery Court violated the Charter of Privileges of 1701, which consigned all legal proceedings over property matters to the "ordinary Courts of Justice."[53] Although that phrase was open to interpretation, it was clear that the Assembly which endorsed the Chancery Court differed radically from its predecessors, which in the heyday of David Lloyd had made opposition to a centrally appointed equity court a rallying cry of antiproprietary sentiment.[54]

By 1720 the influence of the Philadelphia merchants in affairs of government was stronger than it had ever been in the previous four decades of the colony's existence. The identical men, frequently linked by ties of blood, marriage, business, and religion, controlled the Council and Assembly, dominated the Corporation of Philadelphia, sat on the Philadelphia County and City Courts, and handed down decisions from the Provincial Appellate Court and the Court of Chancery. In the city of Philadelphia their rule was un-

---

[53] *Votes of Assembly*, II, 1329-1330, 1334-1335, 1339; *The Registrar's Book of Governor Keith's Court of Chancery of the Province of Pennsylvania, 1720-1735* (Philadelphia, 1941), 1-11.

[54] The Chancery Court erected at the Assembly's insistence was the only separate equity tribunal ever instituted in Pennsylvania.

challenged. And while landowners of lesser status managed county affairs, they deferred to the Philadelphia merchants in the provincial Assembly, as is evident by the election year after year of one of the leading merchants to the Speakership.

The new degree of structure in social and political affairs did not mean either that the middle and lower classes which David Lloyd had so effectively mobilized would fall into a permanent political sleep or that faction would be eliminated in provincial politics. Lower class restiveness would recur in Pennsylvania as in other colonies, especially during periods of economic hardship. When this happened, the leaders of the community again found themselves challenged and occasionally overwhelmed. The best example of this periodic reversion to the earlier pattern of unstable, unruly politics came between 1722 and 1727. For five years following his arrival in 1717, Sir William Keith had ruled with the greatest success of any governor of Pennsylvania since the colony's founding. Enjoying the confidence of both the Assembly and Council, which were dominated by the colony's most prestigious landowners and merchants, Keith had been able to establish the court system, wring a declaration of loyalty from the Lower Counties, obtain royal approval of the Quaker affirmation in lieu of the objectionable oath, and even gain Quaker acceptance of a militia law.[55] He had established "a perfect peace and good understanding" in Pennsylvania, James Logan pronounced in 1721 and later wrote of his great contentment "to see all Affairs of

[55] Keith, "Sir William Keith," *PMHB*, 12 (1888), 1-33; Lokken, *David Lloyd*, 208-224. The most careful consideration of Keith's governorship is Thomas P. Wendel's unpublished dissertation, "The Life and Writings of Sir William Keith, Lieutenant-Governor of Pennsylvania and the Three Lower Counties, 1717-1726" (University of Washington, 1964).

Government carried on without the least Division or Opposition."[56]

By the summer of 1722, however, the political calm of Pennsylvania was shattered. A decade of economic prosperity had come to an abrupt halt about a year before as the colony felt the deflationary effects of the panic and recession in England caused by the bursting of the South Sea Bubble. Prices of Pennsylvania produce fell precipitously, trade decayed, and an acute shortage of gold and silver dampened internal trade. By 1723 the downward economic spiral had depressed land values, left the Philadelphia shipyards almost empty, choked off trade, and left hundreds deep in debt.[57] "Families who had lived well," the Assembly later reported, "could scarce find Means to purchase necessary Provisions for their Support; and therefore both Artificers and Traders were obliged to quit the Country, in Search of Employment and Sustenance elsewhere."[58]

Economic depression led directly to the return of a radical mode of politics. At the October 1721 elections, which Logan complained were "very mobbish and carried by a Levelling spirit," many of the conservative stalwarts of Philadelphia were swept out of office and men who fifteen years before had attempted to impeach Penn's Secretary were elected in their places.[59] The burning political issue became paper currency, which a group of Philadelphia merchants, led by the former Keithian Francis Rawle, proposed to issue

[56] Logan to Simon Clement, April 1721, quoted in Johnson, "A Statesman of Colonial Pennsylvania," 538; and Logan to ———, April 12, 1722, Logan Letter Book (1716-1732).

[57] The paper money controversy is carefully analyzed in Richard A. Lester, *Monetary Experiments: Early American and Recent Scandinavian* (Princeton, 1939), 56-111.

[58] *Votes of Assembly*, III, 1828.

[59] Logan to Henry Goldney, April 9, 1723, *Pennsylvania Archives*, 2nd Ser., VII, 75-78.

in large doses as a cure for the stagnation of internal trade. Governor Keith vigorously supported the paper money plan which all segments of society clamored for by 1723 except the wealthiest merchants, such as Logan and Norris, whose considerable resources put them in a uniquely favorable position to weather the economic storm.[60]

For the next three years, as the split between Keith and Logan widened, the Governor resorted more and more to tactics perfected earlier by David Lloyd in his campaign against the political rule of the proprietor's friends clustered around James Logan. Keith called for legislation for the relief of debtors and for a second issue of paper money, sprinkled his political dialogue with caustic references to the "Great, the Rich . . . [and] the learned," and energetically mobilized the lower classes of the community for political purposes.[61] Logan did nothing to narrow the rapidly widening gap by implying in political tracts that paper money was a dangerous scheme of those whose "luxury, Idleness and Folly" could be blamed for the economic depression. The wealthy, Logan imperiously told the Philadelphia Quarter Sessions Court, owed their riches to "Sobriety, Industry and Frugality."[62]

By 1723 politics had returned to the superheated state of the early eighteenth century. David Lloyd, who had quit the political wars in 1718, came out of retirement to lead the Assembly in 1723 and 1725 and to champion the popular cause. Logan and Lloyd, who for ten years had forsworn political dueling, took up their old grudges and waged war

[60] Lester, *Monetary Experiments,* 67-71.

[61] *Votes of Assembly,* II, 1459-60; J. Langhorne to Alexander Hamilton and Clement Plumstead, Feb. 10, 1724, in Hazard, ed., *Register,* VI (1830) , 225-226.

[62] *Votes of Assembly,* II, 1471; Logan, *The Charge Delivered from the Bench to the Grand Jury* . . . (Philadelphia, 1723) .

against each other anew. The use of the press by both sides brought forth a torrent of provocative and sometimes scurrilous pamphlets which contributed to the combustibility of the atmosphere.[63]

Keith's attempts to develop a broader political base ultimately led him to even more radical measures than David Lloyd had taken two decades before. The numerous Palatine Germans who had flooded into the colony were an obvious source of support and Keith by 1725 was sponsoring bills to naturalize them almost upon arrival—a political stratagem, Logan charged, to swing the electoral tide in his direction, or as Isaac Norris put it more graphically, to create "a sinister army."[64] By this time Keith had also organized two political clubs in Philadelphia, the Gentlemen's Club for his more substantial supporters, and the Tiff Club for the "leather aprons" of the city. Isaac Norris was convinced that the workingmen's club was populated primarily by the "new, vile people [who] may be truly called a mob."[65] With the lower class mobilized for political purposes, inflammatory political literature rolling off the press, and men of parts condemned as enemies of the people, conservatives could only lament with Logan that once more Pennsylvania had become "a scene of the vilest, most extravagant Licenciousness." At the 1726 elections Logan had further reason to despair at the revival of the old style of politics: riots and disorder erupted at the polls and a victory celebration for the popular party ended with a burning of the pillory and

[63] Lokken, *David Lloyd*, 208-213; Wendel, "Sir William Keith," 155-170.

[64] Wendel, "Sir William Keith," 174.

[65] James Logan to H. Taylor, Aug. 22, 1726, *Pennsylvania Archives*, 2nd Ser., VII, 95-97; Norris to Joseph Pike, Aug. 28, 1728, Norris Letter Book (1716-1730).

stocks—the symbols of authority and social control.[66] On
the first day of the new General Assembly Keith rode into
Philadelphia at the head of eighty mounted gentlemen supporters, followed by a far larger number of artisans, mechanics, journeymen, apprentices, and common day-laborers.
"His doctrine of reducing all to a level suits mighty well the
inclination of the poorer sort," wrote one of the Governor's
upper-class critics.[67]

After 1726, however, control of the political process
slowly swung back to the merchants of Philadelphia
and the more conservative landowners outside the city. The
Keithian party in Philadelphia was able to achieve electoral
successes almost to the end of the decade but rarely could
it control the Assembly as it had from 1722 to 1726. Keith
was replaced by Patrick Gordon as the second quarter of
the eighteenth century began and Pennsylvania, enjoying a
new period of rapid growth and prosperity, entered a period
of political calm that lasted for more than a decade. Once
again government was left to the upper stratum. So long as
its members were responsive to the needs of men lower in
the social order, they were able to control the machinery of
government. If government did not threaten burdensome
taxes, military duty, or religious restrictions, most of the
people found no need to engage actively in politics. Political
acquiescence, in this sense, was a result of political contentment or of satisfaction with the existing government.[68]

[66] Logan to John Wright, Jan. 25, 1725/26, *Pennsylvania Archives*,
2nd Ser., VII, 91-94. The 1726 elections are described in Patrick Gordon
to John Penn, Oct. 22, 1726, Penn Papers, Official Correspondence,
I, 247, and Logan to John Penn, Oct. 17, 1726, *ibid.*, 237.

[67] Wendel, "Sir William Keith," 185-191; David Barclay to Thomas
Penn, [1727?], Penn Papers, Official Correspondence, II, 43.

[68] Perhaps of greatest significance in the second quarter of the
eighteenth century was the growth of a non-Quaker elite which chal-

Legacy of the "Holy Experiment"

By 1726 only a handful of those who had participated in the launching of the "holy experiment" were still alive in Pennsylvania. New men, many of them native Pennsylvanians who had never seen England, took their places in the forefront of provincial affairs. But in keeping with the changes that had overtaken politics since 1710, they represented for the most part the established leaders of the Philadelphia mercantile community and the prosperous landowners in the country. More and more, social position and political power became mutually supportive, restoring the traditional relationship between the structure of society and the political system—a nexus which had been disrupted in the early stages of colonization.

Though the social bases of politics returned to more familiar forms, the political disequilibrium of the early years had lasting effects on the style of politics in Pennsylvania. It was part of the legacy of the "holy experiment" that whenever particularly sensitive issues brought opposing elements of the colonial elite to loggerheads, as happened periodically, both Quaker and non-Quaker leaders politicized certain segments of society when they would in fact have preferred to have these groups remain in a state of political inertia. The middle and lower ranks would never again before the Revolution challenge the organizing values of so-

---

lenged and eventually overtook the Quaker community in numbers, economic strength, and social prestige. By mid-century, according to a recent student of Pennsylvania politics before the Revolution, "political conflict . . . was a jousting at the top" between two Philadelphia-centered elites, both dominated by city merchants but one Quaker in composition and one Anglican and Presbyterian. William S. Hanna, *Benjamin Franklin and Pennsylvania Politics* (Stanford, 1964), 201.

ciety as they had in the period which culminated with the Keithian schism, or control politics as they had in the early eighteenth century under the leadership of David Lloyd. But upwellings of sentiment from below would continue to figure importantly in politics, especially in periods of economic stagnation or external threats.[69]

This recurrent appeal to the people, this need to involve the middle and lower strata in political life, has often been taken as evidence of the march of democracy in Pennsylvania. Though there is still much to be known about the structure of politics at mid-eighteenth century, it is improbable that any "democratic" party, articulating an equalitarian ideology or calling for more democratic institutions, ever emerged in Pennsylvania before the 1770's. A politically autonomous middle class existed only to the extent that potentially such a group could be mobilized by either half of a bifurcated elite for the furtherance of its particular political ambitions. But appeals to German and Scotch-Irish farmers, or to Philadelphia mechanics were rarely based on promises of a larger political voice, greater economic advantage, or easier access to office. The ordinary man, in fact, was rarely presented with significant political choices; his

[69] When the French and Indian Wars shook the Quaker domination of the Assembly, popular support was pursued among the Scotch-Irish and Germans on the frontier, who heretofore had exhibited little desire to participate in the political process. John J. Zimmerman, "Benjamin Franklin and the Quaker Party, 1755-1756," *William and Mary Quarterly*, 3rd Ser., 17 (1960), 291-313; and Ralph L. Ketcham, "Conscience, War, and Politics in Pennsylvania, 1755-1757," *ibid.*, 20 (1963), 416-439. In 1750 Alexander Hamilton wrote that "the standing or falling of the Quakers in the House of Assembly depends upon their making sure the interest of the Palatines in this province, who of late have turned so numerous that they can sway the votes which way they please." Carl Bridenbaugh, ed., *Gentleman's Progress; The Itinerarium of Dr. Alexander Hamilton* (Chapel Hill, 1948), 22.

337

power was essentially negative. Lacking organization and leaders, uninspired by political dogma, and uninterested in the power of political office, the common people rarely acted in programmatic fashion to achieve specific political goals. But because such men had the power to alter the balance of political power by throwing their weight to one side or the other at particular times, they could make it highly dangerous for either half of the provincial elite to pass or promote unpopular measures. The strength of the middle and lower strata, then, was defensive, consisting of the ability to thwart any political faction which might be so careless as to formulate programs which ignored the fundamental requirements of the people.[70]

Just as the structure of colonial society and the particular circumstances under which it developed affected the political dynamics of Pennsylvania, so the combative nature of politics in the early decades altered the terms of the "holy experiment" which Friends had initiated in the Delaware Valley. Penn and his followers, inheritors of the English liberal tradition in politics and unswervingly committed to the principle of religious liberty, had assumed from the outset that Quaker government was capable of reordering society along more perfect lines than had been achieved in the Old World. In Pennsylvania, unlike in England, men would respond to the same principles in government that guided their religious life. Government, as Penn wrote, was "a part of religion itself, a thing sacred in its institution and end."[71]

[70] The culminating pre-Revolutionary example of intra-elite political hassling and the consequent appeal to segments of the population normally outside the political arena came during the Stamp Act crisis in 1765. See Benjamin H. Newcomb, "Effects of the Stamp Act on Colonial Pennsylvania Politics," *William and Mary Quarterly*, 3rd Ser., 23 (1966), 257-272.

[71] Frame of 1682, in *Laws of Pennsylvania*, 92.

Few, if any, of the original promoters of Pennsylvania questioned that a transference of values from the religious to the civil sphere would be accomplished, or that in a traditionally organized society the recognized leaders of the Society of Friends would be conceded political preeminence as well. The same ideas and ideals that bound Quakers together in England would cement their relations to Quaker government in America. Religion was to be the all-powerful mechanism of social and political integration. A universally accepted ensemble of beliefs, capped by a sense of stewardship or obligation to the community, would provide cohesion to immigrant society.

Ideas and ideals, as it happened, were pitted against the brute force of circumstances in Pennsylvania. Exposed to the raw wilderness and to almost limitless amounts of land, settlers dispersed, quested individually after the economic security they had lacked in England, and vigorously opposed proprietary or royal policies issued in the name of the community, whether that was defined as Pennsylvania or the empire at large. Men who had venerated Penn in England became his outspoken opponents in Pennsylvania, not so much because Penn had changed as because they themselves had been changed in the process of planting a new civilization. To Penn it seemed that all too often his colonists acted first as ambitious, covetous settlers and only secondarily as members of an organic Quaker community. Though Quakers undoubtedly possessed a "solidaristic conception of society,"[72] they found solidarity difficult to achieve in the early decades of settling their colony. "Particular men doeth for themselves," complained one leader early in the process of settlement. This thought was echoed again and again—by Blackwell, who was astounded that Quaker merchants would

[72] Tolles, *Meeting House*, 80.

charge fellow Quakers exorbitant prices; by Logan, who charged that self-interest was the dynamic element in Pennsylvania life; by Penn, who lamented the excess of individualism; and by others.[73]

Neither the Quaker ethos brought from England or the administrative apparatus of the Society of Friends could subdue these centrifugal tendencies which beset society on the Delaware. Penn assumed that the "proper relations amongst men" and the ancient sense of deference, which had been ungrudgingly displayed toward persons known "for their wisdom, virtue, and ability," as his Frame of 1682 had phrased it, would be perpetuated by the Society itself.[74] In England nobody challenged the authority of the Quaker Monthly Meeting to discipline any member whose secular deportment endangered the reputation of the Society at large or threatened to disrupt the solidarity of the community. But in Pennsylvania the Society of Friends was almost as powerless to restrain its own members in civil affairs as it was to dictate to the growing number of non-Quakers in the population. Shortly after Penn's departure in 1701, leaders of the Society of Friends were moved to unusually strong language at the Yearly Meeting in censuring David Lloyd and his party, who had "by their Seditious Words, Insinuations, and Practices, disquieted the Minds of others, to the making of Parties and Disturbances." Lloyd was accused of promoting his own "Sinister Ends" out of a revengeful spirit,

[73] John Blunston to William Sharlow, Jan. 23, 1683/84, Logan Papers, XVI, 14. Blackwell charged the merchants of Philadelphia with oppressing "the poorer sort of people" by quadrupling the price of goods imported from England. Not even in New England, for all the avarice of its merchants, Blackwell informed Penn, had he seen such disregard for the principle of a fair profit. Blackwell to Penn, Jan. 25, 1688/89, Society Miscellaneous Collection.

[74] Frame of 1682, in *Laws of Pennsylvania*, 92; Dunn, *Politics and Conscience*, 67-72.

while advertising his particular brand of politics under the "Fair Colours of Law and Priviledges."[75] But as in the Keithian controversy of the 1690's, such attempts to curb disruptive individuals were easily ignored. Their ineffectiveness simply demonstrated that the social and religious leaders of Quaker society were powerless to extend their control to the secular sphere. An important link in the Quaker conception of community had been broken.

Ultimately, Quaker leaders were forced to ask whether their religious commitments would even permit them to participate in governing a pluralistic society—and particularly one which, because of events beyond the Quakers' control, was situated in an area contested by the two great international powers. In the first two decades of settlement it had been the Keithian apostates or non-Quakers, such as John Blackwell and the leaders of the Lower Counties, who questioned whether Quaker principles were consistent with civil government. By the early eighteenth century, Quaker leaders themselves were asking the question.

James Logan, upon whom the burdens of proprietary government fell most heavily in the early eighteenth century, felt compelled to advise Penn that his colony's strategic position on the North American coastline and the growth of a polyglot population made "a due administration of Government (especially in time of War) under an English constitution . . . irreconciliable with our Principles."[76] Isaac Norris, after conducting a kind of informal poll of leading Quakers in 1710, admitted that, despite elaborate denials, Quaker principles were "destructive or repugnant

[75] Manuscript Minutes of the Philadelphia Yearly Meeting, I, 87, as cited in Tolles, *Meeting House*, 14-15.
[76] Logan to Penn, July 19, 1708, Howland Collection, Haverford College.

to Civil Government." It was clear, he wrote, after almost three decades in Pennsylvania, that Friends "must either be independent and entirely by ourselves; or, if mixed, partial to our own opinion." On matters of defense and the oath of allegiance, Norris warned, the principles of Quakers and their detractors were mutually exclusive.[77] Having created conditions hospitable to liberty of conscience, Quakers were forced to stand by almost helplessly as people of other religious convictions, who had nothing but contempt for the Quaker faith, made Friends "dissenters in their own country," as Penn was fond of putting it.

If the Quaker system of beliefs could not prevent social and political disequilibrium in the early stages of settlement, Pennsylvania was not significantly different from Puritan New England, Dutch Reformed New York, Catholic Maryland, or Anglican Virginia in these respects. Social dislocation, political instability, decentralization of government, the materialistic urge, and an erosion of the spirit of community were prominent features in the early history of these colonies as well. And if Quaker leaders later found the burdens of political responsibility incompatible with their religious principles, they would find fulfillment of their original ideals in the concept of "disinterested benevolence"—the attempt to reform the world, rather than withdraw from it, through bold work in the fields of abolitionism, humanitarianism, and civil liberties.[78] In planting their Zion, the Quaker elite had embraced too many con-

[77] Norris to Penn, Nov. 29, 1710, *Penn-Logan Correspondence*, II, 430-431.
[78] The deflection of Quaker concern from politics to social reform at a time when the Society had almost disqualified itself in affairs of government is treated perceptively in Sydney V. James, *A People Among Peoples; Quaker Benevolence in Eighteenth-Century America* (Cambridge, Mass., 1963).

tradictory tendencies to succeed along the lines originally set down in London in 1681 and 1682. But the Society surpassed the expectations of even its most optimistic members in becoming, by the time of the American Revolution, the embodiment of the national conscience. Like others who set out for America with a mixture of motives—economic, religious, and political—the uppermost Quakers had suffered the disorganizing effects of the New World experience. They had intermittently lost control of the machinery of government while groping for stability and political maturity over a period of two generations. But finally, with utopian hopes transformed by the realities of colonial life and their role redefined by the political experience of the first five decades, they assumed an important and enduring role in provincial society.

Bibliographical Note

DESPITE the rich manuscripts available, surprisingly little has been written in recent years of the early colonial experience in Pennsylvania. Thus, though I have been guided and informed throughout this study by the work of other historians, the book rests essentially on a reading of the primary sources. The most important of these is the magnificent collection of Penn Papers at the Historical Society of Pennsylvania, Philadelphia. Containing hundreds of documents and letters of the proprietary family which illumine every aspect of colonial society, the Penn Papers serve as the backbone of this inquiry. Together with manuscripts from many other repositories, the Penn Papers at the Historical Society of Pennsylvania have been published in five volumes under the editorship of Richard S. Dunn and Mary Maples Dunn. Important materials relating to the first half-century in Penn's colony are also widely scattered in other collections of the Historical Society of Pennsylvania: the Blackwell Papers, Dreer Collection, Etting Collection, Gratz Collection, Logan Papers and Letter Books, Norris Papers and Letter Books, Parrish Collection, Pemberton Papers, Proud Papers, and the Society Miscellaneous Collection to mention only the most important. Elsewhere, manuscript collections of particular use were the Penn Letters and Ancient Documents, American Philosophical Society, Philadelphia; the Albert Cook Myers Collection, Chester County Historical Society, West Chester, Pennsylvania; the collections of the Genealogical Society of Pennsylvania, Philadelphia; the early records of the Society of Friends at the Department of Records, Philadelphia Yearly Meeting, 302 Arch Street, Philadelphia; and the Penn Papers, Friends House, London.

Of lesser importance were letters, records, and documents

in the manuscript collections of the Library Company of Philadelphia; Haverford College Library; Friends Historical Library, Swarthmore College; Blumhaven Foundation of Philadelphia; the New-York Historical Society; New York Public Library; Maryland Historical Society; Delaware Archives, Dover, Delaware; Library of Congress; Henry E. Huntington Library, San Marino, California; and the Public Record Office, London. Mercantile activity and land speculation, which figure prominently in the early politics of the colony, are revealed not only in the extensive records contained in the Penn Papers, Logan Papers, Taylor Papers, and James Steel Letter Book at the Historical Society of Pennsylvania, but in the little used seventeenth- and eighteenth-century land records in the Delaware Archives and the Bureau of Land Records, Department of Internal Affairs, Harrisburg, Pennsylvania; the deed books and patent books in the Office of the Recorder of Deeds, City Hall, Philadelphia; the warrant and survey books in the Municipal Archives, City Hall, Philadelphia; the records of the Surveyor General of Pennsylvania in the Miscellaneous Manuscript Collection, 1688–1742, American Philosophical Society; and The Minutes of the Board of Property, published in *Pennsylvania Archives*, Second Series, Vol. XIX (Harrisburg, 1893).

In addition, many letters and documents of the period have been reprinted in the *Pennsylvania Magazine of History and Biography;* the *Memoirs of the Historical Society of Pennsylvania* (14 vols., Philadelphia, 1826–95); Samuel Hazard, editor, *Register of Pennsylvania* (16 vols., Philadelphia, 1828–35); Hazard, editor, *Annals of Pennsylvania, from the Discovery of Delaware, 1609–1682* (Philadelphia, 1850); and in the *Pennsylvania Archives,* especially First Series, Vol. I (Philadelphia, 1852), Second Series, Vol. VII (Philadelphia, 1890).

Beyond manuscript sources, the most important materials

for the study of society and politics in early Pennsylvania are the legal and legislative records. Manuscript minutes of the Provincial Council and the executive correspondence of the Council are at the Pennsylvania Historical and Museum Commission in Harrisburg and are available on microfilm published under the auspices of the National Historical Publications Commission. I have used the printed *Minutes of the Provincial Council of Pennsylvania* (known as *Colonial Records*), published in 16 volumes (Philadelphia and Harrisburg, 1852–53), of which the first three volumes cover the period 1681 to 1736. Minutes of a few sessions in 1692, omitted in this series, are in the *Pennsylvania Magazine of History and Biography*, 11 (1887), 151–159. Manuscript minutes for a number of other sessions in 1691 and 1692 are in the Penn Papers, Assembly and Provincial Council; and Society Miscellaneous Collection, Provincial Council of Pennsylvania. Minutes of the Assembly, edited by Gertrude MacKinney, are published as *Votes and Proceedings of the House of Representatives of the Province of Pennsylvania, Pennsylvania Archives*, Eighth Series (8 vols., Harrisburg, 1931–35). Also of importance are the provincial laws, which for the period 1682 to 1700 are to be found in Staughton George, Benjamin M. Nead, and Thomas McCamant, editors, *Charter to William Penn, and Laws of the Province of Pennsylvania* . . . (Harrisburg, 1879), and thereafter in James T. Mitchell and Henry Flanders, editors, *The Statutes at Large of Pennsylvania from 1682 to 1801* (18 vols., Harrisburg, 1896–1915). Ten laws passed in 1682 that were omitted in the first-cited compilation are given in Marvin W. Schlegel, "The Text of the Great Law of 1682," *Pennsylvania History*, 11 (1944), 276–283. Records of the municipal government of Philadelphia are far from complete, but some information is to be found in *Minutes of the Common Council of the City of Philadelphia, 1704 to 1776* (Philadelphia, 1847).

347

Social and political historians will find a trove of information buried in the court records of the late seventeenth and early eighteenth centuries. Records of the county courts are rarely complete, but for Chester, Bucks, New Castle, Kent and Sussex counties the basic records of the common pleas and quarter sessions courts have survived. Unfortunately, only fragments of the court records for the city and county of Philadelphia and the provincial court of Pennsylvania are extant. For a survey of the court records, both published and unpublished, see H. Clay Reed, "The Court Records of the Delaware Valley," *William and Mary Quarterly* Third Series, 4 (1947), 192–202.

Indispensable to any study of colonial Pennsylvania are the English documents bearing upon colonial administration. By far the richest vein to be mined is the *Calendar of State Papers, Colonial Series, America and West Indies 1574–1737* (43 vols., London, 1860–1963) of which Volumes 10 to 35 concern the period under consideration in this study. *The Calendar* contains abundant letters and reports, only slightly condensed in most cases, pertaining to Pennsylvania and its transactions with the English government. Even more important are the reports of neighboring royal governors and imperial bureaucrats, whose views, though often distorted, are invaluable in unraveling patterns of political and social development. Supplementing these materials are the papers of English officials among whom Penn sought assistance in the *Reports* of the Historical Manuscripts Commission; the reports and debates in the *Manuscripts of the House of Lords,* New Series (11 vols., London, 1900–1962); the correspondence of the Crown's super-agent in the colonies, Edward Randolph, in Robert N. Toppan and A.T.S. Goodrick, editors, *Edward Randolph: Including His Letters and Official Papers . . . 1676–1703.* Publications of the Prince Society, Volumes 24 to 28, and Volumes 30

348

and 31 (Boston, 1898–1909); the journal of the Board of Trade, a transcription of which is at the Historical Society of Pennsylvania; and the papers of the Board of Trade, Proprieties and Plantations General, also at the Historical Society of Pennsylvania in transcribed form.

Studies of economic development and social structure in early Pennsylvania are yet to be written. Much can be learned from a careful reading of the letter books of important merchants such as James Claypoole, Jonathan Dickinson, Isaac Norris, and James Logan; the mercantile correspondence of Edward Shippen in the Logan Papers; and a collection of Early Letters from Bristol and Philadelphia. All of these are at the Historical Society of Pennsylvania. Also helpful are Arthur L. Jensen, *The Maritime Commerce of Colonial Philadelphia* (Madison, 1963); Stevenson W. Fletcher, *Pennsylvania Agriculture and Country Life, 1640–1840* (2 vols., Harrisburg, 1950); John W. Weidman, "The Economic Development of Pennsylvania until 1723" (unpublished Ph.D. dissertation, University of Wisconsin, 1935); James T. Lemon, *"The Best Poor Man's Country": A Geographical Study of Early Southeastern Pennsylvania* (Baltimore, 1972); and Stephanie Grauman Wolf, *Urban Village: Population, Community and Family Structure in Germantown, Pennsylvania, 1683–1800* (Princeton, N.J., 1976). I have tried to reconstruct the role of Africans in the economic and social life of early Philadelphia in *Forging Freedom: The Formation of Philadelphia's Black Community, 1720–1840* (Cambridge, Mass., 1988), and Sharon V. Salinger, "To Serve Well and Faithfully": *Labor and Indentured Servants in Pennsylvania, 1682–1800* (New York, 1987). The changing social structure of early Pennsylvania must be traced by using tax lists, land records, wills, and inventories of estate. The best collection of these materials is at the Pennsylvania Genealogical Society but must be supplemented by the records cited previously.

Among the many published histories of early Pennsylvania, the first, Robert Proud's *The History of Pennsylvania in North America* . . . (2 vols., Philadelphia, 1797–98), is still one of the most satisfactory narrative accounts. William R. Shepherd's *History of Proprietary Government in Pennsylvania* (New York, 1896) is unexcelled as an institutional study and Winfred T. Root's *The Relations of Pennsylvania with the British Government, 1696–1765* (New York, 1912) carefully examines imperial relationships. Of more recent studies, the most perceptive is Frederick B. Tolles, *Meeting House and Counting House: The Quaker Merchants of Colonial Philadelphia, 1682–1763* (Chapel Hill, 1948). Edwin B. Bronner has reexamined the first two decades in *William Penn's "Holy Experiment"* (New York, 1962), and Joseph Illick has provided an informed survey in *Colonial Pennsylvania: A History* (New York, 1976). Other important new studies include Sally Schwartz, *"A Mixed Multitude": The Struggle for Toleration in Colonial Pennsylvania* (New York, 1987); Barry Levy, *Quakers and the American Family: British Settlement in the Delaware Valley, 1650–1765* (New York, 1988), Allan Tully, *William Penn's Legacy: Politics and Social Structure in Provincial Pennsylvania, 1726–1755* (Baltimore, 1977); and Jean R. Soderlund, *Quakers and Slavery: A Divided Spirit* (Princeton, N.J., 1985).

Penn himself has been the subject of several dozen biographies and studies but still remains an enigmatic figure, hidden behind a veil of filiopietism. Of the nineteenth-century biographies, almost all of which fit the romantic mold, Samuel Janney's *The Life of William Penn* (Philadelphia, 1852) is the most enduring. Catherine O. Peare has provided the best modern narrative in *William Penn* (Philadelphia, 1957). Edward C. O. Beatty was the first scholar to deal analytically with Penn's ideas; his *William Penn as a Social Philosopher* (New York, 1939) is still useful. Two more recent studies add much to our understanding of Penn and help to portray the proprietor as a study in contrasts: Joseph E. Illick's *William Penn the Politician: His Relations with the English Government* (Ithaca, 1965); and Mary Maples Dunn's *William Penn, Politics and Conscience* (Princeton, 1967). Other secondary sources, most of which are familiar to students of early Pennsylvania, are cited in the footnotes.

Index

353

156; opposition to Keith, 156, 158; political alignments, 308

Christ Church, Phila., 205. *See also* Anglicans

Christina Bridge, 75

Christina River, 14

Clarendon Code, 169-70

Claridge, Samuel, 16

Clarke, William, 25, 55-56, 58n, 66, 81, 86n, 93, 108, 185, 233

Claypoole, James, 50, 97, 170; merchant, 15-16, 55, 58n, 283; and Free Society of Traders, 20, 23, 61-63, 66; proprietary officeholder, 27, 81, 106, 107n

Claypoole, John, 128, 185

Clayton, William, 85

Clows, John, 51

Coale, Josiah, 5

Cock, Lasse, 64, 185n

Colonial Policy, 71, 130, 134, 181-98, 211, 214-24, 241-48

Commissioners of Customs, 189-191, 222

Commissioners of Propriety, *see* Board of Propriety

Commissioners of State, 105-08, 113, 116-117, 164n

Compton, Henry, Bishop of London, 218, 242

Concessions and Agreements of 1677, *see* West New Jersey

Connecticut, 197, 203

Constitution of Pennsylvania, *see* frames of government

Cooke, Arthur, 55, 58n, 95, 107n, 109, 128, 149, 155, 170, 207, 256n, 281n, 284

Cooke, Francis, 159

Copley, Lionel, Governor of Maryland, 134

Cork, Ire., 12

Cornbury, Lord, *see* Hyde, Henry

courts, officers of appointed, 24-25; provincial court, 24, 66, 80-81, 84, 103-04, 107, 128, 131, 133, 152, 156, 185, 212, 239, 329-30; court of exchequer proposed, 95-96; attempts to reduce proprietary power over, 166-67, 229-30, 234-35; paralyzed by oath controversy, 250; controversy over in 1706, 264-67; courts of equity, 265-67, 328-30; reestablished in 1711 and 1714, 309, 312. *See also* Bucks County, Chester County, Philadelphia, Philadelphia County, Sussex County, vice-admiralty court

council, role of defined in Frame of 1682, 33-42; powers challenged by assembly, 67-73, 111-14; tension with Penn, 99, 101-04, 108, 166; split under Blackwell, 118-19, 122-23; assumes power of deputy governor, 127-28; proposes tax, 143-44; and Keithian controversy, 151; denies illegal trade, 194; reduced powers of under Frames of 1696 and 1701, 200-05, 231; supports Gov. Evans in court controversy, 265-67; and Gov. Gookin, 312-18; pattern of recruitment for, 327-28. *See also* assembly, frames of government

Coxe, Daniel, 135

Crispin, Silas, 26-27

Cromwell, Oliver, 8, 114

Dakayne, George, 317n

Dark, Samuel, 298

Darvall, William, 55-56, 76

Day, John, 155

Delavall, John, 129, 149, 155

Delaware, *see* Lower Counties

Delaware Bay, 21, 25, 83

Ingelo, Richard, 26
Ireland, 3, 16, 115

Jamaica, 209, 324
James II, *as Duke of York*, 6, 35,
59, 68; and Penn's grant, 8, 74;
as King of England, and Revo-
lution of 1688, 115-16, 124
Jennings, Samuel, 149, 154-55, 256n
Jesus College, Oxford, 86
Jones, Charles and Company, 60,
61n, 65
Jones, Griffith, and Free Society of
Traders, 23, 25, 55, 58n; as poli-
tician, 118, 128, 130, 144, 185n,
228, 298, 300; and Keithian
controversy, 156, 159
Jones, Henry, 55
Jones, John, 55, 155
Jones, Robert, 298, 300
Jones, Thomas, 308
justice of the peace, in West New
Jersey, 32; as provided for in
the "Fundamental Constitu-
tions," 38; appointment of under
Frame of 1682, 41; in East New
Jersey, 41-42. *See also* courts

Keith, George, 12, 102n, 145, 181,
228, 289; beliefs and personality,
145-47; and Quaker schism, 146-
61, 179-80, 295-96; returns to
England, 205; agent for Society
for Propagation of Christian
Knowledge, 255-56. *See also*
Keithian controversy
Keith, Sir William, as Governor of
Pa., 318-19, 331-35; and Court of
Chancery, 328-30; and paper
money controversy, 332-35
Keithian controversy, 274, 337, 341;
origins of, 146-47, 179-80; splits
Society of Friends, 147-53; social

analysis of, 153-61, 179-80;
residual effects of, 256, 300
Kendall, James, Governor of Barbados, 138
Kent County, Del., 60, 68, 74; social
structure in, 53, 280; early settlers of, 68. *See also* Lower
Counties
King William's War, 130, 134, 208;
economic effects in Pa., 136-38;
and colonial policy, 181-83

Lamb, John, 139
Lancashire, Eng., 23
land, price, 13; sale, 15-17; dis-
tribution, 18-19, 28-29, 52-53, 77-
80; speculation, 17, 90-92, 322;
proprietary policy, 36, 77-79, 89-
97, 215-17, 227-29, 238, 275-76;
policy opposed, 89-97, 104, 109,
215-17, 220, 227, 254-55; and
social instability, 178-79, 339-40
Lane, Sir Thomas, 135
Langhorne, Jeremiah, 300, 308
Lawrence, Sir Thomas, 243
Lawrie, Gowen, 6, 31n
Lee, William, 159
Leech, Toby, 207n
Leeds, Daniel, 256n
Leghorn, Italy, 321
Lehnman, Philip, 27, 85
Leith, Scot., 55
*Letter to the Free Society of
Traders*, by William Penn, 22
Levant Company, 135
Levis, Samuel, 298
Lewes, Del., 56, 81, 83, 259
Lisbon, Port., 273, 321
Lloyd, Charles, 86
Lloyd, David, 102n, 231; as leader
of antiproprietary movement,
109, 143, 209-10, 238, 240, 251-52,
257-67, 288-94, 306, 327-28, 331,

INDEX

Saunders, Charles, 141, 159, 185n
Schuylkill River, 14, 91
Scotland, 13, 15, 51, 189, 214
servants, 3, 21, 54, 285; numbers of,
    50-51, 176, 279, 321-22; social
    mobility of, 51; social origins of,
    52
Shackamaxon, 3
Sharlow, William, 21
Sharpless, Isaac, 102n
Shelpot River, 14
Shippen, Edward, 197, 225, 231,
    233, 239, 255, 300, 310, 323
Sidney, Algernon, 28, 43, 70
Sidney, Henry, Earl of Romney, 8n
Simcock, John, Chester County
    leader, 21, 25, 54, 107n, 170, 176,
    240; officer of Free Society of
    Traders, 23, 63; opposes proprie-
    tary policy, 82, 95-97, 119n; pro-
    vincial officer, 109, 128; opposes
    George Keith, 149, 155, 158
slaves, 50, 208, 283, 285, 323-24;
    arrival in Philadelphia, 64n,
    278-79n
social mobility, 51, 56, 175-78, 284-
    86, 294
social structure, 24-28, 49-56, 79,
    175-78, 277-86, 294, 321-27
Society for The Propagation of the
    Gospel, 242
Society for the Promotion of
    Christian Knowledge, 255-56
Society of Friends, in England, 4-6,
    11-12, 43, 50-52, 169-71; disunity
    in Pennsylvania, 108-10, 161-80,
    338-40; opposes formation of
    militia, 130-31; split by Keithian
    controversy, 144-60; Yearly
    Meeting, 146-48, 152, 258, 307,
    340; disciplinary function of
    Monthly Meeting, 165, 171, 340-
    41; and structure of Quaker

values, 171-74, 179-80; tension
    with Anglican church, 205-08,
    255-56; and importation of
    slaves, 323
Some Account of the Province of
    Pennsilvania, by William Penn,
    14
Songhurst, John, 70n, 82
Stanfield, James, 59
Stockdale, William, 147-48
Story, Thomas, 225, 227, 233, 239,
    255, 262, 300, 310
Susquehanna Valley, 5
Sussex County, Del., 60, 68, 74;
    social structure, 53, 280; courts,
    128. See also Lower Counties
Swift, John, 298

Tatham, John, 135
taxes, proposed by Council, 143-44;
    opposition to, 156, 160, 211, 254-
    55, 304; proposed by Isaac
    Norris, 307-08, 310n
Taylor, Christopher, 26, 55, 58n,
    81, 97
Teague, Pentacost, 311
Telner, Jacob, 55
Tiff Club, 334
Tolles, Frederick, 102n, 171
trade, in development of Pa., 14-
    15; and Free Society of Traders,
    21-22; with West Indies, 56-62,
    65, 136-39, 252-54; suspension of
    proprietary duties on, 83; dis-
    rupted during King William's
    War, 137-38; evasion of Naviga-
    tion Acts, 182-84, 189-98, 219;
    after 1710, 320-21
Trent, Maurice, 55-56
Trent, William, 55, 253, 308, 311,
    323, 328, 330
Tresse, Thomas, 159
Turner, Robert, Dublin and Phila-

363